EARNING RESPECT:
THE LIVES OF WORKING WOMEN IN SMALL-TOWN
ONTARIO, 1920–1960

Between 1920 and 1960 wage-earning women in factories and offices experienced dramatic shifts in their employment conditions, the result of both the Depression and the expansion of work opportunities during the Second World War. *Earning Respect* examines the lives of white- and blue-collar women workers in Peterborough during this period and notes the emerging changes in their work lives, as working daughters gradually became working mothers.

Joan Sangster focuses in particular on four large workplaces, examining the gendered division of labour, women's work culture, and the forces that encouraged women's accommodation and resistance on the job. She also connects women's wage work to their social and familial lives and to the larger community context, exploring wage-earning women's 'identities,' their attempts to cope with economic and family crises, the gendered definitions of working-class respectability, and the nature of paternalism in a small Ontario manufacturing city.

Sangster draws upon oral histories as well as archival research as she traces the construction of class and gender relations in small-town industrialized Ontario in the mid-twentieth century. She uses this local study to explore key themes and theoretical debate in contemporary women's and working-class history.

(Studies in Gender and History)

JOAN SANGSTER is a professor in the Department of History, Trent University.

STUDIES IN GENDER AND HISTORY

General editors: Franca Iacovetta and Craig Heron

JOAN SANGSTER

Earning Respect: The Lives of Working Women in Small-Town Ontario, 1920–1960

UNIVERSITY OF TORONTO PRESS
Toronto Buffalo London

© University of Toronto Press Incorporated 1995
Toronto Buffalo London
Printed in Canada

ISBN 0-8020-0518-7 (cloth)
ISBN 0-8020-6953-3 (paper)

Printed on acid-free paper

Canadian Cataloguing in Publication Data

Sangster, Joan, 1952–
 Earning respect : the lives of working women in
 small-town Ontario, 1920–1960

 (Studies in gender and history series)
 Includes bibliographical references and index.
 ISBN 0-8020-0518-7 (bound) ISBN 0-8020-6953-3 (pbk.)

 1. Women – Employment – Ontario – Peterborough –
 History – 20th century. 2. Sexual division of labor –
 Ontario – Peterborough – History – 20th century.
 I. Title. II. Series.

 HD6100.P47S3 1995   331.4'09713'680904
 C95-930207-7

University of Toronto Press acknowledges the financial assistance to its
publishing program of the Canada Council and the Ontario Arts Council.

This book has been published with the help of a grant from the Social Science
Federation of Canada, using funds provided by the Social Sciences and
Humanities Research Council of Canada.

To David, for his support and friendship; to Robbie, who has lived with this book for the first five years of his life; to my sisters Carol and Wendy; and to Margaret Hobbs, a friend who has always been there.

Contents

Acknowledgments

My first debt is to the people who agreed to be interviewed for this study. Many former Peterborough workers generously shared their memories of their workplaces; their aid made this book possible. I have drawn a composite picture from their recollections, and almost all the interviewees have been made anonymous by the use of different names. I still hope, however, that some part of the book rings true for any one of the interviewees who reads it.

While writing this book, I secured support from the Social Sciences and Humanities Research Council in the form of a Strategic 'Women and Work' grant. I am grateful for that financial aid, and I also wish to thank the Frost Centre, Trent University, for research support.

My colleagues at Trent in both women's studies and history have provided ongoing encouragement for my research and writing. Their advice and friendship over the last years has meant a tremendous amount to me. Special thanks must go to Margaret Hobbs, Keith Walden, Doug McCalla, Jim Struthers, Elwood Jones, Barb Marshall, and Sedef Arat-Koc. Although none of these people has read the manuscript, all of them have certainly listened to my many complaints and worries about it over the years.

At a small liberal arts university with a strong commitment to teaching, it is often difficult to find any time to write. At the same time, the dedication of my history and women's studies colleagues to the intellectual stimulation and emotional well-being of their students, as well as their commitment to making history accessible and exciting, and to encouraging a critical view of the world, has created a positive atmosphere in which to work and write. I am also grateful to my students, who have questioned, challenged, and inspired me over the years. Four students deserve thanks for help with my research: Helen Harrison, Linda Driscoll, Margaret Phillips, and Rhonda Jessup.

Colleagues elsewhere also provided important support. I want to thank Joy Parr for her comments on a paper drawn from chapter 8, and Greg Kealey and Veronica Strong-Boag for comments on a paper drawn from chapter 6. Ruth Pierson offered useful suggestions on this manuscript and helped me clarify my views on oral history; Jane Arscott, Kate McPherson, Kathy Arnup, Cecelia Danysk, Franca Iacovetta, and Julie Guard have all offered me information and advice. My thanks also go to the Department of History, Dalhousie University, which provided me with office space during a sabbatical, and to my Halifax Women's History group – Judith Fingard, Frances Early, Janet Guildford, and Jane Parpart – for their immense support during my year in Halifax. Bryan Palmer kindly lent me his house when I needed a retreat to finish this book; Linda Kealey and Marg Hobbs offered friendly advice and support in the last stages of my writing. To the wonderful staff at Trent Child Care, who have provided loving and professional care for my children for over a decade, I owe sincere gratitude; thanks especially to Susan Scoffin, for her personal and political comradeship.

My family has lived with this book for many years. Although Kate, Laura, and Robbie sometimes resented its hold on my life, their pride in my accomplishments and their love and affection have sustained me through all the ups and downs of writing. David Poole helped me find the time and space I needed for academic work and gave me unwavering and unending emotional support and sustenance. Without this support, the book might not have been written.

Women working at Canadian General Electric in Peterborough during the
First World War

Women workers at Quaker Oats packing cereal into boxes in the 1920s

The Quaker Oats plant and the bridge to Ashburnham, or East City, in the 1920s

The 1937 textile strike at the Bonnerworth mill. The police gather in front of the building, while curious onlookers assemble on the other side of the street.

Young strikers on the Bonnerworth picket line

Striking women workers at the Bonnerworth mill after the police use tear gas

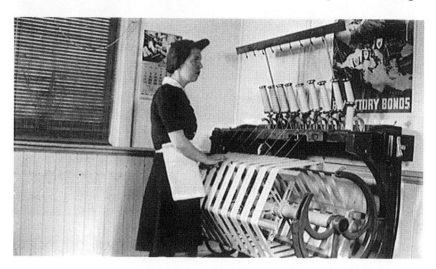

Training women for machine work. In the Second World War the Bonnerville mill set up small machines for women spinners and twisters to test their ability to use the larger machines.

Office work at Westclox. In the 1950s the plant workers unionized but the office workers did not.

Training at the Bell. After the war, white-collar work for women expanded considerably in Peterborough.

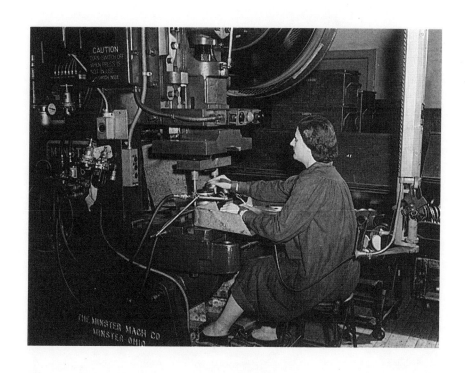

Punch-press work at Westclox

The cafeteria at Westclox

A Westclox promotional shot. Women were encouraged in the company newspaper to see themselves as consumers as well as workers.

A Westclox picture promoting productivity

A Westclox annual picnic in the 1950s

Women assembling clocks at Westclox in 1956

EARNING RESPECT

Introduction: Placing the Story of Women's Work in Context

This study of working women in Peterborough, a small manufacturing city in the heart of old Ontario, examines both the continuities and the changes in the lives of white- and blue-collar women workers from the 1920s to the 1960s. Structured chronologically, but also with reference to women's life course, the book concentrates on six issues: the social construction of women's identity as wage workers; their experiences of occupational segregation and work culture; their accommodation and resistance to wage work; their responses to economic, family, and social crises; and, finally, the gradual evolution of the female labour force from 'working daughter to working mother.'

To explore these themes, I have drawn heavily on oral history as a source, while simultaneously questioning the methodology itself throughout the book. The interviews and examples are drawn from four major industrial workplaces in Peterborough, two with a large female workforce (Dominion Woollens and Westclox) and two dominated by male workers (Quaker Oats and General Electric). Two different though sometimes overlapping age groups, or 'cohorts,' tell their stories: the first group of women interviewed went out to work in the period from 1928 to the Second World War; the second, including more working mothers, took up wage work in the post–Second World War period. In the second group, I widened the scope of my interviews to include more white-collar women, recognizing that the Dominion Woollens mill had closed and that women were flooding into clerical jobs. (See appendix A for a description of the interviews.) Moreover, it is important to note that women changed employment often; they went from domestic work to factory, from factory to home and back, and from one workplace to another, and thus the stories of those interviewed inevitably move beyond these designated factories, indicating the broader experiences of working women.

While my research began with a central focus on the workplace, it grew beyond this emphasis on productive relations, paying more attention to the interconnections between women's familial, community, and workplace lives. To understand the social relations of the workplace and the experiences, consciousness, and choices of women who supported themselves and their families with wages, I found it critically important to explore the cultural and political context and the contours of family and community life that framed these women's work lives.

The manufacturing base, workplace organization, cultural milieu, and labour traditions I describe are distinct to Peterborough, making this a tale shaped indelibly by region and locale. The small city in which these women lived was in fact more like a small town in atmosphere and outlook, because of its stability, insularity, established kin and social networks, and lack of significant immigration – hence the subtitle of the book, even though Peterborough was technically deemed a city. Indeed, as I did my research, this context also became a question: Did small-town life contribute to women's accommodation and consent in the workplace? Did long-standing community relationships or workplace traditions aid or limit women's resistance and unionization (which came relatively late to Peterborough)?

While these questions about accommodation and resistance are connected to ongoing debates in labour history, they are posed with reference to a local and particular setting. Some very vocal Canadian historians have recently decried the so-called fragmentation of history into consideration of the particular and the local and have similarly objected to the concentration on themes such as women's labour history rather than on the grand and masculine nation-building themes of the past. But local studies do offer an important means of exploring the changing organization of Canadian workplaces, the persisting sexual division of labour, and, most broadly, the construction of gender and class relations in mid-twentieth-century Canada.[1]

At the same time, I do not take the 'local' in a poststructuralist vein, as a rejection of the larger theories of historical causation or as a means of particularizing and decentring the past, calling into question the very notion of a continuous and 'explainable' history. On the contrary, a major concern of this book is to address the broader theoretical debates within North American working-class and women's history, as well as in oral history, and, in doing so, to look for common themes and patterns in the organization of work, to explore the dominant ideologies shaping gender relations, and to argue for the efficacy of a materialist-feminist framework of inquiry.

Attention to the controversies in working-class and women's history necessarily means engagement with the theoretical debates in and between Marxism, feminism, and, to a lesser extent, poststructuralism, all of which are current influences on the writing of working-class history. While a detailed replay of these controversies is not appropriate here, their impact on this study is relevant.

With the emergence of the new labour history over twenty years ago, neo-Marxist working-class history began to take a closer look at gender, pushed and prodded to do so by the challenges of feminists,[2] who contended that the lives of working women could not be pressed into the categories of a traditional class analysis that focused on workplace relations cast in a male-centred mould, and indeed that gender was a primary social category of analysis in itself.[3] Evidence drawn from working-class women's history was itself irrefutable proof that a narrow focus on the workplace obscured the vital role of social reproduction (such as the daily, domestic re-creation of the workforce) and the important connections of wage work to household, family, and interpersonal relationships, which were essential to an understanding of the whole working class.[4] Moreover, resilient forms of gender oppression, seemingly rooted – even autonomously – in ideology or in psychic structures, appeared to defy a pat economic analysis.[5]

Even if one looks narrowly at the workplace, one cannot escape gender. It was related to definitions of skill, to the creation of men's and women's jobs, to forms of authority and supervision, and to one's ability to engage in unions or to the experience of unemployment. But as Alice Kessler-Harris argues, gender was also located at home and in the streets, clubs, and unions. It shaped the very process of class formation. It moulded definitions of masculinity and femininity, defining the assumptions and identity that both men and women workers took with them as they entered and left the factory gates.[6]

Indeed, some Canadian historians have recently advocated the practice of a new gender history that would focus on both femininity and masculinity, on gender relations in *all* aspects of history.[7] I heartily endorse this aim, and I have used some interviews with men and have integrated discussion of male workers, masculinity, and gender into this study. Nonetheless, first and foremost, this book is committed to the recovery of women's stories. To privilege gender history over a supposedly more 'limited' women's history is, I believe, a mistake. We must remain committed to both, never losing sight of the extent to which women's stories are marginalized, trivialized, and obscured in our history and culture.[8]

In earlier attempts to understand women's work, including their responsibility for domestic labour, many authors utilized Marxist categories and historical materialism[9] or modified these categories, producing varieties of feminist Marxism, some of which went so far as to argue that women in themselves constituted a class.[10] Other theoretical models were more influential; for example, Heidi Hartmann's dual systems theory suggested that two analytically separate but interacting systems of oppression – patriarchy and capitalism – both with specific, material bases, shaped women's lives. Patriarchy was grounded in men's appropriation of women's labour and control of their sexuality; capitalism was based on the exploitation of wage labour.[11]

The assumption that there are two distinct social systems of oppression can, however, lead to a fragmented understanding of what is actually experienced as unified social life; or it can lead to an inherent privileging of either class or sex oppression, or to the assumption that patriarchal oppression is located in the family, and class oppression in the workplace.[12] As Veronica Beechey argues, it is too simplistic, for instance, to conclude that the sexual division of labour at work was a mere consequence of women's subordinate role in the family.[13]

While grappling with the inherent problems of separating two systems and then trying to argue that they were symbiotically related, socialist-feminist theorists increasingly insisted on a more unified theory of capitalist patriarchy, in which class and gender were interdependent and inseparable. For instance, Judy Lown's analysis of industrial paternalism, which I draw on in chapter 6, suggests that paternalism can only be comprehended by analysing the close connections between capitalism and patriarchy; both owner and worker were gendered beings, members of different classes, and their patriarchal and class interests were compatible or conflicting, depending on the particular historical conjuncture of events.[14] Most studies of working women have now accepted the inescapable links between social relations based on gender inequality and those based on class. Joy Parr's path-breaking *Gender of Breadwinners*, for example, makes a powerful argument that 'any approach that assumes that everything falls into one category or another [such as class or gender] but cannot belong to

more than one at the same time, belies the wholeness of consciousness and experience.'[15]

Deciphering the 'two-headed problematic'[16] of class and gender in
working-class history has itself been challenged more recently by the
integration of ethnicity and race into the theoretical equation. Explorations in Canadian gender history have been in the vanguard of this
encounter, though there are still few integrated studies of women, race,
and work.[17] In this book, ethnicity and race are not as central to my
analysis as class and gender. In part, this is the consequence of studying an extremely homogeneous community with an overwhelmingly
Anglo-Celtic culture, though I have also attempted to analyse the way
in which women and men constructed their racial and cultural identity as 'natural' and preferable. At the same time, any analysis of
ethnicity and culture needs to be historically specific: the major point
of 'difference' in Peterborough was not demarcated by race as much
as by the old Ontario divide – Orange versus Green, Catholic versus
Protestant.

A feminist approach to labour history would ideally employ a holistic analysis of power relations, accounting for culture, age, gender,
ethnicity, race, and culture as well as class. The tendency for class to
dominate in most labour history is still an issue of some debate. The
notion that the social relations of industrial society are patriarchal in
character, for instance, has been flatly rejected by some labour historians. Numerous critiques and counter critiques have dissected the word,
and many Marxists as well as feminists have argued that it offers little
as 'an explanatory concept.'[18]

Admittedly, the concept has been misused in an ahistorical, univer-
salist way, assuming the unchanging existence of a male quest for power
in all societies. Nonetheless, a definition that sees patriarchy as a system of 'practices, arrangements and social relations that ensure biological reproduction, child rearing and subjectivity,' and in doing so
reproduces the subordination of women, is in fact useful for a research
agenda.[19] The social, familial, and psychic structures that shape male
dominance need to be analysed in the historical context of class relations. In other words, we need to 'historicize patriarchy by studying its
many varieties'[20] and its materialist roots.

Like Judith Bennett, I am not ready to jettison the word patriarchy,
nor do I use it only in its traditional meaning of 'father rule.' In this
book it also denotes a social structure dominated by masculine power.
The term does not necessarily mean the juxtaposition of women as

victims and men as aggressors, nor does it suggest inevitable, undifferentiated sexual antagonism, though that theme may appear to be one part of our history.[21] At the same time, we must concede that patriarchal structures are not the only forces shaping women's existence and consciousness. The texture of the past must be unravelled by pulling out the relevant and historically specific threads of gender, race, and class relations, instead of placing theory, like a grid, over women's actual experiences.

Finally, the very words 'experience,' 'identity,' and 'ideology,' already used to describe my project, have recently come under intense theoretical scrutiny. The current influences of poststructuralism and of black feminist theory have reminded us that women have not constituted a unified group whose experience is easily definable by generalizations about gender. Also, many poststructuralist critics charge that the concept of experience is itself ephemeral and unknowable, and that our interpretations of it are mere constructions of past and present discourses. Some critics have also claimed that historians have too easily portrayed working women in a dichotomous manner of binary opposites, as either independent or dependent, as 'working class heroines or victims,' thus obscuring the complexity and complication in their lives.[22]

These criticisms are the reflections of a paradigm shift in feminist theory and, to a lesser extent, of new theoretical currents in history, which draw on poststructuralist writing, especially that of Foucault.[23] In feminist theory, this shift has been profound, leading to a new reorientation, as Michele Barrett says, 'from things to words'; from a belief in the certainties of issues such as low pay to a preoccupation with the way in which they are represented; from grand theories explaining women's oppression to micronarratives exploring the language and representation of that oppression. Materialism – emphasizing the influence of matter on consciousness or the way in which economic structures shape the boundaries of human behaviour – has been decisively pronounced 'decimated' by Barrett, one of its former Marxist-feminist advocates.[24]

It is understandable that feminist historians and social scientists have been drawn to some poststructuralist writing, given the mutual interest of feminist politics and poststructuralism in challenging androcentric epistemologies, critiquing essentialism, and exploring the power inherent in language and representation.[25] Moreover, Foucault's brilliant analysis of the operations of power, through the construction of taken-for-granted 'knowledges,' through disciplinary practices that have shaped modern institutions, and through the very way in which discourses are created, has undoubtedly enriched feminist theorizing.[26] Many feminist writers, of course, have used it only partially, or critically, since they are well aware of the danger of poststructuralism's 'deconstructing notions of oppression and exploitation so completely that they are abandoned.'[27]

What has been referred to as the 'linguistic turn' in American and European history (namely, the emphasis on analysis of representation, rather than the 'pursuit of a discernable, retrievable historical reality,' and the emphasis on language and discourse constituting historical events, rather than vice versa),[28] has been less influential in Canadian writing, the most interest being expressed by feminist social scientists and historians. Historians have not generally welcomed these theoretical currents,[29] undoubtedly because many of the poststructuralist, Foucauldian suppositions – especially Foucault's antihumanism, his emphasis on discontinuity, rupture, and chance in history, his rejection of theories of causality, and, more profoundly, his rejection of the idea that rational analysis leads one to 'better' forms of knowledge – profoundly challenge the dominant methods and suppositions underlying the teaching and writing of history in the West.

Many Canadian and international historians of the working class, with the obvious exception of Joan Scott, have been wary of, if not hostile to, this 'descent into discourse.' They take issue with the overdetermining role of language and the underlying idealism in some poststructuralist writing, the abandonment of notions of historical causality in favour of endless deconstruction, and the blatant refusal to grant significance to the material realities of survival and suffering faced by many working-class people in the past.[30] Some women's labour historians, while recognizing the appeal of this theory to feminists, are critical of its dismissal of materialism – long the basis of labour history – and hopefully wait for the 'present [theoretical] moods to pass'[31] (just as chickenpox always does, I suppose). More useful, perhaps, is Christine Stansell's counsel that we attend more seriously to the way in which language gives form to and constitutes the experience of working-class people, while remaining mindful of the fact that 'language is a process of social articulation indivisible from experience ... Ultimately, it is the activities of real women that press gender into the service of rhetoric.'[32]

All these debates have influenced this book. My analysis consciously works against 'sceptical' or 'ludic' poststructuralist writing, which embraces political agnosticism, emphasizes discontinuity, and collapses all into representation.[33] But it has been challenged positively by the more 'affirmative' or 'resistance' poststructuralist writing, which is interested in the construction of subjectivity; which assumes that deconstruction is useful, not to explode all theories but to create new ones; and which assumes that the 'how' of representation and discourse must be linked to the 'why' of economic interest, political practices, and state alliances.

By and large, however, this study draws more on materialist-feminist analyses, on Gramscian notions of ideology, consent, and hegemony. While it is true that every theoretical view is partisan and has little claim on absolute truth, a feminist-materialist outlook, as Rosemary Hennessey argues, claims that its truth is based on 'its explanatory power ... its success in solving the problems it sets for itself, its effectiveness in critiquing exploitation and the unequal distribution of resources ... and its own ability to produce an interested knowledge.'[34] In the ever-elusive last instance, I take it for granted that structures of material and gender power are realities that shape women's experiences and help or hinder them from altering the discourses available to them, which are in turn part of those power relations. The influence of socialist-feminist or Marxist-humanist traditions of engaged, political if not ideological writing are far more apparent in this manuscript than the 'emotional flatness,' antihumanism, and pessimism about human agency that is ingrained in so much poststructuralist writing.[35]

These theoretical debates are especially prescient in the area of oral history, which was originally portrayed by many feminist historians as a method of challenging the dominant historical paradigms by foregrounding women's experiences, consciousness, and identity.[36] These aims, however, have recently become far more problematic in the face of poststructuralist critiques.[37]

While linguistic theories are far from new in the field of oral history, the more recent turn to poststructuralism suggests a more exclusive concern with both linguistic structure and cultural discourses determining oral histories and, most important, a scepticism that we can locate and describe a concrete and definable women's experience, separate from the cultural discourses constructing that experience. At its extreme, this theoretical imperative implicitly downplays the agency of historical actors by declaring that life histories are narratives that simply 'reflect the cultural models available to us,' or that they 'may be texts which provide a conventionalized gloss on a social reality we cannot know.'[38]

Poststructuralist writing on oral history has encouraged interviewers to give new attention to language and narrative form, to the important cultural and ideological influences shaping women's memories, and to the power relationships inherent in creating this unique historical source.[39] The latter two issues, in fact, have been on the agenda for some time.[40] Oral historians have long recognized that interviews are not 'transparent' stories relaying 'reality,' and that interviews are endowed with meaning through the conceptual and linguistic frameworks available to us. In effect, they are double interpretations, shaped by more than one ideology; women's lives are 'made sense of from a number of vantage points, including those of the women experiencing the event, and those of the feminist scholar who appeals to women's lives as a basis for knowledge.'[41]

The emphasis on deconstruction has also encouraged scholars to examine interviews looking for multiple relations of power, based on age, culture, class, ethnicity, and gender, and to draw out the many, even contradictory, meanings displayed in women's words. As earlier oral historians who drew on concepts of ideology suggested, we need to make the construction of 'memory itself part of our study.'[42] Asking how and why women explain, rationalize, and make sense of their past, for instance, offers insight into the social and material framework within which they operated, the perceived choices and cultural patterns they faced, and thus the complex relationship between individual consciousness and culture.

In analysing my interviews, I have tried to attend to the way in which gender, class, culture, and political worldview create significant differences in how we remember and describe our lives.[43] These differences may be revealed not only through the content but also through the narrative form of the interview. Expression, intonation, asides, metaphors, even silences and omissions, offer clues to the construction of historical memory,[44] and there may be a theme that suffuses the life history, around which an informant shapes the presentation of her life, or there may be collective plots revealing how and why people's memories of their workplaces and communities are created.[45]

Not only is it necessary to have an understanding of how gender and class shape the interviewees' historical memory, but it is also important to acknowledge how our own political perspective shapes the creation of the oral document. Feminist social scientists have long critiqued the model of the interview based on supposed 'detachment' and objectivity, when in reality there is unequal control over the outcome.[46] Even though a detached objectivity may be impossible, a false claim to cooperative, equal sisterhood in the production of oral narratives is unrealistic. As sociologist Judith Stacey argues, feminist research that relies on interviewing is inevitably enmeshed in unequal and intrusive relationships, simply by virtue of our position as researchers and the position of other women, with less control over the finished product, as 'subjects' of study.[47]

These ethical issues are visibly highlighted through the conflicting interpretations that may be embraced by my informants and myself. Of necessity, historians analyse and judge, and in the process we may presume to understand the consciousness of our interviewees. Yet our analysis may contradict women's self-image, and our feminist perspective may be rejected by our interviewees. While I have tried to use the interview method to communicate women's own perceptions and truths, my interpretation of those truths is inevitably given some precedence in this book. We can honour our obligation never to reveal confidences spoken out of the interview and never purposely to distort their lives, but in the last resort it is our responsibility as historians to convey the insights of our interviewees, using our own insight.

At the same time that poststructuralist writing has highlighted these power imbalances we knew to exist, it has not, as Stacey notes, suggested any way of acting to ameliorate them.[48] Furthermore, poststructuralist preoccupations with language may trap us in a discussion of women's consciousness and representation, detached from women's actual social existence; similarly, one wants to avoid a pluralist emphasis on the contradictory consciousness and multiple accounts offered by women, which then conceals the hierarchy of power relations shaping their lives.[49] Finally, we do not want to lose sight of the totality of the historical picture; we need to juxtapose oral history with all our other historical sources, using it to supplement, question, and enlighten other versions of events.

In this study, the cultural influences constructing memory are considered, but they are situated within the framework of social and economic relations and imperatives. I assume that the women's narratives do reflect 'knowable and real' experiences,[50] always mediated by cultural codes, which may in turn come to shape their interpretation of experience in a dialectical sense. While it is important to analyse the way in which someone constructs an explanation for her life, ultimately there are patterns, structures, and systemic reasons for these constructions which must be identified to understand historical causality. Admittedly, each woman's story is unique and her consciousness may even be contradictory; collectively, though, these women's oral histories must be appraised with an eye to the social and historical context of the time, including the material structures of class, the dominant ideologies of femininity, and the pressure and rewards of familial demands. Without a firm grounding of oral histories in their material and social context, and without a probing analysis of the relation between the two, insights on narrative form and representation will remain unconnected to a critique of oppression and inequality.

The idea that we can easily name a clear, singular version of women's experience is admittedly problematic; previous feminist writing has been brought to task for precisely this error.[51] But it may be more dangerous to ignore a concept that allows women to 'name their own lives'[52] and struggles, and thus validates a notion of real, lived oppression experienced by women in the past. Negating an understanding of experience as a lived reality for women will only lead us back to a marginalization, perhaps trivialization, of their historical voices, their experience of oppression, their accommodation to it, and their efforts to resist it. However utopian an aim, however problematic an enterprise, and however difficult a task it may be to uncover those experiences, it should still be on our moral and political agenda. And that is the goal of this book.

1

Peterborough:
The 'Working Man's City'

By the mid-twentieth century, two epithets were used to describe Peterborough. On the one hand, its business and civic boosters termed it the 'Electric City' in homage to its abundant source of water-power and to one of its major manufacturing enterprises, Canadian General Electric (CGE). Less prevalent, but still revealing, was its characterization as 'the working man's city.'[1] During a bitter 1937 textile strike, it was ironically a prominent female CCFer who publicly condemned the absentee owner's exploitation of male breadwinners and called for the resurrection of Peterborough's long-standing good reputation as 'a working man's city.'[2]

Both these representations reveal aspects of the economic and social structure of this small city. Peterborough had emerged in the nineteenth century as a vibrant timbering and manufacturing town and as the local centre of government for the surrounding counties. Its growth, which was rapid until the 1920s, was aided by its easy access to water and rail transport. The surrounding area was originally populated by Irish settlers and by many British half-pay officers, earning it a reputation as one of the most 'loyal' British areas in the province; and the city grew, in large part, because of in-migration from the surrounding countryside, rather than by large immigration from outside Canada.

As timber was displaced, Peterborough became a growing manufacturing centre, with a strong local business élite intent on boosting the city's economic fortunes. 'Manufacturing,' note Peterborough historians Elwood Jones and Bruce Dyer, 'set the tone' for the city's economy, with 'government, tourist and commercial activities' complementing this base.[3]

A central focus of the city's early Industrial Revolution was the establishment of General Electric in 1891, first as a consortium including Edison Electric, and within a short time as the Canadian centre for the American multinational, General Electric (GE). This company was unarguably the largest and most powerful employer in the city; but in the next twenty years, many smaller but still significant employers, such as Quaker Oats, with as many as 500 employees, also became important additions to the local economy. Some businesses began as locally owned concerns but were bought out by the end of the 1920s by larger Canadian or international companies. Outboard Marine, Canada Packers, and the Auburn woollen mill (the latter founded in the mid-nineteenth century and eventually integrated into Dominion Woollens) all fit this pattern. Industrial development added new faces to the existing largely English political élites; the early-twentieth-century town councils, argue Jones and Dyer, were dominated by and reflected the interests of manufacturing and building concerns.[4]

While there were important variations and some ups and downs in women's employment in the city during the twentieth century – occasioned by the Depression, the Second World War, and changes in local economic conditions – nevertheless, a few generalizations can be made. The most obvious pattern over time was women's increasing participation in the labour force. From 1921 to 1961 the percentage of women in the labour force rose from 21 to 31 per cent, with an equivalent growth in their participation rate (appendix B, table 1). This was consistently higher than Canadian averages, in part because of the city's diversified economic base and the availability of jobs for women, though other factors, such as declining farm employment and a laxly enforced school-leaving age also may have been important.[5] Furthermore, this official labour force participation rate by women, drawn from the census, underestimated women's work, since seasonal, part-time, and domestic work was sometimes ignored or undervalued in the gathering of statistics. Chapter 5, which deals with the Depression, carries this argument further, questioning the way in which women's 'official' unemployment obscured women's actual unemployment in the 1930s.[6]

The increasing labour force participation rate by women was linked to escalating numbers of married and older women entering and re-entering the workforce, especially in the 1950s and 1960s. In 1931 the vast majority of women working in the city were young and single; by 1961 these working daughters laboured beside working mothers. In 1961 about 51 per cent of local women workers were married, while in 1931 it had been approximately 11 per cent; moreover, 40 per cent of the female wage earners in the city were between thirty-five and fifty-four, whereas thirty years earlier only one-quarter of women workers had been of this 'middle age.'[7] Over these same years, Peterborough women maintained a strong presence in the manufacturing sector; in the interwar years, this sector employed 40 per cent of the local working women, though perhaps only about two-thirds of these were in blue-collar jobs.

For women's employment in manufacturing, a turning-point had come with the establishment of the Bonnerworth woollen mill in 1911. The mill was originally owned by a manager and two superintendents from Penman's knitting mill in Paris, Ontario: Issac Bonner and the brothers J.W. and Edgar Worth. It started with a mere 35 employees; by 1919 the number was 275, and it drew in two other mills, including the Auburn, to form Canada Woollens.[8] A further amalgamation in 1928, with textile capital from Montreal and Toronto, created Dominion Woollens, the largest woollen-producing company in Canada. By 1931, with new tariffs shoring up the industry, textiles employed about 350 women in the city, the majority of whom worked at the Bonnerworth mill, making worsted yarn. At that time, textiles provided 60 per cent of women's manufacturing jobs in Peterborough and 16 per cent of all their work.[9]

Although women had previously found blue-collar manufacturing jobs in factories such as CGE and Quaker Oats, where they continued to make up approximately 10 to 15 per cent of the payroll, the Bonnerworth mill created a substantial number of new jobs for women.[10] Diversity in manufacturing choices increased even more during the 1920s, when other 'light' manufacturing in food and small appliances, made with modern assembly-line processes, came to Peterborough. Ovaltine, Brinton Carpets, and Westclox – the latter, another child of an American corporation, the Western Clock Company (later, General Time) – were all examples of these new industries. Westclox, the largest of these three, built a new model factory in 1923 and by the Second World War had 800 employees, about 60 per cent of whom were women.

This period also saw an increase in the number of women in white-collar jobs linked to these businesses and to the retail and financial sectors. For example, from 1921 to 1941 alone, the number of women in office jobs appears to have doubled.[11] The numbers again increased dramatically in the 1950s and 1960s. Along with this expansion came a gradual decrease in women in domestic service. Paralleling Canadian trends, women tried to move away from domestic employment, opting instead for manufacturing jobs, or service work such as waitressing, in preference to the unending hours and lower status of domestic employment (appendix B, tables 2 and 3). Between 1911 and 1941, the percentage of domestics in the local female workforce fell (unevenly, because of a small rise during the Depression) from 17 per cent to about 9 per cent, and in the post–Second World War period the number plummeted to about 1 per cent.[12] Although young women continued the long-established tradition of coming to the city, often from surrounding rural areas, and starting off in service, they kept their eyes open for a well-paying factory job or even a white-collar job, which gave them more independence, more camaraderie, and higher wages than housework.[13] Increasingly, older women, with their own families, turned to part-time domestic work as a means of contributing cash resources to their family economy.

Over time, women increased their presence in retail, financial, and clerical work – and, after the Second World War, very significantly in teaching and nursing. By 1961, manufacturing was somewhat weakened as an option for women, who were more likely to be found in clerical and service-related jobs. This shift was most noticeable between 1951 and 1961, when the number of women in manufacturing declined for the first time since the early years of the century. The Bonnerworth mill closed in 1958, and although new post–Second World War factories such as Johnson and Johnson offered blue-collar work to women, in terms of new jobs, manufacturing employment now lagged behind that of the service sector. This trend was to become more pronounced in the next twenty years as many of the city's branch plants downsized or, like Westclox, simply closed their doors.

While women were a significant minority in manufacturing, they were ghettoized, clustered in smaller and 'lighter' manufacturing and in certain tasks within each workplace; both vertical (within job categories) and horizontal (in different occupations) segregation characterized their working lives. In the interwar period, job segregation was probably extremely severe; a recent study has argued that, save for the 1941 census figures, occupational segregation by gender remained quite consistent in the twentieth century until minor changes appeared in the 1970s.[14] Even a cursory glance at Peterborough's census returns unmistakably reinforces this conclusion: decade after decade, women were absent from heavy manufacturing and the skilled trades, and within textiles they were listed as spinners, not loom fixers; in office work they were listed as stenographers, not accountants; in electrical work, as coil winders, not machinists.

In the latter case, women's role in the GE workforce was similar to that in the rest of the electrical industry in southern Ontario.[15] There were fewer women in the Peterborough factory because of its focus on heavy industry, but like women in the Toronto electrical factories, they were recruited for unskilled and semi-skilled jobs in mass production, doing repetitive work such as coil winding. In other ways, however, women's employment patterns in this city were quite distinct, particularly in the diversity and availability of blue-collar work. In contrast to women in northern resource towns, where there was little wage work for females, women here had far more opportunity to pursue both white- and blue-collar work;[16] and in contrast to women of colour in other cities, who faced severe employment discrimination but still had to work for wages, this white workforce was not limited to jobs in domestic service or family businesses.[17]

The most obvious consequence of the sexual division of labour that women encountered here was their lower wages. In the 1930s, for instance, in the electrical industry, male machinists might make over $800 a year, while women were winding coils, making $400 a year.[18] The differential between the average salary of women and men in the city remained a fairly consistent 51 to 56 per cent over this entire period (though, admittedly, there were some periods, such as the Second World War, when women's wages advanced). Within both blue- and white-collar work, there was discrepancy and alteration over time on either side of this average. In 1931, for example, women in manufacturing as a whole made about 45 per cent of men's annual wages, though in textiles they fared a little better, at just over 50 per cent, largely because men's wages were comparatively low, and in electrical assembly work they did better still, making about 60 per cent of men's earnings, though they often had fewer weeks of work. Office workers managed the best of all, making just over 60 per cent of what their male counterparts earned[19] (appendix B, table 4). However one computes the variations in these differentials (and we lack ongoing evidence from all the censuses), an inescapable conclusion remains: jobs routinely done by women were undervalued; women were sometimes paid less even when they had the same education and did the same jobs as men; and, ultimately, their wages made it difficult for them to move outside a circle of dependency within the nuclear family.

Not all working men, of course, enjoyed high wage levels and unending economic opportunity; male textile workers, for example, were notoriously underpaid compared with other male occupations, and Depression tensions revealed ethnic prejudice against workers from minority groups such as the city's small Italian population. At the same time, the positive image of opportunity in this working-man's city was based on the availability of manufacturing employment and on the ability of some men to use fraternal and family networks to secure jobs or apprenticeships, or to set up their own small businesses.

This fluidity between wage work and self-employment became clearly apparent in the 1920s, when an alternative Independent Labour Party emerged and then quickly foundered, as some trade union leaders who were elected to represent 'the working man' found that when they were in office, their loyalties were just as easily claimed by the wider community or even by the board of trade. Peterborough was characterized by a curious combination of class-conscious political identification on one hand and, on the other, by strong non-class loyalties based on a broader identification with the community. In the early 1920s, when a 'labourist' political movement calling for gradual reform and integration of workers into the existing political machine emerged, working-class voters clearly supported these men. As Suzanne Morton has argued, however, this labour coalition quickly fell apart when these same trade unionists supported a reformist and popular local Liberal lawyer, G.N. Gordon; when they deserted the trade union platform to side with other community leaders; and when some of them themselves became small businessmen. The British-born, unionized, skilled élite, who spoke locally for labour in the interwar period, often took whatever pragmatic political route would protect or enhance their economic and social position. As Morton concludes, 'The working class ... at certain times identified themselves by collective action ... [but] the skilled craftsmen were often indistinguishable from small businessmen. In a small community ... personal relationships extended beyond class through many networks. This weakened, but did not eliminate class consciousness.'[20]

Morton's conclusions reinforce my argument, developed in chapters 6 and 7, that both paternalistic ties of loyalty between worker and manager and a class-conscious sense of distinct identity, goals, and values existed in the city. This is well summed up in two oral reminiscences of workers who described their social connection to their managers. On the one hand, a General Electric worker spoke of the managers' and workers' differences in outlook and goals, based on class; in particular, he decried the close connection between the company and the local political élite, which left workers out in the cold: 'GE always had some representative on council. They knew how to control things in this city for their own good.' On the other hand, a textile worker commented on the politeness, care, and respect extended to her by her manager, 'who always showed me to my seat in church.'[21]

Both workers relayed important aspects of Peterborough's small-town life. The GE worker was correct in assessing the close identification of the business élite with local politics, the power exercised by this élite, and the exclusion of working people from that power. Since the late nineteenth century, generous municipal concessions had lured businesses to the city, and despite some protest, the businesses retained their favoured position for some time. As Elwood Jones notes, 'The life of the city was dominated by a small and powerful group of business leaders.'[22]

Moreover, labour unrest and class antagonism were also part of the city's history, as evidenced during the bitter 1937 textile strike and the intermittent labour conflict at CGE and other workplaces. Labour struggles in the city also reveal considerable change within the trade union movement during this entire period, for the local labour movement was characterized by particularly dramatic ups and downs and, after the Second World War, by sharp differences in political outlook.

Although the skilled workers remained the dominant trade union spokespersons in the 1920s, their unions went into a severe decline even before the Depression. In 1919 there were twenty-eight unions in the area, with a membership of one thousand; by 1929 only twenty remained, and by 1933 their number had dropped to a low of eighteen.[23] Labour suffered some significant defeats, which hurt its local influence, until a resurgence during the Second World War and the unionization of CGE into the United Electrical Workers (UE) in 1946. Once the traditional craftsmen were joined by wider industrial unions, the tenor of labour politics changed, becoming more militant. It also became more internally rancorous. Within two years of the founding of an Allied Labour Council representing all workers in 1946, its unions were split, bitterly and for a long time, on political grounds. Rapprochement did not even begin until 1967.

Spatially and geographically, class also characterized the city. Many working people from GE lived in sections of the south end near the plant; those working across the river at the Auburn mill lived close by, in 'East City' (the old Ashburnham village across the Otonobee river).

An analysis of the Bonnerworth wage lists of 1934 shows a similar concentration of textile workers in the city's central area.[24] The women remember a sense of cohesion and familiarity in these areas. In commenting on the closely knit neighbourhood in Ashburnham, one woman said, 'We were East City people ... My mother was born there and went to school there ... and I did too ... I went to St Lukes and Mother's people all lived nearby.'[25]

While class was certainly evident in the community's spatial organization, these divisions were not as rigid as in many single-industry towns. There were no large tracts of company-built housing for workers; white-collar workers lived alongside company presidents in the downtown area; and supervisors and foremen often resided very close to their workers, so that women remember walking or driving to work with their superiors.[26] Even more important, male managers and workers mixed regularly in the city's most popular fraternal organizations, such as the Masonic Lodge and the International Order of Foresters (and perhaps in the powerful local Orange Lodge). Women, too, had close contact with managers, through church, athletics, or even family networks. In a community where worker and manager rubbed elbows on these social planes, a tenuous sense of class accommodation and community could be fostered. Certainly, it was often the women's *perception* that the smallness of the city encouraged a sense of community, rather than rigid social divisions. One factory worker, for example, spoke nostalgically about the small-town atmosphere and sense of community in the larger city, noting that before the Second World War ('when some strangers came in'), she could 'go downtown and talk to practically anybody – you knew them ... It was a nice compact little town, real small-town stuff.'[27]

The sense of community identification was also created within a clearly ethnocentric context. The religious and ethnic make-up of the city remained predominantly white and Anglo-Saxon throughout this period. There were few immigrants, especially from groups outside the existing population of British ancestry. This made for a relatively stable and homogeneous community, though one that was suspicious of outsiders. Even the establishment of a single Chinese restaurant was vigorously protested by citizens in the 1920s.[28] Nor did this suspicion of outsiders who were not Anglo and Christian dissipate easily. Even after a small trickle of European immigrants arrived after the Second World War, a British war bride remembers 'being surprised at how closed [the city] was, how people still said awful things about the

Jewish people in town.'[29] The few non-British European immigrants vividly recall the sense of exclusion and alienation they experienced in the midst of the overwhelming Anglo, Canadian-born population.

As tables 5 to 7 in appendix B indicate, there were almost no Asians or even eastern or southern Europeans in the city through this period, and the local Jewish community, which certainly experienced anti-Semitism, was extremely small compared with that in Toronto and other larger cities. People of Italian extraction, a mere 1 per cent of the population, were one of the largest non-Anglo minorities in the city. The small Native Reserves in the surrounding countryside constituted less than 1 per cent of the county's population, and Native women were less likely to be involved in wage labour or social activism in the city at this time.[30] All these structural factors meant that most workers took for granted, or 'naturalized,' their racial and to some extent their ethnic privilege.[31] While non-white or non-Anglo immigrants may not have appeared a 'threat' to the dominant Anglo-Celtic élite, as they did elsewhere, it is clear that being white and of British origin carried with it a sense of superiority. As one woman noted, once when she was treated particularly badly at work, she equated her position at the bottom of the ladder with that of a woman of colour: 'I said to the foreman, "What is the matter with you? Am I black or something?"'[32]

The most significant 'cultural' difference apparent to many workers were religious differences based on old Irish Catholic or Anglo Orange loyalties. These were even more noticeable in the surrounding countryside, sections of which were notorious, historically, for anti-Catholic activity. These divisions, which were exacerbated by segregation in separate schooling and by a strong tradition of religiously based cultural and fraternal organizations, intruded into the workplace. As one Catholic skilled male worker remembers, access to jobs was shaped by religious connection: 'The toolroom [at one factory] ... was controlled by Masons; I couldn't work there.'[33] Oral evidence indicates, however, that these intense divisions were lessened somewhat after the Second World War.

In the post–Second World War period, a sense of strong British and white identity, even insularity, still characterized the community. In fact, Peterborough's civic fathers boasted publicly of the positive benefits of their ethnocentric, homogeneous city. In the 1950s, a city publication encouraging investment offered the barely disguised racist claim that Peterborough was peopled by a 'pioneer race of British tradition,' characterized by 'courage and industry.' Conversely, it claimed,

'Peterborough has remained free of all problems arising from inter-
mingled races. Less than one percent of its citizens have their ante-
cedents in southern Europe.' Labour troubles, it declared as a corollary, were therefore 'unknown' – rather a puzzling claim, given the
city's history.[34]

This, then, was the 'small-town' city that framed the working
women's lives as they grew up, were schooled, and then went out to
work for wages. The choices and difficulties they faced in the workforce
were delineated not only by the structural shape of local industry, by
the women's employment opportunities, and by the city's class traditions, but also by the women's earliest family life, their schooling, and
their adolescent peer culture – topics to which we shall now turn.

2

Schooling Girls for Women's Work

In the 1930s, when she was only thirteen, Lilly went out to work at the Bonnerworth woollen mill. She secured the job through her aunt, who 'spoke for her' and was able to keep an eye on her at work. Lilly turned over most of her pay to her mother for board, and she happily discovered that once she began work she had fewer chores at home, a recognition that she was exhausted from her nine-hour workday. Indeed, she remembers simply dozing off at the supper table: 'I came home so tired I would *just* be able to eat my supper. I was only 90 pounds, you know. I would just set my plate aside and put my head on the table and fall fast asleep.' [1]

Despite her status as a full-time worker and her responsibility to the household, it is difficult to visualize Lilly as anything but a child. Her story immediately raises a number of queries: Why did she leave school even before the legal and official age? How important was her wage to the family? Did her wage work change her status in the family? Was her choice of job different from those of her brothers? How did her early family life, schooling, and peer culture shape her choice of wage work?

These questions constitute the basis of this chapter. Women's earliest understanding of wage work, adopted and mediated through family, schooling, and peer culture, helped to reproduce the sexual division of labour in the workforce. The 'lessons for life'[2] that girls and young women learned at home, at school, at church, and in the streets constructed their ambition and aims as wage earners. As Bettina Bradbury argues, it is essential that we comprehend how the workforce has 'been gendered before it arrives at the factory gates.' Family needs and strategies for survival, the existing ideology, and social practice regarding gender roles were all crucial factors shaping when, how, and where women went out to work. Underlying these influences lay the tightly linked capitalist labour market and patriarchy, which together reproduced and sustained women's subordinate role in the workforce.[3]

Women's negotiation of the dominant messages about work that they learned at home and at school was, admittedly, individual and unique, but there are some common factors that shaped their views of work: the exposure of young girls to a rigid sexual division of labour, especially in domestic life; a cultural view of extended education being of limited use, particularly for girls; and the socialization of children to a familial ideology of obligation and respect for authority. Children, of course, did not automatically and completely internalize the lessons intended for them. Some resented their imposed familial obligations, while others quietly created alternative family and work relationships; but, more often, the prevailing 'gender and class contract'[4] was accepted, at least in part, by young women.

Some historians of youth contend that school leaving marked a major transition to semi-independence for all young people,[5] but as this chapter shows, the lines between childhood, adolescence, and adulthood were not so definitely delineated for working-class girls.[6] For many females in Peterborough, childhood and adolescence involved unwaged work followed by waged work, but the latter did not necessarily bring financial and personal independence. Clearly apparent was the increasing adult concern over the young women's leisure and moral lives, whether they went to school, stayed home, or earned a full wage. These contradictions simply underscore the danger of 'applying theories of youth as an *age* cohort, without an understanding that this life stage contains within it the broader contradictions of class and gender.'[7] The concern that girls should learn and do domestic labour, the need for their contribution to the household economy, the anxiety about their sexual morality, and the notion that their ambition ought to be different from men's were all tied together, an integrated part of their distinct experience as working-class girls who were being schooled for womanhood and work.

MEMORIES OF CHILDHOOD AND THE FAMILY

Historical debates about children and youth have centred predominantly on the role of children in the family economy, the attempts of reformers and school promoters to 'improve' the lives of working-class children, and the emergence of a 'modern' adolescence in the early twentieth century. The latter was supposedly characterized by increased schooling and greater dependence on parents, a more heterosocial world, and a self-conscious awareness of adolescence as a time of intense psychological and sexual change. This awareness was not only exhibited by youth, but also by adults anxious to extend institutional controls over the behaviour of the young.[8] These three themes – family, schooling, and adolescence – are used here as a means of investigating women's early lessons about wage work. More than any other chapter, this one is shaped by the conclusions gained from oral history.

Nowhere are the possibilities and predicaments of oral history more vividly displayed than in the quest for the history of childhood. Oral testimonies provide a means of overcoming the barriers of age and class that have long obscured the history of childhood. They offer the possibility of 'adult insight into childhood feelings and thoughts unrecognized at the time,' and they provide a means of detailing the most basic structures of work and play, which are usually deemed unimportant in other historical sources.[9] Moreover, oral recollections may modify or even counter the interpretations left by reformers and school promoters, whose writing has been shaped by their own political agendas and class bias.

At the same time, the ideological influences on memory are especially problematic in relation to childhood. Power relationships may be repressed or forgotten, and the expected feelings and cultural images of joy, play, and leisure that are associated with childhood may come to shape one's recollections. As a means of justifying or understanding the present, the women interviewed sometimes constructed a highly idealized childhood. One woman who grew up in the 1930s, for example, cast her youthful years in terms that erased all the social problems of the time: 'We never wanted for what kids do today. We never had much spending money, but we were happy ... There was more closeness then, and we never questioned everything ... We were happy-go-lucky. We never saw things like alcoholism that you do today.'[10] A nostalgic equation, which looks critically on the indulged youth of today and sees early school leaving and early wage work as a healthy, character-building tonic, was a common assumption; this dominant 'script' could then shape the women's descriptions of their family and their wage work in a very profound way.[11] Similarly, the women's oral accounts often assumed the universal existence of a nuclear family – with a male breadwinner, a female homemaker, and dependent children – even though, on closer probing, it was evident that other family forms, including single-parent families, also existed.[12]

Notwithstanding these dilemmas, oral history provides essential insights into the role of young women in the family and the way in which this shaped their later working life. As Elizabeth Roberts argues in her oral history of British working-class women, girls' understanding of their future was grounded first and foremost in family life: 'The family remained the dominant mode of socialization, even more so than the school.'[13] In the work they performed at home, and in their interactions with siblings and parents, children were 'acquiring their class and gendered identities.'[14] Whether one accepts a Freudian interpretation of gender acquisition (and there is reason to be suspicious of a universal, classless psychoanalytic theory) or socialization theories of learned behaviour, it is clear that relationships with parents and siblings, daily games and chores, and immersion in the cultural rituals of girlhood all helped turn females into young women.[15] Their socialization to work roles involved the internalization of important messages about class status and the need for economic contribution to the household, the inflexibility of the sexual division of labour, and respect for parental authority.

YOUTHFUL WORK

What, first of all, were the economic and social conditions faced by the first cohort of women, those who went out to work before the Second World War? Women who became factory and white-collar workers in the 1930s came predominantly from backgrounds where the father but not the mother worked, or tried to work, full-time for wages in similar occupations.[16] At the same time, most women from this age group grew up with the understanding that more than one earner would be needed to maintain their family's economic security. Since the late nineteenth century, a family-wage economy – with pooled resources and more than one earner – was common to working-class life in most Ontario cities.[17] Except for families with skilled and very securely employed men, there was rarely a single male breadwinner during the entire family life cycle. Once the children were of an appropriate age, they were expected to help out. As other historians have shown, various collective family 'strategies,' reflecting shared notions of appropriate work roles, were attempted in order to achieve economic survival. While these strategies were forged within the unequal gender and age relations of family life, offering women few choices, in retrospect, women now stress the consensual rather than constraining nature of their youthful work for their parents.[18]

Women whose fathers were printers, machinists, or bookkeepers often had mothers who did not work for wages, and they were more likely to live in owned homes. But even in these families, there was always a hovering element of uncertainty, created by fears of illness (especially of the adult wage earner) or of temporary lay-off or a death in the family. One woman whose father was a machinist remembered that shorter hours became a practice at General Electric during slack times in the 1930s, thus reducing the family's income and creating a sense of insecurity which they had never before experienced. Another woman, whose father was a printer, felt that the family budget allowed her very little money for things such as clothes, which were so important to high school culture, so she decided to go out to work to help the family. Yet when assessing the level of their family's financial need, the women often compared their predicament to those who were worse off, mentioning others who lacked the two basic necessities of respectability: food to eat and decent clothes to wear. 'We were lucky,' remembered a woman whose father was a skilled worker. 'We always had food and new shoes if they were needed. We had cousins who wore cardboard in their shoes to school until they got their [relief] vouchers.'[19]

Women who came from families with unskilled and especially underemployed fathers remember overhearing their parents' ongoing worries about finances. This left an important mark on their consciousness: '*We* always had to worry about money,' recalled a woman whose father did odd jobs such as cutting wood. Her use of the collective voice signifies how children, from a very early age, saw the family's financial problem as a shared one.[20] In a small minority of families, girls saw their mothers working for wages as well, always doing so in addition to their arduous homemaking tasks. The job a woman chose depended on her skills, the ages of her children, and the state of her household. A few mothers worked in factories or offices, but many more participated in the informal economy. If there was room (for example if one child had left home), boarders might be taken in. More prevalent was the practice of sewing or doing part-time domestic work for pay.

The importance of this 'extra' work to the family is sometimes downplayed – quite unconsciously – in women's memories; their way of remembering highlights the ideological prominence of waged labour, in contrast to the devaluation of unwaged work of the informal economy. One woman, for example, described her parents' household as a traditional male-breadwinner one, since her father worked at General Electric. Yet later, when remarking on her mother's kindness in making her beautiful clothes when she secured a white-collar job, she alluded to her mother's economic contribution to the household: 'My mother was also a seamstress. She made clothes for people. During the Depression, when my father worked ... sometimes he only got two days [a week] ... Mother could support us the rest of the time with dressmaking. I can remember going to bed with her working at her treadle machine. Heaven only knows when she went to bed.'[21] 'The rest of the time' actually made the difference between sinking into poverty and allowing the two children in the family some high school education – a crucial distinction for many working-class families in this period.

Women from the first cohort were also exposed to radical shifts and uncertainty in economic conditions, notably the Great Depression. For the women born between 1914 and 1924, who went out to work from the late 1920s to the end of the 1930s, the average school-leaving age was fifteen. Yet for many of these girls, the economic pressures imposed by the family economy remained the same throughout the entire interwar period. The Great Depression, seen by historians as an economic watershed, was not necessarily a turning point in these women's memories. For many women who came from working-class families there was little difference between the difficult times their families faced before and after 1929. Most of the women of the first cohort believed that family necessity propelled them to work, whether it was in 1928, 1933, or 1937. After 1940, increased wages and a higher school-leaving age lessened but never abolished the need for youngsters' economic contribution to the family. Young people were still expected to find work and 'pay their own way' once they left school, even if their wages were not directly applied to the family budget but were used for self-support. As Isabel, who started work in the 1950s, remembers, her parents believed in the value of work and financial self-support: 'I quit school [at seventeen] and that's when I went to the factory. My mother told me I wasn't going to fool around and do nothing. I had to work.'[22]

The Depression did, of course, accentuate certain economic stresses for many families. The seasonal and uneven work patterns of semi-skilled fathers, underemployment, and fear of debt all increased, so that the pressure for youngsters to help out was felt more intensely. Thus, in retrospect, some women did explain their early entry into the workforce by the onset of the Depression. Still, an equal number attributed early wage work to their membership in large families; and because of this, they often added emphatically that they had resolved to limit their families and offer their own children more opportunity – and most did have smaller families.

Although many of the women at first described their childhood and youth as a time 'before work,' they were also able to list the unwaged work they had performed in the household. The sexual division of labour, while clearly shaped by the sphere of production, was also created within this connected sphere of social reproduction, for children's chores, expected in almost every household, were sex-segregated. Girls performed housework such as cleaning and cooking, but also sometimes did outside work such as collecting wood; boys primarily did outside work. On farms, all the children might help outside at harvest time, but it was the girls who helped inside with the cooking. Even if boys did inside domestic labour, it was not seen as important for them to learn the methods and intricacies of the work; as Neil Sutherland points out, 'the standards [for boys learning domestic labour] were more lax.'[23] In this period, these lessons were clear-cut; few boundaries were crossed. Some girls did resent this division of labour or feel it unfair that they worked at two jobs while the boys had only one. 'I always felt as if my brothers never did as much work as I did [on the farm], but I wouldn't have said that, then [or now],' remembered one woman. Another was more open about gender inequity in this division of labour: 'My mother would send me on an [errand] before school ... and I also did the wood, the boys didn't always do that job. That was my life. My brother sat beside the stove in winter and summer, but I ran. I made the beds on Sunday morning, dusted upstairs before church. I was like a second mother. But it didn't do me any harm. It helped me think about how to treat other people [properly].'[24] The fact that both boys and girls did some kind of work tended to obscure this inequity. As Marilyn Porter has pointed out in a similar study, 'girls saw their brothers working as well, so even if they didn't do the same amount of work or the same range of tasks, they didn't resent them.'[25]

Children's unwaged work involved a wide range of activities, from some scrounging for needed household items to collecting fuel, doing the dishes, and helping in the garden (both in the country and also among families who lived on the outskirts of town and kept small plots). Part of the domestic responsibility of young girls was often helping with younger siblings; indeed, one still finds some examples of girls being kept home from school by their mothers to help out with large families, a continuation of the practice evident in the nineteenth century.[26] This was not so common, however, that it kept more girls out of school than boys on a widespread level: public school attendance was roughly equal for city boys and girls.[27]

Some children gradually took on other small jobs that brought in small bits of cash. A woman who went out to work at thirteen at the Bonnerworth mill had already worked, selling her aunts' homegrown vegetables door to door; another woman, who went to Westclox when she was sixteen, had worked part-time at the candy counter at Zellers. Part-time work also reflected a distinct sexual division of labour.[28] Girls did not take on paper routes or deliveries; boys did not do retail work or babysitting – though the latter was not common in the 1930s, undoubtedly because people had less disposable income, especially for leisure. These part-time jobs were often located through parents or other family members, and they carried with them some obligation of supporting oneself or donating earnings to the family. From the parents' point of view, both unwaged help at home and part-time work provided important lessons in the need for financial self-sufficiency, the moral value of labour, and the appropriate roles for men and women.

When another full-time income was needed in the household, most families assumed that teenagers, rather than homemakers would be the most logical earners. This strategy was shaped by the lack of economic opportunities for married women in the labour market, combined with a prevailing ideology of domesticity, as well as by the practical necessity of having a homemaker perform the arduous tasks of family care. Most families in the 1920s and 1930s were without refrigerators and had wood stoves and, at best, primitive wringer washers, making housework a time-consuming enterprise.

It was not only family income that determined when a child would go out to work. Birth order, the ability of relatives to help out, the number of children, and their mother's part-time work all helped shape economic necessity and the responses to it. The exact time in the family's life cycle was crucial. For the eldest child, with younger siblings coming after, there was often more pressure to earn money, since the mother was unable to work and the eldest was most aware of her parents' financial worries. In the following testimony from a woman who went into the woollen mill at fifteen, many of these considerations are evident. She remembers the material pressures created by the unsteady employment of her father, a sense of obligation to her parents, a feeling of shame that her sister was already helping out, and finally, a strong sense of the inevitability of one's decision – 'that's the way it was then':

I started at fifteen, I think it was 1933. It was during the Depression, I know, and there wasn't enough money to go around. I went to grade nine, but by that time I really had to pitch in. By then, I already had a sister working ... Yes, it was always that way then ... There were six kids in the family, first my sister and me, and then four younger brothers. Mother would go out to clean houses, not all the time, half days, and father would be home. He wasn't working steady. Finally, he got a job at the canoe company. Then, when my brothers were in the services [during the war], my mother took in boarders.[29]

Wage work by the unmarried daughters in the family was clearly the expectation placed on many girls from a very young age. It was just a question of when they would leave school – at thirteen, fifteen, or perhaps seventeen. Although some parents also saw girls' helping out at home as an option, this was far less common than in the nineteenth century. The wage-earning daughter was now here to stay. There were even cases where a young woman's parents wanted her to continue in school but she privately felt that she had a more realistic sense of the family fortunes and so chose wage work: 'Mother wanted me to be a nurse or teacher perhaps. But we were fairly poor. I felt I could work and bring board home ... They really didn't have the money to send me to college.' [30]

The importance of a young woman's wages to the family should not be underestimated. A survey of wages drawn from the censuses of 1921 and 1931 reveals how much teenagers could contribute to the family economy. In 1931, for instance, a man might earn from $800 to a high of $1,000 a year as a truck driver, machinist, carpenter, or mechanic. (Bookkeepers made a little more, averaging about $1,050 for forty-six weeks of work.) The low end of this scale fell below the basic cost-of-living budget designed by the federal Department of Labour. The wages earned by a young female textile worker, factory operative, or book-keeper averaged about $400 a year; but if two-thirds or more of her wages became part of the family income, this could help move the family across the poverty line, providing the income needed for a more secure standard of living.[31]

Intertwined with the realities of economic necessity encouraging girls' wage work was a strong bond of familial obligation and loyalty that cannot be overemphasized as a learned value, shaping women's early understanding of work. In the interviews, the women continually stressed their willing fulfilment of this obligation. In part, this was a means of emphasizing their respectability and good character to me, but they were also indicating how this obligation was taken for granted by their peers and relatives at the time. Many emphasized their desire to ease the burden on their mothers, whom they witnessed attempting to manage the family budget against difficult odds. Their empathy for their mothers' situation points to a strong mother-daughter bond in these working families, a type of bond obscured by later, popular (Freudian) psychological theories, which are often based on a presumption of mother-daughter familial tension.[32] By and large, the women did not describe the pressure to work as oppressive. Wage work was an accepted, reciprocal obligation; their parents had worked for them, and now it was their turn to help their parents. Moreover, donating money to the family budget sometimes brought with it a measure of independence and respect, which young women intent on more freedom were eager to earn.

Not all girls, of course, had close and respectful relationships with their mothers, nor did all children accept their duty to work for the family. An emphasis on family strategies for survival can obscure the differences in bargaining power, the disagreements, tensions, and resentments that also characterized family life. In a family that was helped by the local Children's Aid Society (CAS), the mother made a (common) request to have her teenage daughter, who had been temporarily taken away, come back and live at home. She argued before the board that family solvency would be ensured by the daughter's work in a factory. The daughter, however, was already boarding out and did not want to work in a factory. In fact, she had no desire to return home to help support her biological family. The CAS board was split over whether to endorse the necessity of filial obedience or to allow some autonomy for the daughter, and after a protracted debate it opted for the latter.[33] In another case, an adopted child remembered her parents' financial directives to 'quit school' and go out to work as being authoritarian and cold; and in a case where a stepmother had come into the household, so much tension existed that the young woman felt unjustly pressured to leave and take up wage work. An assumption of obligation, however, still existed. Although sometimes resisted and in some cases grudgingly given, it was invariably demanded and was seldom rejected completely.

Girls' early lessons about respect for family authority went beyond an understanding of the need for financial contribution; they encompassed a recognition of the imperatives and inevitability of authority and hierarchy. Interestingly, a few of the women lauded such values as being indicative of their Anglo or British ethnic identity. They pointed out that one's respectability came from a good upbringing, a respect for authority, politeness to one's elders, and good manners. Despite their association of these as 'English'[34] traits, though, their sentiments were shared by women who came from Italian families, which clearly embraced similar values.

The women's most salient memories of childhood often included punishment for the times they dared to question or disobey their parents. Lilly remembers being chastised for impudence, especially when her mother tried to tell her about the imminent arrival of a new sibling. The mother asked Lilly what the family would like most. Knowing full well what was coming, Lilly answered impertinently, 'A family car.'[35] Her mother corrected and then severely reprimanded her daughter for impertinence, though it is possible that Lilly's feelings were secretly shared by her mother. Other girls similarly remember severe reprimands for disrespect for authority. One sure way to incur castigation was to refer to pregnancy or sexuality in a 'shocking' manner in front of one's parents. One girl, who was already menstruating and was aware of the facts of life from her girlfriends, pointedly asked her mother where her brother came from. When the improbable reply was 'In the doctor's black bag,' June defiantly said, 'I don't believe you, I saw the baby's clothes in your drawer.'[36] She was promptly slapped for her insolence.

It was not only through punishment for these insolent references to sexuality that young girls learned to respect authority. The upbringing of most girls incorporated, either with gentle discipline or with corporal punishment, a regime that stressed respect for the directives of one's elders. Many parents assumed that this authority continued after the girls were earning a wage, and many of the women recalled how parental authority shaped their dating and courting lives. 'We wouldn't have dared break our curfew,' remembered one textile worker.

'If we weren't in at 9:30, my father would come out on the veranda and say, "get in here."' Her brothers, she added, could stay out later, and 'sometimes got away with murder; I guess because they were boys.'[37]

Early socialization within the family thus helped shape expected gender and class roles, preparing girls for women's work. This is not to say, in a functionalist manner, that gender roles in the workforce were determined a priori by family attitudes towards work and sex. The sexual division of labour in the workplace was also grounded in the historical and material structures imposed by advanced capitalism; but these structures were in turn fostered by social practices established in family life and by an ideology of female difference, dependency, and subordination. The subtle interweaving of material necessity and patriarchal ideology, particularly through the learned example of the family's sexual division of labour and one's respect for paternal authority, was further accentuated by the young girls' experience of schooling and adolescent peer culture.

SCHOOL LEAVING

While a recent quantitative study of school attendance in Canada argues for the essential similarity of public education for girls and boys in this era,[38] these oral histories suggest a different story, emphasizing distinct gender differences in the educational experiences of working-class children. Undeniably, the numbers of children in elementary school recorded by census takers and provincial education authorities in the twenties and thirties pointed to roughly equal attendance for boys and girls. Most children completed their 'fourth book' (grade 8), and most left school by age fifteen or sixteen. Low attendance was more of a rural problem, especially for boys, and high school attendance reflected starker class rather than gender differences. In Peterborough, for instance, high school, especially after age sixteen, remained an option for a minority of the city's youth, with girls very slightly more numerous than boys. The occupations of the high school students' parents is significant. Of the 470 students in high school in 1931, almost half had fathers in the professions and commerce, one-quarter had fathers in the skilled trades, 15 per cent came from farms, and a mere 6 per cent had fathers who were labourers.[39] Still, the women's descriptions of their families' views of education indicate that gender as well as family income helped decide the length and especially the type of education they received. Statistics on school attendance must thus be fused with discussion of the different streaming, curriculum, and social life of boys and girls within the school system if one is to create a holistic picture of the education received by working-class girls.

By the interwar period, compulsory schooling and the necessity of a firm background in the 'three r's' was taken for granted by working-class families, and many parents took pride in their children's good school performance. 'When you were graded,' recalled a woman from a farm, 'and your annual report was printed in the local paper, that was a great incentive [to do well] because the whole community could see.'[40] Children's attendance fluctuated according to employment opportunity, with slightly higher numbers in school during the Depression when few jobs beckoned;[41] and for many working-class families, schooling past the age of sixteen ultimately appeared a luxury of unknown benefits.

Although the official school-leaving age was sixteen, it might as well have been fourteen, because an early leaving permit could easily be obtained from both the separate and the public school board officials. Indeed, some women managed to slip out when they were thirteen, indicating a lax attitude on the part of school authorities, who accepted the inevitability of limited schooling for working-class youth. More than one worker remembers a foreman worrying that the factory inspector would discover underage children – or children who looked underage – on the premises. These occurrences, however, are often recalled in a light-hearted way. Stories are told of adolescents being hidden away, not because they might get sent back to school but because it would mean bureaucratic hassle for the employer, who would have to produce their work permits. 'I remember a little fella,' commented a former textile worker, 'they hid him so the inspector wouldn't see this guy; he was small, but old enough. The inspector [also] came around when my brother was there – he was very small – and the boss said to him, "Get down to the cellar and hide in the bales of wool" ... Much later, we asked where he was, and he was still down in the cellar!'[42]

For girls in particular, families engaged in a debate about how much schooling was actually needed, because it was assumed that their long-term future would be domestic rather than wage earning. This debate was also shaped by the level of skill and security of the family; those from economically secure or white-collar households were more likely to set their sights on high school attendance for their children. A woman who came from a nearby rural area distinctly recalls her father's opposition to her proposal that she go on to high school in the late 1920s. Her father had two arguments: only a small minority of local children went, and rightly so because it was not directly related to their need for immediate wages and farm help; secondly, since girls were 'only going to get married,' he couldn't see why they would need high school education.[43] An urban father shared a similar outlook. A skilled working-class immigrant from Britain, he saw graduation from grade 8 as the logical end of his children's schooling. After this, the boys in the family could apprentice to learn a trade; the girls could work before marriage. In this case, the father could not even be persuaded by a visit from school officials, who, having seen his daughter's perfect math scores, argued that she should be 'given the chance to go to high school.'[44] Another girl, who 'loved school,' remarked that 'you would have had to burn it down to get me out,' but a different type of parental pressure intervened.[45] Finding that she was often kept home to help with domestic work, she decided to find a full-time job. This was a step towards independence and adulthood, preferable to the frustrating experience of being absent from school.

For many girls, the material pressures that encouraged school leaving played themselves out in indirect and subtle ways: by their family circumstances keeping them out of school until they were behind in their studies; by feeling guilty because others in the family were already working; or by the exhausting burden of unwaged or part-time work combined with school – 'It was hard to get up at 5:30 ... do the chores, go to school,' remembered one woman.[46] Family crises, such as sickness, could have a cumulative effect on a student's education. As Mary explained, she was kept home to help with sick family members: 'I left [school] at thirteen. I was the eldest. There was always illness, scarlet fever or something. I would just get back to school and the teacher would be helping me and then someone else in the family would take sick. The teachers kept putting me through on trial. In grade 7, the teacher was helping, but I got fed up and quit ... Then, they [the teacher/school] didn't care what age you were when you left.'[47]

In cases of abject poverty, unemployment, or ill health, clothes, food, and doctors' bills made attendance difficult. Few children were as pitifully off as the young girl found in the midst of the Depression living in a tent just outside the city limits, with no heat.[48] But there was a minority of children whose actual physical condition militated against school attendance. Although the truancy books for the school board have disappeared, the board's minutes refer to parents unable to pay for basic health care such as tonsillectomies,[49] and other reports indicate a level of ill health, at least for some youngsters during the Depression, that would have inhibited their wakeful attendance at school.[50] Indeed, records of the Children's Aid Society (CAS) indicate that long before the official beginning of the Depression, children from impoverished families were sent home from school because they were ill-fed or lacked adequate clothing.[51]

Teachers in the Peterborough school system, obviously moved by the disabling effects of poverty on their students, allowed a percentage of their salaries to be committed to the relief association in 1932; and during the worst of the Depression, some socially conscious teachers attempted to work informally, 'trying not to be obvious' (to protect the family's sense of dignity), passing on used clothes and collecting money for milk and cod liver oil for their students.[52] At the same time, Mary's message reveals their contradictory feelings: teachers were concerned about the worst signs of child poverty, but ultimately they too accepted the inevitability of early wage labour for working-class children. One could argue that for these children to overcome the immense barriers to continued education, very active parental and school encouragement was necessary. Saying or doing nothing was tantamount to discouragement.[53]

This was especially true for girls. Teachers must have been aware of the view held by some families that the daughter's schooling could be sacrificed so that they could afford their son's education. 'I graduated from grade 8 at fourteen, and then I left,' explained a woman whose parents were British working-class immigrants. 'Girls didn't get the chance to go to high school. I had a brother who my parents wanted to send to high school, and they felt they could only afford one.'[54] The ethic of family obligation and loyalty so strongly influenced the women who had experienced this practice that many felt it would be improper, even now, to describe it as discriminatory; it was treated as a family secret rather than as an acknowledged injustice, and was not to be publicly aired.[55] The women's reticence to expose this inequality – which is some cases they did resent – indicates again how impermeable the familial ties of obligation were.

Listening to the women's interpretations of their youth, one realizes that their decisions about school leaving were not always made easily or automatically; one cannot ignore the expressions of intellectual loss and the wistful regret associated with unfulfilled fantasies of further education or different occupations. As one woman explained, parental pressure led her to abandon the idea of becoming a nurse, not only for economic reasons but because her mother worried about her leaving home for the nursing residence. Her unfulfilled aspiration remained with her for years, still evoking regret even as I spoke with her.

If a female child from a working-class or white-collar family was to continue after public school, the hopes of herself and her parents were often pinned on at least two years of high school, usually in commercial training. In the thirties, 'most girls [who went to high school] went into commercial,' remembered Monica, 'and that's what I did.' In Monica's case, her commercial education took her directly into a job: 'I went to South Central school in commercial. I started work at the GE office when I was only fifteen. GE phoned up and said they had to have someone right away as someone was sick. My teacher sent me down, even though I hadn't finished my exams yet. I was supposed to be temporary, but I stayed.'[56]

For the children of many working- and lower-middle-class families, a good clerical job represented a significant improvement in status, promising more job security and better working conditions than blue collar work. By the interwar period, the lower ranks of clerical work had been 'feminized,' and commercial vocational training was rapidly expanding in the Ontario school system.[57] As Ruby Heap argues, vocational schooling for working-class girls took on twin goals, emphasizing both commercial courses to train women for future wage work and domestic courses to train them for future homemaking work.[58] Peterborough girls who went on to high school also remember being streamed into the domestic option; indeed, the interwar period saw the highest number of girls ever educated in domestic science in Ontario's public and secondary systems.[59] What could be more important, noted a Peterborough schoolteacher who grew up in this period, than 'teaching young girls about motherhood?' This educational legacy, she believed, was crucial, because it related to the one occupation women would take on for life – domesticity.[60]

Only the more economically secure and those who were very academically inclined took the full academic route and finished grade 12 or 13, for the book fees and, for rural students, the boarding costs, were prohibitively expensive. There were, of course, some families who struggled to make these unusual sacrifices, including some who helped daughters go on to the normal school for teaching training, one of the few 'professions' deemed open to women at the time.

It was not simply material pressures that encouraged early school leaving; these pressures were accompanied by strong cultural feelings of 'separation' or 'alienation' from the whole educational system. As Paul Willis argues for the British working-class 'lads' he studied, cultural values antithetical to the school system developed out of material conditions, but they also took on their own autonomous forms precisely because of their apparent ability to explain the existing economic order.[61] In Peterborough, parents were not necessarily suspicious of the schools' attempts to enforce discipline and moral control – a reaction claimed by historians who stress working peoples' resistance to the values imposed by the educational system.[62] Most of the women remember their parents accepting the authority of the school: 'My parents didn't go and argue with the teachers. Dad would say if you got strapped, you deserved it.'[63] At the same time, there was not a strong feeling of investment in or control over the school system, perhaps because many families did not realistically view the educational system as offering social mobility to their children.

For many working-class families, the school system must have seemed a very remote institution. Voting for the school board was limited to property holders, and the board was dominated by the Peterborough élite, such as local factory managers, middle-class professionals, and, occasionally, homemakers. The schools were staffed by teachers drawn predominantly from rural and middle-class backgrounds, and the women do not remember regular contact between parents and teachers. The visit from school officials to a father, described earlier, was unusual. Because of the very weak interwar labour movement in the city, there was little questioning, as there was in other cities, of the extent and opportunity for schooling of working-class children (and even if there had been, there is little evidence that gender streaming would have been of concern to labour).[64] The minutes of the public school board indicate that labour representatives almost never appeared to discuss, protest, or inquire. Cadet training, vocational education, and the payment of book fees in high school did not become political issues for labour, as they did elsewhere.[65] Moreover, the conservative political proclivities of the school board officials were quite apparent to working-class parents. For instance, the board very quickly dismissed the request from an association for the unemployed to hold a fund-raising tag day in the schools, yet the board was quite happy to offer school space to the women's war service council when the war started.[66]

This culture of alienation extended to the students' views of education and social life. Students were easily estranged by any demeaning or unjust treatment in the schools. When a thirteen-year-old Italian girl was accused of 'stealing a pen,' she decided to 'run away' rather than go back and deal with the indignity of such an accusation. Her mother, who 'couldn't speak very much English,'[67] was probably ill at ease dealing with the school authorities and agreed to let the girl look for work at the Bonnerworth mill. Perhaps not coincidentally (although these women do not name discrimination as part of their memories), another girl with immigrant parents expressed the discomfort she felt when she was forced to repeat grade after grade, following a number of illnesses. Rather than deal with the embarrassment of being older than the other students, she reasoned that it would do better to take a job, which would confer new status on her within the household.[68] Given the strong British and Anglo racism that we know underscored the school curriculum at that time, and given our current knowledge about class streaming within the schools, it is difficult to escape the conclusion that the 'hidden curriculum' particularly encouraged immigrant and working-class girls to follow the pattern of early school leaving and early wage work.[69]

Women who quit school before sixteen often explained their decision in terms of peer pressure and youthful rebellion, which they should have resisted: 'You know, my father did not want me to leave ... but kids all think they know what's good for them.'[70] These recollections, by emphasizing self-blame, reflect an individualist ideology that obscures the more subtle processes of cultural alienation from the school system that were operating at the time. At least one-third of all the women interviewed remembered being bored in school, particularly if they were doing academic work that was seemingly unrelated to the future work roles they could imagine themselves in.[71] 'All my friends were quitting and getting jobs. Why should I stay?'[72] was the thinking of a woman who left after a year of high school. These were acutely pragmatic assessments of the inevitabilities and realities of their lives. It was far more likely that they would join their friends in the workforce than play out some unusual script by becoming a doctor. As Jane Gaskell has argued, the decision of working-class girls to follow traditional occupational paths often emerges from their very realistic assessment of their own family lives and employment opportunities. While ostensibly internalizing the ideology of class and gender inferiority, they are actually well aware of the unequal world around them, and they base their decisions on their own experience and understanding of that world.[73]

Finally, other government and voluntary organizations reinforced the message that early wage work, rather than continued education, should be the lot of working-class girls. The Peterborough Mothers' Allowance Board minutes and some Welfare Department statements in the 1930s indicate that middle-class officials of the state expected working-class children to pay their way as soon as possible. When local women applied for the mothers' allowance, the allowance board's administrators often asked if the teenagers in the family could help support their mother. It was usually assumed that children over sixteen ought to be able to aid the family financially, though in special cases a youth could apply to obtain a letter of support from the school principal if he or she wanted to continue on in school.[74] For children who had been taken from their homes by the CAS (and who were invariably working class or poor), there was a similar assumption of early wage work – unless, like one girl, they wrote to the CAS volunteer 'ladies' requesting special aid in order to have clothes and books for school.[75] In a telling remark made in 1937, a CAS official noted the persistence of the long-established use of youthful CAS wards who were fostered out for farm and domestic labour. 'No one wants to take [an older] boy or girl unless they can work,' he commented.[76] In the minds of these state and voluntary institutions, then, working-class children should not be taxing the state but should be absorbing the work ethic as early as possible.

THE CULTURE OF ADOLESCENCE

Alienation from the school system could take many forms. For girls, one of these was the stigma associated with coming from less affluent circumstances than one's peers. Particularly during the Depression, when some families were dealing with underemployment and had little money to spare, signs of poverty such as old and patched clothes were intensely embarrassing. More than one woman remembers this experience with acuity. 'I went two years to high school. I was going around with the rich kids; three of them invited me to go with them. But they could dress better than I could. So I quit school,'[77] recalled a woman who left high school for factory work. While superficially a form of peer pressure, this problem had material roots, for clothes were part of a symbolic discourse of respectability, and by the high school years, as the student population thinned out and became more affluent, those with little or no money were especially noticeable.

Along with the school, outside cultural influences played a part in shaping a girl's idea of what was probable in her future, what her aspirations could and should be. While it would be wrong to think that teenagers completely internalized the values promoted in movies and magazines and through informal leisure, these images did set some boundaries within which individual meaning and ambition were negotiated. As Mary Vipond and Veronica Strong-Boag have pointed out, the mass media in the interwar period placed new emphasis on the emergence of the single wage-earning woman, but it revealed a continuing assumption that women's happiest and most fulfilling role lay in the domestic sphere.[78] While some young women may have absorbed this message through reading material, the extensive culture of girls' magazines seems to have been less important in Canada than in Britain.[79] Movies, however, were a popular source of teen entertainment, and a pervasive culture of romance that glorified female beauty, heterosexual attractiveness, and marital bliss – even while discussing new female 'independence' – characterized the Hollywood offerings of this period. Indeed, in the interwar period, girls had the unenviable task of living up to diametrically different ideals in popular culture; adolescence was presented as a time of rebellion, independence, and exploration, yet the attributes of obedience, passivity, and morality were still seen as essential for girls.[80]

Girls also absorbed messages about their future as they participated in informal neighbourhood sports and social pastimes and in church activities (a world explored in more detail in chapter 5). Young girls were especially attracted to the drama clubs and sports leagues organized by churches and were perhaps less interested in the religious message offered. But could they simply tune out when the minister's sermons promoted the value of the patriarchal family and domestic womanhood? During the 1930s, for example, a Roman Catholic priest lecturing to Peterborough parishioners argued that young women 'must honour thy father and thy mother'; that married life was women's obligation; and that within marriage 'virtue and duty were the way to heaven.'[81]

By the 1920s, local religious and reform groups had established a variety of organizations to provide leisure activities for girls, usually with the expressed purpose of regulating the moral lives, physical health, and perceived social problems of working-class youth.[82] Whether one embraces a generous liberal view of these reform efforts as being well intentioned or whether one takes a more critical view of the class-biased regulation intended by groups such as the YWCA and CGIT, there is no doubt that this organized leisure was used by and became a meaningful influence on some working-class girls. Again, young women often extracted what they wanted from these organizations, for example, enjoying sports and mixed social events and using the cheap residence rooms at the YW, but avoiding their Bible-study classes. Still, it is difficult to imagine total escape from the overwhelming message of the YWCA, for it pervaded the association's provision of services, boarding, and camp life. This message promoted a feminine ideal, stressing domesticity as well as the importance of a chaste social life for working-class girls.[83]

Other institutions created by the child savers, such as the CAS and the juvenile court (which was not established in Peterborough until 1946) were designed to deal with violence against children, crises in the family, and juvenile delinquency. The latter was not perceived to be a major concern in the city until the post–Second World War period, and even then the number of young girls in conflict with the law was very small. In both the interwar and postwar periods, a small minority of young women challenged school, parental, and community authorities by creating an 'alternative' youth culture, which rejected the work ethic and parental rules and embraced alcohol and premarital sex. In one case in the 1930s, a local judge complained that a teenage girl refused to stay with any domestic job she was given and that she hitchhiked around with friends, was drinking and staying out all night, and engaging in sexual activity with boys.[84] Although the judge blamed this girl's downfall on 'dance halls,' in fact there was only one dance hall in Peterborough, and most parents allowed their daughters to go to it. What did worry parents and police – even more than crimes such as petty theft – was a teenager's participation in 'immoral' premarital sex. This behaviour, which was perceived as melding into prostitution, might earn a teenage girl a stint in the Reformatory.

Reformers and social workers believed that members of the working class, especially the very poor, were more liable to such immorality. In part, they analysed girls' 'troubles' as a result of unavoidable environmental conditions, such as poverty and family dissolution, though well into the 1940s, a discourse stressing moral and religious corruption and 'degeneracy' was also displayed in their pronouncements. By the

1950s, this was increasingly replaced by a social-work practice that stressed the psychological causes of delinquency and looked to strong family ties as a cure for temporary rebellion.[85]

What is evident from the women's recollections, even taking into account that in their interviews with me they may have purposely or unconsciously omitted mention of such misbehaviour or conflicts, is that many working-class families did not deal with such problems. Most families did not have any regular contact with organizations such as the CAS, nor was fear of surveillance by legal and social-work authorities an overarching theme in their lives. Interference in family life by agencies such as the CAS or the court was often equated with a lapse of respectability for working-class families and thus was to be avoided. On the other hand, help from the local police or the CAS might be accepted if it was seen as an effective solution to a family crisis, such as a misbehaving child. One single wage-earning mother remembered with some appreciation how 'the police chief helped me out,'[86] overseeing her son's parole when he incurred a minor criminal infraction. In another case, a young working woman was turned in to the police by her father because he felt that the only way to alter her immoral sexual life, and possibly protect the family name, was to send her away to the reformatory. Thus, historians who suggest that state encroachment on working-class life became overwhelming in these years, debilitating parental and especially fatherly authority, have seemingly exaggerated this process.[87]

CONCLUSION

How girls learned to labour depended on a range of factors: the economic and social structure of the local community; the immediate, material imperatives imposed by the family economy; their early experience of family life and work; and the influence of schools, churches, and the wider culture, through which the dominant ideologies about femininity, ambition, and fate were mediated. The dominant discourses on femininity, family, and work shaped girls' interpretations of the material necessities they faced, at the same time as class experiences shaped girls' images of appropriate gender roles. Women's later identity as workers, both inside and outside the home, often harked back to these deeply rooted images of masculinity and femininity, reconstituted and understood as an integral part of their personal identity.

Women's ambition was thus socially constructed from what they considered probable and attainable, from their interpretation of material necessities, and from existing social practices and gender ideology, as well as from their own abilities and dreams. Women who came from working-class or white-collar families had a clear picture of a possible future. Most women perceived two major choices: if you left school after grade 8, factory work was your main option; but if you had more high school education, especially commercial training, white-collar work was an attainable goal. Women with a more secure family economy and those whose parents emphasized education might imagine a career in teaching or nursing, but even these occupations were perceived by many working-class families as the preserve of the better-off. Certainly, some young women lamented their narrow range of choices, though they generally dreamed not of occupations perceived to be completely inaccessible, such as medicine, but rather of female occupations such as nursing, which were just out of reach for familial or economic reasons. And although the picture of attainable occupations broadened somewhat for the second cohort of women, encompassing more varieties of white-collar work, nursing, and teaching, their choices were still strongly circumscribed – a topic that will be revisited in chapter 8.

For women who went out to work before the Second World War, youth work, both waged and unwaged, was important to the family economy, whereas during the war and in the postwar period, the wages of teens became less important to family solvency.[88] The young age at which girls began work in the interwar period meant that the boundaries of childhood and adulthood overlapped, that children and parents were involved in intertwining economic and emotional relations. As Elizabeth Roberts comments for an earlier period, 'Children had adult responsibilities, and some working youth had child-like relations to their parents.'[89]

The existence of a family-wage economy with pooled resources did not necessarily imply equality of authority among family members. As Marjorie Cohen reminds us, a partnership of productive relations could also embody patriarchal relations.[90] Although young girls going out to work noted their desire to help their mother balance the budget, they also remember their father's continuing authority over their social life. As Jane Synge found in her study of working-class Hamilton, women contributing their wages to the household had less influence in the family than their brothers because of their lower wages, and they had less social freedom than their brothers because of prevailing concerns about women's morality.[91] Family life thus conveyed both powerful images of sexually segregated tasks and important examples of differential power relations. As an integral part of working-class culture and as an aid to the reproduction of a gendered labour force, its influence cannot be overestimated.

Schooling also imparted important messages about the inevitability of working in female jobs and at domestic labour. Educational institutions, as sociologists argue, incorporate and organize relationships that often reproduce the existing class and gender order; the cultural milieu of the schools – from peer pressure to moral values to curriculum – acts as a support for these social relations.[92] This emphasis on the 'social reproduction' of education does not assume the indoctrination of class and gender norms, but it does suggest that schools embody and recreate both subtle and overt messages that shape and often limit the educational options for working-class girls. Within this framework, as Arlene Tigar McLaren shows, women developed their own subjective understanding, interpretation, and actions to cope with the material necessities and gender ideology that confronted them.[93] Individually, they worked out the best possible strategies for fulfilling their sense of familial obligation, their schooling needs, and their personal wishes – and, for a minority, this could even mean opting for more schooling or for an occupation untried by other family members.

It is crucial to stress this sense of involvement in decision making on the part of young women. In one instance, a woman's family felt that she should leave school after grade 8, but her father offered her a choice: she could stay home to do the housework, since her mother was ill; or she could get a job, and use some of her wages to pay a housekeeper. She opted for the second choice with some enthusiasm, because it gave her more money and more independence. Her life, as she emphatically explained it to me, was not without options.

Still, these choices were, ultimately, strategies – whether of accommodation, resistance, or a little of both – to deal with economic realities, using the social and cultural scripts available to women at the time. Ironically, in a society that needed young women's wage work, the images of youthful femininity and work were often contradictory. Girls could have immense responsibility at home but were still carefully supervised when they were in the public sphere; they were soon to be independent working women, but they knew they would continue to live with their families; they were often expected to do jobs that required physical stamina, but they were regarded as more fragile than men.

No neat dividing line marks out working-class girls' independence from their dependence; leaving school was not necessarily a rite of passage that brought with it freedom from parental direction. Their lives were not only distinct from those of their brothers, who had more social freedom and the expectation of lifelong work in different occupations, but they were also distinct from the lives of upper-middle-class girls, whose rites of passage were more likely to be connected to high school graduation and whose future might even include temporary freedom and separation from their families through college attendance. As Rebecca Coulter so aptly argues, adolescence in early twentieth-century Canada was fractured by the intertwining relations of class and gender.[94]

Rather than conforming to an image of dependent and indulged twentieth-century adolescence, many working-class girls in this small city experienced a very different reality. Lilly, the young textile worker who opened this chapter, remembered falling asleep at the dinner table after work and happily spending her 'earnings on candy at the corner store.'[95] She may have seemed to be a child, but she had also become a working woman.

3

Packing Muffets* for a Living: Working Out the Gendered Division of Labour

Harriet was a teenager when she began her white-collar job in the office at the Westclox factory just before the Second World War. She had moved into a boarding house in Peterborough from her family home in the village of Lakefield, and she began her first day by typing letters. By the lunch hour she was literally in tears. Anxious to prove her worth, she had become too nervous to do her job: 'I was petrified, just coming out of school. I remember they asked me to type something and I couldn't get the paper in the typewriter. I was afraid they would think me stupid.'[1]

Many of the women remembered with considerable clarity their first day at work. Despite the excitement of beginning a new stage in their lives, they were intimidated by the number of new faces, overwhelmed with new responsibilities, and daunted by the physical stamina needed in factory jobs. They were also nervous about keeping their jobs. White-collar jobs often had an initial training period of two weeks to a few months, but after the women were shown the ropes, they were on their own. In factory jobs, a three-month trial period was standard; if the women weren't performing, making their quota, by then, they would be warned or fired.

When asked to describe their first impressions of the workplace, the women often stressed very different themes from those that now pre-occupy feminist historians and sociologists. The gendered division of labour, for instance, though a question mark for us, was for these women a taken-for-granted reality. 'I didn't even think about it then,' was a common comment on these divisions, which at the time appeared to be natural and unchangeable. The historical and social con-

---

* Muffets are round shredded-wheat cereal made by Quaker Oats.

struction of occupational sex typing, so apparent to us, was simply not evident to Harriet when she began work.

This chapter is concerned with the nature and conditions of women's work and with the construction and understanding of the sexual division of labour within their workplaces. The fact that women packed muffets but did not bake them, that they worked as spinners but not as straw bosses, and that they typed letters but did not compose them reflected profoundly gendered workplaces, in which women's work was divided from men's, both horizontally and vertically. Women were shut out of some training, such as apprenticeships, but were encouraged to take other training, such as typing. The one constant was the undervaluing of their work, not only in terms of wages but sometimes even psychologically, by the women workers themselves.

We need to explain the tenacity of this gendered division of labour and how it became so hegemonic that it appeared to women to be a natural and common-sense reality of life. The division of work by sex was not the outcome of one set of structural relations but was the product of an interplay of forces, including the existing organization of the work process, the structural imperatives set by industry, a strong ideology of sex difference, and the assimilation and utilization of that ideology at a personal, subjective level by both men and women in the workplace.

To demonstrate the active combination of these forces, I want first to present the women's own memories of the organization of work, then to examine the role of management and male workers in shaping the division of labour, and, finally, to explore women's and men's active participation in a set of familial relations and domestic ideology that sustained and reproduced the gendered division of labour in the workplace.

FIRST IMPRESSIONS

During the 1920s and 1930s, most of the Peterborough women based their job-search strategies on advice from neighbourhood friends, school contacts, or kin. The importance of gender ideology, so crucial to their youth and schooling, was still apparent, and their job inquiries were shaped by their understanding of what was possible and attainable – by the mental pictures they had already absorbed of female occupations. In this process, the direction offered by family and friends was crucial. While the women recalled repeated and difficult searches for work – walking or bicycling from factory to factory, returning day after day – in the end it was usually friends or relatives who helped them secure their first job. As Doris remembers, her first position was completely arranged for her: 'I was out of high school at seventeen and got a job at a local furrier's ... My mother got my first job. She was down at [a store] one day and the man who ran the furrier's was there and she knew him. She told him she had a daughter who had just finished a sewing course and she wondered if there was a job for me. He said he could use a girl and to send me in.'[2]

Of these women, only a minority secured a job through an impersonal application process. The expanded economy and state involvement in hiring during the war encouraged this procedure, and by the 1950s more and more women used the application route, as professional personnel departments were consolidated in many companies. Kin and personal contacts were still important, however. A woman who worked in the office of the Bonnerworth mill in the postwar years noted that even after a personnel department, with job testing, was established, 'the foreman still had the last word.'[3]

If family could not provide the needed contact for a job, a teacher, friend, or neighbour might do so. One woman, for example, secured her desired job at Westclox through a foreman for whom she babysat. Another young woman arranged for a friend who was already at the Bonnerworth mill to usher her into the manager's office: 'I walked up to the Bonnerworth in the rain. I had already tried at GE but they told me I was too small. My girlfriend spoke for me. Mr Merritt [the manager] looked at me – soaked – and he said, "You must really want a job." And I said, "Yes," and I got one.'[4] Companies also had close ties with the high school and business colleges. One manager recalled that he would call up the local head of the high school's commercial section and ask him to send over its 'top students' for a job opening.[5]

When family networks aided a woman's job choice, there were important consequences. Kin connections ensured a certain degree of support for the new employee and helped her training and acculturation to the factory while simultaneously providing a form of supervision and control.[6] In situations of conflict – such as the 1937 textile strike – these networks could also aid oppositional solidarity. Most often, though, the women remembered the feeling of obligation and duty which kin recruitment brought with it, and this was often accentuated by their youth and lack of experience in the workforce. Many female workers were mere teens, who in the 1930s felt lucky to have a job. One teenager, for instance, literally stepped into her sister's job as an inspector of wool at the Bonnerworth mill when the latter left to marry, and she felt a strong responsibility to keep up the family's good name with diligent work habits. And the employer, of course, often reminded recruits that they had been hired because of a personal contact or because of their family name. One woman applying for work at Westclox was asked by General Manager Vernor, 'Are you so and so's daughter?' Even though the father did not work at the plant, in this small city the general manager knew of his reputation as a skilled tradesman and said, 'If you can work as hard as him, you're hired.'[7] This was both a compliment and an obligation. Taking pride in doing a decent day's work was part of the young woman's sense of becoming an adult, and it was also connected in her mind with her family's respectable status, which she wanted to uphold.

Once at work, the physical shock of workplace life was what the women remembered most strongly. For many, the contrast with the school day, which had offered more leisure time and a measure of flexibility, was startling. During the interwar period, women worked on average a nine- or ten-hour day, the longest days being at the woollen mill. Wartime work often brought with it pressure for overtime, and it was not until the 1950s that the average working hours declined to an eight-hour day with assured breaks. Lunch hours were usually an hour long, but two daily rest periods were not available in all factories until the late 1940s. Working conditions varied considerably from one factory to another, General Electric (GE) and the Bonnerworth being considered the most physically demanding, though GE at least offered some material compensation.

While it is extremely difficult to generalize about four workplaces, there were common dominant themes of women's white- and blue-collar work. In the office, save for personal secretaries, women's tasks were segregated, broken down, and highly supervised, though they often involved significant financial and administrative responsibility. Blue-collar women were likely to be machine tenders but not machine fixers. They needed to be attentive and to work quickly, either to make their piecework or to keep up with the line, which was on a form of collective production pay. They answered to a fairly strict disciplinary code, which forbade, for instance, long periods in the washroom, breaks in the workday, and excessive talking or socializing. Although the jobs were physically exhausting, they were not necessarily seen as skilled or demanding. 'People today wouldn't work under those conditions,' remarked a former textile worker unequivocally, remembering the hard labour of her past.[8] Two former Bonnerworth employees began by describing their work on spinning machines as fairly easy to learn, yet later in the interview they both recounted how the work returned to haunt them in their dreams. 'I used to have nightmares when I was on straight time,' remembered one spinner. 'I used to think I was still running the machines. There were about seventy-two bobbins on each side. You had to keep checking them. If one broke ... [they] got peeved at you.'[9] Another former spinner admitted that the intense workpace and the feeling of hot, airless rooms still remains with her: 'After all these years, I still lay in bed and think about it. I couldn't do it now.'[10] Perhaps the best method of illustrating the women's work on the shop floor and in the office is to let them describe their normal workdays. Although the work process, division of labour, and management style for each factory was distinct, the examples chosen draw out the familiar and common themes in women's daily work lives.

SPINNING WOOL

Barbara began work at fifteen in 1932 in the new Bradford spinning section of the Bonnerworth mill. Built with city aid in 1910, the plant consisted of two three-story mills, an administrative building, and a separate boiler house and dye house at the back. The process of making yarn had changed little since the nineteenth century. It was essentially a matter of taking a raw form of wool, or tops, and refining it by combing out the impurities, drawing it out, spinning it, and, finally, dyeing it. A small proportion of women worked on the initial stages of washing and combing the wool with large teethed machines; many more worked on the process of drawing, spinning, and twisting the wool fibres so that they became elongated and straightened into parallel strands of finer yarn. Indeed, this labour-intensive part of the operation was almost exclusively women's work, as it had been in the manufacture of English worsted yarn.

As Barbara remembers, 'It was mostly women, very few men,' on the third floor where she started as a 'bobbin girl.' Paid by the hour, her job was to keep the bobbins full of wool; she then took the job of doffing, or removing, the bobbins full of yarn from the machines and replacing them with new ones for the spinners. 'There were about ten machines in a row, and it was my job to keep them full of bobbins, so the women wouldn't be waiting.' Like many other women, Barbara then moved up to become a spinner. She had two machines to look after, 'to make sure the wool was running down smoothly, not breaking ... watching them as they spun at a furious speed.' She added, 'You were paid by piecework, [by weight], according to the number of bobbins you took off in a day.'[11]

Barbara remained a spinner for many years, but some women moved to the drawing room or to twisting, where the wool was wound together, going from smaller to bigger bobbins. Most of this work required careful attention and physical endurance, for you stayed on your feet all day, tending as many as 120 spindles per machine, watching for breaks and then refastening the wool. While the initial combing process was considered more dangerous work because of the teeth in the machine, serious accidents sometimes happened in spinning as well. Most of the women began by saying that there were few accidents, but those with any longevity at the mill pointed to at least one incident where clothing was caught in a roller or perhaps a finger was lost. Similar accidents were experienced by the men in the weaving mill, the Auburn. One man remembered a workmate shouting frantically when his broom caught in the roller and he was about to have his arm drawn in as well. Another screamed when one of the workplace rats got caught in his machine (understandably an unpleasant sight).[12] Although men claimed that women were nervous about machines, serious accidents could scare men and women with equal strength.

The physical conditions at the Bonnerworth were taxing. The women worked with windows closed to keep in the damp hot air (to protect the wool fibres), and wool flew everywhere. Workers went home with small particles of wool on their clothes, in their hair, in their noses, and in summer these conditions were especially difficult as temperatures in the factory soared. Physical stamina was clearly important, yet the women's fortitude was not equated equally with heavy work, such as lifting the bales of incoming wool, which the men did. For some girls and women, the long hours of standing could be especially exhausting when they were menstruating. 'If you felt really bad,' remembered one woman, 'you could go lie down for a while. But they didn't even have a proper surgery. When young girls were feeling "under the weather," they had a room [to go to]. You had to go through the boiler room [to get there]. Sure, you could lay down for an hour, but all the men were charging through, and you had to ask your foreman to go. You were on your feet the whole ten hours. Even in the washroom, there were no chairs.'[13]

Like Barbara, many women worked for years as spinners with little job mobility. Some workers were transferred to more complicated machines like the ball warp, or into inspecting, but work in the dye house and the positions of foremen and straw boss were completely off limits. Young men came to the plant, however, with different expectations; although they too generally worked as doffers, they were apprenticed as machine tenders and straw bosses, who set up the spinning machines to account for the different kinds of yarn being spun, fixed broken machine belts, and so on.

What appeared at the time to be a natural division of labour was actually the result of different education, for women were never trained in this work. It was assumed by management and foremen that men understood machines (at some innate level) and that women had shorter work lives, thus making their training uneconomic. Yet some women stayed a decade in the mill – longer than the men who routinely left for better paying work – and according to economic rationality, their training costs could have been absorbed by the company. But notions of skill were shaped by a powerful cultural denigration of women's abilities and by a desire to protect certain jobs for male breadwinners. One woman who was particularly knowledgeable about the technology and often helped the other spinners fix their looms discovered this when she was caught by the foreman repairing her own machine. He denounced her actions very 'angrily.' As she astutely realized, she had intruded on his space: 'Though [I knew] the machines ... that was *his* job.'[14]

MAKING FACES FOR A LIVING: WORKING ON WATCHES AT WESTCLOX

In 1935 Mona obtained work through family connections at the Westclox factory and was immediately trained on the assembly line that produced watches. At this plant, there was a wider array of jobs for women than in the textile mill. You might start in the basement, where there was primarily male-dominated tool-and-die work and automatics but where some women worked on small foot presses. After large steel strips were cut in the power press, they were sent to the foot press, where smaller punching work was done; the material then bypassed the second floor, which housed the office and engineering, and went to the third- and fourth-floor production lines and to finishing departments such as the balance-wheel department.

Mona's assembly line was based on a carefully engineered continuous-flow work process, which could produce large quantities of goods relatively cheaply for a growing consumer market. In the interwar period, women provided an important source of labour for many of these new mass-production industries. British sociologist Miriam Glucksmann argues that companies producing goods such as food and small appliances purposely sought out female labour as their primary workforce. Women's presence was not the result of any de-skilling of men's jobs but reflected the conscious decision of management to use cheaper female labour to facilitate the production of wealth within the industry.[15]

Women's work at Westclox was characterized by the machine pacing of the job, by 'direct' assembly (as opposed to indirect servicing, set-up, and organizing of the work process),[16] and by the extensive use of some kind of piecework or incentive pay, or in some cases a production wage that a group of workers had to make together. Many of the jobs women performed were broken down into minute and exact tasks, which were repeated again and again and had to be executed at high speed. Mona, for instance, had her own desk, which was linked to a moving assembly line for watches. She had a plate with holes in it, which she gripped from the back and then put the second hand on. The plate was then put on a block, and a lid with glue was pressed down on it. Mona was guaranteed an hourly rate if she completed a certain quota – in this case, '25 cents for every hundred faces made.'[17]

The pay schedule grew more complex with time, though it retained a basic bias for incentive pay. By the time the union contract was approved in the early 1950s, there were at least three basic rates of pay. For assembly jobs, explained a union activist, 'you had an hourly rate for three months while learning; after that, you had a base (hourly) rate you were guaranteed, then a job rate, which looked like it was less, but since you could do more than 100 per cent of it, you made money on incentive.'[18] Management strongly promoted incentive pay; as one manager put it, 'Whatever we could, we put on piecework. It's the fairest way to pay. Prevents people from loafing off, going to the washroom to smoke. I'm quite a believer in piecework, though I never worked on it myself.'[19]

Management's explanation for why women in particular were placed in these jobs often called up a stereotype of female workers who were easily satisfied with monotonous and repetitive work. One manager, for instance, told a story about women rejecting 'interesting' jobs in favour of boring well-paid ones: 'We had a foreman who tried to move the girls around to relieve the monotony after he had been to a workshop on [monotony] in the workplace. We almost had a revolution. "Why are you taking me off this job?" [the women asked] "I can make good money on that job." They got accustomed to the work and it didn't bother them.'[20] Managers tended to interpret these women's reactions as 'innate personality traits, rather than evidence of their lack of control over the work.'[21] Yet the same manager admitted that 'piecework encouraged women to think primarily about earning more money.' Trained to adapt to a work process in which their actions were a tiny part of the product construction, and lacking control over their work environment, the women developed an instrumental approach to their jobs. Knowing it was unlikely that work strain would be significantly reduced, they chose higher wages over an illusory measure of control over their day.

Some of the assembly work at this plant was notoriously fine and delicate, and by the 1940s women were given finger-dexterity tests before they were hired. Putting springs in watches or fine-tuning balance wheels in a watch also required patience, good eyesight, and careful attention to detail, which managers and workers alike claimed that women inherently had. In the balance wheel department, as a woman hired in the late 1930s remembers, 'You would get trays with balance wheels on them, along with your time card. Five or six women sat at large desks with individual lights, working with small machines which measured the watch wheels to make sure they were properly balanced before they were placed in the watch.'[22]

Such jobs were gruelling precisely because of the attention to detail needed, and the women frequently developed physical responses: one woman began to get terrible headaches after only a year on the job, and her eye doctor said she 'had to be transferred as [her] eyes were deteriorating.'[23] Indeed, women were not usually hired unless their eyesight was good. 'They told me that you had to have good eyesight coming in because girls often end up wearing glasses,' a woman who had considered working there recalled.[24] Surprisingly, though, impairment of one's eyesight was not considered a truly significant occupational hazard by the company or, later, by the union. A tendency to construct women's jobs as automatically more safe, without attention to the risks, was common to a number of workplaces. This was not only because women's work roles were equated with innate abilities (as also were men's). Rather, the actual 'talents' claimed for women were devalued. Women's inborn ability to do fine, delicate work was invoked as a rationale for their job placement; explicit comparisons with knitting and embroidery, which were female hobbies, were often made, thus belittling the proficiency needed for the job.

While the choice of female jobs was somewhat more varied at the Westclox than at the Bonnerworth, and while the dividing line between men's and women's work did shift over time, especially during the war (when women did timing and set-up jobs), there was never a fundamental shift in the gendered division of labour over forty years. As Mona remembers, 'You never would put a girl in automatics [or train them for tool and die] ... Girls just didn't' do men's jobs. Yes, the men were better paid too. We just took that for granted, I supposed because they had families. People just took it for granted that men should make more.'[25]

PACKING MUFFETS

A similar rationale for the gendered division of labour was offered by a longtime Quaker Oats worker, Hilary, who, like Mona, started full-time work in the late 1930s and was a self-supporting worker all her life. 'Did women production workers get promotions to foreman or supervisory jobs?' she was asked. 'There wasn't anything to be promoted to,' was her revealing answer. Clearly, other jobs didn't even appear to exist for a woman. 'There weren't supervisory positions for women at that time,' she continued. 'Women didn't want them. I didn't. I was still a woman, and I don't believe in taking a man's job.'[26]

At the Quaker Oats plant, Hilary worked in the packaging of cereal. Here, the division of labour was often justified by the distinction between hot and heavy work, and lighter work. Built in 1901 and rebuilt in 1916 after a fire, the plant employed at least four hundred in the interwar and wartime period, of which only about 15 to 20 per cent were women. In the interwar period, women worked as sewers of feed bags and in the assembly-line production and packaging of cereal, but they tended to be absent in the areas of the plant where giant furnaces and ovens cooked the raw material. The notion that only men could do heavy physical work was so much a part of the sexual division of labour that many jobs appeared unappealing to women workers even after these jobs were made more mechanized and had changed in content, for sex typing had become an ingrained tradition.

As in other workplaces, there was little job mobility for women. Edna's experience was typical. She started in 1929 and remained on one job on the assembly line until she left three years later: 'One girl had a pile of flat boxes, which she put on the machine, which then shaped the box. The next girl checked to see if the glue was on properly, then filled it under a chute, then it came past me and I checked to see if the other end was glued on properly to make sure the oats wouldn't go all over the place, then I put it through wrapping, and down it went through a chute to be packed.'[27]

Just over twenty years later, another woman went to work on a similar line, and although more of the process was mechanized, the continuous-flow, repetitive, fast-paced work was similar. 'I packed muffets,' Eleanor remembers. 'They came from two big ovens on belts, and we had these little tin boxes and we packed them in. You put two in, then a cardboard divider. We used to pack those things so much [and fast] that you'd wear a hole through your fingers. You'd have blood spurting out the end of your finger. Not from the boxes, from the muffets [because] they were rough.'[28] This job was then further automated; soon, only one woman stood to watch the operation of the machine that packed the muffets.

Like the mass production of clocks, this process involved carefully timed, broken-down tasks, designed to produce consumer products cheaply and quickly. Working on the line at Quaker Oats might involve the same attentiveness, standing, and repetitive motions needed in textile work. Women had very little control over the pacing of the day; they were given little training in how to set up or repair machinery; and they were often part of a collective line of women who had to work quickly and effectively together to make the required quotas.

At Quaker Oats and General Electric, the sex typing of jobs was fairly rigid. Few women were hired, since they were deemed unskilled or incapable of working in the physical environment of the factory. Yet job typing was potentially malleable. Unlike the textile mill, where women rarely saw men working side by side doing similar jobs, Quaker and GE women sometimes witnessed men in similar occupations, either because of a temporary crisis such as the war or, occasionally, because women were engaged in comparable though less heavy versions of male work. Nevertheless, changes to the separate codification and payment of women's and men's jobs did not really come until the 1970s, after a law forbade advertising and seniority lists by sex, and as increasing economic crises created the reality that women with seniority might have to replace men, or that men might have to opt for women's jobs in order to avoid lay-off. Until then, the sexual division of labour remained potentially malleable but fundamentally unchanged.

MAKING MOTORS

Just as the war began, Thelma managed to get a job at Canadian General Electric (CGE). Formerly a textile worker, she was lured to the plant by the promise of better wages and steady employment, a situation far preferable to the constant threat of short time she was experiencing in a local carpet mill. At CGE she secured a job braiding electrical cord. It was 'tiresome,' she remembers, but was less painful than working with the coarse carpet yarn, which had worn through her hands, causing sores. 'She worked on the braiders, where both men and women did similar tasks, though 'men were on the larger wire,' she recalled. 'Before the war, it was mostly men running the braiding machines ... but then women [were hired]. The company liked my experience working with yarn at the carpet mill and so they hired me.'[29] Working at CGE, the largest and most powerful plant in the city, had some benefits; along with Westclox, it offered the highest wages, depending on the value of one's piecework. But it was also, in the words of one woman, 'characterized by monotony, and the jobs were really difficult.'[30]

A physically massive and imposing structure, the Edison plant was founded by a Toronto-Peterborough group of investors in the late nineteenth century and was bought out in 1902 by the American General Electric Corporation. By the interwar period it employed between one and two thousand workers, and during the Second World War it expanded considerably and also administered a government-owned war-production plant, Genelco, which it eventually took over. The Peterborough factory was one of the largest plants in General Electric's Canadian empire. It specialized in industrial rather than consumer lines, producing condensers, switchgear equipment, small and large motors, large generators, and voltage regulators, as well as some smaller equipment such as cables and conductors.

These product lines meant that few women were hired. Working with heavy equipment and machinery was seen solely as men's work. Moreover, the factory had the highest number of skilled workers (such as machinists) in the city, a fact that also resulted in the exclusion of women. The minority of women in the plant were concentrated in punch-press work, armature, fractional (small) motors, and some electrical-assembly work. Their work was coded separately from the men's jobs and was often characterized by piecework pay and by a continuous-flow line. One woman who glazed bulbs, for instance, took planks of fifty at a time, dipping them in and out of the glaze material, before they were passed on to the next woman to be wired. She was paid by the number completed: 'You had to go like mad to make a thousand ... but if you did, you made 25 cents an hour, so you worked [really fast] and did two thousand for 50 cents an hour.'[31]

Many women who worked at the plant started in punch press or small motors. 'Everybody goes through punch press at some time,' remembered one woman wryly, 'and it was a miserable job ... When I worked there, women were on the smaller presses, which made small pieces of metal – like teeth for the motors – which had to be measured to a fine distinction, perhaps a thousandth of an inch. But women were paid less for this!'[32] Winding coil through the small holes of motors or taping the coils of small motors were also typical jobs; while they appeared to be lighter work, they carried with them occupational hazards, from damaged hands to painful muscles, as the tight and quick winding took its toll on women's hands and arms.

Workplace hazards were perhaps the most obvious to women working at General Electric. Some women worked with and near dangerous epoxies, they wound stiff wires around motors with such speed that they had to bind their hands with tape to prevent cutting through their skin, or they worked on punch presses which, even with safety guards, could cut off your finger in an instant if you were not attentive.

The distinction between male and female work on punch presses was revealing. The smaller presses were coded as an 'easier' women's job, while the larger presses with more tonnes of pressure were coded as men's jobs. Yet as more than one interviewee pointed out, 'an accident in either case might cost you a finger.' Whether it was a male or female appendage, the danger was equally horrific.[33] Union activists later tried similar arguments when they argued for equal pay: 'Women's work was on a punch press with 35 tonnes and less crushing power than the men's press. The single trip press was for boys and women. But the union said, "You get your head taken off if you put it under 600 tonnes or 35 tonnes!" The company still claimed it was physical size that counted in the code. That was the kind of difference in men's and women's job codes.'[34]

There were some General Electric jobs that approximated the finer Westclox work. During the Second World War, for instance, women worked on instrument panels for the Lancaster bombers. But overall, the concentration on large equipment, the need for machine-related

skills, and indeed the very nature of the plant, with its massive, imposing presence, brick floors, gloomy interior, noise, and dirt, reinforced
the view that this was a 'man's workplace.' Indeed, some women chose
not to apply there, partly because they worried about the arduous demands of the job but also because of the physical environment of the
plant and because of the notion that work in this atmosphere would
make them appear 'tough,' in contradiction to prevailing norms of
femininity.

TYPING INVOICES: WHITE-COLLAR WORK IN A FACTORY

Molly came from a working-class family. Her father, who was widowed, had trouble finding steady work, so she spent some time boarding with relatives while he travelled looking for jobs. In 1932, at sixteen,
she found a job in the office at the Bonnerworth mill after completing
three years of commercial training in high school. The office manager,
who knew her family, secured the job for Molly, and she felt immense
gratitude, for this was during the Depression, when 'jobs were like
hen's teeth.' Molly was proud of the responsibility she assumed for the
company: 'I went in as a receptionist and switchboard operator and
got nine dollars a week for a five-and-a-half-day week ... I also helped
the girl doing paycards, and typed checks ... I sat at the big switchboard, because we were the head office, you know, taking calls for the
Auburn management too ... The manager was right behind me and he
was very strict. I knew the manager at the Auburn too. I had a fair bit
of responsibility ... We *had* to work. The young getting jobs today want
high pay and no work. We really worked hard.'[35]
   A couple of years before this, Ethel, a young graduate of business
school who had came from a nearby rural farm, was sent to the GE
office by her business school teacher, and she had secured a job typing invoices. At General Electric, some women worked in small offices
within the plant, but far more were located within the large, concentrated office section of the building, which included engineering, payroll accounting, and other administrative departments. Like Ethel, they
often had very specific tasks – typing invoices, preparing payroll - and
at GE, because of the office size, by the 1940s and 1950s they were more
likely to answer to a female supervisor or office manager.
   Both these young women were part of a growing cadre of clerical
workers in Canadian companies. Since the early twentieth century,
the ratio of white- to blue-collar workers in many companies had swol-

len, reflecting the 'growing importance of administration to industry and the re-shaping of industry along modern corporate lines.'[36] In close tandem with the feminization of clerical work in the first decades of the twentieth century, argues Graham Lowe, 'came the massive re-structuring of the means of administering business ... [and] women were recruited for newly created, routine clerical tasks executed under tight management control.'[37] By the 1930s, women with at least two years of high school or business college training were conscripted to the new clerical jobs shaped by the impact of cost-accounting practices, the incorporation of scientific management techniques into the office, and the increased use of technology such as the typewriter.[38]

Ethel claims that many of the office women knew they might make more money in some production jobs, but they preferred positions that offered a more pleasant physical environment, shorter hours, and higher status. Women office workers were encouraged by management to see themselves as a different kind of worker, set off by their superior education, closer contact with management, and responsibility, and by the intellectual character of their job. Small perks were offered by management to reinforce this sense of difference. Office workers at GE, for example, were let out early to 'beat the rush' of the masses of workers from the shop floor.[39]

The notion of a personal obligation and responsibility to one's immediate manager was more successfully fostered in office work, and women often identified closely with the employees and managers in their units. Both male managers and female clerical workers emphasized the importance of factors such as personality 'fit,' sociability, and personal loyalty in their descriptions of the ideal office worker.[40] Indeed, managers could assume the role of fatherly protector or patron. One woman, for instance, commented that the office workers rarely knew others workers' rates of pay, nor did they think it proper to disrupt personal and hierarchical relations by asking. As Ethel explained of her experience at GE, 'There were three floors. The girls upstairs worked for the engineers and I think they had a different status. I don't know if they gave us regular raises; we didn't care. I think your manager went to personnel for you to ask for a raise. Girls in the office didn't know what went on in the top echelons. I didn't even know the wages of the girls I worked with.'[41]

In job content, though, there were similarities to blue-collar work. Some of the women described long hours, and hot airless offices in the summer. Like many production workers, the white-collar women were unlikely to be trained with a comprehensive view of how the firm worked. Women were often assigned very precise jobs, which had little variation. This was especially true in the larger companies that doubled as head offices, such as GE and Quaker Oats, but was less common in the smaller Bonnerworth office. At GE, Ethel typed invoices until the carbon paper turned her fingers irretrievably blue. Other women did billing, typed letters, or prepared the payroll. As one Westclox woman remembers, until the postwar period, she worked on payroll in the most rudimentary way: 'In payroll, I did everything manually. I figured out everyone's pay cheque – looked at the hourly rate or calculated piecework. I did it that way for about ten years until we went to data processing.'[42]

There was some limited job mobility for women in the office, which increased with the expansion of office work in the 1940s and 1950s. Long-term workers might take on more responsibilities, becoming supervisors of other clerical workers, or personal secretaries to managers. At Westclox, some women were able to move from production to clerical work, and from clerical work to secretarial positions. Within many offices, however, most women remained in jobs that were repetitive and standardized, that needed fast pacing and exact results, and were subject to substantial supervision: 'The boss would chastise you if you spent too much time talking ... or too long in the washroom,' remembered one office worker.[43]

Managers sometimes supervised so closely as to be overbearing. One secretary remembers a manager who critically scrutinized her most routine tasks. Since she took pride in her accuracy, she eventually became irritated. One day, after he implied that her margins were wrong, she politely offered him a ruler and said, 'Measure them before you say any more.' Her plan was to humour but also humble him. Unable to confront a manager openly for his disagreeable behaviour – for that would have been interpreted as discourteous – she had to be satisfied with her private knowledge that she knew her job better than he did.[44]

While women white-collar workers did see their jobs as distinct and even superior to blue-collar work, it would be a mistake to characterize them as being hoodwinked by a clever management strategy that imparted a false consciousness about their work. There was more than mere status to the appeal of white-collar work. However standardized the jobs, there was a measure of freedom in the workday which women highly valued. One Bonnerworth clerical worker noted that in running errands or giving out the cheques, she got to take trips through the factory. Another pointed to the relief created by the varying pace of work throughout the day and the month.

Women considered this relative variety and freedom to be preferable to the more tightly disciplined blue-collar jobs. Being tied to a typewriter was not as confining as being tied to a spinning machine, for the order and pace of white-collar work, as Lowe points out, were more difficult to regulate than factory work. Where the clerical workers' tasks were not easily quantifiable – as in some receptionist and secretarial jobs – they were not as easy to control. Sometimes, when there was a slow time, remembered a clerical worker, 'you would put your head on your typewriter and go to sleep, and once [the boss] caught me and said, "Are you enjoying yourself?"... but he didn't blame us for slow time.'[45]

Moreover, however paternalistic the relationship between managers and female office workers, there were potential benefits to white-collar work: women enjoyed aspects of office culture, including the ability to talk with others and to exchange and gain information about the business. Finally, one cannot dismiss women's sense of pride in their work. Many women felt that their jobs had importance to the company; they saw themselves as 'keeping management on track' (and they did) and maintaining efficiency and financial accountability. For those who acted as personal secretaries, they knew that their competency was crucial to someone else's career. While this has been interpreted as an example of women's identification with male management, it must also be seen as a source of job pride for women who had very few choices in the labour market of the time.

MANAGING THE GENDERED DIVISION OF LABOUR

Women's descriptions of their daily working lives emphasize how consistently and clearly the work roles were divided on the basis of gender; they also indicate the kinds of knowledge, experience, and stamina that characterized women's jobs. Unfortunately, the numerical and literacy skills of clerical workers, the rapid dexterity needed on a continuous-flow line, and the endurance of standing before a spinning machine for hours on end were valued less than the qualities apparent in men's jobs. At Quaker Oats the women's work of sewing heavy fabric to make feed bags paid less than the basic lifting by men; although the former may have required more training and experience, its link to domestic labour, and the fact that women did it, meant that it was depreciated in value.

Notions of skill, ability, and job worth, as Barbara Taylor and Anne Phillips argue, are not simply measured objectively; they have an ideological component. Definitions of skill are 'saturated with sexual bias,' and as a result, 'gender hierarchies are integrated directly into capitalist relations.'[46] The concept of skill involves some interpretation: its definition is 'shaped by who has power to define skill, to exclude others from training and to create distinctions between acquired knowledge and inherent abilities.'[47]

Biased definitions of skill were only one component of the sex typing of jobs in these workplaces, and in many cases these prejudices were connected to the long-standing sexual division of labour in the workplace and to employers' attempts to keep close control of both the work process and the gendered division of labour. If we accept the axiom that there is a natural tendency of capital to increase control over labour and the work environment,[48] then it makes sense to explore the way in which management regulated the sexual division of labour. It is important to note, of course, that management practices could vary from one company to another, with different labour market situations, labour processes, and industrial relations policies shaping their choices and strategies. As Ruth Milkman shows for the United States, for instance, the auto manufacturers' offer of a high family wage to male workers in return for their alienating work on the assembly line resulted in the exclusion of women from most jobs; on the other hand, the labour-intensive piecework typical of the consumer electrical industry resulted in large numbers of women workers filling a wide variety of jobs.[49]

Management control was just as crucial in the case of Westclox. Women were hired for less skilled and lower-paid jobs, managers claimed, because of past practice, because of the physical, psychological, and 'innate' characteristics of women, and because of the reality of male breadwinners and temporary female workers. One manager explained that he simply accepted the divisions he found when he arrived: 'It [the sexual division of labour] was already established by the time I arrived in 1930. Women did the lighter work; men operated big presses, did dirty work, heavier ... labour, and work where there was training needed.'[50] Another manager started by saying that education, background, and physical abilities set the guidelines for job assignment: he 'hired the person for the job.' For the punch press, he went on, he only hired 'girls who could handle' the work, such as a 'farm girl who ran a tractor at home.' However, his hiring practices still incorporated images of the appropriate sexual division of labour. He argued that women were naturally and physically better at fine, repetitious assembly: 'You wouldn't hire a man to knit, would you? His fingers were too big and clumsy. Girls were much more adaptable at assembly work, putting parts together. Men [were better] on big machines.'[51]

Managers also had a clear image of women's career intentions and the material compensation they should receive. They maintained that women should not be put in a job needing extensive training because they were merely temporary workers – they would leave to get married – and even if they returned later in life, children and domestic responsibilities would cause a higher rate of absenteeism. However, in some cases, the training argument made little sense. In the finishing rooms, men buffed the clocks and women lacquered them (the latter was actually quite hot work), so the logic of training or muscular strength did not explain the divisions here.

A manager who joined the firm in the 1930s admitted that attitudes about women's familial roles were absolutely crucial in determining their work roles: 'Our attitudes determined the choice of jobs for women ... We thought that men should make more as they had families.'[52] Management policies, such as barring married women from employment, codified these beliefs into a policy that structured the gendered division of labour. Within the plant, then, management determined women's work roles based on closely linked material and ideological considerations; the managers saw women's labour as transitory, malleable, and adaptable, and indeed valued it in assembly jobs precisely for this reason. Women were considered to be a physical and psychological 'fit' for assembly-line work; moreover, their labour was easily compensated and replenishable – a steady supply of female labour in the local labour market, especially from the surrounding rural areas, satisfied the latter concern.

In other factories also, management adamantly championed the male-breadwinner model of employment. In its self-promoting company paper, the *Works News*, General Electric actively advertised the ideal of the male-breadwinner family, featuring pictures and discussions about safety, consumer purchasing, and family life that all suggested that the man was the wage worker and that the woman, at least the married woman, was the consumer who should be at home, using her husband's wages to buy GE refrigerators. Managers saw this family model as the ideal arrangement for their workers as well as for themselves, and they sympathized with the notion that some jobs – indeed, actual physical spaces in the workplace – should be off limits to women. Letting women into the tool room would have been as unacceptable as letting women into their company's clubroom, if not their own washrooms. As Mariana Valverde suggests, a notion of appropriate 'sexual ordering' of the universe, including the protection of certain male spaces, may have played a role in shaping the sexual division of labour and the exclusion of women from some jobs.[53]

The importance of management control in the articulation of the sexual division of labour was echoed in many other workplaces. At the Bonnerworth mill, past practice was a factor in the allocation of work, for many of the managers had been recruited from England, and they brought with them a set notion of what constituted male and female work. Until the 1950s in the English worsted industry, women remained the majority of spinners.[54] Management's active recruitment of youth and female labour for a wide number of spinning and twisting positions also reflected Dominion Woollens' efforts to maintain its position in both the Canadian and the world market. Although it enjoyed a certain degree of tariff protection, the Canadian industry claimed it was difficult to compete with the well-developed British woollen industry, which had an established infrastructure, better access to raw material, and lower wage rates.[55] As the report of the Royal Commission on the Textile Industry pointed out in 1937, Canadian management consciously drew on lower-paid youth and female labour for the labour-intensive part of its operations in order to keep costs low and to remain as competitive as possible.

As Joy Parr points out, however, what appeared to be a rigid division of labour by day was suddenly quite malleable, come dusk. During the 1930s and 1940s, male workers came in at night to use the spinning machines, doing the same work as women, though they were paid higher wages. This was rationalized by management and by the workers in two ways: night work was too dangerous for women, because of the threat to their security after dark; secondly, men assumed more machine-tending responsibilities (though straw bosses were still hired to do some of the set-up).

Within the factory, male managers created a sense of identification with these male machine tenders by offering the promise of upward mobility and also by creating a sense of pride and superiority in their ability to fix and control the plant machinery. This sense of male pride in skill, though, came with little real financial compensation, since the men's wages were relatively low in comparison with other industries.[56] As Joy Parr points out about the Penmans' hosiery mill, the identification of male workers with the sexual division of labour, as shaped by management, created an unequal bargain, which gave the profits to the company and the pride to men.[57]

Management strategies to shape the sexual division of labour did not necessarily remain static. Their key aim was always control, but how this was achieved and rationalized, and what it meant for women's jobs, could vary over time. During the Second World War, for example, the number of women at Genelco/GE rose from 13 to 29 per cent.[58] As women began to do some traditionally male jobs, the company worried that women's wages would increase too dramatically, and male workers worried that the higher-paid men's codes would be transformed into lower-paid women's ones. As a result, a tug of war ensued about what constituted men's and women's work.

Throughout this tussle, the company consistently and vigorously maintained its right to code all women's jobs separately; it argued for a division of labour and pay differentials based on the presence of females in a job, and only secondarily on job content. In 1943, for instance, when the newly unionized workers in Genelco appealed to the War Labour Board for a common starting rate of 50 cents for men and women and for equal pay for equal work, GE management opposed this, claiming that women's wages were based on 'community standards.'[59] Since women were paid lower wages elsewhere, it somehow became a moral imperative for GE to do the same. (In this case, as the largest local employer, the company was setting these standards.) In asserting that the wage packet was socially determined by factors other than objective skills, the company was agreeing – quite unconsciously, of course – to the Marxist concept of a social wage: that labour is compensated not just for what it produces but also according to social standards and values, including gender and race stereotypes.

The company also justified the separate coding of all work done by women by saying that women did not produce as much or as high quality an output as men, even when they were on the same job. It argued that women often did not set up their machines or prepare for work by 'grinding their own tools' – jobs which of course they were not trained to do. Finally, the company argued (without substantial proof) that women's supposed higher absenteeism and turnover prohibited their production of 'equal results.'

In a revealing twist to its argument, however, the company threw in one last suggestion: it was ready to propose a new incentive system that the union could accept, which had no 'distinction of rates on the basis of sex.'[60] What was really at issue was the company's ability to control the job coding and wage system to its own benefit. After arguing that women should not be paid the same, it indicated that it might accept an incentive system with common pay rates – as long as it set the parameters itself.

In subsequent years, the company stubbornly rejected arguments for a narrowing of the gap between men's and women's wage rates or any tampering with the existing job coding by sex. Indeed, as was indicated by the United Electrical Workers Union's 1955 brief to the government on the existing and inadequate equal pay bill, Canadian General Electric had many ways of creating distinctions between male and female labour, from claiming that women and men could be paid differently according to the shifts they worked, to devaluing any machine or technical skills performed by women.[61] The one consistent theme was the company's firm resolve to control the wage codes in the production process and to protect the sexual division of labour by using the rationale that women were of less 'value' to the company.

This GE example also indicates how the state could play an important role, potentially altering but more often reinforcing sexual divisions in the workforce: the War Labour Board allowed coded jobs by sex and unequal pay to continue, despite union pressure to the contrary.[62] There was a long tradition of state support for the sexual division of labour. Government job exchanges and training programs set up in the 1920s and 1930s, for example, had trained women for domestic work, and, in the postwar years, employment exchanges and schemes such as unemployment insurance sanctioned the existing division of labour. As Ruth Pierson shows, the early unemployment insurance plans incorporated the assumption of a male breadwinner and of a dependent female earner, who had limited rights to both employment and insurance coverage.[63]

WORKERS EXPLAIN THE SEXUAL DIVISION OF LABOUR

The last example illustrates the variability in male workers' reactions to the sexual division of labour. While men at GE might argue against coding by sex, pointing to the similarity of men's and women's jobs, those at the Bonnerworth did not do so with regard to night work. The immediate response of male workers to the division of labour varied according to the specific traditions in the industry, the local labour market and availability of work, and the methods of managerial control the workers faced. The presence of a union, and its political proclivities, also mattered.[64] As Ruth Milkman cautions, this variability disputes the assumption that men will 'always identify with male interests,' be they fellow workers or managers.[65] A more useful approach, suggests Judy Lown, analyses gender and class as two sets of relationships and sources of identity, which evolve together in potential conflict and harmony. Historical situations produce different class and gender combinations, with male workers sometimes opposing and sometimes accepting management's views on women.[66]

Nonetheless, Lown also argues that patriarchy, a system with both material and ideological bases, is a factor of considerable importance in labour-management confrontations over the sexual division of labour. Even the most limited definition of patriarchy as a system of male headship of the family – with the power over family members' labour that this entails[67] – would support her contention that the existing axes of masculine power in all classes were crucial in shaping the sexual division of labour. And, indeed, there is a more cynical view to be drawn from the GE example used above: men were more likely to argue against the sexual division of labour when it served their economic aim of protecting male job rates.

While a minority of men – usually union activists in the war and postwar period – were sympathetic to the idea of altering male and female job codes, many more male workers resisted challenges to the existing division of labour and to the notion that women could be equal and permanent workers on the same basis as men. They explained that the preferable family arrangement of women's ultimate domesticity meant that women would be dependent and temporary workers, unsuitable for certain jobs; secondly, they endorsed cultural notions of female weakness and technical incompetence.

'Women were nervous on machines, scared of them,' claimed one male GE worker.[68] This was a common characterization, often stated as if women's antipathy to machinery had an unchangeable psychological basis. 'Women can find more excuses to shut a machine down than you can shake a stick at,' complained a foreman (who, ironically, left one stressful workplace 'because of his nerves').[69] This assumption of women's technical incompetence sanctioned their exclusion from many blue-collar jobs that required contact with machinery; it was often stated in tandem with descriptions of men's superior physical strength and women's physical weakness. Notions of physical aptitude, however, were malleable, though they were invariably fashioned to sustain male control over skills and privileges. One tool-and-die worker, for example, first argued that women were better at fine work that required attention to detail but later proudly showed me the small, exact, and fine pieces of metal he had created by his skill. This man saw no contradiction in his evaluation of work roles, because he also believed that women were working for only a short time and that it was therefore uneconomical to train them for such skilled jobs.

It was not only length of education and training, however, that shaped the ideas of men's and women's jobs, for many white-collar women workers had as much training, in education years, as skilled men, and their work certainly involved financial responsibility. Yet their jobs were still perceived as less deserving of a living wage. As Phillips and Taylor argue, the amount of training may not be the crucial deciding factor, for 'the work of women is often deemed inferior simply because it is women who do to. Women carry into the workplace their status as subordinate individuals and this comes to define the work they do.'[70]

Linked to almost every description of the sexual division of labour given by male workers was one recurrent and strongly emphasized rationalization: the ideal of a male breadwinner or a family wage. Even though this ideal was difficult to achieve and a pooled family wage economy was often necessary, the model of the female wage worker as temporary and dependent, and the male as permanent and with dependents, was tenaciously defended.

Historians agree that the emergence of this ideal in the nineteenth century resulted in the exclusion of women and in the sex typing of certain jobs. They disagree, though, on how and why workers participated in the process. While some argue that the family wage ideal was a working-class strategy embraced by both men and women to protect and enhance the working-class family's standard of living, others suggest that the ideal was pursued as part of a masculinized attempt to protect men's power as husbands, fathers, and heads of households and to secure their identity as 'manly' providers.[71] The actual rationale for the strategy may have changed over time. Martha May argues that while it was a working-class family strategy in the nineteenth century, by the twentieth century the family wage had become a cross-class ideal, with (male) gender interests predominating.[72] Rather than en-dorsing either class conflict or patriarchal control as the modus vivendi, some analyses have embraced both these arguments.[73] Sonya Rose argues convincingly that in the crucible of management's various strate-gies to reduce labour costs, such as attempts at de-skilling, 'gender antagonism' resulted, and consequently male workers often marginalized women in order to protect their status as skilled workers and as heads of households.[74]

While the origins of the family wage ideal are hotly debated, the consequences are not: it created divisions within the working class; it constructed an image of women as dependent and transitory workers, thus making them more dependent; and it ignored the realities of women who were self-supporting or were the sole support of their families, or whose husbands were unemployed, temporarily or perma-nently.

The argument for a male breadwinner's wage, and thus the exclu-sion of women from many jobs, was articulated by workers in all four industries.[75] Night-time male spinners at the Bonnerworth mill never suggested that women should be accorded their higher wages for do-ing similar work during the day; even when women began to work some night hours during the war, the notion that men's wages should be protected was endorsed. During the 1937 textile strike, male work-ers at Dominion Woollens' second mill, the Auburn, emphasized their rights as breadwinners in their confrontation with management. When Dominion Woollens' president, Henry Barrett, made a tour of the mill, a spokesperson was elected to tell him about the men's objections to their low pay. In the midst of this dramatic confrontation, a weaver with a Glaswegian accent pushed his way to the front of the crowd and upbraided the president for denying the men their basic right to a living wage: 'How do you expect a man to support a family on 22 cents an hour?' was the centrepiece of his argument.[76] Appeals for a male-breadwinner wage were not only used as a 'weapon to wield against employers'[77] in labour struggles; they were also invoked in the case of unemployment problems. When Dominion Woollens finally shut down, an employee applauded its policy to 'try very hard for the men, espe-cially the men, to get them unemployment insurance.'[78]

Many men invoked the ideal of the male breadwinner as if it were a moral imperative. It was linked to their masculine pride and was equated with their sense of responsibility for supporting their families without descending into poverty or without other family members being forced to work. As one woman recalled, her husband clearly stated the position when they married: 'My husband said "I will *support* my wife; no wife of mine will go on working."'[79] But the ideal was also fused with notions of social predominance and power, since the male wage was associated with a sense of independence and status, of importance and freedom, and with corollary power within the domestic sphere as well as in the wider society. At its most extreme, this emphasis on masculine power and predominance could have violent consequences: a study of wife battering in Peterborough County reveals that men sometimes withheld their earnings as a means of exerting power over their families, and that contests between husbands and wives over financial resources could result in the husband's violent assertion of his superior position in the family hierarchy.[80]

The male-breadwinnner model could be temporarily altered. One male GE worker remembers that, during the war, men accepted more married women in the plant; but 'after the war, about 80 to 90 per cent of them weren't sympathetic to married women working there.' The men's reasoning, said another male GE worker, was that women should be temporary workers; if women stayed on, they were potentially infringing on men's rightful place and earnings: '"She's going to put me out on the street ... and her husband is already working," is what some of the guys said.'[81] As Paul Willis argues, 'the unholy interlocked grip of masculinity and the wage form ... is a kind of symbol of machismo which then dictates the domestic culture and economy, and tyrannizes both men and women.' It implies a notion of men as productive, active, and heroic; femininity, on the other hand, is associated with domesticity, 'a fixed state of endless reproduction.'[82]

Moreover, in a workplace such as General Electric, which was already associated with male apprenticeships and skill, and was steeped in a tradition of masculine work culture, any potential alteration to the gendering of work undoubtedly appeared more threatening. As contemporary researchers have noted, shop-floor discourses on gender and sexuality in heavy industrial workplaces often equate difficult, dirty, and heavy work with a sense of manhood that 'establishes men's power and dignity in conditions of its erosion.'[83] In such conditions, another observer notes, men may 'compensate' for their denial of dignity in the workplace by 'playing foreman after work'; in this equation, 'the male worker's role as Primary Breadwinner is critical – the economic function of this paycheck is to give him power over the family and status in society.'[84]

It is important to listen to workers' own descriptions of the decision to embrace the breadwinner model. The language used by both men and women in the interviews conducted for this study is extremely revealing. In the majority of cases, men were clearly the authors of the male-breadwinner ideal, both as its executors and as its adamant and insistent protagonists. 'My husband didn't want me to work [in the office] ... he had ulcers,' said one woman. Another recalled, 'Even during the war, I wasn't tempted to work [as] my husband wouldn't hear of it.' Similarly: 'My husband didn't believe in me working.'[85] While the women actively participated in this decision (as will be discussed below), the language patterns divulge a dominant script: men's control of the better-paying jobs and of more secure employment because of the sex typing of jobs clearly gave them a feeling of self-respect, predominance, and power within the household and in the wider society.[86]

The women clearly recognized that the male-breadwinner model carried with it a measure of masculine control in family decision making. As one textile worker noted of her blue-collar husband, 'He wouldn't let me go to work. He said, "I'm earning. You're not going to work."' But after the children were grown, she went to work part-time: 'My husband didn't mind that, as long as I was here to get his meals.'[87]

THE POWER OF IDEOLOGY: WOMEN EXPLAIN THE GENDERED DIVISION OF LABOUR

The sexual division of labour was not only the creation of management and male workers; it was also accepted and rationalized by women themselves. Women's explanations for their placement in lower-paid assembly jobs, their rationale for not demanding supervisory jobs, and their disinterest in challenging notions of skill must therefore also be analysed. It was not passivity that structured their ambitions, but rather their realization of existing power structures, their daily experience of 'female' work, and their participation in an ideology of sexual difference and female domesticity, which in turn became an integral part of their subjective identities as women workers.

Most women participated in wage work under conditions that simultaneously limited both their ability and their desire to challenge the existing gendered division of labour. For the first cohort of women especially – those who went out to work before the Second World War – there was little cultural or familial support for challenging the gendered division of labour. They did not see women heavy-machine operators in their own families, in the movies, or in their neighbourhood, and few of these women remember their families urging them to question their place in the job hierarchy or to change occupation. More often, parental authority urged acceptance and not rebellion at work, since parents feared losing the daughter's contribution to the family economy. Women's choices were also shaped by their limited economic independence; their meagre wages made it difficult to live independently outside a family or household arrangement. Keeping a job, no matter what its content, was thus their first worry.

Secondly, women's immediate work environment made it difficult for them to imagine challenging the sexual division of labour. In many instances of both white- and blue-collar work, women worked under a strict hierarchy, had little overall knowledge of the workplace, and were disciplined by male authority figures. None of these things helped reconstruct women's ambition in new and innovative ways – indeed, quite the contrary. The production process creates its own distinct social relations; the daily experience of the women's work tended to reinforce a sense of little control over job content, rather than encouraging them to think about extending it.

Women could be quite realistic about the rigidity of the sexual division of labour that they witnessed at work and about who benefited from it. One woman in a blue-collar job remembered seeing men getting paid higher rates for similar assembly work, but although she was critical, she knew that complaining would be of little use.[88] Similarly, a woman who worked in a clerical job observed women staying in lateral transfers only, 'with no real promotions,' while men were not only promoted but developed a sense of 'their superiority.' She saw these patterns repeated so often that they came to seem inevitable, though not necessarily fair: 'You just worked hard, and [accepted] you had few privileges – though [you knew] it was different for men.'[89]

If women saw injustice in the division of labour, they might try to compensate for it secretly, knowing that open rebellion would be ineffective. One production worker knew that her 'work was as heavy as a man's,' yet she was on 'a girl's piece rate.' When she had no success with a complaint, she quietly manipulated the piecework system to her benefit: 'I compensated for it myself, I put a little more money into my piecework; but I shouldn't have had to do it [that way].'[90]

Furthermore, many of the women workers realized that women's entry into male jobs could bring with it complications and dangers. Some women who went to work in the 1940s and stayed until the 1960s often expressed surprise, shock, and some concern about later attempts by women to challenge the workplace division of labour. They worried that women would be subject to new physical threats and to the men's poor working conditions, and that women would simply be adding to the occupational hazards they already faced.[91] Others worried that a change in the sexual division of labour would result in loss of job security. As a woman at General Electric explained, 'If women got equal status with men, the company would lay women off.'[92] She feared that, with no financial incentive to hire women, the company would simply do without them, and the women would thus lose the little economic security they had – their 'protected' job ghettos. Given GE's callous managerial attitude towards female labour, her analysis was not illogical.

When asked to explain the sexual division of labour, women pointed to men's superior training and skills and to their muscular strength, and they sometimes made vague references to 'innate' abilities. 'A man could not do some of the fine work with tweezers that girls could; girls could not lift heavy rolls,' commented a Westclox woman. 'There are some things as a woman you can't do. I can't go and lift heavy boxes, but I could do paperwork. But then, I'm of the old school.'[93] Similarly, a woman who worked for many years at Quaker Oats noted that women were not 'equipped for some jobs.' Upsetting the existing gender order was far from her aim: 'Men were here first. They had the heavy jobs and were good [at them] ... I firmly believe women went too far. [Look] what can happen to women if they are not equipped for the work. A running machine is no job for a woman.'[94] Since the sexual divisions in work were something these women grew up with, they became part of a common-sense notion about both work and womanhood.

The knowledge that a marriage bar existed – at least until the Second World War and in some factories until the 1950s – also put closure on the women's mental images of job change. This marriage bar was so pervasive in the local industries that some women believed 'that was the law then.'[95] Moreover, the hostility sometimes directed by co-workers towards pregnant or married women (who in one factory were referred to as 'money grubbers')[96] did not encourage resistance to this barrier. A former textile worker made clear the 'rules of the game' in the 1930s by commenting on what she believed was the proper thing to do and what could be expected if one contravened those norms: 'In those days [you quit when you married]. Your husband kept you. That's why you got married. You got married, stayed home, and had children. I remember a pregnant woman who came to work ... she was told to go home and not come back.'[97]

The marriage bar was linked in women's minds to the impermanent status of women in the workforce and to the family wage ideal; indeed, the latter was their primary explanation for the gendered division of labour. Images of appropriate work were directly tied to images of appropriate wages for women. In the interwar period, the notion that women had limited economic needs was articulated repeatedly. As a Westclox production worker explained, your pay cheque 'should be enough to pay for your keep' within your family, 'but that was all you worried about ... Men got more because they had families of their own.'[98] As Alice Kessler-Harris points out, the wage form contains meanings that transcend economic models of supply and demand, and are tied historically to notions of justice, fair play, and exploitation, and even more generally, to images of 'how people should live.' The idea of a woman's wage, which emerged with industrialization, embodied the idea of survival rather than of supporting others, and it reflected 'what ought to be – that is, women in the home.'[99] This needs-based conception of women's wages, which emphasized the role of women as secondary earners, began to change – although only very slightly – in the postwar years, as women became more cognizant of their rights as wage earners. Even in the postwar period, however, the sexual division of labour remained stubbornly intact, still informed by the earlier cultural notion of the dependent woman worker.

For some women, the existing sexual division of labour had come to shape their very identity; it was firmly linked to their sense of femininity. In the 1960s, a self-supporting woman, who had worked for many years at Quaker Oats, considered that the younger women who challenged the division of labour were 'bold,' unappealing, and unattractive. When she was once asked to get up and do a man's job, stirring the cookie batter in a giant vat, she was quite miffed: 'I told him *I* was still a lady and I wasn't going to do *that* job.'[100] Similarly, a clerical worker who was offered a supervisory position tried to explain why she did not like the particular stresses and tasks of the job and why she eventually decided to give it up: 'I didn't care for it. Management was wonderful, but it was a lot of new responsibility. It was a rotten job for a girl.'[101] As David Collinson has argued, the very practices of gendered work can come to constitute part of workers' subjectivity, with the sexual division of labour offering men and women the security of 'stable,' secure, and comfortable representations of manhood and womanhood.[102]

For some women, their image of femininity also carried with it a commitment to domesticity. While it would be wrong to assume that all women saw their time in the workforce as temporary, many clearly did, or at least hoped that they could leave wage work on marriage. The women interviewed often claimed that they approved of the boundaries on their work roles because they expected wage work to be temporary. A blue-collar worker at GE was transferred after the war to a monotonous job she hated, but she took no action because, as she says, 'I knew I was getting married and it would only be a year before I could leave.'[103] Women embraced the ideal of female domesticity and male breadwinner not because they lacked ambition but because their ambition was to leave the workforce and participate in another kind of work – domestic labour. They regarded domestic labour as important to family survival, they associated it with their feminine identity, and they assumed that it would garner them both familial and social respect. 'I thought my [proper] place was with my husband, looking after him, as my mother had done,' remembered one woman.[104]

This ideology of domesticity, or of 'women's place,' must be seen as part of the overall social fabric shaping the sexual division of labour.[105] The ideal was not always embraced absolutely or without question. Some women clearly chose to live without a male partner. Others, who married, worried about relinquishing the positive benefits of wage work. Nonetheless, many women put their doubts aside and attempted to live up to the ideal – even if, later in life, they also experienced its contradictions and illusions. 'After I married in the late 1930s, that was when a woman couldn't get a job or anything in a factory if you were married,' recalled a former Westclox worker. 'And that's one of the biggest mistakes that ever happened in this country when they let married women back into the factories and the beverage rooms.'[106] Yet her example of women 'overstepping' their bounds by going into factories and beverage rooms was at variance with her own experience, for in the 1950s she became one of the increasing number of working mothers (discussed in chapter 9).

CONCLUSION

While a gendered division of labour has been long-standing in Canadian society, both before and after industrialization, its exact contours have varied over time and place. Historians of nineteenth-century industrialization have convincingly argued that the emergence of an industrial capitalist society intensified the sex segregation of jobs, and that this period witnessed the emergence of the ideal of the male breadwinner – the model which Lown calls the 'closest meeting place' of patriarchy and capitalism.[107] But there is also evidence that job segregation is potentially fluid; it can be shaped by the nature of the labour market, by different work processes, by gender ideals, and by family forms. It was never the simple outcome of objective measurements of strength, skill, and experience; it also involved interpretations of these qualities, which were in turn moulded by the power relations of class and gender.

Men's and women's descriptions of their different work roles in these four Peterborough workplaces do not offer a conclusive explanation for the origins of the sexual division of labour, but they do provide insight into its reproduction and resilience, into how it was justified with ideologies of natural sexual difference. The gendered divisions of labour described here were created not in the workplace or the family alone, but at both sites: women's job ghettos cannot be merely 'read off'[108] as a consequence of their domestic lives, nor were they completely created by a capitalist ethos.

It is true that managerial control was essential to the profile of gender divisions in the workforce. The existing division of labour, set out predominantly by management, created the framework within which workers had to negotiate and struggle. Moreover, employers, in their introduction of new techniques and ways of using labour, in their own reproduction of familial ideology, and in their pursuit of control over the work process and profit, purposely gendered the workforce. The economic structures of capitalist organization do, on one level, create men's and women's jobs, and this power cannot be typified in a Foucauldian vein as ascending, diffuse, or multidimensional: it was very clearly concentrated, controlled, and privileged.[109]

At the same time, the sexual division of labour was sustained and reinforced by ideological representations of femininity and masculinity, and by an image of the nuclear, male-breadwinner family as the ideal. Ideology about gender roles is shaped by material forces, values, traditions, and beliefs – and, importantly, by our lived experience. As it is practised every day, the division of labour becomes internalized, on some level, by the people engaged in it – hence, women's rationale that their nimble fingers secured them assembly-line jobs. This ideology does not seem alien or something that is imposed on women; it is literally created by women through 'their participation in its partial representation of reality which assumes they are *already* its subjects.'[110]

Men and women workers participated in the ideological process of creating gendered meanings of wage work. Male workers engaged, often quite ardently, in the active exclusion of women from some work, assimilating and utilizing the dominant ideological dictums of women's physical weakness and future domestic role in order to explain their actions. Certainly, not all men acted uniformly to protect their gender interests. As we shall see in chapter 7, men's efforts to deal with the sexual division of labour could vary, especially with unionization. Nonetheless, one approach did tend to dominate. Most male workers invested in the ideology of the sex typing of work as a means of protecting deeply held concepts of male pride, responsibility, competence, strength, and power. A crucial ingredient of this process was the way in which notions of male skill and of a more generous 'just wage' for men were developed within familial and social power relations that favoured men's independence and authority: the sexual division of labour was at heart an unequal ordering of power in the workplace, even if that was not women's immediate understanding of their experience.

Women's acceptance of the sexual division of labour was also conditioned by their daily experiences of work, by their familial relationships, and by their absorption of cultural values, all of which reinforced an image of female technical incompetence and male competence, of female domesticity and male breadwinning. Women actually developed their own realistic readings of the structural and material barriers to any alteration in the sexual division of labour, and they too assimilated an ideological representation of work as a profoundly gendered experience; at a deeper level, these representations became part of their own subjective identities as women workers.

The relegation of women to less valued and lower-paid jobs was thus reproduced by the capitalist economies and managerial strategies the workers encountered, along with patriarchal relationships and images, situated both on the job and in the family. These were not separate, autonomous systems; they were interrelated processes that were experienced as one. In order to uncover how women understood the connections between their work and their opportunities for family life, romance, leisure, and friendship, we need to explore in more detail women workers' identities and to ask whether there was a distinct 'women's culture' in the workplace.

4

Women's Work Culture, Women's Identities

In 1948, Marj and Jean, both of whom worked at General Electric (GE), were married on the same weekend in June. On their last day at the factory before the ceremony, their fellow employees stopped work to hold a short celebration. They made speeches and presented the brides-to-be with identical presents – woollen blankets – as they sat on a raised, decorated rolling platform, on which they were then displayed, along with their gifts, to their department. A photographer from the GE paper, the *Works News*, came to take a picture, which was published with the arresting headline. 'Two Porcelain Girls Were Wed Saturday.'[1]

Similar rituals surrounding marriage were repeated, with variations in style, in all these workplaces for the entire period of this study. These celebrations were emblems of women's work culture – the informal and customary values, rituals, and rules that are part of the workplace.[2] The celebrations also revealed the close connection between women's work, family, and community lives, and the way in which feminine identity was both imported into the workplace and constructed on the factory and office floor.

This chapter weaves together an examination of women's social expectations, leisure, and community life with the theme of work culture. By correlating women's workplace experiences to their cultural milieu and to the non-waged areas of their daily lives, we can explore the underlying material and ideological factors shaping women's evolving identities as *women* wage earners, as well as the way in which class and gender identities in turn shaped women's work practices.[3] The cultural values and social customs that women brought to work with them – just as they packed a lunch or carried a purse with personal items – became important resources shaping their coping strategies at work and their understanding of the gendered division of labour, in the same way that their daily experience of the gendered division of labour contributed to their understanding of a 'just' wage for women and their feminine identity.

This emphasis on the interconnectedness of work, family, and community is indispensable to an understanding of women's work culture. Expressed through ideas, oral tradition, and daily practices, work culture encompasses everything from workers' definitions of a good day's work or a good boss, to coping with the work process, initiation rites, and social pastimes on the job. Work culture has in part been the articulation of women's own values, needs, and aspirations as they tried to cope with the problems and possibilities of their jobs. But it is not simply an expression of workers' independent goals and separate space, a form of 'resistance' to management. Because it is shaped within the power relations of the workplace, work culture can also unconsciously draw on management priorities and aims or on ideologies that simultaneously sanction women's inequality. As Sallie Westwood has argued, women's work culture can reflect both acceptance of and resistance to class and patriarchal relations in the workplace, with one emphasis overtaking the other, depending on the circumstances, or with both coexisting in tandem.[4]

Recent debates about women's work culture reveal significant differences of opinion among historians on how we should assess the values, actions, and rituals practised by women in the workplace.[5] Some feminist writers contend that women's work culture (whether women occupy a sex-segregated workplace or share the shop floor with men) has been decisively shaped by their distinctive gender roles, especially their familial and domestic responsibilities, their socialization to 'relational,' caring work.[6] In a slightly different vein, others hold that a distinct, ethnic, racial, and 'gender consciousness' or view of the world exists among women workers as a consequence of their daily concrete 'experience of gendered power relations.'[7]

Other writers are sceptical of such generalizations. Alice Kessler-Harris has warned against the overwhelming assumption that 'domesticity' or 'separate spheres' is always a crucial, defining variable of women workers' identities. Some commentators have suggested that work, not family, may have been the defining ingredient of identity and that factors such as marital status, age, and ethnicity were just as crucial as gender in shaping work culture.[8] More fundamentally, poststructuralist feminist writers have disputed our ability even to locate a group culture or identity, given the multiple variations in women's experience owing to class, ethnicity, marital status, and age, and to the indeterminate refractions of these 'experiences' through the cultural discourses available to us. The very word 'identity' has become problematic. Writers such as Judith Butler posit the idea of women's fluctuating, multiple, and contradictory identities, and they privilege the discursive over the nondiscursive forces shaping these 'instable' identities.[9]

These differences of interpretation (which would seem unnecessarily abstract to many of the women I interviewed, who felt that they knew their own identities quite well) are directly linked to the debates relating to the question of women's 'experience' that I noted in the introduction. Poststructuralist writing on identity has helped expose some of the differences and contradictions in women's outlook and culture, thus disputing a universal, timeless, and seamless gender identity, and it has highlighted the cultural processes shaping discourses about women's changing identities. Nonetheless, like critics of Butler, I am wary of an undue emphasis on the plurality, particularity, diversity, and instability of women's identities created by and through discourses, for it can obscure the role that 'material structures, power, and authority play in shaping subjectivity,' and it can potentially erase the 'self-conscious subject' as an active historical agent of action and change.[10]

This chapter thus remains wedded to the notion of an identifiable work culture, a concept that effectively links women's interpretation of the cultural atmosphere, material practices, and social networks in their workplaces with their lives outside work. Although each workplace spawned its own distinctive culture, there were similarities in the values and practices of the women workers in all these workplaces, shaped by shared family expectations and pressures, by material structures, by the dominant discourses relating to femininity, and by the women's active engagement with (sometimes even their attempts to refashion) these discursive and nondiscursive forces.

THE CULTURE OF FEMININITY

Women who grew up in the interwar period were surrounded by a popular culture that stressed consumption, beauty, heterosexuality, and romance as central to feminine identity. These themes were re-

produced endlessly in magazines (especially those geared towards female readers), newspapers, and movies. In their recollections, the
women interviewed sometimes downplayed the importance of popular magazines and newspapers on their consciousness, perhaps because the memory of glancing through magazines is less outstanding
than memories of movie going and of peer group and courting activities such as shopping, dancing, and skating parties. Nonetheless, the
images of the popular media provided a cultural landscape framing
women's lives that cannot be ignored; they provided recurring and
influential messages about work, life, and love.[11]

The themes of romance and consumption, prominent in popular
fiction and magazines, were often linked together in advertising that
was increasingly directed towards women's buying power; it was suggested that attractiveness, and thus romance, could be easily purchased
at the local department store. An emerging multimillion-dollar cos-
metic industry and a fashion industry that was increasingly concentrating on mass-produced and affordable ready-made clothes directed
their aim at the young working woman. Although some conservatives
at the time saw the fashions of the period, such as shorter skirts and
hair, as evidence of youthful rebellion against existing gender norms,
in fact the desired end was still females' physical attraction to men.
Beauty contests, an invention of this period, 'left little doubt,' Veronica
Strong-Boag comments, 'where female assets [were supposed to] lie.'[12]
Similarly, the apparently 'new' explicit focus on romance in the movies masked the persisting themes of male dominance and the double
standard in sexual relationships, as well as the confining pressure for
everyone to embrace heterosexual coupling.[13]

Messages about women's work roles relayed in mass-circulation
magazines accepted women's work for pay – as long as the work was
temporary and the women remained single. Although the wage work
of single working-class women had been accepted as a reality for some
time, the mass media increasingly endorsed occupations such as clerical work as an option for middle-class women before marriage. But it
was also presumed that the ultimate goal of most women was marriage and motherhood; wage work was merely the rehearsal for their
later, more important, social contribution of raising a family.[14] Significantly, the women workers interviewed often remembered the few
working mothers in their workplaces as unlucky or unfortunate; given
the cultural emphasis on female domesticity, and the division of labour
they witnessed at home, the women knew that to remain at work would
mean doing two jobs. Recalling her desire to leave the workforce on

marriage in 1940, one woman spoke of her sense of identity as a wife and mother, but she also echoed a desire to avoid two jobs: 'When I married I quit, because my husband was in the forces and I wanted to be with him ... [Later] I didn't want to work. I liked to be at home. I wanted to be there when my children came home. [Besides,] when both [husband and wife] are working, the woman comes home and has to do the housework, washing, and ironing. I see [the mothers] now ... and I think, "Good grief ... I just couldn't have done it."'[15]

Since the nineteenth century, it had been assumed that women's inevitable fulfilment would come from marriage and motherhood, but now an emerging ideal of the family was putting more and more emphasis on a family-centred emotional life for both men and women, and on the satisfaction to be gained from the sexual and emotional ties of marriage. Rather than seeing marriage as a partnership based on separate work roles and social spheres, there was an emphasis on companionship, romantic compatibility, and sexual fulfilment.[16] At the same time, family life increasingly came under the scrutiny of professional experts, who offered advice through the media on everything from housework to romance, recommending more scientific, efficient, and psychologically rewarding ways of rearing one's children.[17]

The demographic trends of the interwar period also indicate that marriage and domesticity were important to both men and women. Not only were women increasingly likely to wed in this period, but the age of marriage was slightly decreasing so that most women married in their early or mid-twenties, and smaller families were becoming the norm. Only the economic trauma of the Great Depression temporarily reversed some of these trends, as women and men postponed marriage and put off childbearing, lacking the resources to set up a household.[18]

The images of women presented in the media were only one part of the interwar cultural landscape, and they were always negotiated and translated by women into a language that spoke to their own personal, social, and material worlds.[19] There is little evidence, however, that these popular ideals were directly challenged or thoroughly contested. The emphasis on fulfilment through heterosexual romance, on domesticity as a female career goal, and the portrayal of motherhood as an expression of woman's maturity, indeed as an expression of her natural abilities, were continuing themes in the media throughout the interwar period, despite the dislocation of the Great Depression and an increased incidence of married working women.

How much effect did popular culture have on working-class women, and what were their lives like outside the factory gates? We can try to address this question by asking what kind of leisure and entertainment they enjoyed, as well as what kind of recreational and moral 'uplift' local institutions felt they should offer working women.

WOMEN'S LEISURE

Away from work and home duties, women spent time going to the movies, window shopping, or, most often, taking part in informal sporting events and other neighbourhood-based peer-group activities. Informal and relatively unsupervised leisure predominated. Same-sex circles of friends were formed, though by the age of seventeen, women were also becoming more involved in heterosocial activities. Groups of young women workers often 'hung out' window shopping, talking, and joking. As one woman recalls with laughter, her weekly excitement after having coffee downtown with her girlfriends from work 'was to go and read the funny cards at Hatton's greeting card store.'[20] Inexpensive sports such as bowling, skating, and swimming also claimed the women's spare time. With a river and canal running through Peterborough, skating parties and picnics could quickly and easily be organized without cars.

Once these young women were earning their own wages, movies became a regular and popular pastime, for most of them could spare the Saturday afternoon admission charge of 25 cents, no matter how small their allowance, after they had paid their board. Movies offered escape and entertainment; they also provided images and roles that shaped and 'channelled women's fantasies and expectations' about work, romance, and marriage. The female movie heroines of this period, argues Mary Ryan, were preoccupied with beauty, consumption, and, of course, heterosexual romance. Indeed, during the Roaring Twenties, the heroine who was a working women often used her sexuality to secure her desired escape into the bliss of domesticity.[21] The movies of the 1930s, though admittedly offering more versions of the independent woman, also exposed the domestic tension of Depression life and posed women's independence and lifelong work as problematic juxtapositions to marriage and motherhood.[22]

Movies were sometimes combined with other end-of-the-week rituals, such as shopping, in which the young working women spent (or fantasized about spending) their weekly allowance. One textile worker, for example, went out every Friday night in the mid-1930s with a group of girlfriends from her neighbourhood for dinner and bowling, after which they window-shopped all down the main street. As a pastime, shopping related to women's basic needs, their dreams of luxury, and their newfound identity as wage earners. Up-to-date clothes were an important symbol of respectability and success for many working women, especially those who were earning for the first time, and they were a necessity for white-collar workers, who had to dress well for their jobs.[23] When I asked the women what they spent their money on (after paying for board), many noted the pride of being able to choose their clothes for the first time in their lives. These purchases symbolized new independence and maturity: 'I spent my money on clothes, always on clothes. I came from a big family and when we were growing up, we just didn't have any money for clothes. So, that was my opportunity – when I started to work.'[24] A former factory worker recalled, with self-deprecating humour, a fascination with clothes: 'Dad said if I was old enough to work, I could manage my own money. I loved to buy clothes, and now my closets are still full of clothes!'[25]

Until the steadier employment and higher wages of the 1940s, however, women who were supporting families or who lived alone had to budget extremely carefully, buying large items such as coats on credit. The fact that the women can still describe specific purchases vividly after forty years indicates the time and effort it took to complete them. One woman recounted a purchase in considerable detail: 'It was Friday, payday, and I was going to the Quaker [Oats] Tennis Club for a dinner and party ... And I ran all the way downtown from Westclox to Florence's Dress Shop. [I knew] there was a white linen suit in the window which was $5.35. I had *saved* for that suit. So I bought it ... Mind you, I ate I don't know what for the next week, because then I was broke.'[26] Buying one's own clothes was not only a symbol of independence, but it could also be a means of rebellion. As one woman recalls, she was one of the first to wear slacks in the city in the 1940s, a fact she presents as being positively subversive for the times, and especially for Peterborough![27]

While clothes talk and clothes buying was obviously part of women's culture, some workers concentrated on putting aside items for their trousseaus. One Bonnerworth worker, for instance, gave her mother $5.00 for board in the mid 1930s and kept the remaining $2.50; every week, 50 cents of that went to the creation of her hope chest, as she had already picked out $25.00 worth of linen and china at a local store.[28]

Women's leisure time was spent with peer groups formed around workplace, neighbourhood, and church affiliation, though some women had little to do with their workplace. As one Bonnerworth woman pointed out, she usually had only energy enough to 'crawl home after work.'[29] Another Bonnerworth spinner commented that 'people just did their work and got out of there,' spending little spare time together.[30] (But it is important to remember that in using oral history, the discussion of personal relationships produces especially subjective responses; this woman had worked all through the bitter 1937 strike, and this may have had an influence on how she interpreted the personal dimensions of her workplace.)

It does appear, however, that there were more off-work friendships associated with workplaces such as Westclox, which had a record of employee longevity, many sports teams and less tense shopfloor social relations. As someone going from the Bonnerworth mill to Westclox commented; 'It was like night and day. Westclox was friendlier, like a family.'[31] Still, peer culture was very flexible, and workplace social groups also depended on how long one had worked for the company, on one's family ties to other employees, and one's responsibilities at home, to name only a few factors.

Women were just as likely to spend their time with family, neighbourhood friends, or church groups as they were with workmates. In a city so clearly differentiated by Catholic and Protestant religious affiliation, this meant that women's socializing and workplace networks were also shaped by this religious identification. Church activities claimed significant loyalty for most women, though it was a comradely socializing as much as religious devotion that seemingly inspired their participation in church drama, sports, and skating. Nonetheless, there were women who were especially religious and whose social lives, including their courting, revolved around the church: 'I didn't go to shows', remembers one woman who met her husband through her Church, 'I went to gospel chapel. There was lots of things for us to do ... There was Friday night Young People's, prayer meeting on Wednesdays, and Sunday was church ... The whole week was taken up with church.'[32]

Organizing women's leisure into moral channels was the concern of a number of churches as well as the local YWCA. Even before the First World War, the Peterborough YWCA attempted to influence women workers at General Electric by opening a drop-in centre for them in the city's south end. Following the lead of the national YWCA, the local one offered residence services, and it later provided an employment bureau and also social, religious, and recreational services, with the aim of 'uplifting' the moral and spiritual values of working-class girls and creating virtuous, Christian mothers of the future.[33] In the interwar period, the Toronto YWCA's reform discourses about working women were transformed, argues Carolyn Strange; earlier fears of the inevitable moral corruption of young women 'adrift' in the city were replaced by an increasing acceptance of the working woman and by attempts to foster her growth as an efficient, disciplined worker and, ultimately, to prepare her for healthy motherhood.[34]

In small cities such as Peterborough, a lingering emphasis on moral guidance and supervision for working-class girls alone in the city, combined with an emphasis on healthy, uplifting recreation and Protestant religious education, characterized the YWCA's efforts in this period. In the early 1920s, a full-time industrial worker visited Peterborough factories and offices trying to interest young women in the YWCA, and she had some limited successes building working women's clubs within the organization. For example, a junior and senior girls' club (the United and the Cumjoynus) from the Bonnerworth mill used the gym and pool, and had cooking classes and Bible study. According to the YWCA staff, the Jolly Juniors, a regular group of mill workers, loved to play basketball and also enjoyed a guest lecture by their employer Mr Worth who spoke to them on the edifying topic of 'wool.'[35]

One wonders how many young textile workers really wanted to hear about wool in their time off. The same YWCA employee who described her work as 'difficult and slow' lamented the fact that household workers were not interested in forming clubs, and she once asked her fellow staff for help dealing with the 'uncontrollable' club of Jolly Juniors.[36] Visiting the Auburn mill, she found 'loud machinery' and the discouraging fact that the girls 'scatter as soon as they leave the lunchroom which is also used by men.'[37] Whether the girls scattered to avoid the men or the speech from the YWCA worker is not evident. Progress was also uphill at General Electric, where for many years 'the management and girls' seemed indifferent to the YWCA's overtures.[38]

In the 1920s especially, a few hundred young women passed through the working girls' clubs, though membership was transient and the girls seemed to be primarily interested in recreation (especially the swimming pool), drama, and crafts rather than religious or domestic education. The attitude of the board and the staff towards women workers, as a local history admits, was very 'maternalistic,'[39] not only because of age differences but also because of class distinctions. The reformers who oversaw the programs for working women were better-off homemakers, professionals, and even wives of prominent businessmen; as a result, they were deferential to local employers and regarded cautious 'protection' of women workers rather than radical change and social advocacy as the best strategies for women wage earners. As Diana Pedersen has pointed out, local YWCAs still relied on the largesse of local male businessmen whose agenda of 'efficient philanthropy and a productive workforce' had to be acknowledged by the Y.[40]

In the 1930s the YWCA's efforts were increasingly directed into its employment bureau, which primarily found domestic jobs for unemployed women. A resurgence of interest in offering recreation to war workers led to new factory visits in the 1940s, but interest was uneven, and by the postwar years the GE in-house paper, the *Works News*, noted the Y's concern about workers' lack of interest in its organized recreation.[41]

Although only a minority of working women used the Y, these women endorsed its services and programs enthusiastically. It was the gym and inexpensive housing, not Bible study, that attracted most of them and sustained the negotiated alliance between staff and working women. More than one woman who came to the city from the surrounding rural areas remembered appreciating the Y's residence, which was perceived as a respectable, 'safe,'[42] and cheap solution to their housing problems; and many women used the sports facilities, which were also leased out by local companies as part of their welfare plans. In the interwar period, activities such as mixed dances increased the YWCA's popularity. As Kathy Peiss notes, working women themselves 'set the leisure agenda' by frequenting activities that interested them and boycotting those that did not.[43] Nor would many of these young women have appreciated the idea that their morals needed supervision, for although they loved dances and movie going, they did not see these activities as endangering their virtue.

By the late 1930s, and especially during the war years, heterosocial activity such as dancing was becoming increasingly popular in the city. Women went to the dances either with a group of girlfriends or in couples, often to the large, downtown Brock Arena. It is possible that the culture of dating, first introduced in large urban centres in the 1920s, actually became more widespread here by the 1940s, in part because the wartime agenda made entertaining visiting soldiers a respectable if not patriotic pastime. Until the late 1940s, few couples had cars; courting by walking was far more frequent. While a local scandal and murder case in 1934 indicated well enough that some young couples were 'going parking' in secluded lovers' lanes,[44] lack of access to automobiles actually ruled out this possibility for many working women.

Young women were made clearly aware of the boundaries of sexual and moral danger by parents and community leaders, and even after women were making important financial contributions to the family, their consent to parents' rules and curfews was expected. To disobey, remarked one woman, might mean 'you'd find the door locked on you.'[45] One Quaker Oats worker remembers that even though she was boarding, since her parents lived out of town, her landlord simply assumed that he could tell her father if she came in late, and she would receive a patriarchal reprimand. Her situation was unusual, she added, because her father allowed her considerable independence: 'I had quite a bit of freedom ... In one place when I came in late, they said they would tell my dad. My dad said [to them] if she is old enough to work, she is old enough to know what time to come in.'[46]

Young women certainly pushed on the bounds of the prescribed social rules. As one woman recalls, when the war started she used to slip out to the dances for local soldiers, 'even though I wasn't supposed to be there ... I just told them I was older.'[47] When describing her youthful dating and dancing days, a woman from the second cohort even declined to give me the name of one of her haunts because of its 'bad' reputation: 'It was in the south end, you know, and didn't have a very good reputation, I think because of the drinking, you know ... Well, I won't even mention the name to you.'[48] While young women sometimes resented parental authority over their social lives, many generally accepted the dominant social definitions of moral respectability, avoiding bars and respecting curfews.

Even the scantiest reading of the 'Magistrate's Court' column in the local paper offered clear warnings about the consequences of staying out all night with men, drinking, or giving the appearance of 'promiscuity.' Young women who indulged in such activities could find themselves in trouble with the law, and possibly sent to the provincial reformatory. Indeed, working-class parents sometimes cooperated with the authorities in attempts to correct their daughters' immoral behaviour – even if it meant sending them to jail.[49]

Strict household regulations could encourage young women to see marriage as an attractive option, offering them the opportunity to set their own rules. 'There were house rules,' remembers one woman.

'You had to be in no later than eleven. And if you left home, it looked like you were in trouble and you couldn't come back. Consequently, we got married younger and went out on our own. No, there was no living together without marriage then.'[50] Looking to marriage as a form of independence had its contradictions, however, since marriage could reproduce women's dependency, though in a new form.

The women recognized that young working men enjoyed more freedom than they did. Brothers could stay out later, and they could engage in risky behaviour – 'hide out to smoke'[51] away from home, as one woman remembered. Drinking was more likely to be condoned for men, and a clear double standard underlay judgments about a woman's sexual character. Even as youths, one woman told me, the boys could be more daring: 'There were local swimming holes ... we called them BAB, the bare-assed bum beaches ... There were ropes in the trees and the boys used to swim there, naked. We could see them from down the creek! But the girls didn't have the same swimming holes!'[52]

Although the young unmarried women who lived at home felt the power of parental authority, self-supporting women did eventually carve out their own social and leisure choices. A significant group of working women, who are often overlooked because of the emphasis on the young single women, are the self-supporting single women who worked all their lives. Some of them had important family commitments, earning for aging parents or even supporting siblings, but they also had their own strong networks of friendship and social activity. Their patterns of leisure were different from those of the younger women and, later, from those of the married women workers. The self-supporting women sometimes shared accommodation and had long-term friendships; they recall visiting each other's apartments, playing cards, going to movies, and taking vacations together. By the 1940s, a new trend of some importance was emerging: car ownership. In one case, two women shared a car in order to deal with the expense, but the expense was entirely worth the freedom that cars brought with them. According to their own accounts, as well as to the gossip columns in company newspapers, women increasingly took vacations far from the city, something few women had done in the 1930s. These women carved out a distinctive space for themselves, with church and community activities, travel, and workplace friendships that sustained them throughout their working years and after.

Both self-supporting women and young women living at home found that family duties still claimed their time, limiting their possibilities for after-work leisure. Once wage work began, the women who boarded with parents usually had their home duties reduced, for the parents acknowledged that the women had little time and energy left after spending ten hours at work. Still, many teenagers and young women continued to do some kind of domestic labour, such as helping with dishes, carrying firewood, or minding younger siblings. Their brothers, they sometimes felt, had lighter domestic responsibilities once they were working. This may have been because the higher wages earned by men gave them more 'bargaining power'[53] in the family economy, but it was also because of the resilience of a domestic sexual division of labour that left women with more onerous domestic duties.

For the small minority of women in the first cohort who continued at wage work full-time after marriage and children, domestic duties and anxieties about children were an especially heavy burden. Almost all of these married working women still assumed the primary responsibility for homemaking, even if the husbands helped out. These working mothers often took advantage of a one-hour lunch at noon to go home and feed their children; and after work, laundry, cooking, and attention to children claimed long hours of their time. Some continued to work only because the existence of shift work allowed them to do both jobs. During the war, for example, the Bonnerworth mill had a night-time shift from 5 to 11 PM, which many married women worked on. In their absence, husbands on a day shift or members of the extended family provided care for the children, though occasionally a neighbour was used.

By the war years, some of these working mothers found they could hire part-time help, often older women in the neighbourhood, to assist with housework or mind their children, but the majority worked out their own double shift. These women's heavy domestic duties resulted in different attitudes towards their work and their after-work leisure. More than one woman remembered that a 'seriousness' characterized working mothers, both on the shop floor, where 'we didn't fool around any more, I mean [we] went to work to *work*,'[54] and in their discussion of spending priorities, since most focused their money talk on household needs and filling children's wants. Moreover, married women were less likely to socialize with workmates after work: they just didn't have time.

Family obligations extended beyond one's actual physical household. Women cared for sick parents and sometimes helped provide for them through their unemployment or old age. Indeed, the single unmarried daughter was often the person who was expected to take an important role caring for parents. As one woman remembers of her life after she obtained secure white-collar employment, 'It seemed as if I had more responsibility then. I was helping financially. My parents lived out of town and I sent part of my pay home. Then they moved in[to the city] ... My father was ill, so I helped purchase a house for them.'[55] Family obligations may well have been especially taxing for many working women, since transiency and mobility were minimal in this area, and members of the extended family who needed help often lived close by.

While many women recognized such domestic responsibilities as necessary or even enjoyable, it would be wrong to romanticize all family obligations as being uncomplicated by tension. Some of the women vividly recall chafing under the unequal distribution of work, food, and affection in their homes. Leaving home to live with friends or kin was often the solution to parental demands that one work long hours at home, or to disagreements over how much of one's salary could be kept back as allowance for clothes and entertainment. As for the few married wage-earning women, they still experienced exhaustion and sometimes considerable anxiety and anguish over family problems – everything from their children's school problems to their husbands' desertion.

The contours of women's leisure, peer culture, and family lives all shaped their feminine identity and, subsequently, their work culture. Both an emphasis on family obligation, caring, and duty, and the women's participation in an emerging popular culture of consumption and romance were integral to their outside-of-work lives. Evidence from this small city reinforces but also contradicts conclusions of other North American studies of working women in the interwar and war years. Like other young working women, their leisure was focused on movies and dancing – more so than their mothers' generation. At the same time, they were not yet integrated into the 'car culture,' which American studies such as *Middletown* attribute to the 1920s.[56] While their wages symbolized the possibility of consumption and the enticement of heterosexual socializing, their preference for inexpensive leisure activities indicates their limited resources, for most were helping to support their families. Most of the women remember their first working years positively, largely because of the independence that wages, not the actual work, gave them. They may lament the long hours spent in tiresome labour, but their pay packets, however small, and their social life, however monitored, offered a lifestyle which they now see, almost nostalgically, as symbolizing a new identity and independence.

WORKPLACE CULTURE

Workplace and leisure were often fused through romance and dating. As Dorothy remembers, she met her future husband through her spinning machine. A night worker at the Bonnerworth mill, he courted her by leaving notes on her machine: 'He asked me for dates, and he didn't give up too easy. I had heard [through the workplace] that he was a flirt, so I told him to go out with my girlfriend ... [But] then I married him in 1940.'[57] Women and men went out on dates arranged by workmates, and marriages could emerge out of workplace friendships and romances even in workplaces where men and women rarely met. As two women recounted to me, when they were working side by side in General Electric during the early war years, one introduced the other to her brother-in-law. They later became relatives as well as friends. In a recollection that emphasizes both the youth of the workers and their lack of access to cars, one textile worker remembered fondly that he and his wife 'both worked at Dominion Woollens, and we lived close to each other. I got a bicycle and put her on my handlebars and took her to work. I'd let her off at the Bonnerworth, then ride on to the Auburn.'

During their daily work, the women joked with each other about their relationships and shared friendly advice about their beaux. This shop-floor talk and teasing about romance became part of women's work culture and moulded gender identity as young women 'grew up' on the shop floor.[59] One woman who worked in an all-female area but met her husband at work remembers that she was criticized when she announced her engagement, because her husband was of a different religion: 'I was from a Gospel family, and so another worker came up to me and asked me why a child of the Lord was marrying a child of the devil ... [and my husband was] Anglican!'[60] Another woman recounted how a friend at work quietly let her know that her fiancé was cheating on her. 'She was very close to me, so I didn't doubt her ... I gave back the ring,' she remembered, adding jokingly that she was relieved to know the truth before it was too late.[61]

While teasing about workplace romance was accepted, flirting in order to gain better conditions or work from male supervisors was not. Some Bonnerworth women, for instance, went out with their straw boss on dates, but they made a distinction between socializing in non-working hours and favouritism on the shop floor. 'I remember so-and-so sidling up to the boss, always getting better jobs,' commented a former Bonnerworth spinner with considerable disapproval in her voice.[62] Other interviewees pointed to the existence of some favouritism at the Bonnerworth, particularly in the 1930s,[63] but the dislike of flirting for favours extended to all workplaces. In blue-collar jobs, some women identified the favouritism as an inevitable result of hierarchy rather than simply as a gender issue. As one woman commented, 'The boss always had his pets, men and women both ... I just tried to ignore those people.'[64]

In their assessment of these scenarios, the interviewees often blamed the woman and the supervisor equally, failing to analyse who had more power in the situation. Awareness of sexual harassment was more rudimentary than today (indeed, the term itself is part of a post-1970s feminist discourse), indicating how meanings of unacceptable behaviour change over time, influenced by new political analyses and gender expectations. Nevertheless, the women did see forms of unwanted touching and the demanding of favours as displeasing; they wanted some boundary lines to secure a measure of sexual privacy and self-respect. As one woman remembers, after she moved from Westclox to another plant, she worked for an 'assistant boss who wouldn't take his hands off the girls. You wouldn't put up with that today ... and I quit because he made things really miserable for me.'[65] At the same time, a clerical worker at Quaker Oats could recall, quite unjudgmentally, the actions of a man who always commented on her attire – and who 'ran his fingers through all the girls' hair' – as someone who was simply 'interested' in the appearance of women.[66] Lacking the language and political concepts to analyse what we today term harassment, and perhaps influenced by their uncertain job security, women were sometimes resigned to accept this behaviour as 'part of the job.'

If the company papers are any indication, romance gossip, which was certainly prevalent in the workplace of the 1930s, became even more popular in the 1940s and 1950s. In these gossip columns, marriage was woman's fervently desired goal, and a diamond ring was the sign of personal fulfilment and happiness. 'The gleam in her eye is reflected in the diamond on her fourth finger,' noted a correspondent, describing a workmate.[67] When wedding plans were announced, a number of rituals followed: departmental showers, parties, and the public presentation of household items, such as the blankets given to the

'Porcelain Girls.' Each factory had its ceremonies surrounding engagements and marriage. At General Electric the worker might be drawn around parts of the plant, with her gift on display, and in white-collar jobs, desks were decorated to mark weddings and the birth of children.

Whatever the ritual, these events were an integral part of workplace culture. They allowed women to carve out autonomous space untouched by the pressures of production, thereby making the workday less alienating. Although some celebrations were participated in by both sexes, many were women-only events such as showers, and it was often women who arranged the co-ed celebrations. A former Westclox foot-press worker remembers that the women in her area 'were always collecting 25 cents or 50 cents for communal presents like dishes sets' for other employees' weddings.[68] The women also took time to celebrate other occasions, arranging departmental parties at Christmas or celebrating co-workers' birthdays. Recalling her first year at work in the late 1930s, a Quaker Oats factory employee commented, 'We used to go into the lounge and have a birthday cake. The first time I got it, I never thought about it, and they gave me a nice cup and saucer. And I didn't even know that they knew when my birthday was.' As she reconstructed this event, it was used to exemplify what was most enjoyable about her workplace: the camaraderie, rituals, and friendships that made the workday bearable.

By developing this autonomous space for camaraderie and celebration, women could both create a sense of gender solidarity and 'humanize' the workplace. These spaces were particularly needed in earlier years before coffee breaks were mandated. In the early 1930s, for instance, women at the woollen mill did not receive regular breaks away from their machines, and some even ate their lunches there. Still, many of these rituals were common to most workplaces both before and after this period. In the auto industry of the 1940s, writes Pamela Sugiman, the few women in these factories created their own distinct 'culture of femininity,' centring on discussion of physical appearance and clothing, romance, marriage, and domesticity, which provided both an escape from immediate drudgery and a means of coping with the largely male workplace.[70]

Securing a breathing space separate from work discipline could also become a means of resisting the length of the work day. A clerical worker at Quaker Oats gave a perfect description of the recurring tug of war over separate space for relaxation which she witnessed between women and management. Drawing on existing social networks, the women informally tried to extend their break time: 'We would start off taking five minutes, then stretching it, and stretching it some more, till administration came in and told us to obey the rules. Then we would go back to five minutes, but the process would start all over again!'[71] Creating some autonomous space during working hours could also be accomplished in the most simple way, for instance by talking, joking, whistling, or singing on the line. As one Westclox employee remembers, her supervisor always let women talk, and she would often whistle tunes for her work group. A co-worker indicated that by allowing the women to 'talk back and forth, as long as we got our work done'[72] the supervisor made his own authority appear reasonable and palatable. However, in many industrial situations – such as the woollen mill or many of the GE jobs – noise and employee positioning made such interaction impossible.

A sense of comradeship might also come by means of shared nicknames and jokes or through initiation rites for new employees. Nicknames were used especially for the immediate foremen, the more likable supervisors being made familiar with endearing names, while the few who were disliked were objectified with decidedly unattractive ones. Almost every workplace had a few women who liked to play jokes to initiate newcomers, or even as a regular routine. One textile worker, known among her co-workers as an entertainer, offered her workmates renditions of familiar radio soap opera scenarios, and she occasionally disguised herself to 'fool' her fellow employees. As she remembers, she once 'dressed up like a little old lady, all bent over ... with a white shawl and [made them] move out of the way for me on the street. '"Let the little old lady up the street." I thought they were going to hit me when they [found out].'[73]

Initiation rites in the factory could involve misplacing chairs, putting Vaseline on machine handles, or placing unpleasant objects on a machine or in a pocket. These practices might also be a comment on the workplace conditions: at Genelco during the war, a new woman might find a dead mouse in the pocket of her uniform, a reminder that mice overran the workroom at night.[74] Some workplaces also had specific rituals. Bonnerworth workers from the 1920s remember some workmates being 'blacked' (taken to the cellar and partially covered with lamp black) as an initiation rite, and in one case a new boy was 'blacked by the girls' for purposely eavesdropping on their private talks about romance and then teasing the girls about them.[75]

Although workplace humour was not usually meant to humiliate, it could occasionally take on more negative connotations. One woman remembers her workmates trying to embarrass her out of her extreme shyness with persistent teasing. When she told them she had a boil in an embarrassing place, 'they called in the first aid man, who was kind of an odd creature, to come and attend to me. They knew I would blush. And I said, "No, no, I'll look after it myself." They all knew how shy I was.'[76] Occasionally, too, religious differences intruded into the workplace in the form of cutting jokes or remarks: the Catholic-Protestant divisions that still characterized the city in the interwar years meant that religious tensions could make their way onto the shop floor. The realization that discrimination based on religion is not socially desirable led many women to discount these tensions in retrospect; yet one such woman, when describing a different issue – the foreman intervening in a bitter dispute on the line – admitted that Protestant and Catholic taunting had initiated the disagreement.

Humour was also used by women as a means of suggesting the need for more flexible and good-natured supervision from bosses whom they saw as too strict. Rather than confront a particular boss at the woolen mill 'who wasn't very nice,' the women used a more indirect approach, trying to 'sway him with kindness.' When he refused some of the ritual Christmas practices, such as a small tree, their solution was to sneak one in through the back stairs and decorate it as a surprise. Although 'he wasn't very happy,' she recalled, they confronted his objections by offering him a Christmas gift, which they told him 'to take home with him.'[77] Rather than resorting to open rebellion over the boss's methods of supervision, they saw this as a way of trying to alter his character with good-natured persuasion.

When women came to know their workmates well, socializing and mutual aid went beyond the workplace. Not only did they hold showers and parties for each other but, in times of crisis or need, people took up collections, sent flowers to funerals, or even provided anonymous aid. A young widow who took a white-collar job in the early 1950s, often had trouble making ends meet. She remembers that her predominantly female workplace created 'a bond between women, and they did support each other ... My kids grew up in other children's clothes' (donated by workmates). Perhaps more unusual, she once received an anonymous gift: 'Sometimes I didn't know where our next meal was coming from and I had to borrow ... Though I didn't talk a lot about it at work, [people knew]. One week, when I came home I found a basket of eggs on my doorstep, and I still don't know who put them there.'[78] Another white-collar worker, however, remembers that she and her fellow employees set limits on the sharing of personal problems during breaks and lunches, with an invisible boundary that allowed occasional problem sharing but discouraged ongoing 'complaining.'[79]

One of the most important aspects of work culture was the set of traditions governing help given on the job. Although aid with work was routinely offered, this support had clear limits: newcomers were assisted as they learned the job, but women who were considered lazy or who were subverting other workers were not given assistance. One Bonnerworth spinner remembers that when she was put in charge of new employees, she was told to help them for the first week; but even after that, 'if the person needed help, I was happy to keep showing her for awhile.' Another woman from the same area recalled 'I'd help anyone out, but not when they'd sit there and smoke.'[80]

The women also worked out informal agreements about the pace of work on the continuous-flow lines that had a collective production target. On incentive work, they tried to show newcomers easier ways of doing their piecework, and if experienced women were way ahead, they might 'go and help someone else make some money.'[81] However, women who tried to work inordinately fast and thus put increased pressure on their fellow workers were often given the cold shoulder. By collectively setting these informal rules, the women could try to protect the majority's interests, which they and not the company defined, shaping their own work conditions, if only to a small degree.

At Quaker Oats, for instance, one woman remembers the way a group working on packaging created a 'stint' (the workers redefinition of the work process to create a more livable pace of production). A group of six women were set to work together on a particular packaging line, where one of the jobs was so easy that there was time to sit down and rest. Consequently, the women rotated so that they took turns enjoying the 'rest' position – though they had to be careful not to allow the supervisors or timers to see the easy job and try to eliminate it.[82] In each work situation, the women had some sense of what a fair or good day's work was, and they tried to live up to these notions to maintain the respect of their fellow workers. As Ruth Cavendish noted when she worked in an auto-parts plant in the 1970s, the fast pace and the need for common aid and solidarity meant that other workers were always primarily concerned with 'how you acted towards others at work, not what you thought.'[83]

If other workers broke the informal rules, they could encounter silence or ostracism. 'If you were friendly to [your fellow workers] when you went in,' recalled a textile worker, 'they would never let you struggle. But if you were snarly, well then, tough beans.'[84] In the clock factory, one woman was put on a new job only to find that it had been vastly overrated in its timing, with the result that she was bored and had free time. She asked to be transferred elsewhere because she liked to be busy, but she didn't tell the foreman why, because the other woman on the job would have been angry that a fellow worker had 'revealed' her excessive free time. In this situation, the interviewee explained, silence was the appropriate way of dealing with the foreman, but she did let her co-worker know that she disapproved of her conduct and the inequitable division of work in that area.[85]

Similar informal rules were a part of the men's work culture. For both men and women, the structural organization of the workplace, and ones' place within it, shaped the particular customs embraced by workers. At the same time, the women's coping strategies were clearly gendered; women drew on female friendships and networks for support, and employed the 'cultural resources' – the traditions, practices, and rituals – with which they were already acquainted.[86] Moreover, it is important to note that the women's ability to modify the rules and conditions of work was always circumscribed by the sexual division of labour and by their lower status in the workplace. The fast pace of assembly work, the pressures of the incentive system, and the careful monitoring of spare time even in the office meant that there was little room to create autonomous space and that there were few situations where one could devise a stint or reshape one's workday. Because of the division of labour, women had fewer recognized skills to bargain with and limited control over the pace of their workday. Moreover, because they were women, supervisory methods automatically assumed their subservience to authority. If a woman did try to assert her independence, she could quickly learn it was not worth it. Indeed, when one woman tried to help her employer by pointing to a production problem, she was reminded that her role was to obey, not to think: 'I was told I was there to work, not to tell *them* what to do. So I thought, you can find out for yourself [about the problem]. It kind of made me bitter because the [male] inspector didn't have a clue about my department. But I was accused of interfering.'[87]

This quotation indicates that women's informal codes of conduct did not always work against the company's interests; indeed, the manufacturing of consent, which will be described in chapter 7, was in part achieved through women's acceptance of company rules as intrinsically fair for them too. As a white-collar worker commented, 'Management had the whole picture; they knew the situation best.'[88] The women often explained their assent to work discipline by pointing to the respect they had for their (male) supervisor[89] or, more often, by endorsing the merits of hard work and the golden rule, both of which were ingredients of their notions of respectability. When one woman was reprimanded for sending bad material through the line, she pointed out to her supervisor that it had already come to her with a problem: 'We had to inspect our own work. But some selfish people wouldn't do that [and they let it go through]. I took the [defective] ones out at first, but then I started to let them go through. My foreman discovered and scolded me. He said to me, "But Emma, two wrongs don't make a right" ... [and] I realized how right he was.'[90]

The tendency for a worker to be her own quality-control expert – a Foucauldian internalization of management's disciplinary discourses – varied from one workplace to another. At another local factory that made large machinery, the women described many ways in which the piecework system was manipulated to secure the highest wages possible: 'What is the point of piecework if there is a limit on wages? ... You could hoard it ... and [then] there is no way you are going to sit there and bust your gut to get more done ... You could sit there and talk. The boss could keep an eye on you, but there wasn't much he could do!'[91] Even though this woman showed a disdain for management, her opposition was couched within a framework of acceptance. As Michael Buroway argues, workers' minor manipulation of incentive plans or their manoevring around employers' rules still signified the legitimation of the employer's authority and his right to set the rules.[92]

The degree of alienation women felt at work often affected how oppositional their informal work rules were. At Westclox, for instance, a more flexible authority structure may have assuaged alienation; some of the women may have also been convinced by the company's argument that putting out bad material rebounded on the workers. Countless issues of the Westclox paper, *Tic Talk*, tried to make workers identify with the consumer as themselves. By producing too quickly or letting mistakes go by, it was argued, they would only harm their own purchases. Where jobs were less obviously consumer oriented, such as winding coils for large motors at General Electric, one suspects that financial incentives were more effective than moral suasion in persuading the workers that their informal standards of conduct should approximate the company's workplace standards.

The women's respect for company rules did not come without a price, for they negotiated with managers in informal ways in order to secure the kind of workplace environment they wanted – a subject discussed in chapter 7. They expressed dislike for supervisors who berated them in public, and they sometimes objected to male workers' swearing in front of them. To be treated with respect, noted one woman, was to be treated 'like ladies.'[93] Indeed, women regarded Westclox as an ideal industrial employer because they could make good money while wearing nice clothes and working in a light, clean, respectable workplace. Their status as a 'better class' of worker rested not only on good pay and higher levels of education but on a notion of femininity that was preserved within the workplace and was given symbolic representation in clothing, demeanour, and workplace atmosphere.

For a significant number of women, part of their feminine identity included the perception that wage work would be temporary or perhaps intermittent because they would leave work after they married. As one bluntly put it, 'I was tired of working, so I decided to get married.'[94] The women's daily experiences on the shop floor or in the office made them well aware of their limited economic options and mobility at work, though they were also influenced by a cultural presentation of marriage as a fulfilling vocation. There were thus both material and ideological reasons why marriage appeared a more secure and desirable option than lifelong wage work. This meant that women's identification with wage work was more ambiguous than men's. It is true that the domestic ideal did not always translate into reality; some women found that they had to support their family with wage work after marriage. But when these women explain their work, they excused their wage labour as evidence of family need, rather than celebrating it as breadwinning, as men did; there is a crucial difference in identity reflected in the language used to describe their work.

The women's conscious justification of their decision to turn to homemaking and mothering indicates the importance of the dominant discourses concerning femininity, heterosexual romance, and domesticity in framing women's identity on and off the job. These discourses were in fact ideological, not in the classic (and largely disgraced) Marxist sense of being 'false consciousness' but rather because they worked to create meaning, to rationalize, to legitimize ideals of masculinity and femininity, which in turn provided a set of reasons for the existing class and patriarchal order. For many women, the ideology of femininity seemed to have a deeply-felt subjective validity – it was part of their lived reality, the daily texture of their lives – and it also existed as a more distant, contradictory, unattainable ideal with which women wrestled and negotiated, both inside and outside the workplace.

CONCLUSION

My emphasis on the distinctively feminine cast of women workers' consciousness is echoed in recent studies of women's workplaces by sociologists such as Sallie Westwood and Anna Pollert; they describe a workplace culture of romance, marriage, and family which helped create support systems and a separate space for women but which also reproduced the notion that relationships and family defined women's lives, thus perpetuating their dependency within patriarchal family structures.[95] These accounts avoid a portrayal of women 'duped' by a false feminine consciousness of domesticity, while still critiquing an oppressive ideology that sanctioned women's familial and economic dependence.

Some feminist historians, however, are still uneasy with this approach. Despite a wealth of studies demonstrating that family needs and values shaped when, where, and how women worked,[96] they criticize the view that a patriarchal ideology of domesticity or 'separate spheres' shaped women's actions or identity, claiming that this characterization implies working women's passivity[97] or that it perpetuates the stereotype that all women were 'more transient members of the workforce ... or that women's family life, not their work experience had the major impact on their consciousness.'[98]

These critiques are understandably distrustful of a simplistic 'job model' for men that stresses productive work as the primary force creating their identity and that has an opposing 'gender model' for women, in which an ideology of domesticity shapes women's identity.[99] Moreover, the critiques are influenced by recent attention to the fragmentary and contradictory nature of identity and by the poststructuralist aversion to placing women's consciousness in the simplistic 'binary oppositions' of domesticity/work, private/public, and so on.[100]

It is true that in addition to gender and class, there were many factors (such as religion, age, and marital status) that shaped women's attitudes towards social networks, leisure patterns, and work; the construction of class and gender was fractured on many lines. For example, the diverse historical experiences of working women *vis-à-vis* domestic relationships must be taken into account. The self-supporting woman who remained at work all her life, the working mother, and the younger working woman all articulated different goals, concerns, and ideals in their descriptions of work. Moreover, the gender ideology described here was certainly not monolithic; it could produce more than one meaning and could be internalized or used in different and even contradictory ways by women. Investment in a romantic or domestic ideal, for example, was not understood by all women simply as a vote for family identity *over* workplace concerns, an embrace of dependence *over* independence.

While recognizing the many factors that shaped women's identity as workers, we must especially emphasize some of the dominant themes in their outlook in order to probe the material and ideological factors moulding their work culture and consciousness. The influence of the wider culture – articulated through the mass media, leisure, and peer culture, and emphasizing the importance of romance, attractiveness, and domesticity (as well as the 'justice' of a family wage) – must be acknowledged as one influence on work culture. The codification of women's domestic role and feminine personality in cultural images promoted powerful messages about security and happiness, which affected women's views of their roles and future as wage earners. This is not to say that domesticity was a universal value experienced undifferentially by all women, or that there was a domestic-identified woman worker as opposed to a work-identified male worker. Rather, domesticity, one ingredient of gender ideology, tended to be interpreted differently according to gender: for women, it was an alternative occupation, a full-time job, a moral duty; for men, it signified family headship, breadwinning duties, and a place of rest. Dominant discourses on masculinity and femininity set out the workers' frameworks of understanding and thus came to shape their inner sense of self; patriarchal ideology must be acknowledged as one ingredient woven into the fabric of women's work culture.[101]

Secondly, the structural imperatives of the workplace also shaped work culture. In many blue-collar jobs there were unwritten codes of conduct shaped by the pressures of job structures and the need for worker solidarity. One helped newcomers, one did not tell tales to the foreman, and one did not slack off so much that others were unable to make their piecework rate or do their work properly. Both white- and blue-collar women made efforts to create their own humanized space through celebrations, jokes, and rituals; informal rules, such as the stint, sometimes revealed resistance to management control; and a network of mutual aid characterized the workplace, sometimes extending beyond it, though this aid had prescribed limits, shaped not only by workers' definitions of fair play but also by their response to management's lectures about fair work practices. There were important similarities between women's and men's work cultures, such as the dislike of favouritism, the protection of workers' rest space, and even the joking over romance and courting. To some extent, the nature of the job, not gender, shaped work culture. Also, given the economic power relations of the workplace, both women and men had little room to resist the discipline imposed by management.

At the same time, work culture was certainly not 'gender neutral.'[102] Because the power relations of the workplace were gendered, this affected the shape of women's work culture. Women had to manoeuvre within a workplace hierarchy that duplicated the patriarchal family. The sexual division of labour put limits on women's ability to exercise control over their workday, and it also meant that they were physically clustered together – a situation that encouraged personal interaction and support. As poststructuralists argue, these gender differences then became encoded, through symbolic representations, into the very depiction of men's and women's jobs. The way in which white-collar work was presented as intrinsically female, or the equation of intricate work with female ability to tolerate monotony, had consequences not only for the sexual division of labour but ultimately also for the subjective identity of the women and men who were performing and supervising this work.

Moreover, women responded to the pressures and possibilities of their workplaces by drawing on cultural resources that were gender based. They set up their own support systems, which were shaped by the solidarity created by the sex-segregated workplace; they exhibited distinctive behaviour and values, which reproduced the wider social roles of women, promoting sociability and ritual celebrations; and they engaged in daily shop-floor banter, sharing information on their 'other' lives of romance and relationships. In a sense, women were creatively appropriating and reframing the cultural discourses on femininity in order to build their own space unencumbered by work discipline. Similar concerns, from how to spend their small pay packet to the performance of domestic duties, were shared; and workplace associations were carried into the world of leisure when women shopped, skated, and socialized together after hours.

Women thus produced their own distinctive work culture out of their daily attempts to create a livable workplace, but these attempts were shaped and circumscribed by the structure of the work process, by the power of the employer to define discipline, and by ideals of femininity that were created both within and outside the workplace. The women's sense of identity was also related to their definitions of 'respectable' and, conversely, 'rough' behaviour. We can now turn our attention to an exploration of women's efforts to maintain financial solvency and social respectability in the midst of economic and familial crises, particularly the one occasioned by the Great Depression.

5

Maintaining Respectability, Coping with Crises

'There was an idea of toughness about women [factory workers] ... If you were a good, Christian living person, they thought you shouldn't be there ... that work was for the rough and ready types, the uneducated ... But I didn't let it bother me. *I* was brought up to be honest, to do an honest day's work, so I shouldn't have to worry about what others thought.'[1]

In this reflection, Brenda, a blue-collar employee who began work in the 1940s, set out her view of the social definitions of the respectable and the rough worker. She also quite consciously placed herself within the former camp although, like other women, she sometimes feared that the very image of blue-collar work might jeopardize her status there. Definitions of respectability were not only shaped by the wage work a woman did; they were also affected by her family roles and her place in the community. Exhibited through proper behaviour and adherence to certain customs, values, and attitudes, and, to some extent, represented by material symbols, these notions of respectability were neither fixed nor static for white- or blue-collar working women during this thirty-year period. Even so, consistent themes and continuities can still be distinguished. A belief in the merits of hard work, honesty, and contribution to the family were all important; so were the adoption of appropriate sexual and familial roles for men and women.

Respectability was not something inherited for life, though. It was tested by one's encounter with the economic crises of fate – by unemployment, short time, lay-offs or loss of a wage earner through sickness or death. In the face of massive and ongoing unemployment during the Great Depression, many families had to find coping strategies and develop ways of understanding respectability that took into account the fate of long-term unemployment. For a smaller group of women, the fate of other crises also loomed: desertion, separation, or violence, which affected the economic viability and unity of the family, as well as their own independence.

Women's ongoing efforts to maintain financial solvency and social respectability in the face of economic and familial crises are the themes of this chapter. First, a recapitulation of working women's definitions of respectability offers insight into the prevailing class and gender ideals of the time, and women's attempts to cast the ideals to fit their own lives. Secondly, we need to explore the crises of material need and family dissolution that challenged respectability, potentially pushing women and their families to the opposite end of the social scale – what Brenda called the 'rough and ready' working class.

To explore the boundaries between the respectable and the rough, and women's efforts to cope with adversity, we must examine women's wage work in concert with their non-waged work, as well as in relation to their family lives, the dominant discourses of femininity, and state policy. We must also probe the relationship between the family economy of mutual obligation and support, and the hierarchical family of 'coercion, power and authority.'[2] We need to explore women's innermost fears and problems as well as their hopes and aspirations if we are to understand their experiences and identities as women earners.

UNCOVERING THE MEANING OF RESPECTABILITY FOR WORKING WOMEN

Many labour historians have ventured to give definitions of the meaning of respectability for nineteenth-century workers, especially skilled workers, but there are fewer corresponding studies for the twentieth century or for women workers.[3] Despite the increasing influence of mass culture and the declining insularity of many working-class communities after the 1920s,[4] working people still fashioned and upheld distinct notions of appropriate behaviour and success. Their concepts of respectability were shaped by the existing cultural traditions and gender ideologies, and by the material necessities of working-class life. Respectability was defined in part by hegemonic bourgeois values, but it was also a product of working people's own world view; it was an amalgam of accommodation to the social order and an articulation of the working-class's own agenda.

Respectability was never a static and precise concept; it was a fluid 'process'[5] of creating pride in oneself and one's family that changed over time and took on a particular hue in each community, based on the community's social structure, workforce, and cultural make-up. Capturing respectability in precise terms is also complicated by the fact that it can be defined and explained differently according to who is being addressed, when, and for what purpose.[6] A young working woman in 1938 might describe her values differently when speaking to her girlfriends, her mother, or her employer. The use of oral history confuses this process even more: women may unconsciously reconstruct their family's past values to approximate their world view in 1990 – or to stress their adherence to social norms for an interviewer such as myself. If a woman was arrested for breaking curfew when she was fifteen, it is unlikely she would emphasize this event over a longer-term adherence to moral strictures, but by 'forgetting' the former incident, she and the interviewer are creating a history that stresses women's fidelity to the rules of respectability rather than exposing their challenge to those rules.

Furthermore, the crises women faced, such as desertion or violence in the family, are often hidden from historical view, both by the absence of written and archival sources and by their erasure from women's memories as a result of persisting social taboos and inhibitions. In oral history, silence and omission may in themselves be significant.[7] In response to questions about sexual harassment at work, women's freedom on the streets, or even the dynamics of family life, for example, the women interviewed seldom volunteered information on women's vulnerability to violence. Indeed, some of them compared the absence of violence when they were younger with the more dangerous situation today. Yet their denial of violence in women's lives was a clear contrast to the articles in the Peterborough *Examiner* that noted attacks against women in the street and at home.[8]

The women's silence and the disjuncture between oral and other historical sources can be understood in a number of ways. First, in agreeing to be interviewed for a project focusing on wage work, they may not have imagined that such topics would be relevant, nor were they comfortable with the disclosure of such personal and family memories. Secondly, as I have indicated, the women may have viewed harassment differently, as an unpleasant but unchangeable and unspoken part of working life. Finally, a denial of violence is sometimes an externalization of painful fears that women carry with them, or a comforting means of idealizing the chivalrous past by contrasting it with the 'visible' violence of today.

Because of these inherent limitations in the historical sources, the ideals of respectability described below draw heavily on oral history, but many of the examples of women coping with economic and familial crises are taken from archival and newspaper sources.

'MY MOTHER WAS A LADY': IMAGES OF RESPECTABILITY

By drawing together the women's descriptions of their family life, work culture, and social aspirations, a portrait of respectability emerges. Honesty, hard work, and adherence to Christian values or the golden rule were all ingredients of their sense of individual, family, and class pride. While formal church attendance could be one symbol of respectability,[9] more important was one's adoption of 'Christian living,' mentioned above. As Elizabeth Roberts found, this often meant 'respecting one's neighbour, belief in the work ethic, and that work would be one's salvation.'[10]

The women recognized that they were often hired because of family contacts. More significantly, they also recounted with some pride the recognition, either by other workers or their employers, that members of their family were known to be reliable, honest, or skilled at their work. In their view, respectability was earned and was not simply given on the basis of inherited wealth or status. It might be evinced in material success – home ownership, the ability to take vacations, or the successful education and upward mobility of a son or daughter – yet it was not linked solely to material security or upward mobility; rather, success was the concrete evidence of a life of hard work. Moreover, underlying the women's emphasis on hard work was a collective class pride as well as a sense of individual success; they extolled working people's creation of social wealth and their meaningful contribution of labour to society.

As a result of this emphasis on productive work, some working women looked rather suspiciously on the women who relied on charity, mothers' allowance, or welfare; these supposedly less respectable options implied the rejection of hard work as women's means of survival. And during the Depression, those who were unemployed would often cite their honesty, and especially their desire to work for a living, as evidence of their respectability in the face of adversity.

Financial carelessness and inordinate debts were frowned on by the families of many of the women. 'We were brought up right, we were never in over our heads,' remembers one factory worker.[11] Similarly, a woman who went to work in the plant at Westclox told me that her rural family had a small farm and very little money, but they were still 'upright,' for her parents 'were strict about morals and careful not to run up big debts.'[12] Although this attitude towards debt was undoubtedly shaped by the Depression, it revealed an important emphasis on self-sufficiency and self-help.

Self-sufficiency did not rule out the value of aiding relatives and close friends in times of need. In fact, good relationships with neighbours and the rightful exercise of family obligations were also symbols of respectability. An orderly family life, controlled children, and the appropriate exercise of duty towards other family members formed the contours of familial respectability. Children who were well mannered and disciplined were evidence of a good household. One woman described her mother as 'a lady' who knew 'how to bring us up right.' She added, 'True, she could whip us to discipline us, but the end was [our good behaviour].'[13] For some women, this notion of good behaviour was intimately tied to their Anglo or Celtic ethnic background: 'We were brought up English, we had manners and knew our boundaries.'[14]

With the exception of this quotation, the women were largely silent about the ethnic and racial constructions of respectability in their community. They were certainly attuned to notions of difference shaped by an Irish Catholic or Anglo Protestant background, and some from the Catholic minority felt that anti-Irish anti-Catholicism still claimed a stubborn presence in Peterborough. On questions of race, however, the women were not forthcoming, though their silence on the subject may be revealing: whiteness, and even Anglo-Celtic background, was 'naturalized' and taken for granted as the dominant and most acceptable emblem of citizenship. To be a part of the dominant 'normative'[15] culture meant an implicit acceptance of one's privilege and predominance. The very few women workers who came from very different backgrounds, such as Native women or Eastern European Jewish women, were viewed as unusual, sometimes as outsiders. Although the interviewees stressed these women's inclusion under the umbrella of respectability, they occasionally admitted that the community was not so tolerant. 'I remember when one [Native] woman played on our team,' remarked one blue-collar worker, 'everyone in the stands would start making comments, and I would want to rap their heads together ... It shouldn't matter where you were born.'[16]

Many male workers, labour historians argue, developed notions of respectability that were connected with their skills, work knowledge, autonomy, and solidarity on the job.[17] Respectability, however, was also shaped by familial and gender ideals: 'The domestic realm was a central arena for the expression of respectability governed and guided by women.'[18] Once women were married, their good exercise of familial and motherly duties was extremely important. Budgeting well, nursing the family's financial hopes, keeping a clean house, and producing decently dressed and polite children were all remembered by the women as evidence of their mothers' respectability, as well as part of their own aspirations if they became homemakers. In speaking of the interwar period especially, many of the women emphasized the model of the male provider and domestic mother as the family form that was most socially desirable: 'My mother never worked,' remembered a woman who was a teenager in the 1930s. 'She thought it was terrible that women worked; women with a family should not do that.'[19] A woman whose mother was deserted in the 1930s recalled, 'My mother was seen as some kind of "scarlet" woman by the community'[20] (as if it was her fault). Only a decade later, a woman from the second cohort of interviewees, who divorced in the 1950s and then went out to work, experienced a similar reaction. Not only was she seen as an anomaly for the time, but she sensed that she was actually pitied by some acquaintances because she was divorced.[21]

The sexual modesty of young women and the fidelity of married women was an integral part of this code of respectability. Indeed, one of the reasons why young women remained at home in the interwar period was moral propriety.[22] Even in the postwar period, one white-collar worker turned down a promotion because it might have taken her out of town on trips with her bosses. Her fear that sexual demands might be made on these trips, or even that rumours about her behaviour would result, led to a decision to protect her reputation by rejecting the job.

Women who were described as particularly loud, boisterous, or 'quick to make an argument' were sometimes equated with a 'tougher' class – the 'rough.'[23] In fact, one might define respectability as the opposite of what Brenda called 'the rough and ready.' In other urban studies, the most marginalized have been found to be those who have completely rejected the normal labour market, who indulge in loud, raucous, and often public social lives that often include drinking and visible violence, and who may disregard family obligations and even resort to criminality.[24] The working man who rejected the need to support his family through honest work was suspect in the community, as was the woman who abandoned marital fidelity and motherly duties. Ironically, not only could a woman's emulation of 'masculine' behaviour (excessive drinking, loudness, aggressiveness) condemn her, but so could the exaggeration of supposedly feminine traits – being overly 'sexual' in image or being 'promiscuous.'

Although I have endowed this definition of respectability with considerable coherence, it would be wrong to imply that it had rigid contours or was accepted monolithically by all working women. First, there were some differences based on occupation: white-collar women derived status and identity from their better class of work, which was distinct from the manual labour that was valued by blue-collar women. Second, a rigid polarity between the respectable and the rough obscures the way in which the two overlapped: one could inherit both traditions in one's family life; one could come from a rough family but gain respectability; and one could indulge in occasional rough pursuits – even run into problems with the law – and yet not be permanently marginalized.[25] Finally, there is evidence that the definitions of respectability changed over time. It has been suggested that the increased consumerism after the 1920s set more materially based standards of respectability, over which women had less control.[26] If anything, though, this trend was reversed by the Depression, but it was resurrected in the postwar years with the reinvigorated promotion of consumerism. Moreover, it would be inaccurate to idealize an earlier age when women seemed to control the cultural definitions of respectability. Even though notions of appropriate gender roles and symbols of status changed, one constant remained: women had a tremendous responsibility for protecting respectability but often had limited means and resources to do so.

COPING WITH ECONOMIC ADVERSITY

The fact that many working-class families needed more than one wage, the lack of firm job security in Peterborough's non-unionized factories, and the uneven and seasonal employment for the unskilled meant that economic crises could appear with little warning even in supposedly prosperous times. The loss of a wage earner through temporary lay-off, unemployment, desertion, or death was the most common economic problem that faced women and their families. The skill level of the earners in the family could modify these crises: the presence of a bookkeeper or a skilled machinist enhanced the hope of renewed employment and the probability of using savings or credit. For the unskilled, the prospects were bleaker. One woman remembers that during her teens, her unskilled father was always trying to obtain as many part-time jobs as possible, from cutting wood to hauling ice to casual farm work, and the latter sometimes went uncompensated when farmers were unable to pay. In order to make ends meet, she said, 'he was never without some job ... but we had it hard.'[27]

Working-class families had particularly vulnerable periods – when the children were small and too young to earn or when they had left home and the parents aged – and during these times the economic problems were exacerbated. In the interwar period, mothers' allowances and old age pensions provided only a meagre safety net, for these programs covered only a small proportion of the population needing aid, they offered minimum financial support, and they involved qualifying tests that discouraged many applicants.[28]

Women's wage labour provided a crucial antidote to the unpredictable income and expenditure of many families. The unskilled father mentioned above was a widower with young children, and he had to pay a housekeeper to care for the youngsters while his teenage daughter found wage work, contributing almost all her earnings from the textile mill to the family. Another woman remembered that at one point during the 1930s, her blue-collar wages from Westclox supported the entire family: 'My father was not that well, because of poison gas during the [first] war, so he had to take early retirement from GE. At one time I was the only one working, when my sister was laid off from the [textile] mill.'[29] Finally, it is revealing that local women sent to the reformatory for minor sentences sometimes found their families pleading for their release. When such families faced economic problems because of a serious illness or the loss of a wage earner, they asked that the young woman be let out so that she could contribute to the ailing family economy.[30]

The efforts of homemakers to save, budget, and 'do without' were important coping strategies in times of adversity. While this was true of families in which the earners were temporarily unemployed, it was also a daily part of life for the working poor. One mother of four wrote to the Ontario Ministry of Labour in the 1930s asking that it investigate the substandard wages paid by Dominion Woollens, which were having a disastrous effect on her family's health and well-being; her letter illustrates the absence of economic choices for many families and a sense of entitlement to a decent standard of living in return for their hard work:

The wages paid to my husband at Dominion Woollens are starvation wages. For an eight hour day, he only earns $2.16 and his job is in the washing of cloth which is poorly ventilated and unsanitary ... the floor is filthy and should be inspected. We have four small children and we will starve on this bit of money as my husband only works 5 days and brings home $10.80 ... I am not feeling well myself on this wage, as I have to give the children food and neglect myself. Husband has had pneumonia and pleurisy last year and cannot get his strength back as we give our food to the children. If my husband tries to work extra to make a bit more, the manager kicks about this ... PS My children at school have shoes with their toes through them and no rubbers.[31]

The economic difficulties faced by families were particularly evident during the economic depressions of 1921–2 and the 1930s, though they were not limited to these periods. Steadier employment and unionization during the Second World War and afterwards created a sense of increased job choice and security for women and their families, while unemployment insurance offered a modicum of protection to some earners. Nonetheless, family economies could still be shattered by a stroke of fate. One woman recalled that, when her mother, the lone parent, became ill in the early 1950s, she immediately knew that this 'would be the end of my schooling,' just as her sister knew that she would have to 'return home from her training' in Toronto. It would take both their wages to support their sick mother.[32]

 Economic hard times did, however, take on new dimensions and a new meaning during the 1930s. It is useful to examine women's predicament in this small city during the Depression, since it reveals the prevailing attitudes towards women as wage earners, as well as women's many coping strategies in the face of crisis and their understanding of their work and family roles.

COPING WITH THE GREAT DEPRESSION

Few families in Peterborough were faced with the absolute destitution described in one exposé in the local newspaper: a woodcutter's family was reduced to living in an old tent on the edge of the city – a site which, ironically, overlooked the prosperous, middle-class homes of the west end. The woodcutter's wife stayed in the tent throughout the winter, with little heat, looking after a young child 'with a hacking cough' who was too ill to attend school.[33] While this particularly severe scenario shocked the local citizens, there was a more pervasive reality of unemployment and underemployment in the city itself, taking a daily toil on hundreds of families who were not yet reduced to tents but were certainly clinging to the poverty line.

Depression unemployment varied with each community's economic structure. Because of Peterborough's diverse industrial base and the proximity of some resource and farm production, unemployment was not as consistently high as in one-industry resource towns. Nonetheless, the city's reliance on heavy industry such as the General Electric plant, which was severely hit by lay-offs, resulted in periods of deep distress for many families. Between 1929 and 1933, General Electric reduced its workforce by almost 50 per cent and had more workers on shortened time.[34] During these years, as much as 20 per cent of the population may have been supported by some kind of relief or charity, and in 1933 more than 3,000 people (of a population of 22,000) were on the relief register – a measuring stick that may actually have underestimated need. Unemployment began to decline in the middle of the decade, only to soar again after Dominion Woollens' Auburn mill was shut down in 1938. At the outbreak of the Second World War, more than 2,000 people were again dependent on relief.[35]

The surviving official statistics portray the women's unemployment rate in the city as being lower than the men's by almost one-half.[36] It is true that some employers of large numbers of women, such as Dominion Woollens and Westclox, maintained a reduced but fairly even level of employment throughout the decade, avoiding massive lay-offs. This was because of their increased tariff protection, their competitive place in the industry, and the nature of their products. The sex segregation in some workplaces also gave woman a marginal degree of protection. In jobs firmly typed as 'female,' such as some clerical positions, spinning in the woollen mill, and sewing feed bags at Quaker Oats, women were unlikely to be replaced by men – though this was not true of jobs that were more easily defined as male or female, such as the punch-press work at General Electric. As Margaret Hobbs has found on a wider scale during the 1930s, women were, to a limited degree, sheltered by their ghettoization in the workforce and possibly by the value of their (cheap) labour to employers.[37]

Yet the statistics that claim a lower rate of unemployment among women are deficient in both a quantitative and a qualitative sense; they obscure women's lost time and unemployment.[38] First, many surveys omitted women. When a poll of the local unemployed was taken in Ontario in 1931, civic officials agreed that only men need register.

Indeed, the federal and provincial governments intended the word 'unemployed' in the survey to refer to men only.[39] As well as indicating how unreliable these statistics are, this forcefully demonstrates how women's unemployment was literally made invisible – and was obscured by political will, social policy, and public opinion. Even more significant, Margaret Hobbs has shown that the entire process of counting the unemployed during the Depression was 'structured by conservative gender assumptions,' which took male lifelong earning as the norm and discounted the more varied kinds of informal, seasonal, intermittent labour that women performed. Women who were searching for jobs were not counted, and other women were assumed to be 'doing domestic work' at home or not making 'significant' contributions to the household. Unemployed married women were the group most discounted. To the statisticians and policy makers, 'to be an unemployed wife/mother was simply a contradiction in terms.'[40]

Furthermore, a crucial distinction must be made between complete unemployment and underemployment, or the worsening of one's employment conditions. The latter was a prevalent experience of women during the Depression. During the economic crisis, women in better-paying jobs such as teaching were forced to take wage cuts; despite the women teachers' protests at the severity of the second round of cuts in 1933, their voices went unheeded by a less than sympathetic Peterborough school board.[41] Evidence also indicates that the movement of women into better professional and clerical work that began in the 1920s was halted by the Depression, for they were forced back into lower-paid service or blue-collar work. Women teachers trained in the 1930s recall men taking more positions at the normal school because 'they couldn't get jobs in other places,' and more than one teacher had to rely on factory work.[42] Another woman stated that although she graduated from high school in the middle of the decade with commercial training and part-time office experience, she had to be satisfied with blue-collar work until the war came: 'I applied for an office job, but there were only openings in the plant. At 22 cents an hour, I was glad to get any job ... and I stayed there until 1942 when I could [move into the office].'[43] Furthermore, the ever-present awareness of the unemployed led women to ignore workplace grievances and accept poor working conditions for fear of losing their jobs. 'Working was a privilege'[44] that you did not jeopardize, was the view of many of the women who had jobs then.

Nowhere is this downward push on women's employment choices

and conditions more evident than in the influx of women into domestic work. Domestic service was the 'only occupation during the 1930s where demand exceeded supply.' Moreover, the only retraining program offered to women by the federal and provincial governments educated them for domestic work.[45] Although no official retraining centre was located in Peterborough, similar thinking dominated local institutions such as the YWCA in their approach to women's unemployment. By 1933, more than four hundred women a year were using the employment bureau set up by the YWCA, though it primarily advertised for temporary domestic work. In 1937 the bureau received eight hundred inquiries, but it placed only a small proportion of the women registering (which probably indicates their reluctance to take casual, part-time domestic work).

The women who came looking for work were often young (the majority under eighteen) and in search of their first job. The YWCA also aided 'business girls' from other cities or the surrounding county, who stayed temporarily in the residence while they looked for work in the city, usually only to be disappointed. While the Y tried to offer a supportive environment with free afternoon tea, counselling, and occasionally shelter for job seekers, its band-aid solution of domestic work – the long-standing approach of both the YWCA and the government policy makers to women's unemployment – was obviously unsatisfying to many women.[46] Peterborough women had been trying to leave domestic work over the previous decade, with some success.[47] But now they had little choice but to accept such jobs for five dollars or less a week. When the opportunity for factory work came, they usually jumped at the chance to change occupation.

The view that unemployed women were few in number and could always be sent home or given domestic work conditioned the responses of all levels of government to their plight. Single unemployed women, though less likely to be transient than single unemployed men, still found it difficult to obtain relief; the number of women securing city relief was far, far lower than the number registering for work at the employment bureau.[48] The fate of the single jobless women who were most destitute was displayed in the *Examiner*'s court reporting during the Depression. One young woman without a job who refused to return home to her parents or leave the streets was arrested on vagrancy charges and sentenced to time in jail. The few women transients of the period were viewed by the police with apprehension. Some may have been given temporary shelter, but they were then urged to avoid a jail sentence by accepting the magistrate's discharge, on condition that they 'leave town on the noon train.'[49]

Social anxieties about young jobless women focused mainly on their sexual and moral lives, unlike the concerns about men. Some social workers worried that, faced with both joblessness and hopelessness, young people would become resentful of authority and the existing moral codes, and would thus 'develop bad habits';[50] they feared specifically that young women might turn to prostitution. In Peterborough, the number of women arrested for vagrancy did not actually skyrocket in the 1930s, though the number accused of 'streetwalking' did rise in the early years of the Depression. What was especially significant, however, was the magistrate's severe sentencing for these misdemeanours – a reflection of worries about the 'moral decay' which legal authorities feared might accompany economic decay.

By contrast, the crisis of masculinity precipitated by the social dislocation of the Depression focused on the perceived threat to the male-provider role; this implicitly placed women as the 'complementary and natural role of wife/nurturer.'[51] The image of unemployed, transient, and aimless men, with women left alone and even supporting their families, led to repeated calls for a return to 'traditional' family roles, which essentially were the romanticized, invented images of a secure and comfortable male-breadwinning nuclear family, which in fact had never been a reality for many working people.

The crisis also produced a strong current of antifeminism, which blamed married women workers for unemployment and called for the termination of their right to work.[52] Voiced by women as well as men, these calls to fire married women were based on a conception of economic need and the right of every family to have only one breadwinner in hard times; but they also reflected a gender ideology, which saw earning as an unqualified male right but a qualified female right that was limited by marital status and economic background. In a speech, a leader of Peterborough's unemployment movement publicly denounced a lazy, disreputable married man who was 'sending his wife out to work, while he went on relief';[53] the speaker's scorn was directed not only against the misuse of relief but also at the man's rejection of his natural masculine role. The 'unholy interlocked grip of masculinity and the wage form'[54] thus existed both inside the workplace and in the less affluent world of the unemployed. As Ruth Pierson points out, debates surrounding unemployment insurance in the late 1930s focused on the wage-earning man and the equation of his income with his identity as a worker, husband, and father. Woman's identity, on the other hand, was fractured. She was either a worker or a wife/dependent, and as the latter should not be eligible for insurance. State policy eventually embraced precisely this view.[55]

The animosity towards married women working for wages was remembered acutely by those who contradicted these dictums. 'It took two years to get a job in the Depression,' remembered a woman who had two children in school. 'My husband said at first, "My wife is *not* going to work," but then the Depression came and [with him getting only three days' work in some weeks] ... it was another story.' This woman came to regard the hostility towards married women workers as illogical, partly because her job as a winder in the textile mill was a 'woman's' job that no man wanted, and partly because her husband's irregular and low textile wage was simply inadequate to support the family.[56] While Dominion Woollens allowed married women to work, to do so was to risk the disapproval of one's workmates, who labelled one married woman a 'money grubber.'[57] Other employers, such as the municipal and provincial governments, the local separate and public school boards, and companies such as Westclox and Quaker Oats, simply terminated women's employment when they married. Nor were married women the only ones scapegoated by the crisis. Some of Peterborough's unemployed complained that Italians were obtaining too much relief work, and the local county council passed resolutions against immigration, clearly influenced by hostility to eastern and southern Europeans.[58]

The organization of charity and relief in Peterborough accents both the sharpened class tensions of the period and the way in which woman's position as homemaker and dependent was assumed. Faced with a crisis far greater than the 1921 depression, the existing Central Charity Board realized by early 1931 that it could not cope with the escalating demands for fuel, clothing, and monetary aid: at least 190 families had appealed for help in the first month of the year alone, a portent of things to come.[59] At the urging of the publisher of the *Examiner*, the Peterborough Relief Association was formed; it was to augment Charity Board efforts, working with local churches and collecting corporate and private donations. Soon enough, the city increased its own welfare bureaucracy. The city's relief officer, along with four council members and local citizens, established the Peterborough Relief Committee, which worked in conjunction with the relief association to organize, standardize, and provide relief based on a strict criteria of need. This merging of private and state efforts, and the forced evolution of new bureaucratic measures to deal with relief, was common in many of Ontario's smaller cities.

So were the strict, even draconian, measures developed to keep the relief rolls down. Relief policy was characterized by a desire to maintain the work ethic, to limit the city's tax bill as well as its moral responsibility for the crisis, and to keep relief as a discretionary privilege rather than a social right. The relief provided was lower than the wage level for unskilled labour, and those on relief were forced to take farm work if any was available, do casual work for their benefits, or keep gardens provided by the city. Although the concern with the work ethic was directed very explicitly at men, women also were urged to find some kind of work; the relief committee once congratulated itself for finding a woman a job – scrubbing the relief office at night.[60]

Even though Peterborough's per capita costs for relief were smaller than many other Ontario cities,[61] the city council, which was faced with a declining tax base, was constantly worried about the cost of relief and of other social services, such as the Children's Aid Society.[62] The relief officer hired investigators to inspect the personnel rolls of companies to see if any members of relief families were working, and the investigators also monitored the morality, purchasing habits, and cohabitation situations of individuals on relief. To disobey the city's strict code of economic and social morality was to invite interrogation at relief headquarters. In one instance, an unemployed man was told to report about rumours that he had purchased a bottle of wine. Another man, whose daughter, it was discovered, was working at the Bonnerworth mill, was cut off relief. And a woman caught living in the same residence as another relief recipient also was cut off.[63] Benefits such as medical attention were given at the discretion of the relief officer. This official's inordinate power understandably led to bad feeling on the part of some recipients and to more than one demand that he resign. One petition collected by the unemployed demanded that he be replaced by a woman, a call precipitated perhaps by the view that a woman would not misuse such power.

The relief association and the relief committee were both dominated largely by middle-class citizens, with only a token 'unemployed man.'[64] Although some elected officials clearly realized that the crisis was beyond the control of working people, a vocal minority with access to the media insinuated that the work ethic was in crisis and that loafers were collecting relief. In one speech, Alderman Dutton suggested that many relief recipients were newcomers to the city, and he discussed at some length the 'problem of the lazy unemployed husbands who should be taken into Police Court' and forced to support their families. He offered two examples: one of an ungrateful man refusing work on the railroad for two dollars a day on the grounds that it was not enough to support his family, and one of a man who was simply 'drunken and delinquent.' In another public speech, the alderman even claimed that those collecting relief were 'trafficking in illegitimate children' in order to obtain more relief.[65]

Concern with the male provider meant that any direct relief the city provided through paid work (created with federal and provincial dollars) was construction or road work for men, and married men with dependents were considered the most needy.[66] Women were seen primarily as daughters and wives In order to cut back on costs occasioned by women on relief, the Peterborough Relief Committee suggested that women give birth at home, a less costly alternative than the hospital births that were becoming popular at the time. The concurrent attempts of local social service agencies to prop up the traditional male-provider family form was well illustrated by the case of a single father. Rather than have him unemployed, the Children's Aid Society boarded out his baby girl and hired a housekeeper to look after his three older boys, a strategy that it most certainly would never have countenanced for single mothers, whom it repeatedly urged to stay home and care for young children.[67]

The ideology and organization shaping relief also reflected a class bias for those dispensing aid found it difficult to understand those receiving it. The gulf between the economically secure middle classes and those experiencing the precariousness of working-class life is illustrated in a public speech on the economic crisis given by a prominent local lawyer, Joseph Wearing, who often donated his time to causes such as the Children's Aid Society. 'Times are tough,' admitted Wearing, but he added that Canada had had many depressions and Canadians still did not know 'real suffering.' As evidence, he noted that 'for us, the Depression means doing without luxuries like washing machines and cars'; and since women were still 'buying face powder,' and people were still going to the theatre, things could not be all that bad.[68] His statement would have come as a surprise to the wife of the textile worker above, who could not afford to purchase shoes for her children.

A clear sense of social distance was also exhibited in some women's recollections of the crisis. Many hoboes, one woman said, came to her parents' house in East City asking for a meal, and they were often given something. But they knew better than to go to 'snob hill' in the affluent west end, where the doors might be shut on them.[69] Class distinctions were experienced in women's daily encounters with unemployment and the charity and relief system. Waiting for a job and accepting free tea from the staff at the YWCA, asking for medical care from the relief officer, taking second-hand clothes from the charity board, or hearing school board officials deny relief mothers a 'tag day at local schools' to raise money for Christmas presents – all these encounters underscored the social distance between the economically secure and the women who knew the uncertainty and distress of underemployment or unemployment.[70]

While the fear that relief recipients might be shirking the work ethic was particular to some members of Peterborough's élite, the gender outlook of civic and relief officials was shared by the organizations of the unemployed, which concentrated on the need to provide work for male breadwinners and showed little concern for unemployed women. The Peterborough Unemployed Workers Unity (PUWU), which had connections with the left-wing Canadian Labour Defence League in Toronto, had begun to organize by 1933. It sent delegations to Peterborough's city council and requested 'money, not vouchers,' increased relief payments, and more decently paid work, as well as the fair distribution of work among the unemployed. In order to provide a culture of support for the unemployed, the PUWU organized clothing and toy drives, as well as picnics and other events for the children.

This organization placed its demands in the context of working-class notions of respectability: men, it said, wanted 'work, not relief ... [We need] money for our wives and children.' At one meeting, the organizers astutely featured a First World War veteran, who asked why, 'after fighting for the security of women and children for four years, he could not even get coal to heat his house' for his family.[71] Women were part of the organization, and they appeared 'in numbers' when one petition was presented to City Hall, but their public pleas stressed their role as homemakers. They called for cash, not vouchers, to end the humiliation of relief and to allow them to budget for their families as they saw fit. A women's section of the PUWU was formed, ostensibly as a 'sewing group,' though political consciousness raising was undoubtedly part of the group's intent.[72] Noticeably absent from their public addresses, however, was the concern with single women's unemployment that was sometimes voiced by unemployment organizations connected with the Canadian left in larger cities.[73]

The visible public organization of the PUWU may have invigorated local grass-roots protest, for people increasingly voiced their grievances before the relief committee, and some even engaged in public demonstrations. In 1934 a Peterborough family of two parents and two girls (one aged ten and the other ten months) marched on Queen's Park carrying a sign saying, 'Peterborough feeds its children on 25 cents per child a week.'[74] People could also be rallied to protest evictions, as they did when a family with four children was thrown out of a dwelling that had been designated as 'unfit for habitation.'[75] What is instructive about this eviction case, however, is the woman's place in the story. The newspaper article described at length the fate of the unemployed father, who was lame but was penalized by the city for keeping a car so that he could try and pick up part-time work. A brief sentence at the end noted that the mother was summoned home from her new job at Canada Packers when the bailiff came. It is likely that *her* earnings were the family's only means of support.

While women's unemployment may have been obscured by the gender ideology of the family wage, the reality was that many women were sustaining their families in crucial ways. The young Westclox worker who alone maintained her family and the Bonnerworth employee who was discovered by the city to be supporting her father are both examples of the way in which women's low-wage work, held onto during the Depression, kept families alive, just as young Florentine kept her family solvent in Gabrielle Roy's *The Tin Flute*.

Furthermore, women's domestic labour was indisputably increased by the economic crisis as homemakers tried to 'pick up the slack'[76] by adding to their work in the home. As one woman remembers, there were ways she could 'make do' by augmenting her labour when her husband was on short time: 'I took in a few boarders and did all my own bread and preserves. The one year he was out of work I did sixty quarts of tomatoes! ... I could buy scraps of material for 15 or 20 cents and make them into pants and jackets for the boys, and I made my own winter coat.'[77]

Finally, some women also worked in the informal economy. In this small city, homework provided by factories was rare, but many women did tailoring at home. The dollars earned in this way could feed the family or, as one woman remembers, could provide what she saw as 'luxuries' at the time: piano lessons for herself, and the opportunity for her brother to stay on in high school.[78] Women's participation in this informal cash economy could be a last resort to preserve family respectability. Assessing the household of a young female factory worker, a Peterborough social worker praised the girl's mother, noting that 'the father, a labourer was unemployed in the Depression and was lax about family discipline.[But] the mother was determined to keep up middle class standards of respectability. She took in boarders to keep the family off relief, kept a clean house and tried to encourage [her children's] friends of the "right" type.'[79] Often, the women interviewed commented, as an aside, on their mothers' work in the informal economy, or they characterized it as an 'extra' source of income. This way of remembering, however, does not negate the importance of this money to the household; rather, it indicates how women's informal labour, then as now, was devalued in the ideological realm.

COPING WITHOUT WAGE WORK

No group found it more difficult to maintain economic viability and social respectability than single mothers. The experiences of women who had to support the family on their own offers striking examples of women who 'fell through the cracks' of a society that was premised on both gender and economic inequality. Women who lived outside the so-called normal family – the family with a male breadwinner – were often perceived as anomalies and, as a result, their claim on wage work was rife with contradictions. For instance, single mothers were expected to support their children but were discouraged from taking wage work when their children were young. While this contradiction was exacerbated by the Depression, it persisted, encoded into the welfare and wage system, during the war and postwar years. The women's dilemma, moreover, was not simply an economic one, for they might also feel socially marginalized by their status as single mothers. As one of them commented on her experience after the Second World War, 'If you don't have a [normal male-headed] family, your kids are treated like second-class citizens.'[80] While widows were regarded more sympathetically as honourable single mothers and workers, even they sometimes felt that they were implicitly criticized for being working mothers 'without a man.'[81]

Desertion by a male earner was one of the most dreaded crises faced by women. A deserted woman would have to become the family breadwinner herself or rely on the earnings of her older children; female-headed families were clearly more dependent on children's earnings than male-headed households.[82] In some cases, women who had skills sometimes went back to work, quietly covering up their husband's absence even from friends and family.[83] Men's refusal to support their families may certainly have been the result of their own unemployment – as some claimed before the magistrate – but it could also be because of wilful desertion of their responsibilities or, in a few celebrated cases, because they simply moved on to have second families without legally divorcing.[84] Older children also could deny their responsibility to mothers left with younger siblings. The charitable and relief agencies told these women that they were ineligible for state aid if 'their older sons could support them,' as the Mothers' Allowance Board informed one applicant. But when denied family support, the women were the ones who were penalized, not the sons.[85]

Women who were the sole breadwinners for their families often turned to relatives for help, asking a sister or parents to look after their children while they found wage work.[86] Even if a woman could obtain family aid, however, these arrangements could prove unsatisfactory. In one case, the Children's Aid Society (CAS) had to intervene when it appeared that some grandparents were unable to care for their grandchildren properly.

If a woman did not have relatives to turn to, she could appeal for charitable aid. In the interwar period, some parents placed their children in orphanages when the family was facing economic crisis; their hope was that temporary care would aid the reconstitution and long-term stability of the family. Until the end of the 1930s, many children in the local CAS shelter were not orphans, and a high proportion (up to 50 per cent) of children were returned to their parents every year. A 1934 report noted that the 'average' stay for a child was three months.[87] Until the end of the Depression, many teenage CAS wards were sent out to work as farm help or domestics in other people's homes. By the postwar period, fewer children were being put in care or boarded out, though women coping with the problem of earning as well as caring for children continued to try and use the CAS's services to manoeuvre their way through economic crises.

During the Depression, single mothers sometimes turned to the CAS as a last resort for temporary aid; they asked the society to help locate clothes and shoes or to provide temporary care after evictions or when they had to be hospitalized. The perception that the society might help one through a financial crisis was revealed in a letter, written by a separated mother, who was denied relief and felt that she had no other option than to leave her children with the CAS. As the secretary of the board explained, 'The letter said she was unable to properly care and provide for her children, and her husband, who lived apart from her, could not help her. She was willing to place her five youngest children in the care of the CAS until spring, and by then she would endeavour to get a home together and would like her children back.'[88] While the board was sympathetic to these cases, it was harsh in its condemnation of any mother who was perceived to be immoral or to be shirking her maternal role, even by leaving her children alone so that she could engage in wage work.

Without accessible child care, what other options did these women have? Since 1921, there had been a program that allowed widows and some women with incapacitated husbands, if they had more than one child under sixteen, to apply under a strict means test to the local Mothers' Allowance Board for a small monthly allowance, but this allowance was so meagre that it usually needed to be subsidized with part-time work. As Margaret Little has shown, the Ontario mothers' allowance program was designed to keep entitlement limited to a very small group in order to encourage women to remarry (thus returning to the 'normal' and desired male-breadwinner family form) and to regulate women into becoming 'moral subjects – the proper mother.'[89] In Peterborough County, applicants and recipients were carefully scrutinized by a board made up of middle-class homemakers, professionals, and community leaders, who looked into the women's marital and financial status, housekeeping skills, sexual propriety, and moral character in the community. Sometimes negative information came from suspicious or unsympathetic neighbours, who were themselves struggling or poor. The fact that these neighbours would inform on women whom they thought were not 'respectable' enough or whom they suspected of unfairly collecting the mothers' allowance indicates the pervasiveness of the ideology of the deserving and undeserving poor.

The women taking the allowance represented a small proportion of female-headed households in the county;[90] during the 1930s there were about one hundred recipients of the allowance, whereas almost one thousand widows were listed in the 1931 census. The small number on the allowance may reflect women's reluctance to take state aid, though the restrictive rules of eligibility were probably a more significant factor. Many women fell between the cracks of this program, not because they were transgressing the moral norms set out by the board, but because they had one child or had not been deserted long enough, or because they had an incapacitated husband whose illness was not recognized by the Mothers' Allowance Board. One woman who fell outside the purview of the program explained to the Peterborough County board in 1932 that her husband had gone to the United States and secured a divorce by default, and she could not afford to go and challenge it. Yet she was left with five children to support and no maintenance: 'I live with my 72 year old parents, but they only have their pension, and I have three children in school. If I could find any work, that would help, but that is impossible. I want to keep my children in school.'[91]

Single mothers thus faced more than one implacable contradiction. Although they needed to support their families, the jobs open to them did not provide an adequate wage for family support. Secondly, women collecting mothers' allowance found that if they took on supplementary wage work, they were criticized for 'taking jobs away from others'; yet they were criticized by other citizens for taking state money rather than working![92] Nor did these dilemmas disappear in the more prosperous years of the 1940s and 1950s; they were ingrained in the organizing principles and ideological justification for the mothers' allowance and welfare system. Even after the Second World War, some working women remained wary of women on mothers' allowance. 'I would never have taken welfare,' commented a white-collar worker while criticizing those who did. She disapproved because she suspected that these women had been shirking the work ethic.[93] Perhaps, on another level, knowing how close all women were to economic uncertainty, she too had feared a similar fate.

UNDER THE LAW

While the vast majority of women supported themselves and their families with wage work and a smaller number did so with state or charitable aid, there were a few more desperate women who tried illegal methods of earning a living. Making moonshine was attempted by some women in the surrounding rural area, while city women, often those who were older and had few job prospects, were more likely to be found keeping a disorderly house or serving illegally made liquor. Essentially a continuation of the informal economy of the nineteenth century, moonshining was an enterprise of 'last resort' for women struggling to survive in the interwar period.[94] This practice persisted past

Prohibition. In fact, throughout the interwar period, rural women were more likely to be arrested for making and selling liquor than for being intoxicated in public. The local magistrate could be quite strict in his sentencing of these women. If their demeanour in court was especially hostile or unrepentant (as with the woman charged with keeping a disorderly house who loudly protested her arrest in 'two languages, English and profane,'[95] or in the case of an infamous moonshiner from Dummer Township, May Hill), he was especially severe, sending them to the dreary county jail for up to three months.[96]

Women who were without work or were destitute could be arrested for vagrancy. This catch-all charge was used by the police to deal with the visibly poor and the unemployed, or with women who were publicly contradicting the norms of respectable womanhood by being drunk and disorderly, or were begging, 'cutting up'[97] in public, or engaging in what parental and police authorities saw as 'peculiar'[98] or promiscuous behaviour. The vagrancy laws were also used to arrest 'streetwalkers' engaged in prostitution. Those charged with vagrancy were primarily women from Peterborough or the nearby county, not transients, and the largest group of women arraigned between the 1920s and 1940s listed domestic service as their occupation, though some were only casually employed or were unemployed.[99] The low pay, low status, lack of job security, and marginalization associated with domestic work must have led women to engage in the risk of prostitution or petty theft. One young domestic in the Depression, for example, stole eight dollars and a dress from the home where she was working, for which she was given a two-month jail sentence. In another case, an unwed mother stole 'a dollar, some baby clothes and other valuables' from her employer; already marginalized by her marital status and occupation, she probably felt she had little to lose. The magistrate, who was unsympathetic because the apprehended woman was already on a suspended sentence for forgery, sent her to jail.[100]

Far fewer factory workers or white-collar workers found themselves in trouble with the police; not only were they economically better off than many domestic workers, but their employment may have offered them more respectability and status, which was less likely to be 'thrown away' with the risk of crime.[101] The wage-earning women who did run into trouble with the law were more likely to be arraigned on charges of being found in a disorderly house (sometimes simply a loud, raucous party) or minor theft; one young factory worker, for instance, was caught stealing clothes from a bowling alley. Both the one-time offenders (who were the vast majority coming before the court) and the few repeaters were charged predominantly with vagrancy, prostitution, or theft – all crimes that have strong links to economic destitution. While poverty and lack of employment were by no means the only causes of women's lawbreaking (and, certainly, repeaters were often women troubled by addiction or violence), they were contributing factors.[102]

Nor was the Depression the sole cause of women's lawbreaking: those inclined to break the law may have already been part of the 'rough' rather than the respectable, though the two could and did overlap in some instances, as was clearly shown by some parents' reactions to their daughters' problems with the law. Parents who prided themselves on providing a respectable home worried lest neighbours discover their daughters' misdemeanours; one mother, who reassured the reformatory superintendent that 'I have seven children and never trouble like this before,' asked that her daughter's predicament be kept secret, 'for regardless of anything she may have done she is dear to me and I want to help her [but] if the small community finds out it will be hard to reform her.'[103]

One constant in the magistrate's view of women charged with minor crimes was his belief in the healing powers of paternal authority. 'She never had a chance,' he commented on a vagrant who had been deserted by her husband and her father's family. In another vagrancy case, he recommended that a woman 'return to her father's house until her husband can provide a home for her.'[104] Young women, in particular, were to embrace the discipline of parental authority – despite the fact that some were trying to leave their unhappy family lives behind.

The courts were also used by women themselves, in the attempt to redress their economic and familial problems by laying charges against deserting or violent husbands. Because the onus was on the woman to pursue her delinquent husband – a potentially costly and very public tactic – the number of nonsupport charges laid was very small in the interwar years and well into the late 1940s.[105] Informally, however, the chief of police and the magistrate dealt with far more cases in the privacy of their office, which was dubbed by one court reporter 'the chamber of domestic reconciliation.'[106] The chief of police in fact boasted that few cases of 'married troubles' were 'fought to the bitter end,' because he was able to forge 'reconciliations' and preserve 'the marital relationship.'[107]

The nonsupport cases that did come to court were those of repeat offenders who were pursued by determined women or exasperated legal authorities. In one case in the 1920s a husband was tracked by the police as far as Niagara Falls and returned to Peterborough, where the angry magistrate imposed a short jail sentence, insisting that the man contribute five dollars a week to his four children until they could support themselves.[108] The settlement demanded from husbands well into the 1930s was sometimes only six dollars a week, a sum less than the mothers' allowance and below the poverty line for many families. Moreover, an air of pessimism was evident in the magistrate's response to these cases: 'It is the same old tale,' he said to a husband who would not support his family. 'We need to finish this for once and all, so go home and mend your troubles.'[109] Perhaps the magistrate recognized that informal mediation simply maintained the status quo and did little to help many women. In extreme cases, a jail sentence was given to 'teach a lesson' to the man and make him 'realize his duty.'[110] But the magistrate was reluctant to jail the men, not only because some wives offered to give them another chance, but because it did not solve the family's immediate economic problems.

As more prosperous times returned in the 1940s, the magistrate carefully examined the woman's situation and, quoting recent legal precedent, insisted that she be 'destitute,' witout relatives or other means of support, in order to secure the serious attention of the court.[111] After a family court was established in 1946, the number of formal charges for nonsupport increased dramatically.[112] This was possibly because of women's increasing sense of entitlement to their rights, their knowledge of the law, and encouragement from the CAS and other social agencies, who wanted the husbands and not the state to support the increasing numbers of single mothers.[113]

The knowledge that one's wages might prove inadequate to support oneself or one's family could encourage women to stay in families which they found tense, unhappy, or even violent. While these family tensions were not in any way limited to working people – in fact, they were often obscured or covered up in the better-off families – they were investigated, regulated, and policed more severely and openly for the working classes.

Few formal charges of wife assault were laid in this period[114] but there is ample evidence that violence was a hidden, lived reality for some women. Indeed, in a few dramatic cases, the violence was only revealed after it had culminated in murder.[115] If brought to court, the men were usually given a stern rebuke by the local magistrate, who would lecture that the law 'didn't condone wife beating in any way.'[116] In the legal and social thought of the time, however, a woman's right to protection from violence was premised partly on her morality, fidelity, and good exercise of wifely duties – in short, on her social respectability. If her character was unblemished, the magistrate would denounce her batterer as unmanly and as being derelict in his duty to protect his wife. In one such case, the magistrate severely censured the husband for his drinking, lack of control, and relinquishment of family duties; when this man's wife had gone to remove him from a bar, she had been beaten so fiercely that her black eye was still apparent in court. Although this was not the husband's first offence, the magistrate tried mediation, giving the man a suspended sentence 'so he wouldn't lose his job.'[117]

In the 1930s, more than one-third of the cases of wife beating that came to the county court (presumably only the tip of the iceberg) were dismissed or given suspended sentences, and in another one-third of the cases the women agreed to withdraw the charges; a mere 18 per cent of the men were found guilty, and even fewer served a sentence. Nor did these trends change substantially in the post–Second World War period; judges were still reluctant to jail male breadwinners, and they now looked to trained probation officers in the family court to mediate and patch up families shattered by violence.[118] The women who did go to court were courageously and actively protesting their brutal treatment, but many more remained trapped in violent relationships. Faced with economic uncertainty, some women were ambivalent about their husbands' incarceration and sometimes said they would 'offer one last chance.'[119] 'I supposed she is not anxious to have her husband go to jail,' sighed the magistrate when a battered wife decided not to press charges. A suspended sentence was once again given.[120] Even though the number of nonsupport charges rose in the 1950s, women were still reluctant to pursue battering charges, perhaps the ultimate in shame for many families. Situated in an economic system in which they found it difficult to be breadwinners and yet were simultaneously limited by entrenched notions of male authority and control of the family, women had few viable alternatives. The language of protection on the magistrate's part highlighted the connection between family tension and economic livelihood. As long as women had to be protected, they would never be socially and economically independent.

CONCLUSION

The women who began work during the 1930s and those who followed them during the Second World War embraced an image of respectability that encompassed a belief in hard work, moral uprightness, and acceptance of proper gender roles and familial obligations. In the postwar years, many ingredients of this outlook remained, though women's interpretations of proper family roles began to alter in concert with their changing role in the labour force. Shaped by social custom and gender ideals, this view of respectability affirmed the existing gender and social order, though it also reflected the outlook and struggles of those born into the world with few options other than hard work as a means of surviving or of improving their lives.

Abstract notions of respectability, however, could never be completely lived realities, for these ideals were challenged by the pressures of economic uncertainty, by the impersonal hand of fate bringing illness or death, and by the misfortune of familial dissolution. All these threatened the loss of respectability and raised the spectre that the family would sink into the 'rough' working classes. Women's strategies to cope with these pressures – strategies that were sometimes also aimed at family survival – included wage labour but involved much more; the women secured aid from family members, used credit or the informal economy, increased their domestic work, or turned to charitable or state aid.

The Great Depression intensified existing patterns of economic instability and, as a result, modified working people's view of state and charitable aid. Because of the unprecedented scale of unemployment and underemployment, the women now describe their families' reliance on relief or some other form of charity as a respectable option, an understandable survival mechanism. They maintain that one could be both poor and respectable during the Depression as long as one's claim on welfare was premised on an honest desire to work in order to provide for one's family. '*Even* my father had to resort to relief,' recalled an interviewee who was at pains to emphasize her family's commitment to honesty and hard work.

The economic crisis of the Depression, however, did not lead to a fundamental questioning of the work and wage ethic of capitalism; and a person's claim on state aid or charity was still qualified, both in the minds of the officials dispensing it and among one's own working-class neighbours, on the proper exercise of familial and gender roles.

The prevalent suspicion of married working women and of women collecting mothers' allowance who were not considered deserving, as well as the social disapprobation experienced by single mothers and deserted women, indicate that the right to economic independence or support was contingent on one's marital status and moral character, and on the acceptance of appropriate gender roles.

This contradiction reflected the ideological dichotomy between the dependent mother and the female worker which Ruth Pierson maintains characterizes the policy thinking of the 1930s and the postwar years. The way in which social policy and political posturing dealt with women's unemployment and relief in the Depression, for instance, presented women as a group fractured into two distinct roles: single female worker and dependent wife/mother. The former group was never considered to be a significant unemployment problem. Not once did the many young women who were looking for work and were faced only with the prospect of casual domestic labour cause any social protest in this small city. Although the attention given to unemployed women in larger cities was marginal, it nonetheless stands in contrast to a total absence of discourse about the unemployed women in Peterborough. Perhaps the assumptions of paternalism again prevailed. In a small town with little mobility and a nearby rural hinterland, it was doubly assumed that unemployed women could go home or rely on relatives for support.

While the wages earned by women through factory and office work actually supported their families, an ideological contradiction produced their humble denial of their role as breadwinners. The women now speak with pride about the contribution they made to the family coffers, but they also portray their work as a temporary tiding over, and they assume that the Depression 'was especially hard on the men,' who were breadwinners.[121] Their way of remembering, then, reveals the very gender ideology that privileged men's social right to work and assumed women's economic marginalization during the Depression.

These assumptions also left the women who were outside the so-called normal male-provider family extremely vulnerable. Women who were deserted, separated, or without sufficient earners in the family often fell through the cracks of the nascent welfare state. Their coping strategies sometimes included work for wages, but they also used other means to support themselves and their families, turning for help to family, charity, mothers' allowance, or relief, or even trying to gain redress from delinquent husbands through the courts. A very few tried other less respectable means, such as petty theft or the informal economy of last resort, moonshining.

The economic precariousness of women's lives, along with unsympathetic legal and social policy, had a further impact: it was difficult for women to challenge unhappy, tense, or even violent family relationships. While affection, mutual obligation, and support characterized many families, the negative experiences of unhappiness, alienation, tension, and violence troubled an unknown minority of families. Although I have concentrated on only a few examples of this tension, the mere existence of this culture of violence had – and continues to have – an effect on all women. This darker, unhappy side of family life must be integrated into our studies of women's work and the family economy. It has been part of the overall fabric of women's lives and has affected their economic options and ambitions, as well as their personal and social lives. The ultimate, tragic irony for women and children was that familial tension or violence, if hidden, might not compromise respectability. Nor is there evidence that it escalated markedly during the Depression as a result of the frustrations of material uncertainty. Although men might try to convince the magistrate that 'years on relief had caused' their violent behaviour,[122] social service agencies and the local magistrate recognized violence as an ongoing problem. Persisting family tensions over financial resources, power, and authority were to remain for women of the second group in this study, even though their longer years in the workforce gradually spawned new claims for economic and personal independence.

6

Accommodation at Work

I think they made money at *our* expense there, but you know, you have to learn to manage with what you've got.[1]

I don't want anyone to work under those conditions again. But we did pretty well, after all.[2]

The above observations of two former textile workers indicate how women could articulate, in the same sentence, both a criticism of the conditions of their employment and also some acceptance of the rules of the game, as defined by their employers. They capture the way in which we weave together within one fabric our accommodation and resistance to the conditions of our work. There may be situations that spark a more 'pure' response to work; a strike, for instance, crystallizes and sharpens resistance. Yet in the day-to-day functioning of the work-place, both resistance and accommodation are usually present, sometimes intertwined so closely that it is difficult for us to separate them. Indeed, David Collinson has recently argued that it is difficult to theorize about consent and resistance in isolation, since 'both were different sides of the same coin'; namely, the workers' assertion of autonomy and power, and their attempts to manage class and gender insecurities in the face of employer power and control.[3]

Nonetheless, I believe that we must still try to unravel and evaluate consent and resistance if we are to understand the material and ideological conditions in which both thrived, and the reasons why these different strategies were pursued. We need to ask how and why women workers participated in a process of accommodation, what strategies were successfully used by employers to facilitate this consent, and whether there were inherent contradictions contained in these strategies which also encouraged women's resistance.

In the writing of labour history, the operation of consent has been ignored and 'undertheorized,' as Ava Baron argues.[4] While many works in the last fifteen years have explored women as active agents of change – a necessary antidote to an initial emphasis on oppression in women's history – we still need to explain why women workers saw their lower wages as natural or inevitable and, more fundamentally, why they accepted the employers' right to make the rules.

To do this, we need to fuse materialist theories that explore the manufacturing of consent in the workplace with feminist insights on the creation and resilience of gender hierarchies in the family, the workplace, and the wider society. Previous efforts to understand consent and accommodation have emphasized a number of explanations, either separately or together. Materialist analyses, first, have stressed the economic pressures encouraging conformity, while a second approach has stressed the influence of powerful and dominant ideologies in sustaining unequal class and gender relations. Some analyses, focusing on women's interpretations of their lives, have examined the way in which women make rational decisions based on their astute assessment of the meagre economic and ideological alternatives available to them. Finally, more recent explorations of consent have urged us to consider the way in which discourses encouraging accommodation, expressed through language and symbolic systems, constitute women's subjectivity, their very understanding of themselves and their work.

Oral history is particularly useful as a means of drawing out and analysing the latter two themes. Certainly, in retrospect, many women stress their conformity rather than rebellion, in part because this often befits their current outlook – another indication of the way in which memories may divulge a woman's current ideologies and dominant 'life scripts' as much as her actual behaviour in the past. Nevertheless, this emphasis on consent is itself significant, revealing the cumulative power of the processes of accommodation in women's workplaces. Although women may not consciously see their values or patterns of behaviour as accommodation – and, indeed, may not see accommodation in a negative sense – their descriptions of the advantages and disadvantages of their workplaces, their fears and aspirations, and their acceptance of the rules of the game display the complex blend of coercion, unconscious acquiescence, and even active participation that created consent on many levels.

Often, women's decisions reflected a reasonable assessment of the very limited array of choices that lay before them in their work lives. At the same time, the ideological power of certain taken-for-granted assumptions about economic and gender hierarchy are unmistakable as we listen to the verbal patterns of resignation and acceptance in their accounts. These assumptions then reproduced themselves, through an array of symbols, language, and social practice, within the women's very subjective feelings of self, thereby further facilitating the operation of consent in the workplace.

'WORRYING ABOUT MY APPENDIX OPERATION': MATERIAL PRESSURES
TO CONFORM

Consent, it is crucial to point out, is constructed on the edifice of unequal economic power: material constraints provided the essential backdrop for the authority structure and patterns of control in the workplace. As Patrick Joyce noted when discussing the creation of deferential and paternalistic relationships in the nineteenth-century workplace, 'power relations are a precondition for [paternalism] ... vulnerability sows the seeds of deference.'[5] Keeping one's job, securing jobs for kin, working a full week during the Depression, choosing where one wanted to work within the factory – all these were the kinds of material realities and pressures that employees had to consider when interacting with their superiors.

Fears about losing one's job, not getting enough hours of work, or being denied job mobility were some of the women's most graphic and vivid memories about their wage work. There is no doubt that women who joined the workforce as adolescents or young adults in the Depression experienced a far greater nervousness about job instability than women who joined the workforce during and after the Second World War. This is well summed up in a textile worker's overall assessment of her work experience in the 1930s: 'Work was so hard to get ... you just "took it" [the conditions at work] and you didn't say anything.'[6] For these women, the image – often reinforced by management – of a line-up at the factory door of people ready to assume their jobs was always in the back of their minds.

More precise economic concerns were also important. That the women can be so specific, and indeed intense, when describing these worries forty years later indicates the immense pressures they created. 'I was just worried about paying for my appendix operation,'[7] recalled a textile worker who had to return to work to pay off her medical bills in the late 1930s. Another woman, who married and then went back to work after the war began, had similar concerns. She remembers being very concerned that she keep her job because she was working to help support her only child, who was already a major cause of anxiety. Since her child was often very sick, she was 'just working for the medicine, just to get the medicine' to help him.[8] Whether they were helping support their parents' household or their own, the women worried that dismissal or lay-off would result in health, housing, or other economic problems for the family.

'How did the employer decide who to lay off?' I asked many of the women. Especially before unionization in some factories in the late 1940s, there was one overriding perception: the bosses decided who would go. Although many of the women then went on to endorse the decisions made by management, usually on the basis of seniority but sometimes on the managers' assessments of individual workers' needs, they were well aware that it was always the bosses' decision. Many women remember worrying about reprimands for inadequate work even when they were extremely conscientious. A white-collar worker who started at General Electric in 1929 said of her first months: 'I remember always worrying that they would fire me and get someone else [if I didn't perform well].'[9] Even more evocative is the memory of a blue-collar worker who began in the 1940s yet still pictured her dismissal every time she 'saw someone approach with a sheet of papers ... When I was first there, I thought, *oh oh*, here are my walking papers.'[10]

It was not only the possibility of losing their jobs that caused the women concern. It was also their status at work, their job mobility, and whether or not they could secure work for other family members. Most workplaces were quite tightly controlled by managerial prerogative, and until after the Second World War, a number of managers and foremen were influential in hiring, firing, and assigning work duties. Hiring, remember some of the former workers, seemed personal and arbitrary. One worker at Westclox remembers General Manager J.H. Vernor talking to him briefly, 'making a few scratchy notes,' and then saying, 'You're hired.'[11] In 1945 a separate personnel department was set up by Westclox at the urging of the parent company, which feared that its unorganized workforce would be stirred by the wave of unionization sweeping North America. Even after this, Vernor and other managers took a personal interest in hiring, with recommendations of family and friends carrying weight in their decisions. As a former Westclox manager put it, 'There were names that immediately boded well for you, but others that meant instant disaster ... Forget this talk about nepotism ... it was just a form of reference.'[12] Nor was this untypical. Well into the 1950s, many workplaces still relied on family recruiting networks and informal recommendations.

Women who received their jobs through personal contacts often developed a sense of debt to their employer, particularly during the Depression. As Joy Parr argues in her case study, workers felt 'they owed their jobs to their patrons.'[13] During the worst of the Depression, factories such as General Electric reduced the work week and instituted job sharing in order to keep people at least partially employed, a measure that accentuated a sense of obligation to the company. Obligation could easily slide into a more demanding form of conformity to the employers' aims, as one Bonnerworth worker remembers. A woman in her workroom 'crossed the picket line' in the 1937 strike because 'her brother, who had helped her [work there], was a foreman.'[14]

Prospects for job mobility also figured in the women's decisions. One way in which working-class women, especially those who had to leave school by sixteen, could alter their working lives was to move from the factory floor to a white-collar job. This opportunity, made available particularly at Westclox, became an inducement to stay with the company and, of course, to conform to company rules and priorities. While it certainly could not compare with the more lucrative career possibilities for men in the company, the potential advancement by women into jobs considered more interesting, flexible, and of higher status should not be discounted when assessing the creation of consent.

Furthermore, the work process, as we have seen, was especially tightly controlled in the case of both white- and blue-collar women workers. In most offices, for example, women's work was closely supervised, and the politeness of their demeanour was noted when it came to promotions and raises, which were individually assigned. Indeed, in many companies, job-posting systems did not exist until the postwar period, so employees would not even know about a new job prospect unless they were told about it by management. This method of assigning promotions was a major impetus to follow the rules of the game. One white-collar worker at Westclox learned that women were not supposed to assume they had an automatic right to promotion. As one of her fellow office workers recalled, 'One girl got a raise and told the girl across from her. *She* then immediately went in to [the boss to] ...

ask, "Why not me too?" Then the [first] girl was taken in again and told, "When you get a raise, it is between you and the company, you don't tell anyone." [That was] the way things should be, I think.'[15]

Finally, in a society that more generally celebrated the values of individualism and competition in its political, cultural, and social systems, it is not surprising that some women abandoned the sense of factory consciousness and solidarity created within their work culture, and worried about their own job advancement, even if it meant trying to secure someone else's position. In the woollen mill, for instance, one woman who never joined the 1937 strike indicated her bitterness about a fellow worker who was primarily concerned 'with having my job ... She tried to convince the foreman she could do it better than me.'[16] Like the textile worker described below, who endorsed management's stringent washroom rules, these women had absorbed, at some level, an individualist outlook as well as one that endorsed managerial priorities as their own.

Economic power and coercion, not to mention the level of exhaustion most women felt by the end of the day, thus provided a basic framework for the production of consent in the workplace. As Terry Eagleton argues, we should not dismiss the many mundane powers of 'negative social control' available to produce consent: 'If people do not actively combat a regime ... it may be because they are too exhausted after a hard day's work, too fatalistic to the see the point, or they may be frightened of the consequences of opposition.'[17]

MANAGERIAL STRATEGIES AND WOMEN'S RESPONSES

Employers' open opposition to worker protest is one example of this negative social control. When Peterborough textile workers began to organize in 1937, other employers openly addressed the question of unions for their workers. An office worker from Outboard Marine remembers the general manager delivering a warning to his employees, telling them not to imitate the Bonnerworth, for he would not countenance an international union at *his* company: 'I can still see Hugh Campbell up on a box beside the time clock ... and that box just trembled. I brought this company over here from the States in 1928, [he said], and I can damn well take it back again.'[18]

The textile strike in particular provided lessons that were not long forgotten. 'I was terrified' after that strike, remembers a woman who was a child at the time but whose brother worked in the mills. 'There were chains and police there. I was scared when I heard about it.'[19] Another woman, who found work at Westclox during the war years, still had bitter memories about the strike, for her husband had lost his job when the Auburn mill shut down soon afterwards: 'John worked at the Auburn. We had three children already. Then they went on strike and it [closed]. He was forty-eight before he got a steady job again because they were blacklisted because that was the first union in town.'[20]

The message that organized protest or unions were unacceptable, or at least had negative consequences, was also offered in less overtly threatening ways, for employees were provided with the 'facts' about unions to discourage organizing. A white-collar worker at the Westclox, for instance, explained why the office never unionized, even after the plant did in 1952: 'The personnel officer would come in and explain it to us. Really we wouldn't be any further ahead with a union. He pointed out that we got whatever they did [financially] without having a union.'[21]

At the same time, more than the raw power of coercion or even subtle pressure was involved in producing consent. In assessing accommodation in the workplace, one needs to analyse the whole range of managerial strategies utilized by employers to facilitate consent. As Philip Scranton argues, these schemes must also be situated in their wider context; the method by which the employer tried to create profit, and the cultural, material circumstances of the community in which he operated shaped the success and failures of managerial attempts to establish harmony and consent in the workplace.

Management's attempts to encourage workers' sense of loyalty, obligation, and commitment were also based on the carrot of material benefits and financial incentives (often referred to as 'welfare capitalism') or on the promise of mutual loyalty, concern, and informal aid ('paternalism'). Businesses might use more than one of these managerial strategies; contrary to the initial characterization of Canadian business history by some sociologists, there was not a mechanical evolution of business strategy over time, with most workplaces moving from scientific management at the turn of the century to welfare capitalism by the 1920s and to modern personnel management by the Second World War. In actual fact, companies, influenced by economic considerations, the local labour market, and social structure, employed these strategies differently according to an assessment of their profitability and their fit with local conditions. Paternalism and welfare capitalism, for instance, were particularly effective at Westclox precisely because they were used together. To illustrate managerial attempts to create consent in the workplace and women's responses to those strategies, it may be useful to concentrate on the more successful Westclox example and, secondly, on the less successful Dominion Woollens, with occasional examples from other workplaces.

The material rewards of welfare capitalism were clearly part of the bargain of accommodation worked out between women workers and managers at Westclox. The company's early attempts to establish good pay and benefits compared with other industries in Peterborough helped create an informal peace treaty with labour. By paying one or two cents more an hour than other factories and by providing paid vacations, the company hoped to procure better-educated workers, to increase productivity, and to secure a stable and nonunionized workforce.

From the outset, the company carefully 'planned production almost a year in advance in order to regularize employment,'[22] thus avoiding the instability of industrial employment that was still prevalent in the interwar years. Because this was not a one-company town, Westclox management felt that it had to compete for skilled male labour, but the managers also extended this strategy to include female workers. According to a former manager, when the longtime general manager, J.H. Vernor, first established female wage rates in the 1920s that were one or two cents more than the wage rates at the larger Canadian General Electric, a prominent CGE manager 'stormed up the hill' to demand a rollback. But Vernor argued that in order to recruit a workforce from scratch, Westclox needed some tangible economic inducements.[23] The company also persuaded community members of the superiority of its white-collar work. When looking for new secretarial help, the personnel manager would call the head commercial teacher at the local high school and ask him to send over the top three or four women in the graduating class for interviews.

While many companies assumed that women were not interested in long-term material benefits, women did consider this part of the allure of employment and a good reason to stay at Westclox.[24] On top of paid vacations, which were available after five years of service (one of the most attractive benefits), there was a group insurance plan, which had been instituted from the beginning and which the employer paid. From the 1930s on, employees could also contribute to a jointly paid sick leave plan, though a pension plan did not appear until 1940. There were also several less costly benefits, which the company loudly advertised; for instance, tennis courts on the grounds, an infirmary, and a cafeteria that served cheap hot meals.

Compared with other large Ontario companies, these were good but not outstanding benefits. A 1927 study done for the Ontario government on the physical, recreational, and financial benefits offered by businesses revealed that many companies offered cheaper benefits, such as recreation and cafeterias, while fewer offered the more costly employer-paid vacations, sickness insurance, pension plans, and so on.[25] Later analyses of welfare plans by the Canadian Manufacturing Association in the 1930s indicated that in comparison to large enterprises, Westclox was now lagging behind.[26] Still, it is important to compare Westclox with other Peterborough industries;[27] in contrast to the low wages and the absence of benefits at the large woollen mill and the notorious authoritarian management style at CGE, Westclox 'looked great'[28] to prospective workers. And although Westclox policies were designed to prevent unionization, this was not a central concern of the young women seeking jobs in the 1930s and 1940s. On the contrary, the women remember that there was competition for the few openings at Westclox.

While many of the benefits offered by Westclox were standard ingredients of welfare capitalism, an important element of the company's approach was the personal and discretionary way that benefits were imparted. In a confidential survey returned to the Ontario Department of Labour in 1927, the company revealed that in 'deserving cases, money was sometimes lent on the quiet for house buying'; but at the same time, the survey recorded that 'Vernor hates anything paternal.'[29] While understanding the pejorative connotation of the word, Vernor was still willing to apply its principles. Nor was this unique to Westclox. Over the years, Quaker Oats also became known for its benefit plans and deliberate paternalism. Indeed, a Quaker questionnaire in the same file revealed the same discretionary paternalism. There was 'no formal pension or sick plan,' said Quaker, but 'the Company takes care of needy and deserving cases. No one is allowed to suffer.'[30]

The discretionary benefits offered by Westclox reveal the careful integration of both welfarism and paternalism. In nineteenth-century paternalist enterprises, the employer, drawing on previous forms of deference within the church, the community, and especially the household, attempted to incorporate these social relations into the factory regime. Often assuming a very visible role on the factory premises, he tried to create the feeling of an organic community, equating the factory with an actual or imagined family.[31] This form of paternalism, as Judy Lown argues, was also a form of patriarchy, for it sustained a hierarchical system in which older men dominated younger men, women, and children;[32] it was premised on a conception of 'mutual rights and duties connected to the unequal relations of authority ... found in the household.'[33]

The twentieth century supposedly inaugurated the professionalization of paternalism with the introduction of welfare plans and a trained workforce of welfare and personnel specialists.[34] Replacing the fatherly factory head was the corporate practice of organized, efficient welfare capitalism, which still contained some of the basic principles of paternalism: the familial metaphor, the endeavour to create a company culture of consensus, deference and accommodation, and attempts to maintain a loyal, long-lasting, and, of course, nonunionized workforce.

In actual fact, paternalism extended well into the twentieth century, as examples from this city show. Employers' discretionary aid, only one example of this, reveals many instances of management's attempts to create a culture of accommodation and harmony. At Westclox, until a union contract in the 1950s, there was no official bereavement leave and pay, though management created, on an ad hoc basis, similar benefits for some employees. A longtime employee, whom Vernor had known well, remembered the situation when her father died. Not only was she given time off, but Vernor lent the family his car for the funeral, and when he came to pay his respects, he shook hands and discreetly left a twenty dollar bill behind – a personal contribution to funeral expenses, which families sometimes found hard to meet.[35] While most of the women reported similar instances of sympathetic paternalism, one of them noted that when her mother died, the company sent for her at the funeral home to come and finish some special typing, which only she had done in the past. Paternalism, in other words, was arbitrarily applied.

These discretionary benefits were extremely important, for they reinforced ties of loyalty and obligation between boss and worker, sometimes so successfully that the women began to interpret their legal rights as personal gifts. Even after a sick benefits plan was introduced, Vernor told one employee to let him know if she ever needed time off because of sickness in the family – an incident that was translated as evidence of his flexibility and concern. Another employee praised Vernor for his concern for the personal safety of his female employees, who were taxied home after midnight shifts during the war years. Although she was vaguely aware that this was required by law, she primarily saw Vernor's hand in it: 'The taxi driver had to wait until we were in the door ... and if he didn't, we were supposed to notify Mr Vernor about [it].'[36]

Financial incentives and benefit plans, combined with the informal creation of a sense of personal obligation, were also used in other plants, with varying degrees of success. General Electric, too, created a sense of obligation by offering jobs to kin. On the other hand, this larger, more impersonal company had more difficulty extending the private, paternal hand to all employees. Moreover, one of its main financial incentives for employees in the early years was its system of monetary rewards for suggestions to improve production, a plan geared more towards male workers.

In the textile mill, paternalism was also used, though less extensively. Since it was integrated into a highly competitive, low-wage industry, the mill did not offer the same material benefits or welfare plans that Westclox and eventually Quaker Oats and General Electric did. Still, managers could attempt to apply their own prudent aid to employees, thus creating a sense of employer generosity and mutual obligation. A woman who could not live with her family and was self-supporting remembers her constant fear that she would be laid off. Her boss, she recalls, 'was really good to me. He knew about [my situation] at home and he would try and keep me as long as he could when time was short ... though sometimes if others really complained he would have to lay me off too.'[37]

The operation of paternalism was also linked to the work process and the methods of supervision used in the workplace. These were especially crucial in the textile mill, since it had so little to offer in terms of financial incentives. Women working at the Bonnerworth recognized that their lower wages might be assuaged through considerate methods of shop-floor control and a level of sociability that would temporarily compensate for low monetary benefits. They were especially concerned that the supervision should be both fair and flexible, conditions that could in fact be contradictory, given the above example of the woman who was favoured over others when it came to lay-offs. Straw bosses, they said, should avoid favourites, should allow a measure of joking, talking, and socializing, and should treat women with respect; these were some of the basic ingredients of good supervision. When fair supervision vanished or speed-ups occurred, the women felt justified in resisting – by leaving, by trying to change their supervisor's behaviour, or even by striking.

At Westclox, supervision and the practice of paternalism also interacted on one another, with the paternalist philosophy of the company shaping the nature of authority relations in the workplace. A certain degree of flexibility characterized supervision in the factory; for example, women might be allowed to 'sneak out' a few minutes early to catch a train home for the weekend,[38] and they could talk, joke, or sing on the line to alleviate boredom.

Even more important, foremen were trained to listen and mediate rather than reject complaints, and they were especially to avoid embarrassing or humiliating the women workers. The women commented positively on the manner in which their male foremen dealt with conflict and grievances. 'We were taken aside, never embarrassed in front of others on the line,' recalled one woman.[39] 'I learned never to dismiss a complaint,' said a former manager. 'J.H. [Vernor] once took a strip off me for brushing off a complaint ... I listened, even if the complaint didn't seem [justified].'[40] Some of the women claimed to prefer this conciliatory method to later union practices, because the latter tended to be more confrontational, drawing attention to the aggrieved, since 'the union was always looking for an issue to hold over the company's head.'[41] Perhaps women's own methods of conflict resolution learned in the family at this time made them appreciate the private, mediated approach.[42]

While the previous analysis of women's work culture has shown how the women had their own code of behaviour and sense of solidarity, which was not simply equated with a company's interests, Westclox's labour relations were still compared favourably to shop-floor relations in other factories where these women had worked or had relatives working. Westclox's 'laissez-faire supervision' thus tended to 'mystify labour/capital relations';[43] significantly, it was also construed by the women workers as evidence of the company's familial style of management.

Indeed, whatever the level of success of paternalist strategies, what is revealing in the oral histories is the importance placed by women in many different workplaces on these welfare and paternalist measures. For example, a former Quaker Oats woman cited the company's Christmas bonus plan as evidence of company generosity; a Westclox woman described the company-donated dinners and social events in some detail; and a woman who had found work at Outboard Marine lauded that company's benevolence because, she claimed, she was given the job precisely because she was the widow of an employee. In an aside, she noted this as a kind of charity on the company's part: 'They would hire the widows ... otherwise I wouldn't have had a job.'[44]

GENDERED PATERNALISM

Welfare capitalism and paternalism were managerial strategies geared towards placating both male and female workers, yet there were gender differences both in the application of these strategies and in the workers' responses to them. For example, paternalism was justified with direct references to the sexual division of labour in the factory. Accounts of why and how the these gender divisions existed are characterized by a familial discourse within which the women workers assume the role of daughters and maiden aunts, while the men assume the role of sons. In the Westclox example, the latter role was constructed in a patriarchal manner, with younger men under the control of older ones – but always with the prospect of advancing into positions of power as supervisors or managers. Many company rituals, such as foremen's picnics, fishing trips, and poker nights, further solidified gender solidarity among the men. This was true in other workplaces as well. Outboard Marine, commented one observer, 'was renowned for its annual deer hunt ... over one hundred and fifty [male] employees went on the trip during the 1950s [and those who went] cut across management/workshop boundaries.'[45]

On the other hand, women were not integrated into these networks, nor did their wage work lead to the possibility of significant advancement and power. In the equation of mutual obligation, they were perceived as needing some protection but not the same opportunities for promotion as men. The different type of paternalism directed towards men and women was underscored by the way in which sons could prosper in the family while women could maintain only secondary roles. Earlier research has argued that both male and female workers were 'rendered childlike' by paternalist managerial strategies, which 'undermined [men's] sense of identity as breadwinners,'[46] but this obscures paternalism's inherent rationalization of the patriarchal organization of the factory.

Gender differences were also apparent in the moral protection and notions of respectability the company offered to women but not to men. American studies have pointed to the efforts made by employers of the Progressive Era to emphasize feminine skills and moral protection in their welfare plans for women.[47] It is often assumed that such moral paternalism was unwanted and did not persist past the Roaring Twenties, yet at Westclox quite the opposite was true: anxiety about marriageability and respectability remained a subtext of concern well into the twentieth century.

Managers made clear their emphasis on morality and respectability in various ways. These included commenting to their office workers on the necessity of appropriate 'ladylike' dress and deportment; admonishing their women softball players to stay out of bars in order to protect their good image; and even directly interfering in the women's personal budgeting and debt problems.[48] As one Westclox manager commented, 'We hired very nice girls. We were careful about that, to hire good girls, respectable girls. You could be a preacher's daughter and work at Westclox, you know ... [whereas] the mill had a tough name, you know.'[49] Former workers, it must be stressed, often made the same connection, implying that Westclox drew in a more educated and thus respectable class of women: 'We took the cream of the crop ... we even had school teachers there ... But after the war, it was harder to find people and we had to take some we didn't really want.'[50]

The company's attempt to champion the respectability of its women workers was not entirely unwelcome with the female employees, for this dimension of paternalism offered women, especially those in the plant, some reciprocal psychological benefits by countering what they believed was a negative image of factory workers. Blue-collar women, as we have seen, sometimes felt that their labour was stereotyped in the public mind as rough and even 'degrading'[51] – and they resented it. As an Outboard war worker noted, 'My coveralls felt like a jail uniform ... I felt embarrassed if I had to go to the Doctor because people stared at me.' Though she tried to rationalize: 'Who cares – I was making more money than them!'[52] Women who worked at Westclox, however, cited the impeccable reputation of the plant as evidence of their better class of employment, especially in comparison to 'dirty, dark' General Electric.[53] Management's participation in this process was crucial in reinforcing an image of commitment and concern for its women workers.

It was not only by providing material benefits and buttressing an image of respectability that companies like Westclox sustained the impression of concern and notions of mutual obligation. Other fringe benefits such as the company's on-site clubhouse and tennis courts (which created a homelike atmosphere), and company rituals such as Christmas parties, picnics, and celebrations of long service were also very important. Many who attended the Quarter Century Club (twenty-five years and over) and retirement dinners characterize these events as lavish affairs, which they see as evidence of the Company's magnanimity. In her interview, one employee proudly repeated, word for word, the acceptance poem she had delivered when she received her twenty-five year award.

Initiatives such as the encouragement of recreation and athletics for employees were also utilized by companies to create consent in the workplace. At Westclox, for example, J.H. Vernor supported the creation of industrial league teams for both men and women and donated money to rent the YWCA for team sports, sometimes personally passing on the cheque through an employee. Westclox's community name, however, was best known for its women's softball team.

The women workers were sometimes ballplayers scouted out by coaches who were more concerned with team needs than with manpower needs in the plant. One woman remembers that even before she finished high school, 'they were hot and heavy after me to play softball for them ... but my mother put her foot down as she wanted me to finish my business training.'[54] Another woman was recruited by her sister, who was already a Westclox athlete: 'I went there to play in the sports. I think you'll find a lot of the girls did the same thing. They got jobs to play softball, basketball. My sister got the job first, then Mr Vernor, who was the president, needed another player [so I was hired].'[55]

The women on the Westclox team practised regularly, competed fiercely, and did well; in 1945 the team was runner-up for the provincial championship. The company outfitted the women with uniforms and paid for buses to transport them across the province, and although the women were not supposed to get extra perks at work, some lateness might occasionally be accepted when they were playing for championships out of town. When one ballplayer sprained her ankle, Vernor sent a truck to pick her up every day so that she could make it to work.

Sports were used by employers to create a sense of company loyalty, suggesting competition with the outside but team effort inside. As well as advertising the company's name in the community, they were supposed to create a disciplined and committed workforce that strove to give its best performance on and off the job.[56] Many previous studies of industrial-sponsored sports have focused only on the companies' recruitment of skilled male workers or on the attempted inculcation of 'manly' attributes of competition through sport,[57] or they have assumed that these programs were of little effect after the 1920s.[58] Feminist analyses of women's sports, on the other hand, have been critical of the ways in which sport was moulded by male medical and educational experts intent on controlling women's bodies and preserving traditional notions of female physical weakness.[59]

Listening to the women's subjective memories of industrial sports suggests that the actual meaning sports had for the women players may have differed somewhat from the intentions of the industrial team promoters.[60] Women who played on Westclox teams enjoyed the physical competition and, for some, the public visibility involved. The ballplayers recall with pride the spectators, especially the other Westclox employees, who filled the stands. 'Years later,' a star player remembered nostalgically, 'someone would come up to me on the street downtown and say, "I remember you pitching for Westclox!"'[61] Moreover, the women's teams drew together a closely bonded female community, which offered the women support and companionship sometimes even after they left work; one Westclox woman continued to play on the team while friends minded her children. A woman who had been on a Genelco (General Electric) team recalled that during the war, 'with many men away, there was a special bonding. We were not only competitive and had fun playing ball, we became very close. It was a difficult time and we helped each other ... We did everything together, bowled, went to picnics and other people's homes.'[62]

While workers who participated in sports may not have directly shared in the company's goals, these leisure activities arranged by the company still had a positive influence on their attitude towards their employer. In the case of Westclox, some of the women ballplayers remained for years with the company; once established there, the existence of benefit and pension plans encouraged one's decision to remain. Moreover, the team united office and plant workers, who rarely socialized in other companies; and for some women, excellence in sports seemed to provide a source of personal identification that helped overcome the limitations of the glass ceiling encountered at work. As an English historian has shown, sports teams could create a sense of harmony in small communities, even temporarily muting class differences.[63] A similar outcome was accomplished here: women came to identify their enjoyed sport and leisure time with their workplace. As a result, 'the softball solution' aided the company's effort to manufacture a consent in the workplace.

If team sports supplied one glue to cement the Westclox family together, another was the company publication, *Tic Talk*. As Stuart Brandes has argued, company publications were a well-planned strategy to persuade the worker that she had a stake in the company's success, that the company had the economic sense to run the show, and that it cared about its employees' personal goals and family lives.[64] Westclox introduced an all-Canadian version of *Tic Talk* in the late 1930s when Peterborough's General Electric started its own paper, the *GE Works News*. Although GE boasted in the *Financial Post* about its success in 'spreading the news' through its paper,[65] few GE employees seem to have read it, whereas many Westclox employees wrote for *Tic Talk* and remember reading it; even union activists offered to lend me copies they had saved.

Company publications attempted to create support for their own objectives and to socialize workers to a corporate point of view. Basic lessons in the rationality of capitalist economics were standard fare. For instance, concepts such as 'capital formation' were made familiar by comparisons to homes and gardens. 'Capital formation,' lectured *Tic Talk*, 'is just the same as when you set up a garden; you buy the necessary tools, fertilizer ... It is what every company needs to provide jobs for all of us.'[66] In both the GE and Westclox papers the Horatio Alger myth was also a theme, illustrated with examples of office boys becoming managers, while the company's commitment to full employment, its concern for health and safety, and its importance to the community were stressed.

Companies also attempted to create an image of the workplace as a 'family.' In the Westclox paper, family ties were mentioned as a theme underlying plant relationships, thus creating an image of caring and concern rather than discipline and profitability. During the war, sections of Westclox were encouraged to adopt Westclox boys overseas, sending them collective presents. In turn, the soldiers' letters of thanks were reprinted for the employees (largely female) to read. In one, which was addressed 'Dear Mother,' the soldier noted how much the Westclox present meant: 'You know it was like being a kid on Christmas morning ... it was like receiving my first toy.'[67] The reporting also reinforced accepted notions of women's and men's gendered work and family roles; for instance, women's domestic and mothering duties were lauded approvingly, and biographies of longtime employees often confirmed their status as good family men. Especially after the Second World War, the GE paper promoted a picture of woman as homemaker and consumer, her husband as the breadwinner. As Mrs. Consumer, the woman was to buy the GE products that would keep her home comfortable and her husband in work.[68]

Nowhere are distinct gender roles more clearly accented than in the extensive gossip columns sent into these papers, often by worker-writers themselves. In the Westclox paper, the dominant social prejudices of the period were replicated with little or no critical comment, especially in relation to the dating and mating game that preoccupied many writers. Women were supposedly consumed with mating impulses and, once successful, were then 'out of circulation' and no longer a potential conquest for the company's bachelors.[69] With marriage, it was assumed that women would 'now retire to take up another job, homemaking,'[70] while men would continue to work at the plant. Few references to married working women were made, even after they were increasingly employed at the plant. Until the 1960s, one image of the family was made to seem natural and inevitable in these columns as well as in the illustrations: the nuclear, home-owning, mother-at-home, father-at-work family.

According to these articles, the sexes were bound together by dating and mating, and ultimately 'marriage comes highly recommended';[71] but at the same time, men and women were oceans apart in character and ability – an implicit justification for the division of labour. Women were concerned with beauty and appearance, men with technical knowledge and physical strength. Women's known love of shopping was mentioned frequently, while fishing and hunting were clearly pursuits that preoccupied male departments. Cars were a man's joy, but women were 'the plague of our highways.'[71]

Tic Talk's use of graphics and pictures also exhibited the familial theme. Not only were company events profiled, showing workers and managers enjoying leisure hours together, but many employees sent in their own pictures of family and fellow workers. Here the contrast with the *GE Works News* is noteworthy, for while the GE pictures were usually posed ones taken by plant photographers, the Westclox ones were submitted by the workers themselves; they are often off-centre, unfocused, and completely homegrown. It was this lack of professionalism, ironically, that was probably responsible for *Tic Talk*'s success, for a feeling of active participation rather than company manipulation was created by the 'family album' approach. Moreover, although both companies used their publications to promote such things as pension plans, GE used its paper at least once to denounce its union – a mistake that Westclox did not make.

Although the *Tic Talk* gossip columns were occasionally edited, they were also the product of shop floor banter, which many workers clearly enjoyed. One aspect of work culture already noted was women's creation of their own social networks which celebrated life rituals, offered mutual support, and broke down the anonymity of the factory.[73] By integrating these social networks into its company publication, Westclox was able to promote the image of a humane workplace that was concerned with the workers' lives outside the factory. While the company calculated this as a means of securing worker satisfaction and loyalty, the workers participated for other reasons: to alleviate boredom, to engage in daily gossip, to connect with other people, and to make the workplace as livable and human as possible. At the same time, by participating in the company-initiated magazine, which supported management priorities, and by endorsing images of the male breadwinner and the female dependent, of male competence and the female technical scatterbrain, the workers were legitimizing the economic and gender power structures in the factory. While trying to make the workplace livable, they were unconsciously reproducing its gendered hierarchy.

Other workplaces tried similar strategies (such as sports, company papers, and various rituals) to manufacture consent, with varying degrees of success. One of the most difficult plants to unionize, General Electric encouraged sports teams, a cash-for-production suggestions plan, special interest group organizations such as foremen's clubs, and an employee-run mutual benefits society. As at Westclox, family employment characterized the plant. But GE was not as successful in creating a reputation as a superior employer for women, despite its high wages. Not only was employment there assumed to be more physically arduous, but GE was known for a more autocratic authority structure; and for women, this was accompanied by rumours of sexist favouritism in some sections of the plant.

Nor was the Bonnerworth mill, which was a major employer of women, nearly as successful as Westclox in creating a sense of loyalty to the employer, though the women did stress their respect for particular straw bosses. One explanation for this was the company's managerial style. In the interwar period, there was an unpopular general manager, described as a 'cool, English aristocrat type,'[74] and a distant, absentee president, Henry Barrett, who appeared to make decisions with primary concern for the stockholders and with no regard for the community of workers. Even some of the supervisors at the mill felt that 'profits were being skimmed off in Montreal, with nothing left for [employees] here.'[75] There was no company paper to try and persuade employees that the decisions made by management were good ones; nor did management try to create that strong sense of identity, noted at Westclox, of a more educated, 'respectable' group of workers; and no paternal and concerned patriarch like Vernor sat in the cafeteria talking to the employees every day, listening to their grievances, watching who was hired, and carefully educating supervisors in management techniques.

Secondly, material benefits at the mill were few and far between. Not only were wages lower than at GE and Westclox, but there were no paid holidays or bonuses to compensate for this drawback. The company did attempt to create a unified and harmonious social milieu by offering sports, picnics, and other social events, but such activities were less ostentatiously funded by the Bonnerworth than by other companies. In any case, some of these initiatives came after the 1937 strike had already set the tone for tense relations.

As in the case of Westclox, paternalism at the mill offered men and women some possibility of job protection or advancement though, overall, both women and men were limited by the structure and economic health of the factory. The only real opportunity offered to men was advancement to foreman, a position that was still not as well paid as other skilled jobs in the Peterborough area. The benefits of paternalism offered to women were even more limited. Possibilities of job mobility were fairly restricted in the plant; and there was less protection against temporary lay-off, because of the company's tight financial resources (especially in the 1930s), its seasonal production, and the ready availability of young unemployed labour in the immediate community. Given this context, it is not surprising that the Bonnerworth mill could not effectively compete with the image of the Westclox as 'the' place to work in town.

WOMEN INTERPRET AUTHORITY AND ACCOMMODATION

Whatever the success of the Westclox and the Bonnerworth in creating consent through material incentives and paternalist strategies, there was one commonality in the operation of accommodation: consent was a two-way process in which women participated for obvious and concrete as well as more subtle and unconscious reasons.

Workers tried to use welfare plans, financial incentives, and paternalism for their own ends, extracting certain economic and moral obligations from the employer in return for their loyalty. At Westclox, for example, the women and men used the rhetoric of paternalism to obtain their own rewards from the company. The men could benefit from a degree of autonomy on the shop floor, hope of upward mobility, a sense of male privilege and camaraderie, and reinforced identification with the image of the masculine breadwinner. The women could try to use paternalism to make their workplace more humane, less confrontational, and more flexible, to provide mobility within female job ghettos, and to reinforce a sense of dignity secured through their status as moral working women.

Thus, while accommodation and loyalty seemed on the surface to symbolize deference to one's employer, a more negotiated bargain was involved. The paternalist pact meant acquiescence, at least to some extent, to economic inequality and a gendered hierarchy at work. At the same time, a distinct notion of the dignity owed to women and of the respectability of women's aspirations and lives was promoted and defended by the workers.

This negotiation becomes more clearly apparent when one gives close attention to the women's explanations of their acceptance of the employers' rules and outlook. In some cases, the women appear to have internalized their employers' definitions of fair play as their own. At the same time, their oral testimonies reveal the intangible as well as the more obvious benefits they received in return for their accommodation, and also their astute assessment of the meagre alternatives available to them and the barriers preventing their rebellion.

In analysing the form and presentation of women's recollections, it becomes clear that they emphasized their acceptance of the company's right to make the rules rather than their attempts at collective resistance, unconsciously revealing how difficult or futile resistance was perceived to be. This attitude was typified by a Westclox worker's comment: 'My manager said we really didn't know half of what went on' or how the workplace operated, and 'I guess he was right.'[76]

For many women, workplace hierarchy was accepted as an inescapable reality, just as their parents' right to set household curfews was. The women remember accepting stringent regulations, in part because they had little choice and in part because some rules (such as incentive plans) could help them make money, but also because some regulations were perceived as fair and justified. More than one woman for instance, spoke positively of the way that use of the washrooms was regulated: 'I had no complaints about [the Bonnerworth]. They had nice washrooms. They didn't want you frequenting them too much or too long. I've seen them knock on the door to see how long someone was taking. I think the employee was often at fault. It's not fair to go and smoke in the washroom. You are not getting paid for that.'[77] Some workers even punished those they felt were disobeying the rules; work discipline was maintained 'through the lateral displacement of conflict' onto other workers.[78] For instance, in the textile mill, a spinner who thought the woman beside her was spending too much time in the washroom taught her a lesson by 'turning her machine off,' thus completely messing up her work.[79]

The women's decision not to challenge workplace organization and rules also emerged from their assessment of the alternatives and outcomes. When analysing the sexual division of labour and women's relegation to lower-paid jobs, for instance, they assessed the benefits and problems of breaking down job codes. As we have seen, the women feared that making a claim on men's jobs might result in loss of their own job security; they also believed that few women would be able to pass the physical tests of endurance needed for these jobs or be able to handle the antagonism which this process might engender in the male workers. Similarly, when describing their loyalty to their employer or their opposition to unionization, the women carefully assessed the pros and cons of going against their employers' obvious antipathy to unions. The opponents of unionization at the Westclox, for instance, compared their wages with those at other workplaces and worried whether the existing flexible shop-floor relations would continue with a union. Some also feared that they would endanger the benefits of a harmonious workplace – the special privileges they enjoyed, even the praise they received for their work.

One white-collar worker, for example, made a virtue of putting in extra time at Westclox, rejecting the union argument that overtime should be paid. She explained that pride and a sense of contribution to a collective enterprise were her rewards: 'At end of the year, they would give in a piece of paper with the number of hours overtime you put in and you would feel proud that you had given the company that. It was a different line of thinking. You never got paid overtime. Never.'[80] Although this employee emphasized the pride she felt in donating overtime, she described her relationship to her boss in a revealing way: 'He was boss, and when he asked me to do something. I would do it – right away. That was the nature of [life]. You don't argue with the boss.'[81]

The women's deference to authority and their internalization of management's definitions of a good worker must therefore always be placed within the context of the employer's immense power to define work relations, including promotions, transfers, hiring, and firing.

Bound up with women's recognition of the material realities and the existing power structures was a measure of acceptance for the natural placement of men over women and the juxtaposition of jobs as superior/inferior, important/unimportant, which simultaneously encoded male/female in people's minds. The terms, language, and ways of understanding work roles brought with them notions of femininity and masculinity that perpetuated the existing power relations. Women's accommodation to the gendered hierarchy at work was thus deeply entrenched, not only in material practices but also in the very language of work and the meanings of male (authority) and female (passivity) which workers experienced in the family and community, as well as on the job.

This is perhaps most clearly articulated through white-collar jobs, where the position and attributes of a 'good' worker were described in terms that underlined a paternal relationship between female worker and male supervisor. Good work habits of clerical workers – punctuality, preciseness, politeness, pleasant personality – were essentially equated with 'female' attributes. The ideal personal secretary was expected to act as an intermediary and buffer to the outside world; she must be adaptable and should defer to the opinions of the employer; she should be efficient but not too independent; she should be a good listener and should have a nice appearance. The very language used to describe this ideal secretary in fact 'cast her in a female role as office daughter/wife.'[82] As Rosemary Pringle has recently argued, the metaphors of family and sexuality literally inscribe descriptions of power relations between men and women in the office. She notes that managers worry about finding the 'right' woman for the job and inquire into a woman's family situation in doing so; male supervisors 'go into the secretaries' offices unannounced, pronounce on their clothes and appearance ... expect them to do overtime on short notice and ring them at home.' Such infractions on privacy would never be countenanced in the opposite direction, precisely because of the gendered and paternal assumptions involved.[83]

It was not only in white-collar jobs that acceptance of gendered hierarchy and rightful exercise of authority existed. On the shop floor, too, women had a sense of respect for some of the male supervisors, given their greater skill and knowledge, and simply by virtue of their position. Women's acceptance of gender inequality in particular, one could argue, replicated the patriarchal familial relations reflected in the household and the wider culture, which were then reproduced within the workplace. The women's apparent deference extended beyond the youthful worker, an indication that the gendered hierarchy of the workplace, entrenched in material and ideological practice, became an integral part of job definition and worker identity.

Women's consent to management rule was thus expressed as acquiescence or resignation to the inevitability of this authority, even though we may comprehend such 'accommodation' as a strategy to confirm a stable identity, to seek dignity, autonomy, or power. The construction of women workers' identity and consciousness, portrayed in chapter 4, can therefore be linked to the processes of accommodation described here. Like the construction of work culture, the process of accommodation was shaped by material pressures and constraints, as well as by powerful ideological influences that outlined the proper gender roles for women and rationalized both gender and class inequality as an inevitable part of social life.

CONCLUSION

However much consent may have been negotiated or experienced as a two-way street, we must still try to separate out the reasons for its success. The dominance of management was achieved through a whole range of strategies that elicited consent from women workers. A combination of overt material aid and benefits, subtle and less tangible inducements, and obvious opposition to employee resistance all produced consent in the workplace. Personnel strategies, shaped by each employer's methods of creating profit, emphasized the different means of encouraging accommodation; some employers used direct threats of dismissal, while others used the carrot of benefits or the promise of paternal protection. Often, more than one approach was attempted. As Craig Heron points out, welfare capitalist strategies developed by businesses in the post–Second World War period often involved a 'velvet glove' approach, combining both the appearance of mutual gain and more direct opposition to rebellion.[84]

Indeed, the successes of Westclox, as opposed to the failures of the Bonnerworth, can be attributed to its use of more than one astute management strategy, *combined* with local and international economic conditions that were temporarily favourable to its economic health. Westclox's position in the market allowed it to use the lure of material benefits along with the process of discretionary paternalism to secure the long-term loyalty of its workers; though, even here, the workers eventually rejected paternalism for unionization – when the material benefits declined in the early 1950s.

At Westclox and at other small workplaces of five hundred or fewer workers, the process of accommodation was facilitated by the small-town atmosphere of Peterborough. The geographical proximity of worker and manager in some neighbourhoods and churches, the close knowledge of family networks, and the stable social hierarchy bolstered the hegemony operating within the factory, creating the illusion of an organic community in which class and community interest were one and the same. Earlier work has suggested that class-consciousness could be 'reinforced by the community solidarity of small towns with stable, homogeneous and familiar populations.'[85] Similar conditions in Peterborough, however, could also foster an acceptance of class inequality and promote the illusion of a community rather than a class-divided city.

Last but not least, management's hegemony was facilitated by the ideological creation of consent. Recent poststructuralist writing has shied away from the concept of ideology, rejecting its links to economic determination and Marxist class analysis, and sometimes rejecting the epistemological affirmation that any ideas have more inherent 'truth claims' than others.[86] Instead of jettisoning the concept, it may be useful to employ it, in a Gramscian-feminist vein, to consider how consent was 'produced within systems of social relations that shape women's daily lives.'[87]

Ideology – the production and articulation of systems of social meanings, values and belief systems – can simultaneously embody the operation of power relationships: 'Our ways of seeing the world are shaped within the context of ideas, symbols and representations produced within structures shaped by those with the most economic and social power.'[88] These power relations help sustain a broader cultural and intellectual hegemony, in which ideology works to create meanings of class and gender, legitimizing, rationalizing, or naturalizing the existing design of material and social organization, the status quo of both economic and gender power.[89]

Ideology is also reinforced in lived social practices, so much so that it appears to be 'common sense' and 'natural,' even while it is mystifying existing power relations. Accepted social norms of both gender and economic hierarchy encompassed women's lives; they were 'subtly diffused through their habitual practices, interwoven with the culture in which they lived, and inscribed on the texture of their experiences from home to work to home again.'[90] This was not a conscious managerial strategy as much as the inevitable product of a society that was already fundamentally based on sexual difference and inequality, not only in the workplace but also in the family and the wider community.

This emphasis on hegemony allows us to understand the subtle, dominating pressure to accept existing gender and economic hierarchies, and women's apparently consensual acquiesce to inequality in the workplace. Ideas that women were suited for certain jobs, had less claim to good wages, and had to accept the rules of the game set by the employer were taken for granted as inevitable 'common sense' conceptions of women's material and social world; they were so strongly imprinted in language, communication, and daily knowledge that they became linked to one's very subjective identity, internalized as one's own. Yet, tragically, these assumptions also explained and made 'natural' relations of female subordination.

Still, as the women's recollections and rationales for consent powerfully remind us, ideologies are not simply 'bad dreams of the social structure.'[91] They also work as forces actively organizing people's lives in ways that seem to make some sense. While the women at Westclox accepted the model of respectable femininity promoted by the company, they had valid and worthwhile reasons for buying into this view, both in terms of material security and in terms of a personal sense of dignity and respect.

Moreover, it is crucial to remember that women's common-sense view of the world did not simply include an acceptance of female subordination. Ideology can also be incoherent and fragmented, assuming a number of perspectives, not simply consensual ones but also contradictory and even oppositional ones. The dominant assumptions about gender and class can also be precarious, with hegemonic understandings potentially challenged or altered. Thus, while women accepted a measure of hierarchy in the workplace as inevitable, they were willing to resist when conditions made that hierarchy unbearable or unacceptable.

At Westclox, for instance, despite a long history of paternalism, the women proved ready to challenge these patriarchal relations when they felt aggrieved or misused. Indeed, the language of respect and mutual obligation which had long justified paternalism could be appropriated, used as a rationale for women's rebellion against injustice. When the company began to fall short of its promises to offer good benefits and wages in the city, the women joined a successful movement to unionize in 1952. And much later, when the company tried to deal with falling profits by rolling back the women's wage rates, they protested. Alarmed that the (male-dominated) union was apparently wavering on this issue, a female union member wrote an indignant letter, warning the union leadership that women workers were very upset over reported 'secret negotiations' between the male management and male union leaders. She indicated that women at the plant did not want to be 'sold out' in such negotiations.[92] The paternalist bargain and the process of accommodation thus clearly had its limits. This example is only one of many instances of women's opposition to existing power structures in the workplace. We need to turn now to the flip side of the coin of accommodation: women's resistance.

7

Resistance and Unionization

Harriet was an extremely efficient and valued white-collar worker at Westclox, but after seven years on the same job, and knowing that there were 'no promotions' for women, she was becoming bored. Her solution, she remembered, was to leave her job just after the war and to travel, taking the risk that she would find similar work when she returned. Kitty, on the other hand, who worked at General Electric at precisely the same time, responded to dissatisfaction with her conditions of work by becoming active in the newly organized United Electrical Workers Union.

Kitty's dissatisfaction found an immediate avenue for expression in an existing militant union that claimed to speak for women. By contrast, Harriet knew that she had few legitimate avenues through which to voice her dissatisfaction, so she took a private, individual solution. We are accustomed to seeing Kitty's response as a form of protest, while Harriet's solution would not be characterized as such. Both women's actions, however, constitute forms of resistance – the process of questioning, challenging, or rejecting one's status or conditions at work.

Women's workplace resistance encompassed a broad spectrum of thoughts, spontaneous actions, and well-planned protests. The tactics they selected were shaped by the social and economic context and by the immediate alternatives and possibilities available. Like Harriet, many working women responded to boredom or dislike of their jobs by quitting and moving on to other employment. Others tried to alter unpleasant conditions by individually persuading a superior to change the workplace routine or by drawing on the collective traditions and gendered solidarities of work culture to alter working conditions informally – for example, by creating a 'stint,' by carving out more time for workplace celebrations, or by opposing the authoritarian style of a manager. All these practices can be interpreted as resistance to workplace rules, even though some may have been simultaneously intertwined with accommodation.

A small minority of women also engaged in collective organized protest and unionization, though even fewer became union leaders. Although such organized resistance was not a daily staple of life for all women workers, it occupies a central place in working-class history, in part, admittedly, because historical records are more plentiful for women involved in the labour movement and in walkouts and strikes. The ideological sympathies of labour historians have also shaped the research agenda. Critical of the inequalities inherent in capitalist organization of labour, we have been eager to probe its vulnerabilities.

It is not simply historians' ideological proclivities, however, that have led to an emphasis on resistance. The study of women's protests also highlights the social agenda and cultural values that women brought to work with them and reshaped on the job. Whether they engaged in the spontaneous washroom protest described below or in a protracted public strike, the women rebelling exhibited their own distinct vision of good conditions and wages, and their definitions of personal dignity. By exploring resistance, we can also get a better understanding of the political, social, and economic conditions that led women to oppose, in a sustained manner, their working conditions and their status in the workplace, and the ways in which they drew on dominant as well as more subversive discourses to justify this opposition. Moreover, a focus on the organized labour movement reflects the recognition that unions were indeed an important arena in which women could express their dissatisfactions with work, could organize with other workers, and could try to change the workplace.

Finally, resistance may reveal gender as well as class conflict. Unions and labour disputes have historically become arenas of gender conflict, mediation, and resolution, even at the same time as they reflected and promoted class solidarity. By examining the daily workings of trade unions and the evolution of walkouts and strikes, the different and sometimes contesting understandings of men's and women's work and family lives become apparent.

While recognizing that women's resistance and accommodation were intertwined, and also that women's resistance was often invisible, individual, and informal, this chapter will concentrate on women's organized resistance and on their involvement with the trade union movement. After delineating some brief examples of women's informal resistance and the history of their connection to the union movement in Peterborough, I want to use two detailed illustrations – women's role in the 1937 textile strike and women's later involvement in the United Electrical Workers at General Electric – as a means of analysing how, when, and why women resisted, what the barriers to their protests were, and what could be accomplished and lost through collective organization. The women's own interpretations of their participation in collective protest are especially important in this regard. Although the women concerned remember the strike of 1937 differently, these differences reveal the dynamics of class and gender relations, the dominant ideologies, and the women's own attempts to negotiate the all too meagre array of choices in their working lives.

PLAYING CARDS IN THE WASHROOM AND OTHER INFORMAL PROTESTS

Peterborough working women were not without grievances. An *Examiner* reporter was surprised to find that the 'shop girls' he interviewed had a long list of complaints about their work, ranging from 'unfeeling customers' to difficult working conditions.[1] In a similar vein, textile workers resented the unfair distribution of good yarn to spin; electrical workers complained about heat and close air in the factory; and white-collar workers objected to condescending managers. Yet few women had the means, energy, or facilities to organize collectively to alleviate these problems.

Many women dealt with grievances individually like the woman who quietly left her job because her boss was sexually harassing her. 'Voting with one's feet' had long been a strategy of women workers for dealing with unpleasant bosses.[2] Walking the thin line between protecting oneself and opposing the boss was often the dilemma women faced when they criticized their workplace. A secretary who worked in the office of a local factory recalled that she was once instructed by her boss to go to the washroom and find out 'who was playing cards,' since the office women, denied a coffee break, simply rebelled by taking their own break time in the washroom. Her solution was to enter the washroom with her eyes shut, telling the women to 'leave by the time I was out of the cubicle.' She then could report to her boss that she 'didn't see anyone,' but she added, 'I don't expect to be a spy for you.'[3]

Women also used informal though more visible protests to change the workplace. Before the Second World War, spontaneous protest was the most likely form of rebellion, for women rarely had formal structures, either unions or grievance committees, to utilize. In some cases, the women could join in the petitions of others. At Quaker Oats, for instance, the female office workers signed a silent protest asking for 'fair treatment and goodly increases' in salaries in order to deal with the inflation of the years following the First World War. Pointing to the substantial increases already given to plant workers, the office workers demanded similar treatment, signing their petition with a circle of names to avoid any recrimination against the ringleaders.[4]

In a more militant protest, women at one of the city's textile mills, the Brinton Carpet factory, walked out in an informal protest in the 1930s. These textile workers had had their wages cut during the early years of the Depression with the promise that the wage level would be restored when times improved. By 1937, impatient with unfulfilled promises, they asked that the 25 per cent cut from their pay be terminated. When the employer refused, twenty-three girls from the setting department walked out, and they were later joined by the more skilled and powerful male weavers, who already made twice the wages of the girls. In response, the company offered a 10 per cent increase, and workers returned to their jobs.[5]

Similarly, in 1942, women at the newly established Genelco, a subsidiary of Canadian General Electric (CGE) that had been established to produce for the war effort, initiated a slowdown and brief walkout when recruiters appeared from a Malton factory trying to entice women workers away with the promise of Toronto wages, which were considerably better than Peterborough ones. In order to highlight the inequity of their wages, the women hired to make gun carriages 'sat down' on the job, and the men followed suit. After a meeting with company officials, the women agreed to return to work, pending a review of their piecework rates.[6]

While informal resistance was a significant weapon for non-unionized women, there is evidence that once women had the protection of a union behind them, they became even more inclined to create informal and innovative protests – undoubtedly because they knew they had some protection against lay-off. More than one woman who had worked at the unionized CGE recalled that in the postwar period women engaged in planned but not necessarily union-inspired protest. For instance, Kitty, a union activist, devised a scheme in her section that drew on women's sense of humour and their feminine culture while also making a point about the cynicism of management. The problem had begun when a government safety inspector came in and the foremen ran ahead of him, telling the women winding coils for motors to 'clean up their benches' and letting them go on the (easier) day rate while they did so. The only recommendation the inspector made, however, was for the women to wear hats. The women hated wearing the headgear, and with good reason: 'We weren't working on any machines that could have possibly caught our hair.' The demand, along with the company's hypocrisy over the clean up, angered the women. So Kitty organized her work group, and the next day they all appeared with elaborate hats covered with fruit, feathers, and flowers. The foreman gave in and said, 'Okay, okay, I know who the instigator is here ... just take them off.'[7] By adroitly drawing on and then inverting traditional images of femininity, the women enhanced their own sense of solidarity and power in the workplace; they achieved their goal of reversing the hat rule, but without appearing to use unacceptably 'masculine' or 'aggressive' tactics.

Similarly, another CGE worker remembers how some women in her area who worked with poisonous epoxy resented an effort to speed up their work by having them clean equipment with 'faster varsol-based cleaner' rather than with water as usual. They solved the problem by continually going to the nurse's station to have their blood pressure taken, until the company reneged and altered the work process.[8] Women also drew on the informal codes and networks associated with work culture to resist unwanted rules. As one CGE worker remembers, she and the other women saw it as an invasive affront when an overbearing supervisor started watching and timing their trips to the washroom. As a solution, they got together and collectively warned him that they would respond by embarrassing him in a very public manner if his harassment did not stop.[9]

These examples, which are only the tip of the iceberg, offer a glimpse of women's informal attempts to alter the workplace. In order to secure lasting and ongoing change, however, they needed unions as a safeguard. But until the late 1930s, women were almost entirely invisible in the Peterborough labour movement.

WOMEN IN THE EARLY UNION MOVEMENT, 1919-1939

The small number of unionized women in Peterborough was related not only to the city's small size but also to the structure and membership of the local unions and to the fortunes of labour politics in Peterborough. By the time of the First World War, some women at the large General Electric plant had established their own local of the International Brotherhood of Electrical Workers (IBEW), probably encouraged by the men's IBEW local in the plant. In the Labour Day parade of 1919, these women rode proudly on decorated automobiles, along with their union brothers.[10] By 1921, however, the women's local had disappeared from view, and until the textile revolts in the 1930s, women remained largely excluded from the local unions.

In the first two decades of the century, the Peterborough labour movement was characterized by an overwhelming dominance of craft unions, especially in areas such as transportation and construction. Unions in manufacturing, the life blood of the city, were few and far between. Moreover, in many trades there was great fluidity in union membership, with members leaving to become contractors and small businessmen themselves. This pattern further reduced the vigour of the local labour movement.[11] Finally, hurt by the unemployment and depression following the First World War, as well as by management's attempts to create an open shop, the local labour movement went into a tailspin in the 1920s from which it did not recover until the Second World War. Whereas in 1920 the local labour council had boasted twenty-eight affiliated unions, by 1937 it was listing only eighteen, and by the late 1930s, it was not even making its regular report.[12]

Labour's doldrums were in part the result of failed confrontations with management. In 1920 the IBEW, along with one of the strongest unions at General Electric, the International Association of Machinists, was defeated in a summer strike, and some union members were subsequently blacklisted after strikebreakers had taken their places. The company blithely ignored the recommendations of a conciliation board, successfully divided the two unions involved, and ultimately weakened union prospects in the plant for years to come. The largest workplace in Peterborough and the leader in local industrial relations, GE reaffirmed its commitment to the open shop, setting the example for the entire city.[13] The lessons were not lost on other workers. Indeed, GE's immense power exhibited through the strike became a central part of labour lore in the city.

At the same time, unionists in the early 1920s became discouraged by the failure of the political labour party that had been formed in the city. Shortly after the First World War, inspired in part by national trends, an Independent Labour Party was organized in Peterborough. It managed to elect city aldermen after the ward system was temporarily abolished,[14] and in 1920 it also elected a provincial MPP, Thomas Tooms. Labour's euphoria with its newfound power, however, was short lived. Dissension between the Trades and Labor Council and the elected labour aldermen increased, particularly when the latter put what they saw as 'the interests of the community' ahead of a labour platform.[15] In the next civic election the local paper pressured against bloc labour voting, but labour itself was in conflict: some trade unionists broke ranks with the Trades and Labor Council, including those who supported a lawyer and Liberal reform alderman, G.N. Gordon.

Always the preserve of skilled craftsmen, especially the minority of British immigrants in the city, the Independent Labour Party foundered on the basis of its limited clientele and in confrontation with small-town paternalism and the political allure of traditional Liberal-Labour alliances. As Suzanne Morton argues, class voting and working-class consciousness, though part of the city's history, could be fractured and co-opted at particular periods in time.

Not only was the organized labour movement struggling with its own base and identity, but there were few signs that women were encouraged to become involved in this struggle. On the very rare occasions that local unions discussed women workers, they usually reaffirmed a protective approach, such as urging a limitation on women's hours of work.[16] Despite the Independent Labour Party's efforts to import a speaker on women's rights, women's names are noticeably absent from both the party and the labour council – in contrast to women's active interest in other cities.[17] Less than ten years later, however, women became the focus of one of Peterborough's most violent and polarizing labour disputes, the 1937 Dominion Woollens strike.

WOMEN ON THE PICKET LINE: THE DOMINION WOOLLENS STRIKE OF 1937

To some observers, the 1937 textile strike emerged out of the blue, a violent interruption in an otherwise peaceful city, which prided itself on harmonious community relations. Yet the seeds of discontent had clearly been growing for some time, and the impetus to organize Dominion Woollens' two mills, the Auburn and the Bonnerworth, was part of a larger movement of industrial unionism that was sweeping Ontario. The United Textile Workers of America, the fledging union of the Congress of Industrial Relations (CIO), had already made forays into Peterborough in the spring of 1937, responding to the walkout of Brinton Carpet workers, and it had signed up some of the (largely) male workforce in the Auburn weaving mill, which had staged a brief protest over piecework rates in 1936.

By 1937, many textile workers were becoming increasingly angry over Depression conditions and wages. All across Canada, textile wages had fallen below the average manufacturing wage, a situation that meant bare survival or the need to have more than one earner in the family. This was also the situation in the Peterborough mills, with more than one family earner being necessary in order to create a livable family economy; the mills were the primary local industrial employer of boys and girls under sixteen.

Although the Royal Commission on the Textile Industry, which reported in 1937, claimed that wages might average 20 cents an hour for women, or about $11.74 a week, the Dominion Woollens wage sheets tell a more depressing story.[18] In 1934 women working at the Bonnerworth mill were earning as little as $11 a week, and the highest wage most women could receive was about 20 cents an hour for a fifty-hour week.[19] The women interviewed uniformly remember a learning rate of 12.5 and 13 cents an hour in the early 1930s, and they said that piecework made it difficult to earn anything over $11 a week. Indeed, Dominion Woollens workers lost ground over the 1930s, with a slight decline in their wages and buying power, especially after the cost of living increased slightly later in the decade.[20]

Even before the strike, letters of complaint to the provincial minister of labour pointed to the 'long hours the girls worked' and the 'starvation wages' paid to the Auburn men. But as the minister pointed out in his replies, the mill was working within the bounds of the minimum wage laws, which sanctioned a fifty-hour week as well as lower wage levels for 'small towns' such as Peterborough.[21]

While the textile industry, including Dominion Woollens, was fond of parading the lower British wage rates as justification for higher tariffs and their own low wage rates, they also admitted privately that their wage bill was cut to the bone as a result of the Depression. Explaining the company's failure to achieve economies in the early 1930s, its president, Henry Barrett, wrote to stockholder O.A. Dawson that 'in the woollen and worsted branch of the textile industry, wages never rose to a very high level, even in the most prosperous times, and consequently the economies which can be effected in other industries by wage reductions cannot be effected in our case.'[22]

In contrast to some other Peterborough employers, Dominion Woollens had been able to maintain a fairly stable workforce through the Depression, despite an aborted attempt to close the Auburn mill in 1930.[23] At the same time, the company proved to be a disappointment to investors, who had hoped to see it corner the market and produce substantial profits after a 1928 merger made it the largest woollen producer in Canada. The company's financial woes, according to a confidential Royal Bank assessment, came not so much from the Depression as from 'bad management' in the Auburn mill, some imprudent buying of wool (which had spin-off effects for the next years), and dated machinery that needed replacing. In response to these criticisms, the company made some management changes and installed new automatic looms at the Auburn, and this brought slight financial improvement and profits for 1936 and 1937. The bank and the company both recognized, however, that the most profitable part of the overall operation was always the Bonnerworth mill, the main site of the company's female workforce.[24]

The textile workers' resentment, then, emerged from their long experience of underemployment and stagnating wages. This particularly grated, because when the company's fortunes seemed to improve in the late thirties, workers' salaries did not. Management style in the Peterborough mills was also problematic. President Henry Barrett ruled his woollen empire from far-off Toronto and was seen as a robber baron who was out of touch with local concerns. Even the local foremen were suspicious that the company was milking the profits of the Bonnerworth mill for the larger Montreal textile empire of O.A. Dawson, a major shareholder.[25] Meanwhile, the Auburn workers complained of unfair supervision, citing a foreman who gave the best jobs to those who brought him beer on the weekends,[26] the authoritarian style of certain managers brought in from the United States, and especially the unfair distribution of piecework. Similarly, Bonnerworth women, though they often respected their foremen, resented rules that denied them regular breaks yet let them sometimes stand idle with no piecework and therefore no pay.

By the spring of 1937, United Textile Workers (UTWA) members had signed up the majority of their fellow Auburn workers, and on 29 June, 85 per cent of that mill – some three hundred workers – went on strike demanding union recognition, wage increases, and better distribution of piecework. The Bonnerworth women were tacked on to the Auburn agenda two days after the strike began. A UTWA organizer, Alex Welch, arrived on the scene almost immediately from Toronto, but it was a young Auburn weaver, Elmer Hickey, who decided to devote himself to organizing the Bonnerworth 'girls.' Few of the Bonnerworth women had any idea of the union's presence until they went to work on Thursday, 2 July, and found a picket line set up and a man with a megaphone at the gate. Some women went inside and discovered that their straw bosses were secretly sympathetic: 'I just came back to work from the July 1st holiday and found a strike ... and my straw boss said, "You'd better get out there, there's a strike on."'[27]

From the very beginning of the strike right through to its aftermath the next year, the agenda of the strikers was a gendered one, with internal, unrecognized contradictions. Male workers at the Auburn mill initiated unionization and were the focus of many of the union's arguments for better pay, yet women strikers at the Bonnerworth mill were at the centre of strike publicity and tactics. Women strikers controlled access to the most profitable section of the company, though they were never seen as the most important 'breadwinners' in the strike. And while women were often the most militant picketers, they were an afterthought in the union's initial strategies. Tragically, the failure of the union to draw women into its orbit may have been one reason why the union was unable to survive in the years to come.

In the early days of the strike, most women workers immediately identified with the demand for higher wages; they were well aware of their status at the bottom of the local manufacturing ladder. On the other hand, those who were extremely young at the time sometimes downplayed the seriousness of the event: 'We kids didn't know what the strike was about ... for some of us it was a heyday for the summer; we had street dances and went downtown [for tag days].'[28] Women were more likely to support the strike if they were long-term employees or if they had union supporters in the family, though some fathers who endorsed craft unions were nevertheless not sympathetic to their daughters' involvement in the strike. The young women (most of whom lived at home) whose parents were suspicious of or opposed to the strike were in the most difficult situation. As one who crossed the picket line remembers, her parents told her not to get involved and 'just to mind her own business.'[29] Another young worker, whose father owned a small store, was forbidden by him to participate, and when her workmates approached his store to ask for strike aid, he thundered, 'Wouldn't you rather be in there, collecting your pay cheque?' 'No,' one of the women replied quietly, and they left.[30]

In order to help organize the women, the union astutely asked Edith Frizelle, a married woman with children, to join the UTWA committee.

Frizelle had worked at the Bonnerworth for quite some time and was known as someone who was not afraid to talk back. She came from a large working-class family, many of whose members had been employed at the mill at some time. As an elder child, she had felt she had to go out to work quite early, yet she had become determined to create a better life for herself and her children.[31] Later, younger women from other departments, such as Lucy Ronco, part of a family team in the mill, were added to the committee, though women remained a minority on the strike committee. Considering how quickly executed the strike was, the extent of female support was remarkable. The women soon developed a list of demands relevant to their Bonnerworth conditions. Publicly, though, their defence of the strike tactic sometimes downplayed their own problems and stressed the inability of male workers to support their families. As Frizelle argued, support for the strike emerged because the company paid men with wives and children to support a mere 25 cents an hour. 'How could you [support] your family on that? It would buy a loaf of bread, but it wouldn't put butter on it.'[32]

Within a few days, the tone of the strike was established. On Friday, while trying to block trucks from entering the Auburn, men were clubbed by local police and later treated for injuries. In the days to come, mass picketing, police protection for strikebreakers, and violence on the picket line all became part of the pattern. Picketing was focused especially on the Bonnerworth mill, where local and Toronto newspapers reported the girls' vehement opposition to strikebreakers in terms that stressed their youthful excitability or feminine hysteria. As Joy Parr has argued for a later textile strike, the police and the press cast the men and women in roles that reaffirmed notions of innate gender differences.[33] The Peterborough police pronounced the male strikers cowards who pushed women into the front of the picket line, while the mayor claimed that the girls caused all the trouble because 'they are more excitable and they get the men excited by yelling.' In the mainstream press, the picketing young women were portrayed as cat fighters, clawing, screeching, and screaming, while the men were seen as the radicals and ringleaders behind the union.[34] Although left-wing papers sometimes portrayed the women as young and vulnerable, and in need of protection from exploitation and picket-line violence, they also contradicted this view by communicating examples of women's assertive militancy. Not surprisingly, the strike began to take on the aura of street theatre. People who did not work at the mill went to watch, and in one case, a spectator was hit by a police billy. 'Everybody would gather near the hill, and the streets would be lined,' recalls an onlooker, 'Then, as soon as the workers would come out, the strikers would get in there and the "nice" policemen would bang them up.'[35]

The strikers secured a good deal of community support. They astutely denied any connection to the communist, or radical causes that sometimes were associated with the CIO, and reaffirmed their 'loyalty to King and Council' as well as reiterating that their main desire was to bring up their families decently with a living wage.[36] The *Examiner* editorials suggested that the industry should heed its workers, who were entitled to fair wages;[37] and the local Liberal lawyer and alderman, G.N. Gordon, spearheaded the formation of a relief committee, which was endorsed by aldermen and church leaders, and which raised money through tag days and collected hundreds of dollars in groceries from local merchants. Gordon, a radical Liberal who served one term as an MP, was an outspoken populist who often tried to speak for the working man. While something of a maverick in the midst of the local Tory compact, his public denunciations of the company reflected the suspicions of other middle-class citizens that Dominion Woollens was an irresponsible corporate body, guilty of stock watering, and that it was now trying to starve out its workers.[38] Gordon was particularly worried that as a result of the company's failure to pay a decent wage, local men would be forced onto relief, thus burdening the civic government.[39]

Perhaps as a result of this community pressure, the company agreed to meet with some workers, though only after union organizer Welch was removed from the negotiating committee. A company proposal, made at a meeting in Peterborough on 15 July, agreed to some of the non-wage demands, such as eliminating the grading of work, paying the pieceworkers during idle time, allowing rest periods for female workers, and exhibiting no discrimination against union members. However, it offered no raise in wages, except to the more skilled male weavers (who the company perhaps thought could be bought off). The company claimed it was unable to pay the wider increases demanded, and it threatened to close the Auburn plant. The workers, including the weavers, continued their strike.

By 27 July, a second effort at negotiation, which included provincial mediator Louis Fine and labour lawyer J.L. Cohen, acting for the strikers, also failed. The strikers were becoming increasingly well organized, cognizant of the moral support of nearby unions such as Oshawa's United Auto Workers, and it was especially encouraged by the recent decision of the Cornwall textile workers to strike as well. At a mass meeting in the East City town hall, they shouted down an offer that raised wages only very marginally.[40]

At this critical point, G.N. Gordon assumed a more prominent role in the strike, bypassing the union and wiring the Ontario premier, Mitchell Hepburn, urging him to intervene by setting legal minimum wages for men and women in the industry through the newly formed Ontario Industry and Labour Board. Other local leaders, including the mayor, began to push for a similar resolution. The company finally agreed to be bound by the findings of the board, but it insisted that it would reopen the mills without any further negotiations. While the local politicians supported the company's initiative, the strikers were not even given time to meet with their union to vote on a decision before the provincial police were brought in.

In the aftermath of this company manoeuvre, some of the worst violence occurred. The local police, aided by the Ontario Provincial Police – nicknamed 'Hepburn's Hussars' by the workers – attempted to open up the Bonnerworth mill using clubs and tear gas. The mayor, trying to assist in the reopening of the mill, became the centre of a riot, and when the strikebreakers advanced, chaos ensued, with fist fights, pepper throwing, and, finally, tear gas. Three women and twelve men were arrested. As one of those three women, Dorothy remembers that the police simply grabbed whoever was in the way:

I remember being on picket line. That's all I was doing. I was really surprised how wild [the police] were ... The chief of police came and grabbed me from behind with fingernails in my neck – you could see the marks. I was trying to kick out at him: I couldn't figure out why he was picking on me. He shoved me under the gate ... By that time I was crying and ... started to run out ... Another girl [Ethel Eason] came to rescue me from Chief Newall, and they threw her in [to the paddywagon] too. They made us go to city jail and we had 'a bit of a trial'... The chief of police charged me with throwing pepper in his face, and I never even *had* any pepper!

Dorothy recalls that her family later teased her about her assault on the chief for she was 'a mere 110 pounds.' She joked that her friends and family then developed mocking nicknames such as 'public enemy number one' and 'the jailbird' to describe her.[41]

Angered even more by this brutal treatment, the strikers voted to reject Hepburn's offer on 10 August. However, the company's agreement to accept the Industry and Labour Board's findings and the loss of community support in the aftermath of heightened violence, marked a turning point for the strikers. Gordon claimed publicly that the rank and file of the strikers would have been glad to go back to work if they had known of the premier's undertaking, 'but these leaders do not want the strike settled. I am through with them.'[42]

More than one hundred employees trickled back to work, and by 15 August the strikers had agreed to another meeting at Queen's Park with Hepburn and Paddy Draper of the Trades and Labor Congress. An agreement was reached, but it was essentially the same one proposed in July by the company, with the addition of a commitment to abide by the Industry and Labour Board's recommendations. The strikers were persuaded by the UTWA, by Cohen, and by their leaders to accept the agreement, but they knew they were taking a risk in hoping that government intervention would bring them higher wages. Ominously, union recognition and collective bargaining rights were never part of the agreement.

Nor did conflict end with the agreement. When they returned to work, the Auburn workers found some of their jobs filled by strikebreakers and previous piecework grievances unsolved. They walked out again. Barrett came to Peterborough to solve the crisis, but although he agreed to rehire the men, he was furious when they offered a show of hands to indicate their union allegiance. He pounded his fist on the table, part of his confrontational style, threatening that 'anyone who goes over the line of discipline in our mills is subject to discharge.'[43]

The Bonnerworth workers also found new problems. When a young spinner who returned was told there was no work for her, even though a strikebreaker was still running her machine, she went straight to Edith Frizelle, who replied 'Well, we'll see about that!' With Frizelle's help, the young woman got her job back.[44] In September, Elmer Hickey wrote to Cohen, asking if he could intercede again, since the women had found that conditions had not improved; indeed, the pace of work had been increased.[45] The workers attempted to sustain the union through an elected grievance committee, many of whose members had been strike supporters, but in both workplaces the union had problems. A woman who was elected steward did not want to be involved after the strike. As she recalled, 'I was elected steward at a meeting. I nearly flipped because I wasn't even at the meeting. I didn't go to any meetings.'[46] The elected grievance committee at the Auburn mill complained that it was unable to solve contentious issues such as unfair distribution of piecework. Moreover, it also had to compete with a newly formed company union.

In fact, when the Industry and Labour Board hearings about wage rates opened in Peterborough in the fall, much of the testimony was taken up with charges by the Auburn union men that the company was intimidating their members, pressuring them to join the company union. The board was not sympathetic, pointing out that it was the supervisors and not the company who were organizing the union – a moot distinction in the eyes of the unionists. When the board reported in January of 1938, calling for slightly increased wages of $16.00 minimum for men and $12.50 for women, the strikers rejected these as minimal increases that could be subverted through the piecework system or shorter hours. The women interviewed agree completely on this point: 'Before the strike I had two machines, when I went back, I had four ... Wages were a bit better, but working conditions were tougher.'[47]

Some strike leaders were eventually fired, supposedly because, as Hickey was told, his production level was unsatisfactory; and when the new minimum wage was announced, some men were replaced by lower-paid youths, despite complaints from the city relief committee that the company was dumping its employees on the local relief rolls. Finally, the Auburn mill was closed entirely in 1938, causing severe problems for the city's relief bill. By the end of the decade, there was no longer a viable textile union in the city's large mills, and the number of unionized workers in the city had returned to that of its lowest point in the Depression.

One of the most important legacies of the strike was the subsequent difficulty of Auburn men to find jobs. Strike leader Mike English finally gave up and headed for Alberta to escape his local notoriety. Elmer Hickey found a job at Outboard, but as his son remembers, 'within two hours he was identified [as a strike leader] and he was out. He was blacklisted.'[48] In order to support the family he had started with the fellow striker he had married (the former Ethel Eason), Hickey eventually joined the army. This persecution made an important impression for years to come, not only on the men but on their wives, sisters, and daughters.

This abbreviated description of the strike reveals a story involving a growing sense of entitlement on the part of textile workers, heightened class-consciousness on the part of both men and women, immense structural barriers to labour organizing, and, ultimately, the defeat of the union. Yet the strike needs to be analysed in three other aspects, examining what it reveals about class relations in this small community, what gender scripts were being played out within it, and how the women themselves interpreted and understood these class and gender relations.

CLASS RELATIONS AND GENDER SCRIPTS

Paternalism, while never very successful as a personnel strategy at Dominion Woollens, was an important theme underlying the larger class and community relations shaping this strike. Members of the local political élite, both Liberal and Conservative, provided some support early in the strike, for the well-known difficulties of the strikers' working conditions and their absentee, uncaring employer made them suitable objects of sympathy. Other community leaders, such as the Rev. Barr of the Presbyterian Church and Dean O'Sullivan of St Peter's Cathedral, also offered their aid on the relief committee, as did a local CCF leader, Dr Lorna Cotton Thomas.

By August, however, the support of political and church leaders was waning, and it was not simply the question of violence that changed people's minds. Rather, the increasing threat of a broadly based working-class militancy and the spectre of widespread unionization were creating tremendous uneasiness. Protecting the right of men to a breadwinner's wage and shielding girls against undue exploitation by a rapacious employer were acceptable aims; encouraging the spread of the CIO was not.

G.N. Gordon was a bellwether of this growing fear. While undoubtedly motivated by a sincere aversion to the economic exploitation of the workers, he was also concerned with maintaining a traditional balance of deference in the community. He expressed anger that the company might force men onto the relief rolls, thus overburdening the local taxpayer, and also that the company had 'kept labour in turmoil for the last ten years and ... created an uneasy labour situation, where there should be harmony.'[49] By August, he was being even more blunt, declaring that he distrusted the strike leaders and warning that Dominion Woollens had created a class-consciousness that was 'likely to affect the management of other companies in this city, where working conditions are good, and unless these labour unions are headed by men and women of good judgement and sense, we are likely to have labour conditions which will put factories in a continuous turmoil.'[50]

Gordon's fears were well founded. As more and more speakers appeared at the strikers' meetings, they indicated that the union agenda went far wider than Dominion Woollens. The United Auto Workers organizers from Oshawa, other UTWA leaders, and also Communist Party organizers who appeared to support the strike made it clear that the agenda was the organization of all industrial workers in Peterborough.[51]

Other employers were decidedly afraid. As an office worker from Outboard Marine remembers, encouraged by the Bonnerworth example, the employees began to talk about using a strike to get higher wages. Manager Hugh Campbell, however, made it clear that he would close the company before he accepted a union. Fearing for their jobs, and also because 'they respected Mr Campbell,' the employees rapidly dropped all talk of a union.[52] As well as employers, other community notables began to oppose the union. Bill Hickey remembers his mother Ethel Eason talking about the interference of the Roman Catholic Church: 'They got the strike leaders together and told them that this had gone too far and it had to stop.'[53]

A letter to the local paper by a former textile worker who supported CIO unions indicated that both workers and employers saw the radical potential of union success in this strike: 'I work in a south end factory, there is a craft union there it works for the skilled men. Now most of us in the factory are unskilled. This skilled body of men ... don't even let the unskilled men to join them. They enjoy regular hours, while we, and the girls have worked 12 to 13 hours a day, and even the odd Sunday. Now you see the value to organize the industry as a whole and everyone shares in the results.'[54]

Organizing the industry as a whole was precisely the agenda that local employers feared; and encouraging socialist propaganda like that distributed at union meetings was precisely what church leaders opposed. Ironically, most strikers were unaware of or unconcerned with the political infighting between the local CCFers and communists within the union and of Welch's rumoured connection to the Communist Party. These connections, however, were of concern to community politicians and church leaders, who saw them as a threat to the 'harmony' of the existing paternalistic class relations – in reality, an uneasy alliance constructed on the edifice of unequal economic and social relations.

Inequity also characterized the gender relations in both the strike and the union. From the very beginning of the strike, men and women were perceived as having different roles, both as workers and as strikers. The initial impetus to organize the Auburn mill focused on its largely male workforce and on the perception that the weavers in particular had a skill that could be used as a bargaining tool. The right of these men to a decent wage to support their families was also central to union organizers, particularly in their public pronouncements.

This agenda became even more apparent during the post-strike Industry and Labour Board hearings, which were intended to ascertain what a decent minimum wage would be, 'based on the cost of living, [and] the ability of the industry to pay.'[55] Acting for the UTWA, Cohen noted that women, primarily in the mending department at the Auburn, were not earning the minimum wage because of the fixing of piecework, but that they were so intimidated after the strike 'being in the wrong with their [supervisor] Miss Pattison that they wouldn't come to testify.'[56]

Still, far more attention was focused on the average wages for Auburn men. Presenting his evidence to the board, Cohen continually referred to the men, noting their marital status and sometimes the number of children they were supporting: 'Warp Room: 2 [men] with 17 and 7 years experience – [paid] $18.00 – one married and one with 5 children.' In this critique of the wage rates, he asked: What are people expected to live on, 'let alone maintain and bring up families or dependents?'[57]

Strickland, the local lawyer acting for the company union, was also concerned with the men's marital status in his presentation. Asked what he thought the minimum wage for men should be, he replied that they should get twelve dollars a week if they were married. Single men, he added, could be paid lower rates. Board commissioners ruminated on whether single men should be paid less and what constituted a family wage. 'Do you think an adult male of 22 years should get as much as this [a higher rate] to give him the possibility of getting married and bringing up a family?' they asked Strickland. 'Do you think he should have that chance?'[58] After all the men at the hearing had enjoyed a moment of relaxed fellowship, joking about the idea of wage scales being changed in June of every year and the possibility that married rates would discourage divorce, they went on to examine female wage rates.

Although the board generally saw a clear-cut division of pay, in which women would automatically receive a percentage of the amount men received, one board member did ask why night (male) spinners were paid more than the women spinners who worked during the day. The company's lawyer answered that night work was inherently worth more and that textile wages should not be compared with wages in other manufacturing, because textile work was lighter, needing 'a small expenditure of physical energy.' Moreover, he noted, women were simply working for 'supplementary' wages to aid the family income. His major argument, however, was that female wages should be paid according to the competitive costs of production, not according to the costs of living. While Cohen was rightfully sarcastic about the portrayal of textile work as being near 'health resort conditions,' he did not refute the notion that women were supplementary workers.[59] Both Cohen and the union men appearing before the board repeatedly drew on a language of working-class respectability that emphasized men's claim to a decent family wage as a manly right and an emblem of citizenship; this gendered definition of respectability clearly placed women in a supportive and 'supplementary' role in terms of their earning power.

Indeed, the women themselves described their labour as supplementary in the sense that they contributed to the family economy but could not afford to live on their own. These women stressed their right to a decent wage, not to a family wage. With Edith Frizelle, they agreed that it was a tragedy when men did not receive a family wage, and many expressed the hope that their wage earning could be temporary, ending when they married. While this image of supplementary work certainly existed, they would have been horrified to hear their work described as light and easy, and they believed they had the right to fair working conditions and good wages, similar to those paid in other manufacturing jobs done by women.

This does not negate the women's important role in the strike. Although the strike leaders constantly rejected Barrett's claim that the Auburn mill was not in good economic shape, it is possible that they knew that the Bonnerworth mill was more profitable and thus concentrated their picketing there. Moreover, there is no doubt that in the radical press, and to some extent in the mainstream press, the presence of young women and the ever-present threat of violence and tear gas to these 'vulnerable' girls were used to gain sympathy for the strike as a whole.

There is little evidence, however, that women were seen as long-term union activists or leaders. Drawn in at the last minute rather than recruited as a central party of UTWA strategy, the women provided essential leadership during the strike but found it hard to sustain their organization afterwards. Mere teenagers at the time, the women remember that they did not really know what was going on with the union. This may have been partly because of their youth and their understandable hesitation to become politically committed, especially to such a radical concept, when they were barely fifteen. But it was also because the union considered women to be less important than the Auburn weavers to the long-term life of the union. This turned out to be a disastrous mistake: it was the Bonnerworth mill that needed the investment in union education and leadership, for by 1938 the Auburn mill was closed permanently, soon to be razed to the ground.

WOMEN INTERPRET THE STRIKE

An examination of the strike through the press coverage and the Industry and Labour Board hearings suggests that both class solidarity and gender differences underlined the experience for women workers. Interviews with the women who participated in the strike provide many dimensions to this picture, for their recollections sometimes downplayed the violence stressed in the press and questioned the burgeoning class-consciousness that was apparently feared by the city's employers. While I expected to find women who, like an onlooker, would stress the bitterness after the strike and the radicalizing potential of such an intense conflict, I also found women who had crossed the picket line, who remember the experience as a heyday, and who downplayed its importance in their lives.

In order to examine their consciousness as reflected in strike memories, it is worth exploring a few representative examples. The women's strike stories varied significantly, despite similarities in their biographies: all the women who are quoted below came from working-class families; they were all working at spinning and twisting by the age of fifteen; they all contributed their pay to the household, and all of them left the mill for married life by the early 1940s.

Rosa was a second-generation Italian immigrant who had to leave school at thirteen, even though she was very clever, and find wage work. She soon became a trusted, versatile employee, a talented machine operator who was often moved to difficult jobs throughout the plant. Indeed, she believed that her privileged position made her the envy of at least one woman, who tried to convince the foreman that 'she could do my job better.'[60] During the strike, Rosa stayed away from work for a while, then crossed the line, encouraged by her parents' opposition to the strike and by their admonishment to mind her own business. Although acknowledging that the money was not good, she felt that she was getting by and that she owed her boss, who had supported her job mobility, some loyalty.

Rosa stood out as an anomaly within the Bonnerworth's small Italian population, most of whom supported the strike. Yet her response may have been a personal reaction to the social situation she faced. Living in a dominantly British city that was often ambivalent to immigrants, and coming from an unskilled working-class family, she may have been reluctant to throw away her newfound respect in the workplace by joining those on the picket line like the woman 'who wanted her job.' The experience of being called a scab was nonetheless a traumatic one, which both obscured her memory of strike events[61] and led to her overall denial of the conflict involved and the importance of the strike in her own and her workplace's history.

Similarly, June, a teenager whose parents were English working-class immigrants, downplayed the strike and joked with me about it being a heyday for the young women involved. She described the strike as an abrupt, puzzling event, which the women in the mill did not create, though they did become involved in strike aid, making sandwiches for the night picketers, collecting funds, and helping at the union office. During the strike, it was an opportunity 'for us to go downtown together ... The girls I chummed with weren't bitter about it ... it was almost a heyday ... we had street dances. I don't remember any tear gas. Us kids didn't know what the strike was about.'[62]

June's depreciation of the seriousness of the event, her denials of a leadership role (though she was later elected a steward), and her self-distancing from other 'radicals' in part reflected her youth at the time of the strike, but her memory was also shaped by her later, more conservative political views, which became apparent during the interview. June had no desire to assume the persona of a working-class radical in the city's history, perhaps because of her view that combative and outspoken militancy negated women's feminine respectability. Moreover, for young women workers – mere teenagers – the strike could have been 'a lark,' a rest from the long, hot hours in the factory. If the family had other wage earners (as hers did) and could scrimp by, then why not enjoy this unexpected vacation?

There were also women who did not fall into the category of either supporter or strikebreaker. Amelia, a farm girl who had come to the city to find work in the mill, recognized that her pay was very low but did not want to be seen as a 'complainer' taking part in the 'brazen' actions of the strikers, so she told them she lived too far to come and picket: 'I wasn't much of a politician then, and so I just went with them [the strikers] because I didn't want to be seen against the strike.' Amelia was most disturbed about being off work, because she was saving up for her wedding, 'and I wasn't saving anything on strike.' Strike events took second place to her marriage plans: 'I remember being fretful about going on strike ... There was a settlement suggested in August when I was getting ready for my wedding ... Yes, I knew it ended before I got married because I [used my] back pay to buy new curtains for my home ... I guess I missed the violence, but I was really preoccupied with my upcoming plans.'[63]

On the other hand, some women certainly remember the strike as an intense conflict and emphasize the lingering bitterness after its end. As one strikebreaker noted, she was denied the ritual wedding present when she left work the following year, for one reason: she had crossed the line. In a slightly different vein, Dorothy, the young woman who was arrested for 'assaulting' the police chief, believed the strike was precipitated by poor working conditions, and she recognized the violence involved. Her ten years of experience as a worker solidified her support for the strike, even though she was not involved in its planning. At the same time, she avoided any depiction of her role as heroic, even describing the ordeal of her arrest with humour, and she harboured little antipathy to management or to the strikebreakers, trying instead to understand why the strikebreakers continued to work: 'Maybe they ... needed the money more than we did.'[64] Never concentrating only on her own story, she related the strike and its consequences to the lives of her workmates and her family – a common characteristic of women's oral histories.[65]

Edith Frizelle's clear-cut and fiercely moralistic attribution of guilt to the employer stood out in contrast to these narratives. Her description of the strike seemed to offer evidence of women's oppositional, class-conscious outlook: 'The whole thing was wages. The strike was about wages. Dominion Woollens paid starvation wages and everybody knew it.'[66] At the same time, she did not see class antagonism as inevitable. Although Frizelle portrayed Dominion Woollens as an unscrupulous employer and the police as unworthy accomplices, she did not extrapolate this view to embrace a wider, class-conscious view of the city, especially after the strike. She remained somewhat suspicious of Welch's politics, as he was a suspected communist, and her critique was primarily focused on Dominion Woollens; indeed, she emphasized the difference between Dominion Woollens and her later employer, who treated employees far better.

The women's ways of remembering the strike offer important insights into the nourishment of and the limitations on women's resistance. The diversity of these women's voices underlines the variability of working-class women's experiences, the way in which a woman's gendered and class identity can produce a contradictory and fragmented consciousness, and, given the barriers to class solidarity, how fleeting women's protracted, intense resistance to their working conditions may be. Even in the crucible of conflict, working-class consciousness may be oppositional, accommodating, or a mixture of both.

The dissimilarity of the women's views, however, should not be construed as evidence of their 'individual' rather than class experience, or as confirmation of claims that there can be no 'truth' or 'reality' outside our multitudinous constructions of them, especially given the multilayered and highly interpretive use of oral sources. On the contrary, if we examine the power relations of age, gender, ethnicity, and class, as well as the dominant gender ideals of the time, these apparently diverse stories assume more discernible patterns. Thus, the social and material context of the conflict must be examined in tandem with the women's subjective interpretations of the strike.

The social dynamics of the family, the economic limits and possibilities of the women's lives, and their own reactions to these possibilities were all significant forces pressuring and shaping their conduct during the strike, as well as their later memories of it. All these women were expected to contribute to the family economy for basic survival; many were subject to parental authority on pain of losing the roof over their heads; and they were influenced by a dominant political ideology that feared communism and radical union activity.

Rosa, who crossed the picket line and has downplayed the conflict involved, is telling us something about her difficult status as a member of an ethnic minority in a WASP city and her purposeful memory of her hard-won battle to achieve respectability in the workplace. Like the other interviewees, Rosa is also revealing how difficult it was for young women to contradict the power of parental authority.

Amelia's preoccupation with her wedding reveals much about the dominant gender ideals of the time, which stressed women's private, marital, and family lives. Her memories reflect the priority given to the ritual of marriage and investment in the ideal of domesticity as a fitting end to a woman's time in the labour force. Perhaps the strength of these gender ideals helps explain why some of the younger women, such as June, did not remain interested in the union. At the same time, though, June's testimony also speaks to the male-dominated, exclusive power relations of union politics. Younger women were not adequately integrated into the union and were seldom informed of strategy or considered potential leaders; the result was their 'disinterest' in the union. Moreover, like June, many of the strikers were mere teenagers: they were not women with immediately dependent families, nor were they older women with a long workforce experience (except, significantly, the female leader) like those who have often been visible in recent strikes.[67] Their youthful rejection of serious political commitment thus becomes more understandable.

Finally, the role of political ideology in shaping memory is important. Given June's later emphasis on respect for authority and loyalty to mainstream political parties, which was apparent in her interview, her early union involvement might be more embarrassing then heroic. In a city where radicalism remains a fringe ideology, not a respectable one, especially for women, her dismissal of her early activism becomes entirely comprehensible.

Given this dominant political culture, Edith Frizelle's strong public support for the strike and her continuing pride in that role become all the more interesting and exceptional. Frizelle played an extraordinarily vocal and militant role in the conflict. She was often the only woman in some bargaining meetings, and in fact her radical persona led to some criticisms that she was not acting in a proper wifely and feminine manner. Her ability to proceed in spite of these criticisms and her courageous assumption of a public role, indicates that dominant gender ideals, though influential, have been challenged by women of exceptional intellectual bravery.

Rather than individual or near-fictional constructions of the past, these women's memories provide further proof of the difficulties hindering women's concerted resistance to their wage work. Coupled with the other sources, they highlight some of the barriers to women's resistance: an unsympathetic state, a powerful ideology of female dependence, and fears of isolation or poverty. Women's class-consciousness – a sense of their own interests as opposed to those of their employer – existed, but it was only temporarily expressed in direct and organized resistance. Moreover, it was interwoven with complex, competing power relations of family, ethnicity, and gender; for these women strikers, class was 'experienced in gendered terms, and gender was classed.'[68] In view of these barriers to resistance, one has to marvel that the women did organize themselves, at least temporarily, with such determination and ingenuity, on really no more than a moment's notice.

WOMEN AND THE LABOUR MOVEMENT IN THE 1940S

During and immediately after the 1937 textile strike, trade union supporters saw new hope for the organization of women workers into industrial unions and for the resuscitation of a community-based labour movement to return Peterborough to its 'former position as trade union citadel.'[69] With the closing of the Auburn mill and the failure to sustain the United Textile Workers, these hopes were delayed until the propitious conditions of wartime aided union organization and produced the Allied Labour Council, a new coalition composed of older craft unions and recently formed industrial unions. A rejuvenated union movement spawned two concurrent forces within local labour relations in the 1940s. On the one hand, more workers questioned the older-style paternalism of their workplaces and embraced unionization. On the other hand, by the late 1940s, the labour movement was engaged in bitter intra-union battles, which divided workers from one another and weakened the unions; hopes for community-wide labour unity were again negated until well into the 1960s, even beyond.

The United Electrical, Radio and Machine Workers of America (UE) was a central player in these battles. In the fall of 1937, UE organizers had made their first unionizing efforts at Canadian General Electric, one of the keys to overall organization of the Canadian electrical industry. They failed. Union activists claimed that the fiasco of the textile strike had created a climate of fear, made worse by the use of industrial agents at General Electric to spy on the union. By 1938, winter lay-offs at GE, including those of union men, had worsened the climate. In March 1938, the UE organizers gave up, leaving the task to a local citizens' committee but vowing to return.

It was the Second World War that provided the legal protection, full employment, and increased social approval of unions needed to spur local organizing to a successful finish. In 1942 the UE dared to hold its first public meeting in four years; the next year it captured Genelco, the war-production plant owned by the Government of Canada and run by GE; and in 1946 it finally succeeded at GE. During and immediately after the war, other local factories began to unionize: Quaker Oats and Canada Packers certified into the United Packing House Workers; and the UE began a vigorous organizing drive at Westclox, De Laval, Peterborough Lock, Hobbs Glass, and Raybestos, succeeding, at least temporarily, in the last three.

By 1952 even Westclox had succumbed, though only after more than one union attempt and only when a moderate union, the International Union of Electrical Workers, appeared on the scene. Westclox workers became sympathetic to unionization when they saw the material benefits of the older paternalist bargain seriously eroding: as other major Peterborough plants secured good benefit packages, Westclox's former generosity began to look deficient. Once the gap between the promise of paternalism and the reality became quite wide, disappointment set in – perhaps even more strongly because of previously raised hopes of fair dealing on the company's part. Unionization was perceived as a necessary (and by some, even unfortunate) last resort to defend the benefits initiated by company paternalism. While this pattern was replicated in other companies, paternalism was by no means dead: it persisted as a management strategy in a number of workplaces, with varying degrees of success and with ever-changing priorities. In the postwar period, for instance, the profit-sharing plan at Quaker Oats occasioned considerable employee support, forming the centrepiece of the company's long-standing commitment to welfare measures and paternalism. [70]

The Second World War also brought with it changes in women's employment: more women, including married women, were coaxed into heavy industry in the city. Wartime growth had a particularly dramatic effect on female employment at General Electric, since Genelco and GE were designated essential war industries and were thus key targets for government labour-recruiting strategies. Within a year, Genelco had increased its blue-collar female workforce from 1 to 36 per cent, an all-time high, while GE went from 13 per cent in 1941 to a peak of 29 per cent in 1945. Female white-collar workers also increased their numbers, though not quite so dramatically: at GE they remained about one-third of the clerical staff; at Genelco they rocketed from 17 to 52 per cent, though most of these women were laid off or reintegrated into GE after the war. Recruiting for GE war work in particular extended beyond the city limits; in 1941 the company was appealing for housing for the thirty women sent in monthly by inspection boards across Canada for industrial training. At the height of the war effort, the government was aiding in the relocation of women from northern Ontario and even from Nova Scotia to supply labour for the plant, though by this time the local vocational school was also providing special classes for women going into industry.

Nor was General Electric alone in augmenting its female workforce. By 1943, more than two thousand women were engaged in industrial war work; in numbers, they equalled the entire population of Peterborough's working women in 1931.[71] In some factories their presence was a first. At Outboard Marine, for instance, manager Hy Wood had vigorously prevented any woman from working on the shop floor: 'You know, if I had my way, I wouldn't hire a woman in the factory, it will cause nothing but trouble; but things are changing and I'm forced to by the government.' Women were at Outboard to stay.[72]

With their increased numbers in these male-dominated plants, women were able to construct stronger social and support networks, which provided an enhanced basis for collective resistance. However, their incursion into the masculine work environment of factories such as General Electric, created anxiety, both for management and for some male employees. Although the workers' concerns were framed in terms of safety or equal pay issues, their anxiety clearly had deeper roots. Cartoons in union papers showing an attractive female war worker distracting her male fellows, or a blue-collar woman leaving her baby in the arms of her feminized househusband, reflected the men's anxieties that women's presence would disrupt their masculine domain or upset the existing patriarchal family order.

The company revealed its own concerns about women's sexuality and femininity. When searching for housing for its new female workers, it made an effort to find chaperoned homes for the women, and its publicity tried to emphasize the 'nice' character and respectable backgrounds of these out-of-town 'girls,' some of whom, it reassured the public, had been 'teachers' in another life.[73] The company appointed a female welfare worker to look after the personal problems of women and to encourage wholesome leisure pursuits at the local YWCA. A new column, 'Listen Girls,' was instituted in the company paper, offering advice on relaxation, grooming, and fashion; in the latter case, the guidance emphasized women's safe and practical clothing, as opposed to ostentatious and flashy work attire.

As Nancy Palmer has argued for U.S. electrical plants, management efforts to dictate 'decent' (that is, not sexually provocative) clothing, to regulate women's social intercourse in the workplace, and to appoint female counsellors all reflected a strong sexual anxiety about the women they claimed were 'flooding the workplace' during the war.[74] Reflecting its own class bias, she argues, management implicitly saw these working-class women as more 'promiscuous' and as prone to flirtations and affairs with co-workers. These 'wartime jitters' that working-class femininity would become sexually 'out of control' were also a part of government thinking.[75] As well, they found their way into the mass media. In the Peterborough *Examiner*, columnist Dorothy Dix ominously warned wives of war workers that the new women workers in the plants were turning men who were 'previously as faithful as ... domestic house cats' into 'philandering Casanovas'; the real threat to the 'homefront,' she insinuated, might be the 'pretty young girls flocking to the factories' looking for a wild time.[76] Such caricatures help explain why blue-collar women felt unjustly targeted as 'unrespectable.'

Wartime changes in the sexual division of labour also occasioned social anxiety. Women did some non-traditional work at GE on drills and turret lathes, and there were a very few women who were welders and crane operators,[77] though women were still concentrated mainly in female-typed jobs. A woman who worked on Lancaster bombers remembers that her workroom was populated largely by young women on an assembly line, soldering small parts into aircraft instrument panels. Nonetheless, the preservation of women's femininity in the midst of heavy industry remained a public issue. In part, this was assuaged by the deliberate 'feminization' and 'domestication' of such work.[78] The *Examiner* assured its readers that women's natural skills of adaptability and dexterity, and the 'light touch' of 'their slender hands' for precision work were only temporarily being channelled into making armaments rather than baking cookies.[79] Union papers relayed similar messages. The UE paper, for instance, reprinted a cartoon of a female manicurist carefully polishing armaments – which were made to look like nails. The message was clear: after the war, she could easily return to her old job.[80]

In order to preserve the existing familial status quo, government policy at first stressed the importance of recruiting single rather than married women. But by 1943, the government, in concert with local businesses, was becoming more aggressive in its approach to recruitment in the face of increasing labour shortages. The required registration of all single women and a job permit system were adopted; and in September 1943, the federal government used Peterborough as a small-town test for the new policy of getting housewives to take up service jobs for three months so that single women could go into the factories. In its concern that Peterborough, 'a very conservative city'[81] would not respond well to appeals for female industrial labour, the feds asked local women's organization to aid with registration and publicity campaigns, including a special fashion show to allay fears that women war workers would be forced to don unfeminine overalls.[82] The local Council of Women, whose president admitted she had not worked outside the home in thirty-eight years, couched its appeal for factory workers in patriotic terms. Likewise, the GE *Works News* and the Peterborough *Examiner* often featured stories of industrial women working to back up the boys at the front. In fact, many war workers were working-class women who were primarily attracted by more secure employment and higher wages, though many were also war supporters.

Once the UE became more sympathetic to the war effort, after the Soviet Union's entrance into the war, it lent support to these campaigns, astutely combining recruitment sentiments with pro-union appeals as well as with calls for women's equality on war production lines. Irma Locke, secretary of the UE local that was organizing General Electric, appeared on Peterborough radio, urging support for the production of guns 'so that my brother and your brother can hurl shells at the Hitlerite enemy.' She also used her airtime to argue that the soldiers at the front should be 'protected by unions at home, so they could return to good working conditions,' and she put in a pitch for equal pay for women 'who are often working side by side with men on the same machine, and turning out the same work ... but paid far less.'[83] The nascent Women's Auxiliary of UE Local 524 also intervened in recruiting, and in 1944 it urged the Ontario minister of public welfare to set up a day nursery program in the city as a means of freeing women to work in industry. In a city of 28,000, the auxiliary pointed out, 'there are no facilities ... If the government is to recruit more women, it must provide such facilities.'[84] In the face of local apathy, however, its lobby failed.

In the midst of this altered war situation, the UE reasserted its influence. After certifying Genelco, the union began a long and difficult process of building union membership in Canadian General Electric. Management antipathy to unionization was apparent from the beginning. As one organizer remembers, the union once booked the YWCA for a special meeting for women workers – only to find that 'permission to use the room was quickly withdrawn' after the GE management intervened with the YWCA.[85] Apparently, swimming at the YWCA was an appropriate and wholesome recreational activity; organizing unions was not.

Ironically, the image of Canadian General Electric as an anti-union employer was different from the image promoted by the U.S. corporation, which had became known in the interwar period for its benefit plans and for its attempts to cushion Depression lay-offs with its own unemployment insurance scheme, as well as for its various methods of internal education and promotion.[86] Not all these benefits, though, were automatically extended to Canadian plants, which during the Depression had also suffered severe pay cuts to wages that were already lower than those in the United States. As one GE manager remembers, 'Really top-notch benefits [in Canada] were not achieved until the early 1950s, as a result of union pressure.'[87] Moreover, in the United States, some benefits were abandoned in the worst of the Depression, and discretionary aids – such as preferential seniority for the more 'needy' – were increasingly seen as discriminatory. The resulting worker disillusionment brought unionization; by 1937, General Electric in the United States had come to tolerate the UE as a national bargaining agent.[88]

Peterborough workers, though, missed this decade of supposed toleration and unionized just as the American owners were about to assume a more aggressively anti-union stance associated with Boulwarism, a tough 'take it or leave it' approach to bargaining, which came to dominate in the postwar years. Certainly, it was not management largesse that aided unionization in Peterborough: rather, the Second World War provided the conditions needed.

Even in wartime, union organizers privately bemoaned the near impossible task of organizing in what they perceived to be a conservative city. 'The rest of the world could be atomized all to hell,' despaired UE organizer Bob Ward, 'but the staid little borough of Peter goes on unruffled as be damned.'[89] Other organizers agreed that there were major structural impediments, based on cross-class ties of ethnic exclusivity and on a history of labour defeats: 'The city is 99% Anglo-Saxon community, with a well-knit manufacturers group, led by GE ... and a background of defeat back to 1919,'[90] commented Ward. The fact that there were few 'foreign born' meant that 'ethnic organizations could not be called on for support,' but the union had to cope with the racist Anglo-Saxon prejudice of workers who 'claimed that the union was run by Jews from New York.'[91] Old Orange versus Catholic antagonisms also became intertwined with union and anti-union sentiments in some areas of the plant.

Perhaps even the organizers were surprised when General Electric was finally conquered in 1946. Shortly after the first contract of 1948, however, serious internal union conflict surfaced. As a result of growing anticommunism in Canada, fostered especially by the state, and the long-standing hostility of CCF trade unionists to communists, the UE came under fire from the Canadian Congress of Labour (CCL). The UE leadership had always contained a few obvious and vocal communists, and for years it had been a vociferous left-wing critic of CCL policies;[92] moreover, it steadfastly refused to join the CCF-labour alliance advocated by many CCL leaders.

In 1949, following the lead of the Congress of Industrial Organizations (CIO) in the United States, the UE was thrown out of the CCL, ostensibly on the basis of late payment of dues, though essentially because the CIO leadership wanted to get rid of the UE at the first opportunity because of its political orientation.[93] A rival union, the International Union of Electrical Workers (IUE), was chartered – in fact its organizing had already begun in the Peterborough plant. Yet this plant, which appeared to be the most likely one to switch to the IUE, became its central failure. Partly because of the expert manoeuvring of the UE leadership, but also because of critical mistakes and lack of unity within the IUE, the UE survived three bitter and tumultuous raids by its rival in 1950, 1951, and 1952. After these three attempts, the IUE finally relented, turning inward with recriminations against its own staff.

UE Local 524's persistence can be attributed to four factors: the Peterborough UE leadership was still positively associated with the recent and difficult organizing campaign and with the first major contract gains of 1948; the UE's emphasis on democracy and its very active shop steward organization gained the respect of rank-and-file workers; the members of the opponent IUE were clearly identified with the CCF, while the UE did not officially endorse any party; and the UE leadership remained united, disciplined, and centralized throughout the battle.[94]

The UE remained the largest electrical union in Canada, in contrast to its position in the United States, where anticommunism was stronger, but there was a price to be paid. The union was isolated, not only from its international headquarters in the United States (due to the American bar on travel by communists) but also from the whole Canadian labour movement. And not only were Canadian electrical workers divided between the two unions while a few large companies dominated the market, but the experience of anticommunism meant that the UE was increasingly anxious about political dissent and was sometimes unreceptive to internal debate. Ultimately, the only real winner of this internecine battle was General Electric. The losers were the workers themselves.

WOMEN IN THE UE IN THE POSTWAR PERIOD

Despite the negative effects of dual unionism, some historians, as well as older members of the UE, maintain that political isolation also brought unforeseen political opportunities. One historian argues that in the United States the Cold War battles encouraged the UE's sympathy for women's rights, because the union's status as an 'outsider' and its left-wing views enhanced its identification with the doubly oppressed worker.[95] In Canada, argues Julie Guard, this isolation allowed the UE to promote its own militant brand of social unionism (extending workplace struggles into the community), and it developed a political discourse of oppositional class conflict that contradicted the conservative Cold War tenor of the times. This oppositional discourse in turn allowed union women an opening to create their own image of 'respectability,' which endorsed the assertive, militant, and class-conscious woman fighting for her union and her rights as a 'contributory breadwinner.' Such an image, notes Guard, was in part a subversive reaction to the dominant postwar image of domestic and passive femininity.[96]

Certainly, the Cold War did not deter the union from discussing gender issues. Two interrelated workplace issues dominated Local 524's agenda on women workers in the postwar period: separate seniority by sex, and equal pay. By the late 1940s most North American trade unions were determined to defend the principle of seniority as an absolutely crucial part of their bargain with management.[97] At the time, trade unionists believed that the 'first in, last out' system was the fairest one. This represented a decisive rejection of earlier corporate paternalism, which allowed management to designate who was the neediest worker to keep on. At Genelco, for instance, the UE was gradually able to remove the company's right to determine seniority according to marital status and number of dependents (which obviously worked against women more than men) from its contracts over the war period, and in 1946 the union voted to resist seniority by marital status for men at Genelco's larger parent plant, Canadian General Electric.[98]

At Canadian General Electric, women had historically been accorded seniority on a separate basis from men; this was a key means of preserving the gendered division of labour. This practice persisted during war and postwar alterations in women's work, with little major objection from rank-and-file workers. After the war, the UE publicly defended the right of all women to work, calling for full employment and not the firing of women workers as a reconversion solution. Although quite radical for the time, this demand could theoretically be reached with separate seniority designations for women and men; indeed, full employment with such 'separate spheres' was probably easier to sell to returning veterans and skilled male workers than the more revolutionary idea of integrating male and female seniority lists.

The Peterborough factory, with its focus on heavy industry and its large male labour force of skilled and semi-skilled workers and only a minority of female workers, was very different from the more evenly balanced mixed-sex electrical plants in the United States and Canada. The latter, claims Ruth Milkman, more forcefully opposed separate seniority as well as wage differentials. In Peterborough there were no public protests by women over loss of seniority and reassignment to female jobs after the war. Admittedly, this was partly the consequence of the immense power of management to reimpose female job ghettos through new hiring and through the careful transfer of women from Genelco war work into traditional female jobs at General Electric; but it was also because of the workers' and the union's tacit acceptance of a gendered division of labour and because of the many informal barriers to the integration of male and female seniority lists. In one of the few references to women's postwar grievances, the local noted that women were most concerned with problems *within* their specific job areas: speed-up in their jobs, loss of lunch time, unfairly timed rates and unjust transfers and dismissals.[99]

Seniority within women's separate sphere became an issue in 1949 when some female workers began to suggest that single women should have preferential seniority over married women. A resolution to this effect was passed at a local union meeting for women workers and then forwarded to the national office, with the request that it be a major focus of the UE's upcoming women's conference. The resolution said that local 524 single girls wanted preferred seniority in women's jobs unless a married woman could show her need to work, in which case she would be treated as an honourary single woman.[100] Despite lack of support at the women's conference, some Local 524 delegates defended their motion, drawing on the same rhetoric that had decried married women's work during the Depression. 'I know of cases where married women who work have so much money that they can afford to save enough to buy either $1,000 bonds or fur coats,' declared the Local 524 delegate Marie Gavreau, 'while single girls, who have no one to look after them, eat onion sandwiches and have to wear cheap dresses!'[101]

UE national president C.S. Jackson was furious when he saw the resolution. He castigated the local executive for allowing such a discriminatory resolution to pass at a union meeting. 'It would seem to me,' he wrote, 'that there was insufficient appreciation of the obligations of leadership on the part of those conducting the meeting in permitting this subject to reach a point of decision, contrary to established policy of the District.' The resolution, he pointed out, was both discriminatory and divisive, and perhaps the result of 'employer inspired prejudice against one group of workers.'[102]

A major furore resulted. The local leader accused Jackson of suffocating union democracy and freedom of speech, and of defaming them by insinuating that they were in the pocket of management. Jackson responded that their letters were full of half-truths, and he implied that their management of the union was naive at best, discriminatory at worst. Not coincidentally, the Peterborough renegades included John Morton, a CCF election candidate and an arch-opponent of the UE leadership before he eventually headed up the rival IUE.

The women's seniority issue became part of the ongoing political battle within the UE which eventually resulted in the establishment of the IUE. The issue reflected the different political styles and priorities of the two opposing camps. Jackson and other left-wingers believed in the importance of strong leadership and direction of political education by the union central.[103] Morton disagreed, not simply on the grounds of decentralization and the need for locals to have freedom of speech, but because he abhorred the UE's 'communist' political views.

More important, though, was the fact that the issue threatened two basic concepts which UE leaders George Harris and C.S. Jackson believed should be defended militantly: first, that preferential seniority based on marital status was discriminatory, and therefore married women should have the same right to work as single women; secondly, that any modification of seniority was a dangerous thin edge of the wedge that might allow management to water down seniority provisions for all workers. This two-pronged analysis formed the consistent basis of the UE's official stance over the next decade.

It was no accident that editorials about preferential seniority immediately appeared in the *UE News*, which was controlled by the left-wing Toronto leadership. Discrimination against married women was the result of 'boss propaganda,' said an article by UE staffer Jean Leslie, while another editorial stressed women's economic need to work, as well as the dangers to men of discriminatory seniority. 'When jobs are scarce,' it warned, 'workers sometimes look for a scapegoat in women ... They forget that in one third of our homes men and women have to work ... They forget about widows.' The editorial added that discrimination based on marital status might encourage employers to pursue discriminatory seniority based on other factors, such as age; the only solution was to oppose all qualifications to the seniority structure: 'Seniority must be based on years of service not whether one wears pants or skirt ... Any violation of seniority undermines seniority for everyone.'[104] The leadership's defence of married women's right to work was influenced in part by the left-wing ideas and background of some union leaders; it was also shaped by a practical desire to defend existing principles of seniority.

Although Morton claimed that his intention was to allow the women freedom of speech, there is evidence that he was willing to use the more skilled male workers' discriminatory fears of encroaching female labour to advance his own political agenda. In the fall of 1949 he supported a company proposal that complex 'flow charts' could be used in lay-off situations, with some workers offered more chances at job change than others, based on factors such as skill. Morton's question – 'Can a girl on light assembly work replace a man on heavy manual labour?'[105] – revealed his attempt to use divisive fears of female dilution in the seniority debate.

Left-wing UE opponents criticized Morton for abandoning the basic principle of seniority, noting that one result would be that 'long service girls would be laid off while less service men stay.' Indeed, this fight inspired the UE's most radical statement over gender and seniority; ideally, it said, 'anyone should be able to bump into any work group within 10 cents of one's rate pay and there should be equal rates regardless of sex ... with men and women holding same seniority rights.'[106]

The irony was that, radical statements aside, separate women's and men's seniority within the plant was an established and even accepted fact. As Jackson admitted, 'Because of separate seniority lists, women are denied plant-wide seniority.'[107] Management's active promotion of separate lists was definitely a major factor here, but one cannot escape the conclusion that there was a gap between the official policy of the union and the rank-and-file opinion within the factory, with the result that the union did not consistently pressure management to change these separate spheres. As we have seen, many men believed that women ought to be in separate job categories because they were not able to do heavy industrial work. Furthermore, as more than one union activist remembers, many men had ambivalent feelings about women's absolute right to work: 'They opposed married women working at this time. Especially when lay-offs came, they were not sympathetic to married women, but more so to single women.'[108] Thus, although the union executive spoke of nondiscriminatory seniority and of having only one seniority list, it is unlikely the union would have ever gone to bat over these issues.

Nevertheless, the UE leadership continued to claim that gender equality was a feature of its platform which distinguished it from the rival IUE, charging that women's fight for better pay and an end to differentials would be severely hampered if the IUE triumphed. Part of the UE's claim to militancy on this issue focused on its ongoing support for a group grievance pursued by women working at Induction Motors. Although we shall never know how women voted in the contest between UE and IUE, the UE's clear support for these women, and its astute use of the *UE News* to publicize the Induction Motors arbitration protests, made it appear more vigilant in its defence of both male and female workers.[109]

Still, it is revealing that the grievance the union chose to focus on was one that could unify women and men – potentially a more popular issue than calling for a single seniority list.[110] This grievance had started in 1947 when GE women working in Induction Motors found that their rates had been altered downward when part of the job had been changed. It is quite possible that the change in rates was part of the company's long-term agenda of reducing women's wage rates,

which had definitely been pushed up during the war. Since the contract stated that rates could not be altered unless there was a change
in the method of manufacture, it was taken to a grievance, and in
February 1949 the provincial arbitration board ruled two to one in favour
of the union. But the company refused to pay.[111] It claimed that it had
sought only 'clarification' through the arbitration board and, furthermore, that the board had given a contradictory judgment by admitting
that there had been a change in method.[112]

The union responded by holding illegal work stoppages and demonstrations, and it promoted the women's cause in the *UE News*, de-
nouncing the company for refusing to abide by the arbitration. The
company used its own in-house newspaper to defend its actions; since
it rarely debated with the union in this forum, the grievance was clearly
an issue on which it feared it might lose face. Significantly, General
Electric appealed to the same sentiments as Morton, implying that the
new rates would be too high for female work: 'The judge would have
us pay $3.00 [an exaggeration] an hour and this is not as it should be ...
Surely the skilled man rightfully feels he should have higher pay than
the unskilled.' [113]

The union was never able to make the company pay the new rates.[114]
But the union did win in terms of its own image, and possibly in its
campaign against the IUE. While the Induction Motors grievance was
a cause that women workers naturally supported, it could also gain
male sympathy since men, too, feared the retiming and reduction of
their piecework rates, just as they feared the substitution of female for
male labour.

It was the latter that often sparked unionists' interest in the second
key issue of the period: equal pay. Since the war, the UE had persis-
tently agitated against any modification in men's work that would result in their job codes being broken down into new jobs, for which
women and boys would be hired at cheaper rates. To protect against
this, the Genelco union had insisted during the war that before a
woman or a minor could be placed on a job previously done by a man,
the reasons must be set before the local executive board by management.[115] A cartoon in the UE paper was intended to bring the point
home to both male and female workers: the boss was shown placing a
man on the lower-paid woman's job, while the woman was being
shown the door.[116]

During the Second World War, equal pay had taken on new life as a
trade union issue, because male workers were worried that the substi-

tution of women workers would result in their wages being depressed to lower female levels. Indications of this new trade union emphasis can be found in labour's presentations before the War Labour Board. J.L. Cohen, appearing for the Canadian Congress of Labour, no longer emphasized the family wage, as he had done at the 1937 textile inquiry, and instead stressed that 'women were now a permanent part of the industrial workforce and that equal pay should be the letter of the law, adequately enforced by the board.'[117] Both the Canadian Congress of Labour and the Trades and Labor Congress passed equal pay resolutions, as did many union conventions; moreover, in the wartime context, the public increasingly supported the concept of equal pay.

The UE attempted to draw on this public sympathy. As soon as Genelco was unionized, the UE made a case before the Ontario War Labour Board for a common minimum starting rate of 50 cents an hour for both men and women, and equal pay for equal work. As discussed in chapter 3, the union's attempt to alter the electrical industry's entrenched differential starting rates and to obtain equal pay was adamantly opposed by the company, which claimed that it had to follow 'community standards' of pay[118] and that women's work did not produce equal results at equal outlay of cost.[119] Although the War Labour Board rejected the cost argument, it supported lower starting rates for women and the company's emphasis on equal results – which of course were easily 'proven' by the company, with its manipulative control over workplace statistics. As in the textile inquiry, the state became a buttress to the employer's agenda of maintaining unequal pay by gender.

Moreover, as a way of avoiding the equal pay issue, the company maintained the prewar division of labour in its plants through its postwar reassignment of jobs and hiring. Women did do some traditionally male work during the war, but when they were reassigned to postwar jobs, they were carefully placed within female classifications. At a UE meeting held in Peterborough, the union noted that many plants offered lip-service to equal pay but always put the girls in a particular department on a type of work that they had agreed beforehand was a cheaper class of work.[120]

In lieu of offering either equal pay or the same starting rate, the company increasingly advocated new incentive systems in the 1940s and 1950s which supposedly offered both men and women better chances of making money. These systems were attractive to some women working in the plant because they allowed experienced workers better wages once they had produced more than the standard timed rate. The national union, however, criticized incentive systems for differentially discriminating against women. It claimed that more women were on incentive pay and that differentials were higher here than on day rates. The union warned that women needed protection from the health implications of the incentive plans: Jackson explained, 'Women are under greater pressure for production ... and speed-up robs women of earnings, and of their health ... there is no need to tell the women here of the nervous exhaustion, nervous breakdowns, heat prostration that they are subject to.'[121] On the other hand, a UE leader has claimed that despite Jackson's criticisms, the incentive systems did have some popularity with workers in prosperous times of good rate increases, though incentives could ultimately allow the company to divide workers and buy off some with the illusion of higher pay.[122]

In union publicity and education, the fight for equal pay and an end to wage differentials merged into the union's general denunciations of the capitalist exploitation of female labour; the 'community standard' argument used by General Electric, for instance, was exposed as the self-serving immoral cop-out that it was. Drawing on educational material provided by the American UE, the Canadian union argued that unequal pay was the deliberate attempt of business to squeeze extra profits from its workforce. At the same time, it was stressed, there were valid economic reasons why women had to work to support their families, and they therefore had a right to be in the workforce. This was especially emphasized in the *UE News*. 'It is the bosses that promote the idea that women are less capable,' the paper argued. 'We still hear [from union members] that women shouldn't get the same rates as men ... As a result of this propaganda, women earn 60 per cent of men's wages. Men have to see this as an overall attack by the bosses.'[123]

The UE promoted both higher wages for women and equal pay by making these issues part of its national education programs, by featuring the issue at its regular women's conferences, and by urging locals to add these demands to contract negotiations and grievance tactics. The national organization suggested that locals secure a common hiring level for men and women, and promote job evaluation systems that would objectively measure job content rather than concentrating on the sex of the worker.[124] On a political level, the UE urged a provincial equal pay law and, when the inadequacies of the 1952 law became apparent, exhorted the government to put teeth into it.

In practice, though, the union admitted that contract changes were few and far between, especially after the war years.[125] In 1953 it self-critically commented that 'most of our locals have not raised this struggle for job opportunities and equality of wage rates for women in any full way.'[126] In 1953 the Peterborough union submitted its demands to a board of conciliation, asking for an across-the-board increase and elimination of male-female differentials. But the union later compromised and accepted an increase of 7 cents for women and 6 cents for men, admitting that sex 'differentials of 11 cents in 1946 had now *risen* to 20 cents differential separating men and women.'[127]

In negotiations, compromises were made on both equal pay and lower starting rates, though equal pay was often seen as the more critical principle to defend. Differentials in starting rates might have to be accepted in bargaining trade-offs, but equal pay was related to the protection of men's pay and status as well. Time and again, the local union executive expressed its concern with situations such as the following: 'Girls are working on the same size of motors as men and given girls' codes ... The Company is breaking down jobs performed by men, and spreading them amongst the girls.'[128]

Asked whether separate seniority lists were an issue at the time, a Peterborough union activist admitted there was little concern, but he added that equal pay was most certainly an issue: 'The UE had good policies on paper, but within the union, where there were few women, it didn't get worked out very well. When we talked about unequal pay, it was how to narrow the gap; we didn't dream of abolishing it. I think equal pay was important because it protected men's jobs too, including breaking down of jobs into boys.'[129]

The women's grievances that were taken up by the local union in these years were often ones that the union saw as important to the protection of both women's and men's job rates and seniority. In one group grievance, women from General Electric's phased-out meter section found that their transfer to other departments was fraught with difficulty. Some who were sent to Induction Motors were faced with a foreman who claimed that their work was unsatisfactory, while another woman was discouraged from trying a job in punch press because the company told her it was too heavy for her. These women subsequently submitted a grievance over their dismissal and the failure of the company to recall them on a seniority basis. Meanwhile, the union fully supported their attempts to secure similarly paid jobs within the factory. As the union representative explained to the Toronto office, the grievance was important because it involved a larger issue of protection of seniority and transfer rights that affected all workers. It was dangerous, he said, 'to accept the company's view of seniority ... that regardless of years of service, if one can't do a job that one is transferred to, one is dismissed ... The Company will be able to get rid of employees whenever they chose to.'[130]

Supporting grievances over equal pay, on the other hand, sometimes exposed all the contradictions of union views on this issue. In one such grievance, the men working in armature noted that the company had installed new air presses and had promptly recoded the job at a girls' rate. The union argued that the same male rate should apply for work on the presses. But in its attempt to prove its point, the union reasserted the company's emphasis on a 'natural' gendered division of labour. The male workers insisted that the 'girls only do five hours a week on the new presses as the work is too heavy for most women ... A girl could not stand the full range of work [involved].'[131] Not only did the men lose the grievance, but they inadvertently reinforced the notion that women could not and should not do men's jobs. Although the union sometimes argued that the skills associated with women's jobs (such as women's 'natural' dexterity) were undervalued and should be better paid, in cases like this one the union reinforced the idea that the gendered division of labour was a natural rather than socially constructed one and that it reflected men's superior physical abilities.

Not all the union's grievance work contained such contradictions. The union did pursue cases based solely on the justice of equal pay for women. Some UE leaders saw women's lower pay as a dangerous wedge preventing working-class unity, while others were motivated by abhorrence of discrimination. In one grievance, for example, the executive tried to expose the ridiculous practice of paying the women who cleaned washrooms less than men who did the same work; in another case, they argued that a woman, ostensibly a clerical worker, was doing the same job as a tool attendant for lower rates. The inadequacies of the existing equal pay law, which narrowly defined work tasks and avoided questions of comparable worth, were manifest in the company's victory in this case. In order to win its point, the company argued that since the woman did not sharpen tools like other tool attendants, she was not producing 'equal results.'[132]

Moreover, the UE cast its political agenda beyond its own union, arguing for better provincial equal pay legislation and criticizing taxes and UIC regulations that discriminated against married working women. Employing a class analysis, the union argued that unemployment was a shared problem of all workers and that married women should not be subject to the discrimination under the Act, as indeed they were. At the same time, the union often took up the cases of women denied benefits, appealing for specific needs arising from pregnancy or family responsibilities. In 1951 when Local 524 activist Flo Farrance, a single mother, tried to move to Toronto to find work and was disqualified from unemployment insurance, the union defended her claim on the basis that 'continued residence in Peterborough was a moral hazard to her daughter.' Her decision to place maternal concerns first was represented by the union as legitimate and not as a cause to deny her benefits.[133] In Peterborough, a UE member sat on the UIC appeal board in the 1960s and clearly took women's cases seriously. When local UE activist Kathy How won her UIC case, which protested gender discrimination by the board, the local union paper publicized her victory as a means of promoting the union and encouraging other women to follow her example.[134]

The union's actual practice on gender issues, therefore, was contradictory and a product of mixed motives. While the union did make attempts to raise women's wages and while it spoke out for equal pay, it was less adamant about eliminating wage differentials and separate seniority lists. Sympathy for equal pay could be more easily generated because it also symbolized the protection of male wages, though some unionists had genuine political sympathy for the elimination of women's lower pay rates. The more difficult and contentious issue of merging seniority lists and thus potentially allowing women access to the skilled jobs, long the preserve of men, was less central to union actions. However much the union sloganized that 'a fight for women is a fight for the whole union,'[135] the prospect of actually sharing jobs and seniority raised fears of men losing status in the workplace.

The reasons for this local's difficulty in challenging women's inferior workplace position can be explored in more detail by examining both the barriers and the successes that women themselves perceived in their union organizing.

ATTEMPTING TO ORGANIZE WOMEN IN THE UNION

Women who became actively involved in the UE were the minority. The others, those who remained mere bystanders, remember feeling that activism was not appropriate for a variety of reasons: because they never thought about making a career of work; because of the competing claims of domestic duties at home; or even because the militancy of the union frightened them. 'They made you feel as if you had to join ... and I felt too pressured,' said one woman, explaining her antipathy to the UE in the late 1940s.[136] Another woman, who had in fact wanted to become involved, felt a similar pressure to demonstrate uncritical loyalty to the union. Because of the constant attacks on the UE through the fifties, she reasoned, the executive developed a protective shield, fearing uncontrollable dissent; as a result, one was supposed to get on their slate of candidates for office and never challenge existing political priorities.

The white-collar women working at the plant who had remained in the IUE were also hesitant about becoming involved in their union. They worried about a close association with blue-collar union tactics, such as strikes, and were more closely tied into paternalistic relationships with managers. Unlike the factory workers interviewed, some cannot recall the name of their union – surely an indication that it was a less than effective public presence – but they do remember relying on the plant workers to set standards for benefits, which the company then offered to them: 'I think we got the same raises as plant people did if they went out ... Usually if the UE was on strike, we could still go into the office though.'[137]

Women who became more involved than merely attending union meetings often exhibited a personal and political conviction that was unusual for the time. The barriers to women's activism were immense: the competing demands of family, housework, and child care made union work too exhausting a prospect for some women, while the inhospitable popular culture of the postwar period offered few role models for women's workplace militancy. The prevailing political climate in the city was also crucial; the intense anticommunist ideology, which not only surrounded the fights between the UE and IUE but lingered in the community's view of the UE for the next two decades, impeded women's association with the union. To become involved would have meant going against the dominant notions of 'decency' that were promulgated by powerful community spokespersons and often repeated by one's own family members.

Political attacks on the UE came not only from rival unions in the CCL, but also from the local media, the political élite, and even some churches. During UE attempts to organize other workplaces, and at the existing UE locals at Lock and Raybestos,[138] Peterborough's workers were inundated with leaflets and speeches by rival unions which declared the UE to be agents of Stalin in Canada.[139] The Peterborough *Examiner*, while claiming to be neutral in the conflict between the UE and the IUE, implied that many UE activists were communists: 'Is the UE's voice the kind Peterborough workers want, a thin hollow echoing, as the CCL alleges, from the Kremlin's turrets?'[140] On another occasion, it informed its readers that the UE was providing money for notorious U.S. communists engaged in subversive activity.[141] Similarly, a Peterborough business leader informed the local Council of Women, at one of its meetings, that 'these [UE] union men were trained in Moscow.'[142] Some church leaders, too, were suspicious of the union.

The women remember this anticommunist propaganda as a clear impediment to their union involvement. One, who was in the UE women's auxiliary in the 1950s, recalled this fear of involvement and, more important, the interference of church leaders in creating this anticommunist fear. 'The label of communist meant some women wouldn't have anything to do with it. ... None of the men were really communists. I even called our minister [and] had a talk with him. He told me that churches were going to condemn [the UE]. We had a fight with my sister, and she got scared and went home ... One priest told a friend he would be excommunicated.' Her analysis was shaped by a clear image of a class-divided city. 'The problem was that the elders in the church were high up [in the local companies] and didn't want to hear about working conditions. Ministers didn't want to offend [the] elders, who make big contributions ... One guy said to us, the minister of Murray St Church has a list of communists and *you* are on it. My husband just said, well, I hope I'm on top of the list!'[143]

This woman's perception of religious interference bore a similarity to the memory of workers involved in the 1937 textile strike, and her allusions to the Catholic Church's obvious antipathy to the UE was repeated by other interviewees. As one union activist remembers, women's attitudes towards the union were affected by such associations. 'Women used the grievance procedure,' he recalled, 'especially where there were large numbers of them. Where they were isolated, or very religious – church going – they were less likely to.'

The strong arm of the company was another barrier to women's union participation. On the one hand, they feared that intimidation on the job might result; on the other hand, the company used paternalistic pleas of common interest to undermine union loyalty. Appealing to the women at Induction Motors to abandon their protests, the works manager assured them that he had the best interests of the whole General Electric 'family' at heart: 'I've grown up here at GE for the last 25 years. I know the people personally and have been on good relations with them. I want a good workforce.'[145] While the company's use of the velvet glove affected men too, women were often in a more vulnerable position: they were spread throughout the plant and were a minority of the workforce; they relied heavily on the good graces of supervisors for job transfers; and they were subject to different kinds of harassment than men.

Moreover, the company's postwar labour policy, Boulwarism, may have had especially severe effects on women. Boulwarism used the immense wealth and power of the company to follow a set pattern in labour relations. To avoid endowing the union with legitimacy through bargaining, the company, after claiming to look at the financial demands of workers, stockholders, and management, made a final offer that was said to be in the best interests of all, and the offer was then promoted in the plant and the community through media blitzs.[146] Lacking similar access to public relations systems and to total financial information, the union was greatly disadvantaged.

This style of bargaining hampered the promotion of women's issues, which often relied on appeals to equity, fairness, and morality – not on rationalizations based on the 'bottom line.' A Local 524 official recalled an occasion when women were injured by Boulwarism: 'I remember one time the girls complained about a percentage increase, which meant they didn't get as much [as the men], but that was the company's final offer ... Maybe we should have protested more vigorously, but we wouldn't have proposed that [then].'[147] At the same time that Boulwarism was introduced, Canadian General Electrifc underwent a massive reorganization and decentralization, with more pressure put on semi-autonomous units to 'show their own profits.'[148] Attempts by managers to cut production costs in order to do this may well have adversely affected women workers, who were predominantly semi-skilled, were in a narrow range of jobs, and were more likely to be pieceworkers.[149] Thus, since it was operating within the context of both anticommunism and Boulwarism, the union was limited in its ability to pressure for women's equality. As Lisa Ann Kannenberg has argued, these two forces explain why gender issues were side-tracked in the United States during the 1950s.

In the Canadian union, however, the Cold War was moderated by the UE's triumph over the IUE. We must also assess how union culture and politics played a role in the stifling of gender equity. No matter how many times the union officially said it welcomed women, union culture offered a different message. From the 'smokers' held by the Allied Labour Council (which had very few women associated with it) to the physical fights at union meetings, women must have acquired an uneasy sense of exclusion. This problem was undoubtedly accentuated by the bitter battles between the IUE and the UE. As one man recalled, his baptism into active union participation – literally – was during a fist fight at an acrimonious meeting.[150] In view of women's less secure sense of physical safety in the world and their small numbers within the union, one can sympathize with some women's desire to avoid such intimidating encounters. While battle with the IUE could encourage a sense of comradeship with male workers – one woman remembers the UE's victory parade around town as her initiation into the union – it is also likely that some women did not relish these battles.

The visual images and stories of women promoted in the *UE News* also provided contradictory messages about women's role in the union. On one hand, women were portrayed as fellow union members, with equally important voices in conventions or on picket lines; contradicting the image of domestic and passive femininity in the mainstream media, Julie Guard argues, the union attempted to recast 'femininity as compatible with wage work and union activism.'[151] But on the other hand, as Guard concedes, the union also used stock images, which equated tough masculinity with good unionists, implied the need to offer chivalrous protection to the more vulnerable women, and stressed the man's role as head of the household and provider. Simultaneously, women were portrayed in graphics or stories as beauty queens or, conversely, as the tireless auxiliary worker, wife, and supporter.

Auxiliary work, admittedly, provided an avenue of resistance for working-class homemakers and occasionally connected plant women with the wives of other workers.[152] Nonetheless, there remained a dichotomy between women's expected role as auxiliary supporters and their possible role as union sisters, for the image of women as workers remained problematically fractured, and fractured in a masculinist mould. The union auxiliary also stressed the male-breadwinner image. Women in the auxiliary spoke of the importance of supporting husbands who worked in terrible conditions, and some reasserted the notion that women did not belong in 'men's jobs' in the factory.[153] In public appeals, the auxiliary emphasized the need for an improved family wage for their husbands, which they could use for raising their families. Although the Canadian union used some innovative radio scripts from the American UE, which critiqued the company for appealing to women consumers while at the same time paying low wages to women who had to work, the Local 524 auxiliary focused predominantly on the need for a male family wage.[154]

The particular structure of the Peterborough factory definitely accentuated these problems. Ruth Milkman's *Gender at Work* argues that the historical and particular structure of an industry decisively shapes its division of labour and the union responses to these divisions. While she contrasts the more 'co-ed' American electrical industry to the male-dominated assembly line in the auto industry, there was much in the Peterborough factory that approximated the latter. The Peterborough works had always produced a high proportion of capital goods, such as turbines, large motors, and, later, nuclear equipment; the heavy industry focus of the plant and its need for a large cadre of apprentices and skilled workers meant that the factory was historically associated with male workers and that, within the factory, socially constructed notions of gendered skill and a culture of male strength were evident. Like the auto industry, General Electric offered relatively high wages in exchange both for the skills and for the physical risk involved in such heavy work. Moreover, many of the women working in the factory, who were already socialized to these gender divisions, did not welcome a collapsing of gender roles.

Furthermore, in the postwar years, women may have become even more isolated in the factory; some female jobs, such as those in the meter department, were moved elsewhere in the 1950s, with the result that the number of women workers dropped. By 1961, women made up only 8 per cent of the workforce, a decline of at least 5 per cent since 1939. As a union member recalled; this meant that 'women were spread throughout the plant, and [for the union] this was a problem.'[155]

A wide spectrum of structural and ideological barriers thus explains the small number of women in union work; by the late 1950s, sometimes the only role filled by a woman was the stereotyped one of recording secretary on the executive. More women did, however, become involved as shop stewards (for female-dominated areas) and in the union's separate organizations of women. The latter provided one of the union's most supportive and innovative means of encouraging women to challenge both specific workplace grievances and their lower wages.

WOMEN'S COMMITTEES AND THE MILITANCY OF SEPARATE SPHERES

Even before the union was certified, it held separate meetings for plant women, recognizing that women had different issues of concern and that organizing might be more propitious in smaller, female-focused groups. Also, during the war, the Genelco UE organized its own 'girls' committee for equal pay.' By 1949, Local 524 was sending representatives to women's conferences sponsored by the national organization; indeed, the first meeting held to elect such representatives resulted in the infamous seniority resolution about married women which so angered the national UE. By the late 1950s, the executive was often appointing delegates to these conferences, rather than electing them at mass meetings.

In the early 1950s, Peterborough developed its own women's committee. At their inaugural meeting, the women decided to concentrate on issues of fair wages for the work done by women and to make sure that equal pay was enforced. To do this, they concluded, 'We should take an aggressive stand against the bosses.'[156] They used Local 524's own publication, the *Voice of the Worker*, and special plant-gate leaflets to persuade women to join them. In public statements, the women's committee often tried to reassure male workers of the nonthreatening if not positive impact that women's self-organization would have on men's rights. A union pamphlet, 'Calling All UE Girls,' which was distributed in the plant, argued that 'women are exploited by the company ... They do same work for lower wages ... The company tries to get men's jobs done by women at lower rate. They want two seniority lists, and equal pay on paper only. Women want fair treatment, not to be used to take jobs away from men, nor cause unemployment for men by doing their jobs at lower rates.' [157]

The local women's committee attempted its own research on wage differences in the Peterborough factory; it held socials, such as women's after-work dinners; and it put on educationals designed to acquaint women with the widespread problems of women in industry, as well as with the immediate, practical issues of contract language.[158] Local 524 Women's Committee also tapped into the national organization's educational program, sending delegates to annual women's conferences, which discussed issues such as equal pay and worked out strategies on how to lobby for better legislation and contracts.

Some Peterborough women also participated in special weekend retreats for union women at the UE's Clearwater Lodge in the Muskokas. These sessions, in a sense early consciousness-raising groups, were central to women's understanding of gender-specific issues in the workplace. Lodge sessions explored workplace and contract issues, such as women's specific health and safety concerns, but they were also designed to encourage a critical perspective on the Canadian economy and government by stressing the broad historical and social background to women's industrial participation.

In small groups, women discussed such problems as child care, family support, and harassment at work. As one Peterborough woman remembers, the discussions were wideranging: 'Once we took twenty-five girls up at the Lodge. We had a whole weekend to talk. We talked about women coming into industry: we were there because we had to be there, because it takes two salaries to live ... We talked [about] care for children, babysitters, the attitudes of men towards women in industry – because some [of them] did fight us.'[159] Women unionists benefited from the sense of gender solidarity created at these events; talking about issues such as child care reinforced their radicalization, even if it did not appear to them to be timely or realistic to pursue these issues as public priorities.

The women also remember these getaways as providing important emotional sustenance. The sense of shared experience and comradeship was extremely important to women, such as those from Peterborough, who were a minority in their own locals but could benefit from contact with the larger group of gender-conscious female activists in Toronto. In one woman's memory, cooperation and comradeship remain as central to these events as discussions about contracts: ' I remember each table organized and would take turns serving a meal ... Then on the last night, we would have a party ... [Sometimes] we would all take the time to "let our hair down!"'[160]

These UE women initiated a collective process to raise women's economic status and independence, and though they were primarily focused on issues of equal pay and bargaining, there was also an understanding that women's different life cycle and reproductive role – thus, for example, the need for maternity leave – must be fused with their right to equality. In the so-called era of the feminine mystique, their activism was both innovative for the union movement and distinct from the concerns of more middle-class women's organizations – a form of 'working-class feminism' – though it was not labelled as such at the time.[161]

In a sense, a 'militancy of separate spheres' developed in the UE in the 1950s: women activists, supported by the union, vigorously protested the exploitation of women within their own sphere in the factory, and they actively pursued women's self-organization on this basis. And when the exploitation of women directly addressed male fears of dilution and speed-up, the union was always supportive. Rhetorically, the union also supported an end to separate seniority and wage differentials, but in reality, as one Peterborough woman concluded, 'We mainly fought for women's seniority over other women.'[162]

While the union leaders supported women's self-organization, they believed that class and union unity were paramount, and after the initial women-only conference, they insisted that the conferences be open to all unionists. Although the women usually concurred with the leadership publically, they nevertheless expressed their misgivings about how thorough the union leadership's commitment to equity really was. After the 1949 conference, Flo Farrance expressed precisely these views in a private letter: 'Men in the union do not seem to understand the girls' problems and therefore do not fight for the girls. This gives the girls the tendency to feel they are not important enough for the men to bother about.'[163]

Five years later, Evelyn Armstrong, a longtime UE stalwart from Toronto, noted that since the inauguration of the women's conferences in 1949, 'we have increased the role of women in the union, but we are still not involved in proportion to our numbers in union ... Questions of equal pay and one seniority list are not pursued in negotiations ... [and] the right of a married women to job is still [under fire].' On another occasion, she pleaded with her own union for more understanding: 'We [women] are not asking for *favours* ... we want to be treated with decency. You say women are not interested [in the union]. You have to make women feel like human beings and that you are interested in their problems.'[164] A male unionist from Local 524 put it even more bluntly, stating that in the in overall scheme of things, 'the women's committees were not that important' to the local.[165]

Ironically, in the period after the re-emergence of feminism in the 1970s, the UE women's committee was renamed the Equal Partners Committee. When women were no longer focusing their ire only on the company but were also challenging men within their unions, and when seniority lists were finally to be merged by law, and the feminist movement was providing an analysis of male power, the notion of women's self-organization had become more threatening. The neutral name, agreed to by women and men, was to reassure male workers that women did not oppose their interests but sought their cooperation.

In fact, this was a continuation of the union leadership's long-standing proclivity to endow class with more pre-eminence than gender issues. Rather than a healthy tension or oscillating authority between the two, there was simple dominance; as a result, women were absorbed into a politic of class unity, while at the same time accepting separate spheres of action. It is revealing that the activist women reconstructed their radicalization for me by emphasizing most strongly their emerging class-consciousness, even though many also acknowledged that they had a different 'standpoint' and needs from their fellow male workers. They stressed the physical environment of the Peterborough plant and the oppressiveness of management authority, noting how both became unifying forces for workers. 'It was so overpowering and [oppressive] ... even I was surprised at how dirty and physically hard the jobs could be,' one woman remembered. 'And as soon as they found out I was [outspoken], they [the company] tried to give me the worst job they could.'[166] Union education, as a form of ideology, undoubtedly reinforced the class-consciousness of the blue-collar women workers, who saw the union as an instrument that might rectify issues such as speed-up and unsafe working conditions, which they accepted as being differently experienced by men and women, though both sexes were affected.

Another activist, who stressed how the daily and sometimes petty power struggles between workers and management acted as a radicalizing force for her, made a revealing comment on where she chose to work in the factory. She preferred her job in armature, she explained, because she wanted to work with other women. She was less interested in being in punch press, where men and women both worked, because of the gender antagonism there: 'There was more strain there ... The presses were sometimes large and ... well, I guess some men thought *they* should have the jobs.' Uneasy with this statement, she added that maybe the men 'just thought it was too much for the women.'[167]

Still loyal to a notion of worker and union unity, her comments were shaped by an understandable impulse to defend her union brothers' motives as chivalrous. My analysis is somewhat different. A sense of male privilege and claim on certain jobs, and the image of a physically superior man and an inferior, weaker woman also lay behind the strain and acrimony she pointed to in this area when men and women worked together. By the end of the 1960s, when social and political conditions had changed, some women's assessment of their union was to be more critical. However innovative and progressive the UE's working-class feminism was in the 1950s, it would not be enough for women influenced by feminism of the 1970s, which did not accept separate spheres in the workplace.

CONCLUSION

On more than one occasion, women from other Peterborough work-places went to the UE office asking for advice or aid; the fact that other women sought out the UE indicates that its reputation as a militant union, willing to fight for women, was more than superficial self-congratulation. In 1967 this reputation was confirmed when the UE supported the local Tilco strikers – women workers in a small workplace who were battling an intransigent employer who was set against union recognition. The strike became a *cause célèbre* for Ontario labour, and it marked a thaw in labour's Cold War, for UE men picketed with the CCL unionists, who had shunned them for almost two decades.

The isolation imposed by the Cold War had contradictory effects on the union's program *vis-à-vis* women. On the one hand, it allowed the leadership and women activists to develop a progressive platform on gender issues, and the union's status as political pariah, as well as its left-leaning proclivities, encouraged it to exonerate itself as the more militant defender of women workers' rights. However, the UE was also cut off from any friendly criticism or aid from other unions. And the Cold War battles wasted union time, channelling members' energies into fist fights that could only alienate female membership. Tragically, as more women entered the local workforce in the 1940s and 1950s, internecine warfare and not gender issues preoccupied the local unions.

The difficulties of persuading women to join in collective protest cannot be attributed only to union politics and culture. Both the Dominion Woollens strike and the UE's attempts to organize women in the postwar years demonstrated some of the most forbidding barriers to women's collective, organized resistance. These barriers included a gender ideology that saw women as naturally weaker and as being far more tenuously attached to wage work; the conservative pressures of church or family authority and duty; apprehension of being made an 'outsider' in the community because of one's political orientation; and the tacit support of the state for the employers' agenda.

The twin pressures of company paternalism and coercion, and especially women's fears of job loss or deterioration in their conditions of work, were also major stumbling blocks to activism. It is important to emphasize that employers were the primary defenders of unequal pay and separate seniority: at every opportunity during the 1950s, General Electric opposed all union suggestions that women's pay be brought closer to men's.

Not all women, of course, regarded unions as their defenders or as an effective means of resistance. Many women wanted decent treatment, changes in their workplace, and more collective power, but they did not see unions as a means of providing these things. In 1937, though, faced with an organizational *fait accompli*, the unionized textile workers at the Bonnerworth mill, who arrived at the factory gate to find a ready-made picket line, embraced the union tactic of a strike. The women textile workers turned to collective resistance in response to a sense of economic injustice, shared physical and emotional experiences of work, and, importantly, because they were being offered an opportunity to imagine an alternative to their current working lives.

The leadership and ideology of the union, as well as its educational process, were therefore very important in encouraging and shaping the women's resistance. In theory, unions could create an inclusive process of organizing that drew all workers in, validating the importance of their specific problems and points of view. In practice, however, the unions maintained an exclusive perspective which, through its gendered assumptions about women's work roles and the means of organizing, limited women's role in the labour movement. Admittedly, organizing around both equality and difference was a difficult task: on the one hand, women's workplace culture, networks, and concerns had to be respected and used as organizing tools; on the other hand, an alliance of men and women workers had to be forged which recognized existing gender interests but which also strove to overcome them with a more equitable version of class-consciousness.

Both unions found that organizing within women's separate sphere of wage labour could have positive results. The textile union recognized that its success depended on the appointment of respected women leaders, such as Edith Frizelle, who understood the particularities of women's work culture and their workplace grievances. Although women were never a majority of the United Textile Workers' leadership, their numbers and participation were crucial to the outcome of the strike. However fleeting their association with the labour movement, the experience gave them 'a language to connect their plight to that of other workers.'[168] Looking back, Frizelle still remembers that the issue was clear: 'The strike was about wages ... starvation wages.'[169]

The UE, too, had some success in utilizing women's networks at work to draw women into the union. Aided by these networks, it militantly defended women workers in their own sphere, encouraging grievances and workplace protests that protested health conditions, timing, or speed-ups which the women saw as unjust. Breaking down the separate spheres of the workplace, however, was not a priority in either the 1937 strike or in the postwar work of the UE. This was also true of many of the women activists, who were socialized to the prevailing gendered division of labour.

Moreover, it is important to stress that separate spheres were certainly not equal spheres. In the 1937 strike, the strategy of organizing women was tacked onto the United Textile Workers' agenda, rather than being integrated into union plans from the beginning – a fatal mistake. In the UE, women's separate education was used to encourage them to become union activists – not to develop a feminist agenda that might potentially challenge, in a radical way, the gendered division of labour in the plant or in the union leadership.

The very issues tackled by the UE, however, were harbingers of a changing workplace, changing labour movement, and changing city. Whatever its failings, the union rhetorically stressed that working-class women needed to work for economic reasons, and it protested discrimination against married women in the workplace. Attempts to use unions as instruments of social change, women's right to equal pay, and the right of married women to collect unemployment insurance were all issues that stood in marked contrast to the gender issues surrounding the 1937 textile strike. At that time, the participants had been more concerned with establishing unions and with the needs of single women to a decent wage, especially in the absence of any social assistance measures such as UIC. Although the ideal of a family wage was still very strong in the 1940s, it was clearly an ideal fraught with increasing contradiction as more and more married women joined the labour force.

No sooner had men in the city won postwar wage increases and new benefits, often appealing to the ideal of a family wage, than more married women began to remain on the job and trickle back to work after childbearing. While Ruth Pierson correctly concludes that social policy during the Second World War resolutely reaffirmed a traditional gender order and the sexual division of labour, the end of the war nonetheless marked the beginning of a new era that saw an increasing number of married women participating in the labour force. For working women, the war was a watershed in that it broke down the marriage bar to employment in local workplaces and sometimes destroyed the complete ban on female employment, as it did at Outboard Marine. Married women's right to employment and the consequences of married women's wage work were to become contentious issues in the 1950s and 1960s as many women increasingly found themselves doing two jobs: wage work and mother work.

8

Doing Two Jobs:
The Wage-Earning Mother
in the Postwar Years

You were supposed to be married, stay married and have your husband bring home the bacon. But that didn't work out [for me] ... I started to work because I had to.[1]

Doreen had begun work as a domestic in the early 1930s. She quit when she married and had children, but was forced to look for work after her husband lost his job at the Auburn mill and was blacklisted in 1938. When the war started, she secured a well-paying job in the buffing and lacquer department at Westclox, but she felt she should leave after the war to return to domestic life. Later, after the birth of another child, she found that the family needed her wages again, so she took a waitressing job in a downtown restaurant, with hours that allowed her to combine child rearing with wage work.[2]

At the same time as Doreen was looking for work in the early 1950s, Beatrice was job hunting for the first time. She left high school in grade 10 because her mother, a single parent, was taken seriously ill, so Beatrice and her sister had to get jobs to support her. Beatrice found work in the expanding Bell Telephone office, and even after her marriage she continued to work. She took a short respite when she had two children, but she was soon back on the job, doing shift work and using babysitters, since her husband was unable to support the family. Beatrice remembers resigning herself to the fact that she would now be doing two jobs.[3]

Rather than returning permanently to domestic life after the Second World War, some Canadian women like Doreen and Beatrice continued in full-time jobs after they married, and a growing minority were combining child rearing with full- or part-time work for pay. Doreen and Beatrice represent the two major groups of women entering the workforce in the twenty years after the war. Many, like Doreen, were over thirty-five and were returning to work after their children were in school or had left home. The second group were younger women who had come of working age during and after the war, had joined the labour force at a later age, married younger, and were more likely to continue working after marriage than the women who went out to work in the interwar period. A minority of this group, like Beatrice, continued to do both domestic and wage work even when they had pre-school children.

In the twenty years after the end of the war, the participation rate of women in the Canadian workforce declined from its wartime high, and it was not to reach war levels again until the 1960s. At the same time, the reduced but ever-growing workforce was undergoing a significant change: more married women and women with children were going out to work.

Wage-earning wives and mothers were certainly not a new phenomenon; indeed, their numbers had been gradually increasing during the twentieth century. There had always been significant regional, ethnic, and racial differences in married women's work; as Franca Iacovetta points out, in the postwar period, immigrant women were more likely to work for wages than Canadian-born women.[4] Much of the public anxiety over working wives in this period thus betrayed an ethnocentric and to some extent class bias. What was of concern, apparently, was not that mothers were doing wage work – for many poor and non-white women had historically had to work – but rather the gradual influx of white, Anglo, and supposedly middle-class women into the workforce.

Moreover, as an Australian author has argued, the increased employment of married women in the 1950s and 1960s may simply reflect the penetration of capital into the informal economy, in which married women had been diligently working, producing goods and services for many years.[5] Still, married women's expanding role in the formal economy was certainly a phenomenon of special significance, particularly in a city like Peterborough, where it transformed the existing marital and family profile of the female labour force. These women found that their work was the focus of debate in the popular press, which continually questioned the necessity, consequences, and appropriateness of working mothers.

Sadly, their daily struggles, worries, and satisfactions were less than visible in this media debate and in the popular culture of the time, and their needs were inadequately addressed by social policy. Despite this lack of support and sympathy, however, these women represented the future; they were the harbingers of a radically new workforce, which was marked by a shift from the working daughter of the interwar period to the working mother of the contemporary period.

We need to assess the conditions of work, the division of labour, and the women's own vision of opportunity in this period, noting whether the second cohort of women – those who began work after the war – had a tangibly different understanding of their work for pay and their identity as wage earners. Secondly, we need to examine how these working mothers evaluated their need to take on wage work. How did they respond to the popular debate about working mothers, and how did they manage, and interpret, the balancing of pregnancy, childcare, domestic labour, and paid work?

There were familiar continuities from the interwar period in the economic rationale for women's wage work, the sexual division of labour, and the conditions and opportunities which the new generation of women workers faced. Discontinuities, however, were evident in the emergence of a new form of family wage economy and in the increasing significance of married women workers to the economy. The discrepancy between women's important role in the labour force and the persisting antipathy to married women's wage work foreshadowed a crucial contradiction: changing economic structures were still intertwined with a resilient patriarchal ideology. What, ultimately, were the long-term consequences of the asymmetrical variance between change and continuity that became evident after the war? Although this era was not sympathetic to the plight of working mothers, the impetus for future protest and the blueprints for change may well have been in the making.

THE RADICAL CHANGES AND RESILIENT CONTINUITIES IN
WOMEN'S WAGE WORK

In the two decades following the end of the Second World War, the number of married women, and, secondarily, women with children, in Ontario's workforce increased dramatically. At the beginning of the war, only one in twenty married women worked for pay; by 1951, it was one in ten; by 1961, one in five. In the mid-1960s the census indicated that one-third of the Ontario workforce was female and crucially, that over half of these women were married, a marked contrast to the interwar period.[6]

The most rapid increases were among women between thirty-five and forty-five, who had left the workforce while their children were young and were returning to wage work. By the 1960s, the age of women rejoining the workforce after childbearing was declining, and the number of working women with pre-school and especially school age children was increasing dramatically. At the end of the decade, the labour force participation rate of working mothers in Ontario was growing by about 7 per cent a year, far outpacing the increases in any other group.[7] Many economic experts and planners in the 1950s had not imagined or predicted such rapid and sweeping changes.[8]

These dramatic changes were the result of both demographic and economic forces. Because fewer women had been born in the 1930s and because girls were entering the workforce at a later age in the 1950s, there was a demand for female labour in the postwar period; this demand, which was augmented considerably by the economic expansion, was especially prevalent in the service sector. At the same time, the earlier age of marriage and childbearing throughout this period meant that women were ready to rejoin the workforce by their late thirties.

In Peterborough all these trends were evident. By the 1950s, the average school-leaving age had risen slightly; more girls from working-class as well as white-collar families were securing some high school education, often their junior matriculation.[9] On leaving school, some of these young women found jobs in local manufacturing establishments, but an increasing number went into the clerical and service sector, while others went into the expanding areas of education and health care. A long-term move away from manufacturing was only beginning, but it was appropriately symbolized by the closing of the Bonnerworth mill in 1958. Once one of the city's most important employers of women, the woollen industry was now in an irreversible decline. Overall, the expanding female workforce was still concentrated in female occupational ghettos, with lower wages than men's (on average, from 50 per cent to 60 per cent lower), and in sectors where women had limited means of vertical mobility.[10] Studies showed that married women in particular were more likely to be ghettoized in the service sector and to be part-time workers with fewer benefits than full-time workers.[11]

By 1961, women constituted 30 per cent of the local labour force, and about 50 per cent of these working women were married, divorced, or widowed.[12] The actual number of women working for pay was undoubtedly even higher than the census claimed, since the official statistics missed out women who were doing seasonal, part-time, domestic, or babysitting work. Some women still used the informal economy, such as dressmaking, to help increase the family income, and many more turned to part-time work in the retail and service sectors. Many of the women interviewed who began work before the war at first claimed to have left the workforce on marriage, yet they later referred to intermittent, seasonal, or part-time work taken up once their children were older; they returned to office jobs or found cleaning or factory work, or, in many cases, looked for jobs in stores, which consciously sought out women as a source of cheap and flexible labour.

For many women, part-time work was their only means of earning money while they were rearing children. Ramona, for instance, noted that her husband, a blue-collar worker, was not enthusiastic about her returning to work in the 1950s, but her choice of a job helped convince him: 'My husband didn't want me to work, but [my daughter] was in school and I saw an ad in the paper, for Sears, part-time help, just before Christmas. I didn't say anything to my husband and children. I went down to apply. Eventually I told my family. My husband didn't think too much of it, but I told him I was tired of doing the same thing.'[13]

The most striking continuities between the first and second cohorts of women workers was the persistence of this sexual division of labour. Although women were spending more time in school by the 1950s, they were well aware that their career options were different from those of the male students. A woman who went out to work in the 1950s made this quite clear. For women in high school, she remembers, there was an overwhelming emphasis on secretarial work if one did not aspire to be a teacher or nurse. University was simply out of the question: 'In my vintage, I had only one friend go to university. You just didn't. It wasn't the thing to do. There wasn't the money ... I can't remember any counselling; we were not told anything [about careers].'[14]

Occupational designation was also shaped by one's class, cultural, and even geographical background. One woman noted that, especially in the village near Peterborough where she grew up, even nursing was a rare ambition: 'Nursing was not talked about in a small town. In fact, careers for women were not talked about. It was expected that *if* a girl did go on, she would be a school teacher or a secretary.' Did she ever consider medicine, I asked. Her answer was emphatic: 'It was too expensive to train and also it [was] just not heard of [for women.]'[15]

Although the women are now more aware of the gendered streaming process of the schools, they admit that they did not necessarily 'see' it at the time. One woman, who came from a rural area, now feels that she was doubly disadvantaged: 'It was hard to move from a small town where everybody knew each other to school in Peterborough. And I found out later – and, by the way, all through school I had been first or second in the class – that when I came to PCVI [the high school], they just put me in the home economics stream. That's where the women went. And that's where people from surrounding towns went ... You had to have money to go into the academic stream then ... Girls could be a secretary or teacher. [With no typing] and grade 10, you could go to Bell or to a factory.'[16]

It is true that by the postwar period more women thought of white-collar options, such as telephone operating, bookkeeping, and secretarial, yet these were not 'new' job options for women; they were already feminized, though certainly they were expanding sections of the workforce. Thus, for the second cohort of women, there was still a narrow range of job choices, even though many women from the first cohort imagined that the next generation had far more options than they did.

Once in the workplace, a division of labour was taken as a given, despite the increased number of women with high school education and despite the minority of women who had worked in jobs designated for males during the war. Although a few women held onto blue-collar 'male' jobs such as time keeping, the reimposition of a prewar sexual division of labour was quite thorough. Employers adamantly protected and nurtured these divisions, and both men and women continued to explain them with references to the family wage.'Men made more than women – quite a bit more,' remembers a woman who worked at Quaker Oats in the 1950s. This had consequences for other benefits: 'We used to get a profit-sharing bonus. Some years it was pretty good for the times – between two and three hundred dollars in June. [But then] some of the men got *great* ones. This never came up in union meetings. It was accepted. We had a job, enough to pay your keep. That's all you worried about ... but I imagine that men had heavier jobs ... and men had families ... It [the division of labour] was accepted.'[17]

There is no doubt that men did earn more. In 1960, the starting

Quaker Oats wage for a woman was $1.38 an hour; for a man, $1.56.[18] Similarly, at General Electric, a plant worker on women's codes averaged $2.07 an hour, while those on men's codes averaged $2.47. Moreover, women tended to remain in the lower job codes, while men, especially skilled tradesmen, could reach substantially higher rates.[19] Still, with a mere 15 per cent separating men's and women's wages, these were actually some of the best-paid women's blue-collar jobs in the city. In Peterborough workplaces that represented the clerical, service, or professional sectors, the differentials between men's and women's wages were far wider, with women making from 33 to 50 per cent less than men.[20] An indication of women's lower rates and of the continuing emphasis on the pre-eminence of men's job security was expressed in a dispute at Westclox in 1969, as already noted. Faced with falling profits, the company proposed a rollback in the female rates of pay. Some women at the plant believed that the male union heads and the company were secretly collaborating in this exercise, both assuming that women were more temporary workers. In a letter to the union, however, a female unionist made it clear that the women would not accede to the wage cuts: 'We have made our stand with the Company and there will be no cutback in wages.'[21]

As the above example suggests, in the more affluent postwar period and with heightened unionization, women did alter their views of economic entitlement, increasingly seeing some workplace benefits as rights rather than as privileges. Their greater willingness to make such demands may have been encouraged by the growing age diversity and experience of women in the workforce, which gave younger women the chance to benefit from the experience of women who had been in the workplace for a long time.[22] This could also aid women's resistance; significantly, Julie Guard discovered that almost half of the activist women at UE conferences were married, many of them with children.[23]

Women's sense of entitlement was aided by unionization, for they developed new expectations, including the right to raise grievances about problems and to anticipate pay raises. 'We attended the union meetings regularly, for 3 cents an hour extra, you would,' joked a Quaker Oats plant worker. 'When you're young,' she added, 'you don't pay attention to great detail ... Most of it was men. They were the breadwinners. They had to be there. There were no women on the board ... Women didn't talk in the meetings. We were conditioned to that because at home father was the head. We [just] went and voted for our 3-cent raise.'[24]

As this quotation indicates, women's sense of entitlement had limitations. First, most white-collar women did not join unions (even if one existed, it could be extremely weak), and some blue-collar women in unions clearly felt alienated from the union process, which was largely run by men: 'Women didn't always [speak] at union meetings ... They [the leaders] argued on stage, and we didn't know what they were talking about. They just laughed at you ... [if] you stood up and said something. And there was a bar [at some meetings] ... to me that was wrong.'[25]

Secondly, vestiges of paternalism remained in many workplaces: families secured jobs for kin, and a range of fraternal, church, and sports organizations tied workers to bosses in relationships of mutual obligation. As well, in the postwar period, employers such as Quaker Oats emphasized new and expanded benefits (for example, a popular profit-sharing plan) to enhance worker-employer ties and labour peace.

Because of the sexual segregation of the workplace, women continued to shape a work culture distinctive to their goals and needs. It was characterized by attempts to create humanized space and to establish collective definitions of fair play. Mutual aid, on and off the job, was also important. As a white-collar woman remembered, 'There was a bond between the women, and they did support one another.'[26] This support, however, sometimes stopped short of extensive sharing of advice about child care. Many women were aware that being a married worker was acceptable, but working when you had young children was frowned upon. Women 'didn't talk much about child-care problems,' recalled a woman who worked at the Bell then. 'There was an unspoken rule that you didn't talk all the time about babysitting in the staff room ... Maybe you talked to your best friend, but not with everybody. You didn't want your boss to know you were having problems.'[27]

A NEW FAMILY ECONOMY

The growing presence of wives and mothers in the workplace was part of a new family economy, distinct from that of the interwar years. The long-term trend was for mothers, rather than their teenage children, to provide the wages needed by the family. This is not to say that teenagers became pampered consumers, as some social commentators worried in the 1950s. In working-class families, children were still expected to support themselves once they left school. As one woman remembers, her mother made it clear 'I wasn't going to fool around if I quit school: I had to work.'[28] Moreover, as Beatrice, who had to leave school to support her mother, indicates, teenagers could still have heavy family responsibilities. Even so, a much heavier family reliance on wives' and mothers' wages was becoming the norm.

This revised family economy was the product of new economic pressures and inflation, rising standards of consumption, and changing opportunities for women. Some women's image of work and womanhood may have been slightly modified by the war experience. Despite the resilience of the sexual division of labour and the strong ideology of female domesticity promoted after the war,[29] the postwar period did indicate some incremental changes in women's sense of identity. When surveyed, many women stated a desire to work after marriage, and some declared that childbearing did not spell an end to their work lives.[30]

The opportunity to work was crucial. One of the largest barriers to married women's work in the 1930s had been the vigilant enforcement of a marriage bar by employers.[31] One woman described how she had tried in vain to get a job at General Electric in the late 1930s: 'The foreman asked me if I was married and I said "yes," and he said "what did you get married for?" [If you were married] you didn't get in, no way ... Then, when the war came, [factories] were happy to get married women!'[23] As 'women's productive rather than reproductive labour was increasingly valued by business and the public sector'[33] in the 1950s and 1960s, the marriage bar was gradually abandoned. Indeed, for many women in the city, the relinquishment of the marriage bar offered proof that the war had indeed transformed women's work roles. Some of the women interviewed remembered the exact moment of the policy change, because the dismantling of this barrier was so significant. For example, a woman who worked at Westclox recalled: 'Until the war, married women could *not* stay on in the office. Vi was the first girl they kept on. She married Joe, from the plant. [Since she was a manager's secretary,] we held our breath to see what would happen. She was a good secretary and it was hard to get help during the war. She stayed on, and that was the start of it.'[34]

Although the marriage bar was broken, a new invisible maternity bar did remain; and in some workplaces it was not so invisible – there was a declared company policy to terminate the employment of pregnant women. Returning to work after one had children (a practice seemingly more common for blue- than white-collar women) usually happened only after the children were in school, though there was a minority of married working women with pre-school children in the 1950s and 1960s.

Given the negative or, at best, uncertain view of working mothers presented by the mass media, it is not surprising that the vast majority of women stressed the immediate economic necessity that compelled them to go out to work. Women with children also made their decision by assessing the availability of child care and, in a minority of cases, their own educational achievements and career goals.

Although the workforce as a whole offered more security and stability than it had in the Depression years, wage earners, especially in blue-collar manufacturing, still had to deal with temporary financial crises, illness, lay-off, and short time. One war bride remembers how she had to find work only ten days after the birth of her third child, because her husband became seriously ill and his sick benefits from General Electric did not start for three weeks. As soon as she was out of hospital, she found part-time waitressing work at night to tide the family over.[35]

Many of the women who had married by the early 1940s quit work, hoping to make domesticity their only job, but found this impossible. 'I did not like working ... I liked to be at home. I wanted to be there for the children after school ... I was a homebody. Still am,' said a woman who left her job at Westclox in 1939, on her marriage. But she later found that her husband's blue-collar wages did not allow her to fulfil this dream entirely. She took in dressmaking part-time, then found that she had to return to work in a store when her husband's wages on piecework at Outboard Marine went down: 'He was used to doing piecework and getting good money. They brought in a new motor and they couldn't get the bugs out of it [and so the men] went on day rate, and the pay was terrible. So I worked to help make ends meet.'[36]

Both provincial and national studies concurred that family needs were the common denominator pushing mothers into the workforce. 'Economic motives' were cited as the reason for their wage work by 75 per cent of the married women surveyed by the federal Women's Bureau in 1958; most working wives were in lower-income families, where their salaries meant the difference between bare subsistence and a more secure though certainly not affluent lifestyle.[37] In the mid-1950s, many working wives in Ontario made less than two thousand dollars a year, and in some cases their wages were the essential means of pushing the family income above the poverty line. For instance, a woman who worked primarily as a domestic in this period explained that her spouse was without a skill and was usually seasonally unemployed. Her earnings kept her family eating: 'My husband really didn't want me to work, but it was our main source of income ... I hated the work, but loved the money!'

Moreover, definitions of economic need were changing in the postwar period. The purchase of a car, some appliances and especially home ownership increasingly became important family goals. Women who started work during the insecurity of the Depression were often anxious to offer their children choices in education and occupation which they had never had, and the younger women who went out to work during and after the war had expectations shaped by economic prosperity and Reconstruction promises of income and social security. A woman who started a factory job after the war and took four maternity leaves, each time returning to work, indicated that her earnings were the only means of giving her children something she had been denied: 'If they were to have an education, then I had to work.'[39]

Women who began work in the postwar period were more forthright about their dreams for economic advancement, and especially for home ownership. At the same time, even when home ownership was a mutual goal, they sometimes had to convince their husbands of the need for their wages. One woman remembers her husband's profound uneasiness when she resumed work as a typist, even though her children were in school. 'My husband didn't want me to work ... but without my job we couldn't have afforded new things [appliances] ... nor this house.'[40] The women often felt, then and even in the interview, that they needed to justify any family money not spent directly on food and shelter. One war bride at first referred to her wage work as 'purely selfish' because she used her earnings to take her children home to Britain to see their grandparents. On one level she recognized the importance of sustaining these ties; but on the other, she found it difficult to challenge prevalent stereotypes about women working for 'extras.' [41]

Mothers who went out to work had to balance the knowledge of their own and their families' needs with a public perception that they were working for unnecessary or selfish reasons. The extent to which women were viewed suspiciously varied according to their family situation. As a Bell operator expressed it, if your husband was alive, you were 'just working for extra money ... you were seen as sort of selfish.'[42] On the other hand, widows were deemed more worthy wage earners.

One widow explained how her employers 'understood' her need to support her children and have specific hours of work.[43] Moreover, a widow's determination to work rather than go on mothers' allowance was often lauded by employers and fellow workers.

Single mothers who were separated or divorced were caught somewhere in the middle of this hierarchy of need. A divorced woman told me that people 'felt sorry' for her because she was divorced – and in a small city one's personal life was often an open book – but they also understood her need to work outside the home.[44] On the other hand, a woman whose husband was an alcoholic and did not support the family was treated less sympathetically. When she looked to her priest for advice, he said, 'Well, Jean, you made your bed ...'[45]

Although the women remember their wage work primarily in a context of economic need and a desire to improve their family's standard of living, they also note the consequences of personal satisfaction, independence, and camaraderie that they experienced in the work world. Women in white-collar work, and most particularly in professional jobs such as teaching, drew upon professional pride to explain why they continued to work outside the home. 'I taught for the fulfilment, not the money,' joked a woman who worked in a number of rural schools.[46] Women who had striven to secure a postsecondary education, such as teachers or nurses, were the most vocal about their sense of professional satisfaction, and many of them pointed out that they had been lured back to work by employers desperate for their labour in these areas: 'We were urged to come back to work [by the hospitals]. But when we did, we felt shunned by our peer group ... [for] neglecting our home duty ... As a result, we worked afternoon and nights so no one would see us working.'[47]

The independence of having one's own pay cheque (even if it was barely enough to raise a family on), combined with a liking for the workplace community, contributed to the women's positive, self-confident sense of identity as workers. One white-collar worker put it succinctly: 'I left work a number of times but always came back. I loved the girls ... and I loved my independence.'[48] As a child, she had seen her mother work, and she said she knew the independence and satisfaction it could bring, despite the double day.[49] Once they gave up their jobs for homemaking, some of the women greatly missed the workplace: 'The few weeks I spent at home after I quit work [at Quaker Oats], I nearly went crazy. I missed the girls, I missed the pay cheque. If you get a pay cheque from the time you're fourteen until a few years after you're married and it's just gone, it's terrible ... I kind of wish I had gone back ... Then I would have a pension now, something for myself.'[50]

With the emergence of this new family economy, married women increasingly joined younger single women and long-term career workers as permanent members of the workforce. Throughout this period, though, their presence was questioned, debated, and sometimes criticized by other family members, by community leaders, and by professional experts in social work, psychology, and medicine. The debate about working wives and mothers was different from that of the interwar period. Many opponents of working wives during the Depression had endorsed the merits of the family wage and claimed that women were taking jobs away from men; the contours of the debate now shifted to a grudging acceptance of married women's work for pay, but there was deep concern, even hostility, to mothers' attempts to do two jobs.

WOMEN LISTEN TO THE POPULAR DEBATE ABOUT WORKING MOMS

Despite the mounting evidence that women were spending more of their lives in the workforce than out of it,[51] public opinion surveys reflected the view that women were perceived as 'until workers,'[52] with less claim to jobs, pay, or benefits than male workers. Married women workers were well aware that they did not enjoy unqualified social approval, and mothers in particular felt that they had to 'rationalize their choice to work' with considerable proof of economic urgency of their wage work.[53] As a federal Women's Bureau researcher noted, the criticisms of working mothers were so prevalent that it would have been difficult for a woman to admit working because she wanted to, rather than because of economic need. In her interviews, working wives often deferred to the notion that their husbands were the 'real' breadwinners because 'loyalty to their husbands would not permit' them to challenge his claim to breadwinner status.[54] Women's reluctance to claim the true value of their work was related in part to the ongoing popular debate about working wives and mothers; lacking unqualified ideological support for their dual working lives, they could become apologetic, defensive, and sometimes even guilty about their wage work.

Many of the popular images in film and television and in the mass-circulation magazines during the 1950s and early 1960s presented the wife and mother who worked in the home as the archetypal, normal, and indeed superior model for North American women. As Ellen Tyler May has argued for the United States, the era of the Cold War was accompanied by, and indeed helped to sustain, a domestic ideology of nuclear family 'containment,' which extolled home and family centredness, pronatalism, and heterosexuality, all the while celebrating the security of traditional gender roles for men and women.[55] Similarly, in Canada, full-time motherhood was continually lauded in the popular press as women's natural choice, *Chatelaine* articles of the 1950s portrayed women who spurned heterosexual marriage as abnormal, while a wife who chose not to have children was 'selfish.'[56] The messages offered in early Canadian television also reinforced traditional gender roles and 'underlined the naturalness of patriarchy.' According to television's national historian, the advertisements showed women pursuing either 'beauty or the cult of domesticity,' and the programming let women play only 'supplementary' decorative, and sexually stereotyped roles, while the men became 'the masters of argument and fact.'[57] Popular images of womanhood were not without exceptions and contradictions; nonetheless, the dominant and pervasive images of womanhood and the family at this time emphasized heterosexual bliss, female attractiveness, and domesticity.[58] It is not surprising that many working women do not remember looking to the popular media for role models. As a single working mother put it, magazines and television could 'annoy me, because they weren't in touch with reality.'[59]

Despite a strong emphasis on women's homemaking roles, the emergence of wage-earning mothers did not go unnoticed in magazines and newspapers; both supporters and opponents of working wives strongly argued their cases in the Canadian press.[60] As Veronica Strong-Boag has argued, however, the overall assumptions of this debate distorted the reality of married women's work for pay; by assuming that it was simply a matter of choice whether or not a woman went out to work, it ignored the economic need that compelled women with families to work outside the home, and it erroneously portrayed Canadians as entirely middle class in income and outlook.[61] Opponents, for instance, portrayed working mothers as evidence of an increasingly materialistic society on an unnecessary consumer binge – 'on a treadmill, to buy frills.'[62] Magazines, especially in the 1950s, seldom examined the lives of single working mothers, and they offered typical portraits which were highly ethnocentric: the women were inevitably white and Anglo, and often suburban.[63]

The popular debate followed public opinion polls that showed a grudging measure of acceptance of working wives by the 1960s (not surprisingly, with more acceptance by women than by men) but strong opposition to working mothers with small children.[64] Would women's wage work hurt marriages 'or cause children to suffer?'[65] the experts fretted in the media. The opponents of working mothers based their arguments on the disastrous effect this wage work would have on marital relations and on the children's well-being. It was suggested that reversing or undermining the anchors of traditional masculinity and femininity – breadwinning and domesticity, respectively – would result in the 'unmanning'[66] of the husband, denigration of women's homemaking role, and, possibly, divorce. Most of all, it would have harmful psychological effects on the children. Popular Freudian psychology was used to buttress the contention that only adherence to traditional roles (which meant an idealized image of women in the home) would result in well-adjusted children. As one woman remembers of the 1950s, 'The magazines then, even *Chatelaine*, [said] if you were a working mother, your kids were going to be convicts in time to come.'[67]

This concern with the supposedly adverse effects on children was also suggested by some of Peterborough's religious leaders, indicating how the lectures against working mothers went far beyond the popular press. The Peterborough *Examiner* reported various local sermons that criticized working mothers.'Being a mother is a full time job,' declared a Protestant minister, while a priest implied that working mothers were responsible for increasing delinquency.[68] Some of these condemnations drew on a broader current of mother blaming, which even working mothers had trouble shaking off.[69] One teacher, herself a working mother, recalled, 'In the staff room I remember hearing men talk, and if anything was wrong with kids, it was because mothers were working.' Yet she, too, was critical of maternal care: 'Sure, there are a few bad apples whose mothers were working ... but there were other [problem] mothers who were out on the golf course, then having a few drinks before dinner.'[70]

In the light of the public suspicion of working mothers, their public supporters were frequently apologetic and defensive, and they often implicitly reinforced the sexual division of labour. For instance, they stressed the beneficial economic consequences of women's work and argued that work outside the home allowed women fulfilment and intellectual stimulation which would reflect well in their roles as wives and mothers. Moreover, they reassured their readers that women were not taking traditional male jobs but were being induced into the workforce by labour-hungry employers, who were looking for workers in pink- and-white-collar jobs. In fact, the business press was far more likely to see married women workers as a solution to their labour shortage problems than as instigators of familial and social problems.[71]

Women working in white- and blue-collar jobs were certainly aware of the image of the bad working mother; indeed, many of the working-class women I interviewed did not return to wage work after they had children precisely because they and their husbands believed it was preferable to have a home-centred mother when the children were growing up. Although a large number of the working mothers claimed not to take great stock in advice literature in the magazines, they noticed the lack of role models in the culture around them, and at some time during their working lives they had felt worry, uncertainty, or, at worst, guilt about working outside the home.

The contentious public debate these women heard in the media did not generally take the economic needs of their families, or the basic right of women to wage work, as starting points; rather, the issue of mothers' wage work was measured in relation to its perceived effect on family 'psychology.' Moreover, there was an implicit assumption of 'maternal deprivation' but never 'paternal deprivation' in these critiques of working moms. As a woman pointed out in *Saturday Night*, it would be unthinkable to ask, 'Should married men work?' or 'Are Married Men People?' yet women with families were constantly being subjected to similar questions in the work world.[72] Given the media's emphasis on family togetherness and on the need for devoted mothering as the foundation for well-adjusted children and healthy communities, it was difficult for the women to reconcile their two roles without having some contradictory feelings.

The women whose families were in need, however, coped ideologically, because their definition of family welfare was more likely to incorporate a materialist sensitivity to the family economy, in contrast to the definition of family welfare promoted in the mass media, which concentrated more exclusively on a constructed psychological image of the well-being of the child. As a former director of the Ontario Women's Bureau has noted, there were distinct class differences in the way one viewed mothers' work outside the home: middle-class mothers 'just didn't work' in the 1950s, but working-class women usually 'had to' go out to work and thus surveyed their own decisions with less guilt.[73]

BALANCING PREGNANCY, CHILD CARE, AND WAGE WORK

Many of the women working in blue- and white-collar jobs felt strong social pressure to resign once a pregnancy became visible. Depending on the workplace, they also knew that they might simply be fired. It is important to note that the prejudice against working married women and working mothers varied considerably across occupations. In some professions, married women encountered unstated but inflexible marriage bars. For example, one of the Peterborough married women 'didn't even bother applying to the school board' just after the war, because she knew the board would favour single women – though she eventually did find employment in one of the less popular rural schools.[74] Strong prejudice against hiring female spouses also surfaced when a new university was founded in the 1960s.[75] But where tradition was less élitist and labour shortages more severe, as in white- and blue-collar work, women might find that marriage was accepted, though maternity was viewed dubiously. By the 1960s, about half of Ontario's employers had developed some kind of maternity leave policy, and a few union contracts stipulated leave, but women had no legal rights to maternity leave and job security.

Few women considered working straight through a pregnancy and returning to work soon afterwards as a particularly attractive choice. It was more likely to be a necessity. If a woman did stay at work while pregnant, it could be the result of 'a favour' from management. At Westclox, a woman who reluctantly gave in her notice in the 1940s was asked by her foreman if pregnancy was the reason, and he then offered her an easier, sitting job for a number of months, since she was the sole family breadwinner at the time. But this informal paternalism – or 'kindness,'[76] as she interpreted it – was a long way from a legal right to a job.

Older women who were in the second phase of their working lives tended to see 'leaving when you became pregnant' as close to a legislated imperative: 'It was just the thing you did.'[77] More than one woman remembers the shared expectation that the plant nurse would keep an eye on women workers in order to detect pregnancies. In small workplaces, after women married (and in this small city, one's marital status was well known), the company kept a lookout to see if the women became pregnant. Younger women who began work in the postwar period also expected to be routinely asked in interviews if they were married, had children, or planned to have children.

Yet there were few cases where the physical condition of pregnancy interfered with the women's jobs. A woman who was a recent immigrant from Britain remembers that her 'combined morning sickness and whooping cough' made winding motors at General Electric 'so unbearable' that when the foreman asked her to leave, she was secretly relieved.[78] But her case was the exception. More often, it was the social disapproval of having visibly pregnant women on the job that lay behind dismissal.

There were some health and safety concerns for pregnant women, particularly in blue-collar jobs where there was exposure to heavy lifting or chemicals. But this was not the only or the major reason why women resigned or were fired. When maternity leave was first discussed in the 1960s, male medical experts were often called on to offer opinions on where, when, and for how long pregnant women could work. In many cases, their replies acknowledged that most women could work during pregnancy without 'the threat of physical damage,' but they still commented extensively on whether these women should ultimately leave work and offer 'consistent maternal care' to their children.[79] Maternity leave, in other words, was still a moral issue as much as a health issue. Knowing this full well, the women occasionally disobeyed the informal rules and used subterfuge to keep their jobs. For instance, a Quaker Oats worker simply 'wore large clothes and a girdle, and kept my mouth shut [about being pregnant].' As a result, she joked, 'I just about had my baby on the muffets line.'[80]

These younger mothers who began their working life in the 1950s after the marriage bar had been broken, came to see the pregnancy bar as the next frontier, and they increasingly questioned (and occasionally resisted) dismissal on pregnancy. 'I wanted to keep the independence of my own pay cheque,' recalled a woman who worked at Quaker Oats. 'If I had been given seventeen weeks leave [in 1951], I would have been happy. [But] they wouldn't even let you come back [after having a baby]. That was to keep the married woman home, barefoot and pregnant! '[81]

If a woman actually protested her dismissal, she was likely to find management a difficult adversary. In 1960 a separated woman in the Peterborough Quaker Oats plant was fired when her pregnancy was detected, and she courageously took it through the grievance procedure as wrongful dismissal. The union, the United Packing House Workers, supported her and brought in Mary Eady from the Canadian Labour Congress as its Board of Arbitration nominee. The woman, however, lost her grievance. The majority of the board agreed that the company had the right to decide on the marital, family, and financial status of its workers. Noting that the company had a firm policy of hiring only single women, management added that if a woman married, she could continue only until her sixth month of pregnancy, and she should not be re-employed unless 'she is the sole supporter of a family due to the husband being disabled or dead.' This was unwritten but 'well known' company policy, and the management considered it both moral and justified because it was the same as that of other companies. The company also used specific information from the personal record of the employee to justify her dismissal. But as Eady noted in her minority report, all this was irrelevant to the issue of unwritten, informal, and unfair management rights: 'If a worker could do the job, she should not be discriminated against because of pregnancy or marital status.'[82]

Such protests were few and far between. Most women did not have a union to appeal to, and they simply complied with the pressure to leave work, usually at the point when their pregnancy became visible. Until some limited legal rights to maternity leave were established in 1970 with the passage of new provincial legislation guaranteeing some (unpaid) maternity leave, such moral judgments, social inhibitions, and inconsistent employer policies acted as the arbitrary law of the land.

Even more difficult than dealing with pregnancy was the issue of child care. 'The hardest thing' about working, women said again and again, 'was concern for your kids.'[83] This concern, along with the dominant social emphasis on female homemaking as full-time work, produced contradictory self-judging on the women's part. One 1958 Canadian study on working wives, for example, quoted a working single mother who felt that 'every woman with three children should be at home all the time for her children's sake. I think my kids lost something along the way.'[84] Similarly, some of the women I interviewed who had to work when their children were young expressed regret, either individually or with the general trend: 'I would have preferred to be at home with the children' ... 'I know women that are working [now] while their husbands are getting good money' ... 'Why don't they stay home and mind their children? Parents aren't home now to raise their kids.'[85] The women's regrets are sometimes the direct product of the exhausting double burden that most working mothers carried. Those who decided not to return to work after having children were often quite clear about their attempts to avoid a double day: 'Even now,' commented one, 'I look at the woman coming home and having to prepare dinner [for her kids and] I think, I just couldn't have done all that.'[86]

Many working mothers coped with combined mother and wage work by accepting part-time or seasonal jobs, which allowed them to shape their work around their children's schedules. These jobs were usually low paying and less secure. The women also coped by trying to be model mothers and by taking on the primary responsibility for their children. Even in families where there were two working spouses, the women invariably looked after child-care arrangements as well as many extra child-care duties. 'It was just understood that I would stay home if a child was sick' ... 'Of course, I was the one to stay up at night with the children,'[87] explained two women in different occupations. If the husband was unenthusiastic about a woman's work, she would feel even more pressured to assume the responsibility for child care.

Women's uneasy feelings about leaving children while one worked depended on the children's age (with pre-school children always occasioning the most worry), who they were left with, the mother's sense of her own need for wages, and also her occupation. The worry of leaving children was linked to the practical problem of finding someone to care for them. A 1967 Canadian study showed that the majority of working women with pre-school children were using relatives and friends to care for their children for free, though sometimes reciprocal services were given. The next most popular choice was a babysitter, while only 1 per cent were using a day nursery or day-care programs.[88] The women in Peterborough followed these trends, save for the last one, since no full-time child-care centre was established until 1967.

Many working mothers relied on immediate family to care for young children, or else the parents shared child care by working shifts. Married women who worked at the Bonnerworth mill during and after the war usually took the afternoon shift, when their husbands were home (from 5 to 11 PM). Similarly, nurses worked at night while their husbands were at home with sleeping children. The majority of working mothers had school age children, and thus family aid, short-term babysitters, and latch keys were all used as child-care solutions. Nieces were sometimes asked to babysit, or the older children helped. As one single mother remembered, 'My eldest daughter was literally my right hand.'[89] In this small city, women also found, by word of mouth, older women, often widows, who would look after their children after school.

Those who relied on nonfamilial babysitters still recall the worry of calling home constantly to check on the home front. One single mother came home to find 'her sons outside in the rain' and was told by her six-year-old son that the babysitter had a visitor: 'The babysitter had been inside with a boyfriend in my bed ... She denied it, but do six-year-olds make up stories like that?'[90] The babysitter was promptly fired, but finding someone else became a new problem.

Women's child-care options were drastically curtailed because of the lack of supportive social policies, both provincially and locally. Public child care has historically been used to encourage or discourage women's labour force participation; the federal and provincial withdrawal of funding for child-care centres after the Second World War was precisely for the latter reasons.[91] In Toronto, a few centres survived the postwar cutbacks, and the memory of publicly funded child care remained an important political stimulant for some parents who continued to press for day care. But outside Toronto, as a relieved politician commented in 1949, there was 'no pressure for the establishment of daycare centres.'[92]

In Peterborough, no centre was established during the Second World War, despite the efforts of the UE women's auxiliary to secure one for war workers. In rural areas and in small cities and towns, there was no history of full-time creches or child-care centres, and often little public support for subsidized aid for working mothers.[93] Since local initiative was crucial to the provision of day care, municipal parsimony was also part of the problem. The local reluctance to spend money had a strong ideological component, for day care violated the concept of the nuclear, patriarchal family, which many local politicians felt must be defended – particularly because more married women were now working. When the issue of a municipal centre was first broached in Peterborough in 1966, the city's welfare committee and administrator said that the city was uninterested. Two of the aldermen on the welfare committee voiced their opposition in no uncertain terms. One raised the financial issue, saying that 'taxpayers' money' should not be used to look after children whose mothers were working. The other made clear his ideological opposition: 'I am a firm believer,' said Alderman Curtin, 'that all children need proper, and if possible a mother's care.'[94] However, even the local newspaper found their opposition questionable at a time of increasing female participation in the workforce.

A year later, the city's first day-care centre was established, on the initiative of the local Children's Aid Society (CAS) and the Community Chest, with aid from the Peterborough Health Unit and Family Counselling. The centre was set up to aid single mothers and children who were seen to be at risk. A former social worker recalled that the CAS had financial reasons for its involvement, since it thought the centre might help reduce the CAS protection budget. Another participant remembers that it was not intended to provide care to all working parents, but rather to 'prevent disintegration of family life and to offer security and attention to children ... where there was a need for assistance.'[95]

By the early 1970s, Peterborough social workers and the community organizations that aided women and children finally began to call more strongly for child care. But for the first postwar generation of working mothers, organized child care remained an unappealing option. In a society in which organized pre-school care had weak cultural traditions, the women felt hesitant and worried about placing their children with strangers, even qualified ones. They also claim that they would not have used day care, for it was associated with welfare status and low-income people. If women already felt under seige because of their wage work, they felt vindicated when a close family member provided care for their children, for this offered the respectability of keeping children within the privacy of the family. 'We coped entirely on own,' remembered one woman proudly, adding that she did not have to go outside the family.[96]

Despite their personal experience of worry and exhaustion, publicly funded child care remains one of the most unacceptable ideas to women of this generation. This may be related to a misunderstanding of the financial costs of day care and a sense of pride in their individual survival. A union activist, who began factory work in Peterborough in the 1960s, stated it succinctly: 'Many women were unsympathetic to day care when we raised it, because they had coped, so why couldn't we?'[97]

GROWING CONTRADICTIONS

Child care was not the only problem working mothers faced. Families, and husbands in particular, were sometimes less than supportive about their work. The women remember their husbands' fear that their status would be diminished if their wives worked: 'It was a sort of feather in his cap then, you know, if the wife didn't work'[98] In other households, the necessity of having more than one income led to a readier acceptance of women's full-time wage work. One war bride, who secured white-collar work, explained that her husband was supportive 'because it was simply a financial matter,' but she added, 'Mind you, he never changed a diaper.'[99]

Husbands worried that their wives' wage work would detract from their domestic and child related duties. The fathers who performed a substantial amount of domestic work traditionally done by women were a distinct minority; most working mothers worked a double day, and then some. The long-established practice of women's unpaid work in the home left women 'ironing until one or two in the morning'[100] in order to finish both jobs, though they did develop various coping strategies. These ranged from establishing 'a regimented household' or purchasing some household services to lowering their expectations. 'Eventually,' admitted the above 'my kids had to wear some wrinkled clothes.'[101]

The expectation that women should both iron the clothes and earn money indicated the sharpening contradiction of this period: while a growing number of women continued to work after marriage, their responsibility for family care did not in any way diminish. The effects of the postwar social dislocation, argues Elaine Tyler May, were to accentuate the emphasis on traditional female domesticity and male breadwinning. Working mothers thus faced very high expectations for their standards of maternal care and domesticity at the same time that rising costs were forcing them into the workforce.

As a result of this contradiction, women expressed pride in their wage work while also apologizing for and worrying about it. The reality that women spent much of their time raising the family, combined with the pervasive popular image of the nurturing mother, meant that balancing mother work and wage work could produce conflicting feelings. The women interviewed still vividly recall their mixed emotions and the guilt they sometimes experienced: 'Once my son broke his ankle and had to stay home alone and I had to go in. I felt so terrible ... If I needed to work on weekends to make ends meet, I felt bad about leaving the kids, but you know, I just had to.'[102]

One response to the conflicting pull of two jobs was that women internalized the dominant 'ideology of mothercare'[103] and the experts' warnings about the psychological consequences of their work. In some cases, they coped ideologically by attempting to distinguish their individual needs and circumstances from broader social experiences. Some women lamented or regretted their need to work, claiming that it was hard on their children; others justified work in their own particular situation but expressed social disapproval of other mothers, such as those with pre-school children or working spouses. Such paradoxical thinking was evident in a woman who began to work at Westclox during the war. She remembered feeling that she should resign when the war ended: 'They would have kept the married women on, but I had five kids and I thought I should quit.' On the other hand, she did want to keep her job: 'I would have liked to have worked [because] Grandma was good with the kids ... I was getting 57 cents an hour then, and I thought I had the world by the tail!' Ironically, her overall assessment of the more recent increase in working mothers is somewhat negative, betraying the contradictions underlying her own balancing of mothering and wage work: 'I don't know, I think that's one of the biggest mistakes that ever happened in the country, when they let married women back into the factory.'[104]

While women could easily mix together feelings of guilt with the knowledge that they had work or wanted to work, it is revealing that one woman who was actively involved in union politics and attended many conferences on women and work during the 1950s was better able to concentrate on women's economic needs and rights, and had little patience for those who focused on questions of the morality of mothers' work. Her intellectual metamorphosis as a union activist helped her see the negative side of the motherhood myth and acknowledge the sheer economic necessity of mothers' wage work. In contrast to the trade union publications of the 1930s, those of the 1950s were slightly more sensitive to the reality of married working women. Although a certain ambivalence prevailed, especially in many workplaces, most unions publicly acknowledged the economic needs and even the rights of married women workers.

When analysing their past, the women were well aware of the contradiction between their need for decent wages and the fixed barriers they faced in the workplace, in terms of occupational choice, lack of upward mobility, and the outright opposition to pregnant women or mothers working. They often described the division of labour and the limiting rules set by employers as inevitable or unchallengeable. For instance, they had to accept that some employers would not hire or promote women with families; and they had to comply with the paternalistic rule that they 'bring a note explaining they had a babysitter'[105] before they would be allowed to regain their job after having a child.

The women described these barriers and the prejudice against working mothers with various degrees of criticism and acceptance. Those in the first cohort, who had begun wage work before the war, tended to see the restraints as especially immutable; some even criticized later attempts by women workers to challenge them. The women from the second cohort, however, were more aware of these barriers even if they did not see any immediate means of overcoming them. Moreover, both groups were insistent that we judge their strong commitment to mothering, and even their decision to follow female occupations, not merely in the light of discrimination but also as positive choices that reaffirmed an important part of their feminine identity.

The immense contradictions that working mothers faced, though difficult to live through, also had the potential to shape new goals and new identities for women wage earners. A woman's identity as a worker was still shaped by the sexual division of labour in the workplace and the home, and by the work culture and popular culture she was immersed in, but the new life cycle of family and work that was evolving was to have incremental effects on her self-definition as a woman worker. This was most particularly true of women who joined the workforce after the war and had been in it longer. They identified with their role as breadwinners as well as homemakers; they spoke of achievement in the workforce as well as in the home. Although this generation's self-image as workers was still fractured – even ambiguous and sometimes self-effacing – there were signs of a more complex self-portrait in the making, which involved competing sources of pride, purpose, and identification, and included a more firmly fixed notion of lifelong wage work existing together with family and domestic commitments.

CONCLUSION

As Alice Kessler-Harris argues of the immediate postwar era, its most important legacy may have been the long-term 'radical consequences' precipitated by evolving 'incremental change' in women's working lives.[106] Perhaps it is in the subsequent generation of daughters, raised by this postwar generation of working mothers, that those radical consequences are most clearly evident. This is well illustrated in two stories of mother-daughter relationships taken from my interviews. The woman worker from Quaker Oats who lamented the loss of the 'independence' of her pay cheque and expressed some wish to return to work after marriage, 'though they wouldn't let you then,' noted with some pride that her daughter had developed even more radical views on this issue: 'Today, things are different, my daughter is altogether different. Boy, she's for equal rights right down the line.'[107]

The second story concerns a woman I knew who urged me to interview her mother, who had worked at Canadian General Electric after the war and at other jobs throughout her life. She indicated that her mother might not readily volunteer because she was too unassuming and did not see her work as important enough. Yet the daughter viewed her mother's wage work in a very different light. She told me how her mother had gone out to work ten days after she was born, and she saw her mother as a pioneer and, indeed, as a strong and courageous woman. Both these stories indicate a different comprehension and sensibility towards wage work on the daughters' part; both stories suggest that the mothers' wage work and influence were factors shaping the distinct view of their daughters.

In the immediate postwar period, however, working mothers had to understand, justify, and interpret their wage work in a cultural and social context that offered them little positive ideological reinforcement, legal protection, or practical help in terms of social policy. The knowledge that they could be dismissed on pregnancy or because of their marital status offered a clear message that mothers did not enjoy the right to wage work. Given this inhospitable atmosphere, the women's contradictory feelings about their working lives become understandable. The ideological – not to mention physical – wear and tear of combining motherwork and wage work took its toll.

Women's memories offer us a means of understanding the reality which they themselves saw, the economic and ideological premises on which they based their choices, and the way in which they negotiated the profound contradictions not only in the popular perception of working mothers but indeed in their own minds. The domestic ideal promoted in the wider culture, along with women's lower wages and lack of job mobility, meant that many women, particularly those in the first cohort, saw homemaking work as opposed to wage work as a sensible, sometimes inevitable, and certainly socially respectable career choice. Moreover, leaving their jobs on marriage, though certainly not desired in every case, was often interpreted as a sign of family economic well-being and as one way of avoiding the double day. This embrace of domesticity seemed a logical choice in a world of few choices, though, as we now know, the long-term consequence of this 'defensive strategy of domesticity'[108] was the perpetuation of women's economic dependence and social subordination.

Women, however, also discovered that various realities intervened to complicate their choices. At least half of the first cohort and the majority of the second had to combine domestic labour with work for wages at some point in their lives – in the informal economy, through part-time work, or (for a growing minority) through full-time work. Whatever the supposed moral consequences of working mothers, business and government saw a need for female labour in the expanding economy, and families found that there were important economic pressures – as well, sometimes, as the women's more personal needs – encouraging women's labour force participation.

It was primarily the knowledge that their wages were needed by the family, or that their work was socially productive, that gave them the fortitude and pride to persist. In hindsight, women stressed the importance of their outside work to family security and advancement, as well as the positive consequences for their children's development. Indeed, given the massive influx of mothers that occurred in the decades after 1970, some women take a certain pride in their place as pioneers of a radically altered workforce.

The radical potential of these alterations, however, has yet to be fully realized. Mothers' paid work should raise questions about economic power and hierarchy within the family; about women's responsibility for unpaid domestic work and their 'natural' role of caring for young children; about their right to equal economic citizenship and respect; and about our collective social responsibility for child care. All these issues became points of contention and debate, and also focal points for feminist organizing, in the period after the 1960s. Despite some important changes as a result of this organizing, many of the issues remain unsolved challenges for today's wage-earning mothers.

Conclusion: From Working Daughter to Working Mother

When my husband went back to school [in the 1950s] and I had to go out to work, my mother was very upset. They offered to have me go home and live; they saw this as 'a bad thing' I guess, as hardship for me. But I didn't mind ... [Now] I think my daughters liked having a working mother. Now ... I hear them talking about me with pride.[1]

This woman's recollection indicates the way in which mothers' understanding and advice about wage work, both intended and unintended, were perceived by their daughters. While a daughter might eschew her mother's counsel, she was often affected, subtly or profoundly, by her example. This woman's memory also points to a repeated pattern evinced by these interviews and over this time period: daughters born after the Second World War have been more likely to take lifelong wage work as a norm, thereby reflecting the expansion of the labour force from working daughter to working mother.

The decision of daughters about when to work, what occupation to follow, and whether to combine wage work and homemaking, however, depended on far more than familial example and direction. The working lives of both groups of women – those women who went out to work in the interwar period and those who began work in the postwar period – were shaped by the local economic opportunities, the particular needs of the family economy, and images of what was fit and proper work for women, as well as by the personal ambitions of the individual women. Indeed, a crucial message of this book is that our examination of women's wage work and of the choices women perceived to be open to them must be placed in the broader context of their non-waged work, their family lives, the dominant cultural definitions of femininity, and state policy.

Furthermore, the historical sources we utilize to sketch out both the context and the detail of women's work histories must be questioned and contrasted against each other. Oral history, while an invaluable means of exploring women's daily working lives and the texture of workplace and family relations, must not be seen either as an unmediated, exact replica of women's past or as a mere construction and creation of many discourses relayed to us through language and culture. Rather, the cultural form that memory assumes and the structural context in which it is embedded are connected: two parts of one picture. The ways in which women remember and interpret their histories provide important insight into the material conditions they encountered, the ideological influences on their lives, and the personal choices they comprehended and made. The analogies, metaphors, and patterns of language that women employ to describe – and comprehend – their own experiences are also inseparable from those experiences.

This conclusion speaks to the broader theoretical assumptions and debates between historical materialism, feminism, and poststructuralism that have shaped my research. The notion that productive and reproductive relations are fundamental to an analysis of women's lives remains a basic premise of this book. A study of working women must take into account the context in which women sell their labour power and the evolution of relationships between classes, because the latter set out the structures, limits, and possibilities for women's experience and behaviour. At the same time, historical materialism must be infused with an awareness of the operation of patriarchal social structures and with attention to women's active creation of their own history.

In short, materialist traditions need to be completely transformed by feminist theory. Without the sincere intent to combine an analysis of class with that of the sex-gender system, any comprehension of the tenacity of the sexual division of labour or of women's acceptance of the ideal of domesticity – both central themes in this book – remains elusive. To comprehend the latter fully, we may also have to draw on the insights of theorists such as Gramsci, who saw ideology and consciousness as the lived product of social practice, experience, tradition, and culture. In a feminist appropriation of Gramsci, we can say that although culture is mediated by material life, it has its own 'dialectical dynamics' and reproduces, through consent as well as coercion, the 'hegemony of a ruling gender as well as a ruling class.'[2]

Indeed, my conclusions call for a reconsideration of the tarnished concept of ideology rather than for an analysis of signs and signifiers. We need to analyse the dominant and oppositional ideologies shaping work – not in the classic Marxist sense, simply as automatic reflections of economic realities, but as systems of thought that offer meaningful *reasons* for those realities: as a 'set of *effects* within discourses which contribute to the process of explaining, justifying, legitimating, or perhaps masking and countering, social relationships.'[3] Ideologies are constituted by and express social and political interests, and thus power relations; at the same time, they may be lived and experienced as daily life, tradition, and culture, shaping women's interpretations of their working lives and influencing their efforts to create a life of respect and security for themselves. This understanding, which both attends to the materiality of ideology and its more slippery existence within variable systems of meaning, can be fruitfully used to understand the reproduction of a gendered division of labour, the creation of work culture, and the process of accommodation.

Class and gender, I have also tried to emphasize, are symbiotic relationships, shaped by historical, regional, and cultural circumstances. Moreover, just as class must be seen as an evolving relationship rather than as a rigid structure, so must gender be seen as an equally significant relationship, indeed a *process*, with material and ideological foundations and with shifting meanings and boundaries.[4]

Ideally, a community study like this one offers a window on the specific configuration of class and gender relationships in a local setting, while also pointing to significant contrasts and similarities with working women in other communities and provinces. The availability of blue- and white-collar work for females in Peterborough meant that the experiences of its working women were quite distinct from those of women in primary resource communities, and also from the many immigrant women and women of colour in the larger cities, whose job choices were far more limited. Furthermore, the variety of blue-collar work and the division of labour emphasizing a male breadwinner made Peterborough somewhat distinct from the 'woman's town' of Paris, described so well by Joy Parr.[5] At the same time, common themes are apparent in both locations: domestic labour remained largely the worry of women; and, ideologically, working-class women were anxious to defend their good names as respectable and competent mothers. These similarities intimate the importance of connecting local specificity to the larger story and highlighting the corresponding influences on working women, such as their responsibility for reproductive work, and the dominant cultural images of sexual difference that shaped their perspectives.

Finally, in an attempt to redress existing masculinist historical scripts, this book has stressed the centrality of gender to working-class history, though it consciously focuses on the experience and stories of women. Gender is crucial to organization of the workplace, not just where we expect to find it, in the sexual division of labour, but also to forms of authority and management, responses to paternalism and unionization, shop-floor culture, and the very identity that workers constructed for themselves on and off the job.

Gender differences were created long before women's first day at work. Girls' early socialization in the family, among peers, and at school helped create gendered patterns of work and identity 'before they even entered the factory gate.' From a young age, women absorbed important messages about class status, the inflexibility of the sexual division of labour, and respect for parental authority. Although their negotiation of these dominant messages about family and work was individual and unique, there were common themes apparent in their memories. Particularly prominent were the duty of family contribution and the acceptance of a division of labour, especially women's primary responsibility for domestic work.

Women's ambition was thus socially constructed, shaped by what was seen as possible and probable for young women, by the economic and social structure of the local community, and by the imperatives of the family economy. These lessons were particularly clear for the first cohort of women, most of whom had gone to work while they were young teenagers, still under the parental roof. By the post–Second World War period, it was more often wives and mothers who aided the family with wage work, though young women, especially those from less economically secure families, still felt the pull of family obligation. The pressure to help support the family was sometimes resisted or resented, but more often it was fulfilled; women from the first cohort especially felt that they owed their parents some economic aid.

For these women, earning respect was both a strategy and a goal in itself. For teenagers of the first cohort, going out to work for wages was a strategy designed both to aid the family economy and to enhance their own independence in the family. Once in the workforce, this quest for respect was often stymied by the lack of job control and mobility, and by the rigid and gendered authority patterns women faced on the job – though the women certainly negotiated, as best they could, to obtain decent treatment from fellow workers and management. Furthermore, women's lower earnings, which reflected the social devaluation of women's labour and the assumption of female dependence, seldom gave them the means of achieving real economic independence and security.

During the Depression especially, an overwhelming sense of job insecurity, fostered by management as well as by the economy, encouraged women to accept extremely arduous physical conditions. It is revealing that the heat, the worry, and the rows and rows of spindles to be tended at the Bonnerworth mill remained not only a memory but literally a recurring nightmare in one woman's mind. Indeed, these Peterborough women stated a relative preference for Westclox and similar factories, not only because of the physical conditions, but because managerial authority was exercised with a degree of flexibility and there were at least limited possibilities of lateral movement into white-collar work, which offered less arduous working conditions, more workday freedom, and a higher social status.

Overall, though, mobility within most workplaces was limited, and sex segregation of jobs was the rule. Occupational divisions in the workplace were based both on class and on the privileges bestowed by education, but they were also based on gender: women assembled watches and typed invoices; men designed timepieces and managed the office. Women's recollections of these divisions are revealing; the degree to which they emphasized how natural and taken-for-granted the sexual divisions of labour were, points to the hegemonic strength of the structural and especially the ideological underpinnings of a sexual division of labour. Although each of the four workplaces had its own distinct division of labour, there were strong commonalities in the justifications for women's placement in 'female' jobs. Women's physical difference and inferiority, their so-called temporary wage work, and especially the concept of a male breadwinner were invoked as rationales for the fact that women did the assembling, men the directing. These justifications for the gendered division of work were extremely resilient and became ingrained in the very symbols, language, and meanings attached to men's and women's jobs in the workplace.

The reproduction of these gender divisions was shaped in a crucial way not only by capitalist economies and management's ongoing efforts to restructure the workforce by gender to its own economic advantage, but also by patriarchal relationships and images, situated both on the job and in the family and the wider community. Men and women participated in the gendering of work as they drew on ideological representations of masculinity and femininity, and invoked the ideal of a male breadwinner and female domesticity – though this ideal had a difference resonance, meaning, and outcome for men and women. While one of these factors could take on the dominant role in sexually segregating a particular workplace, in general they were not separate systems but were interdependent, part of one fabric. For instance, although managerial initiative was clearly crucial in shaping a segregated labour force at General Electric, we cannot discount the role of male workers in protecting their skills, wages, and jobs. These threads cannot be easily separated with definitive authority assigned to one or the other cause; after all, we simply do not know what would have happened if male trade unionists had put equality on the bargaining table – because it never happened.

Women's working lives, of course, encompassed much more than the gendered division of labour. Their work culture – concepts of fair work practices, social pastimes, rituals, and interaction on the job – also shaped their identity as workers and as women. Moreover, this identity was created not only from what women experienced, day in and day out, on the line or in the office, but also by the ideas, practices, and traditions they carried to work with them from the family and community. These traditions were mediated by women's marital status, age, and placement in the family, but they were still gender specific. Women created distinct networks of support and friendship for themselves, and they were integrated into a workplace culture shaped by the sexual division of labour and by cultural understandings of a woman's familial role, her feminine personality, and her goals for the future.

Using the networks created by their work culture, women attempted to create an atmosphere and conditions of work which allowed them some flexibility in discipline, respite from routine, recreation, and, very importantly, respect. Indeed, this emphasis on earning respect offers one means of understanding the process of accommodation that women participated in at work. The process of creating and negotiating consent, which is often undertheorized in favour of the more rousing theme of resistance, is of particular interest to this study. Although the compromises of accommodation described in these four workplaces were similar to the organization of other patriarchal and capitalist economies, they also took a distinct form in this small and insular city, with its stable population, its ethnic homogeneity, its history of close family networks, and its small-town pressures and paternalism.

Accommodation was in part an instrumental means of coping with economic and managerial control; on one level, women accepted the rules of the game because the organization of the capitalist-shaped work process left them little choice or room to manoeuvre. However, a more subtle process of manufacturing ideological consent was also at work here, since accepted norms of class and gender hierarchy were dispersed through workplace practices, social relations, and culture, becoming part of a 'common sense' view of life. Gender was central to the creation of this ideological hegemony; paternalism was itself sustained by its incorporation of a gender ideology, and patterns of patriarchal authority were integral to the organization of work; they were ingrained in the workers' subjective understanding of their responsibilities and rights and the 'natural' hierarchy in the workplace. At the same time, accommodation was a two-way process in which women bargained, however informally, for good working conditions and respect on the job. In return for a measure of dignity and security, they might offer hard work and loyalty. But when this tenuous bargain was violated, the women were quite ready to rebel.

While most women's resistance remained informal, sporadic, even hidden, they were ready to embrace the collective organization of unions when wages were perceived to be particularly unfair or the deterioration of working conditions especially severe, or when leadership and an existing organization offered the ideological liberty and structural means for self-organizing. Both the 1937 textile strike and the ongoing organization of women within the United Electrical Workers after the Second World War pointed to the need to organize women with attention to their own distinct working conditions, but also with an eye to integrating them into union leadership – a task that proved difficult in both situations.

When contrasted, these two forms of resistance before and after the Second World War highlight crucial changes in the workforce and in women's role in labour organizing. In 1937 the women demanded a decent wage commensurate with their difficult work and the wage levels in other industrial workplaces; by the post–Second World War period, issues of equal pay, maternity leave, and a recognition that women were in the workplace as permanent workers were far more apparent. This had something to do with the United Electrical Workers' own political agenda, but it also reflected the changing nature of the workforce: working daughters were now being joined by more working mothers.

Despite the apparent contrast between the processes of accommodation and resistance, a central theme emerges in both instances; whether women accepted the manager's rules of the game and the gendered division of labour or whether they picketed, organized, and spoke against the status quo, their actions often reflected an ongoing quest for independence, security, and dignity. Within the broader community as well, maintaining respectability – symbolized by hard work, honesty, contribution to family, and appropriate gender roles – was important for working women. Nevertheless, some women did question and push on the bounds of the dominant definitions of respectability, attempting to break with family authority or establish some independence of leisure, and a minority even challenged the community standard of respectability.

Many women also found that the economic crises of Depression, ongoing unemployment, and familial dissolution threatened their attempts to earn wages and maintain respectability. These crises, though apparently temporary, highlighted a persisting problem; the dominant definitions of respectability could be confining and conservative, dismissing and obscuring the lives and struggles of many women who, without a male breadwinner lived outside the rigid parameters of the supposedly normal nuclear family. Single mothers, for instance, were viewed warily and were offered little means, through social policy or earned wages, to provide their families with real security, let alone prosperity.

There were, of course, meaningful changes in social policy over this time period. The deserted mother of the Depression years, who was forced to take her children to an orphanage, had fewer options than the deserted mother of the 1960s, who could now claim a mothers' allowance and family allowance, however meagre. But the continuities are also clear, both for the workplace and for social policy. Women had to contend with an ideology of the male breadwinner and with different notions of domesticity for men and women; women still faced the prospect of economic dependence and of moral judgments of their right to work based on marital status; and they encountered a persisting sexual division of labour, even if the workforce was encompassing more women in service and public sector jobs, which would rapidly unionize in the 1960s and 1970s.

Structural alterations in the workplace, however, did mean that cracks would develop in these assumptions. By the 1950s and 1960s, there were marginal changes in women's outlook. The war and postwar promises of economic security, the increasing time spent at wage work, the growing experience and age of women in the workforce, and their coinciding responsibility for home and work led to some questioning of these ongoing limitations.

Women who continued to work after marriage in the 1960s were not simply dismissed as 'money grubbers,' as the married woman in the 1930s had been. The Quaker Oats plant worker who contested her dismissal on pregnancy indicated a sense of entitlement and a knowledge of unions that very few women in the 1930s had possessed. The politically astute women who organized into the United Electrical Workers in the 1950s were demanding equal pay and an end to wage differentials, not simply a decent wage as women had done in the 1930s. All these changes reflected different economic and social conditions, and symbolized an altered consciousness on the part of working women. They represented fissures in the existing social hierarchy that would soon be questioned more concertedly and loudly by working women. They were a portent of the more thoroughgoing critique of women's work that was to evolve with the next generation of working daughters and working mothers.

Appendix A
Note on the Oral History Sources

Oral histories were one of the major sources used to research this book. These interviews were done over a three-year period, and they concentrated on women in four companies: the Bonnerworth (a section of Dominion Woollens), Westclox, Canadian General Electric (CGE, or GE), and Quaker Oats. Since women moved from one workplace to another, some interviewees worked at more than one of these companies, and many (at least 40 per cent) had other work experiences which they discussed during the interview. The subjects were volunteers who had heard of the project through newspaper articles or who were contacted by me after being recommended by a fellow worker, a family member, or, sometimes, a manager. This is a snowball sample, then, which does not exactly replicate the demography of these workplaces. The interviews were generally two to three hours in length and, in a few cases, were followed up with telephone information.

Seventy-five interviews with women were completed, ten with men. The majority of these women began work before the Second World War broke out, and a minority began work during the war. There are also twelve women who started their working lives after the war and who worked into the 1960s. They are often referred to as the 'second cohort' of women, while those who began work before the war are called the 'first cohort.' Of the women who began work during the 1930s and then married, at least half returned to work at some time later in life, joining the second cohort in part-time, seasonal, or full-time work.

The analysis of interviews done with these two groups raises some difficult methodological questions. In actual fact, women's lives are not easily chopped up into time periods that have distinct social and economic contexts. A woman who began work in the late 1930s may have more in common with her younger sister (who comes from the same family and the same ethnic and social background but who started work after the Second World War) than she has with a woman of her own cohort. Moreover, women's working lives are often more complicated than men's, for women are involved in many kinds of labour, including reproductive labour, that are not remunerated. A woman might work in the home caring for parents and not go into factory work until after the war; yet in terms of age, she belongs with a different cohort. Or she might do domestic work on an intermittent basis and not even see it as wage work. There are many such variables. In analysing the interviews, then, I tried to be sensitive to these contingencies before drawing generalizations about women from different cohorts.

As well as the eighty-five interviews described, I completed eight interviews with women who began work in the postwar period as teachers and nurses. I have used these for another project, but in chapter 8 I occasionally refer to them in order to describe the social context. I was also given access to eight interviews, five with blue-collar women and three with white-collar women, done for an oral history project by Margaret Phillips on Outboard Marine, a company founded in the 1920s which closed down most of its operation in 1990. These women all began work in the very late 1930s or in the 1940s (for women were not hired on the production line until the war).

Some of the interviews utilized were done under the Work Study Program by Helen Harrison, Rhonda Jessup, and Linda Driscoll, though I listened to all the interviews and usually transcribed them myself.

Only a minority of the people were comfortable with having their names or initials used in the book; they include the better-known labour leaders, who are used to a public profile. The vast majority of interviewees, therefore, have been assigned pseudonyms in order to protect their anonymity.

Appendix B
Tables

TABLE 1
Labour force participation in Peterborough

	1921	1931	1941	1951	1961
Total population	20,994	22,327	25,350	38,272	47,185
Female population	10,941	11,605	12,847	19,846	24,331
Female population of working age	8,931	9,284	9,763 [1]	14,744	16,928
Women working	1,940	2,107	2,791	4,473	5,308
Men working	6,180	6,576	7,394	10,257	11,905
Female participation	21.7%	22.7%	28.65%	30.3%	31.3%
Female: male	1:3.1	1:3.1	1:2.6	1:2.3	1:2.2

SOURCE: *Census of Canada*, 1921, vol. 4, table 3; 1931, vol. 8, table 43; 1941, vol. 7, table 9; 1951, vol. 4, table 22; 1961, vol. 3:2, table 5
[1] Estimate

TABLE 2
Female workers by industry

	1921	1931	1941	1951	1961
Manufacturing	693	841	1,192	2,066	1,282
Construction	2	3	2	10	21
Transportation	53	60	22	106	154
Trade	311	325	388	766	992
Finance	46	59	77	190	250
Service	725	804	1,085	1,460	2,383
Other	110	10	23	23	87
Total	1,940	2,107	2,791	4,640	5,308

SOURCE: *Census of Canada,* 1921, vol. 4, table 3; 1931, vol. 7, table 54; 1941, vol. 7, table 25; 1951, vol. 4, table 17; 1961, vol. 3:2, table 5

TABLE 3
Number of women in specific occupations in Peterborough

	1921	1931	1941	1951	1961
All occupations	1,940	2,170	2,791	4,473	5,308
Manufacturing total	693	565	788	1,179	946[1]
Manufacturing					
Vegetable	42	14	122	n/a	n/a
Animal	34	17	35	n/a	n/a
Textile	349	344	172	199	n/a
Service general	725	713	977	588	1,170
Saleswomen	178	196	219	381	574
Graduate nurse	145[2]	92	85	60	286
Teacher	98	101	112	151	282
Clerical	347	442[3]	629	1,311	1,594
Personal service	177	215	252	89	273
Waitress	18	16	34	118	235

SOURCE: *Census of Canada,* 1921, vol. 4, table 3; 1931, vol. 8, table 43; 1941, vol. 7, table 9; 1951, vol. 4, table 22; 1961, vol. 3:1, table 10
[1] Estimate
[2] Includes nurses in training
[3] Estimate

TABLE 4
Average earnings in Peterborough

	1921	1931	1941	1951	1961
Total earners	3,944[1]	7,373	9,091	14,730	15,975
Male earners	3,130[1]	5,480	6,660	10,257	10,842
Female earners	814[1]	1,893	2,431	4,473	5,073
Average weeks worked	n/a	M 42	M 45	n/a	n/a
		F 45	F 42	n/a	n/a
Average earnings	n/a	M 1,007	M 1,123	M 2,250[2]	M 4,099
		F 571	F 579	F 1,750[2]	F 2,102

SOURCE: *Census of Canada*, 1931, vol. 5, tables 2, 9; 1941, vol. 6, table 2; 1951, vol. 5,
table 18; 1961, vol. 3:3, table 34
[1] Estimate
[2] Mean estimate

TABLE 5
Major racial origins in Peterborough

	1921	1931	1941	1951	1961
English	10,248	10,898	13,069	n/a	n/a
	48.8%	48.8%	51.6%		
Irish	6,142	6,197	6,410	n/a	n/a
	29.3%	27.8%	25.3%	n/a	n/a
Scot	2,866	3,210	3,388	n/a	n/a
	13.7%	14.4%	13.4%	n/a	n/a
Other	97	82	135	n/a	n/a
	0.5%	0.4%	0.5%	n/a	n/a
Total British	19,353	20,387	23,002	33,083	39,572
	92.3%	91.3%	90.8%	86.4%	84.0%
French	701	831	971	1,612	2,272
	3.3%	3.7%	3.8%	4.2%	4.8%
German	135	158	185	480	1,259
	0.6%	0.7%	0.7%	1.3%	2.7%
Italian	345	423	449	634	980
	1.6%	1.9%	1.8%	1.7%	2.0%
Other	460	528	743	2,463	3,102
	2.2%	2.4%	2.9%	6.4%	6.5%

SOURCE: *Census of Canada*, 1921, vol. 1, table 28; 1931, vol. 2, table 34; 1941, vol. 2,
table 34; 1951, vol. 1, table 35; 1961, vol. 1:2.5, table 38

TABLE 6
Major religious denominations as percentage of Peterborough population

	1921	1931	1941	1951	1961
Anglican	5,047	5,700	5,830	8,299	9,314
	24.0%	25.5%	23.0%	21.7%	19.7%
Baptist	1,105	1,203	1,385	1,688	1,962
	5.4%	5.5%	5.5%	4.4%	4.2%
Jewish	136	139	175	232	243
	0.6%	0.6%	0.7%	0.65%	0.5%
Methodist/United	4,909	6,615	8,401	13,315	16,213
Church	23.4%	29.7%	33.1%	34.8%	34.4%
Presbyterian	4,054	2,422	2,231	2,800	3,301
	19.3%	10.8%	8.8%	7.3%	7.0%
Roman Catholic	4,960	5,254	5,912	9,174	12,314
	23.6%	23.5%	23.3%	24%	26.1%
Salvation Army	339	472	522	873	848
	1.6%	2.1%	2.1%	2.3%	1.8%
Other	444	522	894	1,891	2,990
	2.1%	2.3%	3.5%	4.9%	6.3%
Total	20,994	22,327	25,350	38,272	47,185
	100%	100%	100%	100%	100%

SOURCE: *Census of Canada,* 1921, vol. 1, table 39; 1931, vol. 2, table 43; 1941, vol. 2, table 40; 1951, vol. 1, table 42; 1961, vol. 1:2.6, table 45

TABLE 7
Birthplace of population of Peterborough

	1921	1931	1941	1951	1961
Canada	78%	80%	85%	87%	87%
British Empire	18	16	12	10	9
Europe	1	1	1	1.5	3

SOURCE: *Census of Canada,* 1921, vol. 2, table 38; 1931, vol. 2, table 47; 1941, vol. 2, table 45; 1951, vol. 1, table 48; 1961, vol. 1:2–7, table 52

Notes

ABBREVIATIONS

AO   Archives of Ontario
CAS   Children's Aid Society
CGE   Canadian General Electric
GE   General Electric
NA   National Archives of Canada
OMP   Outboard Marine Oral History Project
PCMA Peterborough Centennial Museum and Archives
TUA   Trent University Archives
UE   United Electrical, Radio and Machine Workers of America
WB   Women's Bureau

INTRODUCTION: Placing the Story of Women's Work in Context

1 The best example of the use of a local study is Parr, *The Gender of Breadwinners*. For an example of the 'fragmentation' view, see Bliss, 'Privatizing the Mind.' Two responses are Pierson, 'Colonization and Canadian Women's History' and Kealey et al., 'Teaching Canadian History in the 1990s.'
2 For a few reviews of some of these debates see (in historical order) Barrett, *Women's Oppression Today*; Armstrong and Armstrong, 'Beyond Sexless Class and Classless Sex'; Sargent, *Women and Revolution*; Eisenstein, *Capitalist Patriarchy and the Case for Socialist Feminism*; Walby, *Patriarchy at Work*; and Bradley, *Women's Work, Men's Work*.
3 See, for example, early debates in Raphael, *Peoples History and Socialist Theory*, and Rowbotham, *Women, Resistance and Revolution*. There is

some debate about the extent to which this androcentric mould has been challenged and gender has been integrated into working-class history; as some authors point out, the categories of race, class, and gender are invoked like a ritualistic mantra at public conferences but are then quietly forgotten in the actual writing of books. For commentary, see Bradbury, 'Women's History and Working-Class History'; Buhle, 'Gender and Labour History'; Kessler-Harris, 'A New Agenda for American Labor History'; Baron, 'Gender and Labour History.'

4 Many of these studies attempted to clarify the formulation and reformulation of class and gender as interdependent variables in women's lives. To note a few examples: Stansell, *City of Women*; Cooper, *Once a Cigar Maker*; Benson, *Counter Cultures*; Gabin, *Feminism and the Labor Movement*; Baron, *Work Engendered*; Blewett, *Men, Women and Work*; Lamphere, *From Working Daughters to Working Mothers*; and Frager, *Sweatshop Strife*.

5 For example, Mitchell, *Women's Estate*; Barrett, *Women's Oppression Today*; Barrett et al., *Ideology and Cultural Production*; Coward, *Female Desire*; and Alexander, 'Women, Class and Sexual Difference.'

6 Kessler-Harris, 'A New Agenda for American Labor History,' in Kessler-Harris and Moody, *Perspectives in Labor History*.

7 De la Coeur, Morgan, and Valverde, 'Gender Regulation and State Formation in Nineteenth-Century Canada,' 165. For some excellent recent examples of gender history, see Iacovetta, *Such Hardworking People*; Forestall, 'All That Glitters Is Not Gold'; Morton, 'Men and Women in a Halifax Working-Class Neighbourhood in the 1920s'; and Rosenfeld, 'It Was a Hard Life.'

8 As Judith Bennett points out, these calls for gender history are sometimes repeated by commentators who have long rejected the project of women's history as well as its feminist orientation.

9 On the domestic labour debate, see Benston, 'The Political Economy of Women's Liberation'; Seccombe, 'The Housewife and Her Labour under Capitalism'; and Fox, *Hidden in the Household*.

10 Delphy, *Close to Home*.

11 H. Hartmann, 'The Unhappy Marriage of Marxism and Feminism.'

12 For some of the discussion and critiques of the dual systems theory, see Eisenstein, *Capitalist Patriarchy*.

13 Beechey, *Unequal Work*.

14 Lown, *Women and Industrialization*. For another attempt to use the dual systems theory in a more integrated manner, see Cockburn, *Brothers*.

15 Parr, *The Gender of Breadwinners*, 8.

16 The term is Miriam Glucksmann's from *Women Assemble*, though she was referring more centrally to the process of production and social reproduction.

17 Two examples of works on gender, ethnicity, and work are Iacovetta, *Such Hard-Working People*, and Frager, *Sweatshop Strife*. Some essays in Iacovetta and Valverde's *Gender Conflicts* also deal with women, race, and ethnicity. For discussion of gender, race and women's work, see Brand's introduction to her *No Burden to Carry*, and Morton, 'Separate Spheres in a Separate World.' American women's labour history, of course, has a longer and stronger tradition of integrating ethnicity and race into writing on women's work. Two good examples are J. Jones, *Labour of Love, Labour of Sorrow*, and Janiewski, *Sisterhood Denied.*

18 Rowbotham, 'The Trouble with Patriarchy.'

19 Fox, 'Conceptualizing Patriarchy,' 175.

20 Bennett, 'Feminism and History,' 261.

21 See Alexander and Taylor, 'In Defence of Patriarchy.'

22 See, for example, Turbin, 'Beyond Dichotomies,' and Iacovetta and Valverde's introduction, to their *Gender Conflicts.*

23 In the area of feminist theory, the influence of Derrida and French feminist poststructuralist writers are important. In history, many writers have been influenced by Foucault. On the general principles of poststructuralism, see Weedon, *Feminist Practice and Poststructuralist Theory*, and Rosenau, *Postmodernism and the Social Sciences, Insights, Inroads, Intrusions.*

24 Barrett, 'Words and Things,' 201–2. For definitions of materialism, see Armstrong and Armstrong, *Theorizing Women's Work*, and Jaggar, *Feminist Politics and Human Nature.*

25 Diamond and Quinby, introduction to their *Feminism and Foucault*; Flax, 'Postmodernism and Gender Relations in Feminist Theory.'

26 For a recent example of the critical use of Foucault, see Fraser and Gordon, 'A Geneology of Dependency.'

27 Tress, 'Comment on Flax's Postmodernism and Gender Relations in Feminist Theory,' 197. For other critical assessments, see Walzer, 'The Politics of Foucault'; Jehlen, 'Patrolling the Borders'; and Hartstock, 'Foucault on Power.'

28 Canning, 'Feminist History and the Linguistic Turn,' 369–70.

29 For example, see Toews, 'International History after the Linguistic Turn.'

30 See, for example, Palmer, *Descent into Discourse.*

31 Buhle, 'Gender and Labor History,' 73.

32 Stansell, 'Response to Joan Scott.'

33 On the political agnosticism of 'sceptical' poststructuralism versus affirmative poststructuralism, see Rosenau, *Postmodernism and the Social Sciences*, 23; and on 'ludic' poststructuralism (i.e., emphasis on systems of difference in language) versus 'resistance' poststructuralism, see Hennessey, *Materialist Feminism*, 3.

34 Hennessey, ibid., 28.

35 The term 'emotional flatness' is used by Michele Barrett, who is sympathetic to though sometimes critical of Foucault. She also notes that 'poststructuralism has been caught with the shirt tales of human agency left out' (Barrett, *The Politics of Truth*, 153, 166). On the socialist-feminist tradition of historical writing, see Rowbotham, *Dreams and Dilemmas*, 162–89, or, on Marxist-humanism, B. Palmer, *The Making of E.P. Thompson*.

36 See special issue of *Frontiers*, 1977 and 1983; also Geiger, 'What's So Feminist about Women's Oral History?'

37 Scott, 'Experience,' in Judith Butler and Joan Scott, eds., *Feminists Theorize the Political.*

38 Bruner, 'Life as Narrative,' and Crapanzano, 'Life Histories,' 955. Literary theory and anthropological writing are currently the most important theoretical influences in the field of oral history.

39 These concerns were already apparent, but they have been accentuated and extended. Poststructuralist claims to 'new' insights are sometimes based on existing feminist work. See Gordon, 'Response to Joan Scott'; Flax, 'Postmodernism and Gender Relations in Feminist Theory'; and Alcoff, 'Cultural Feminism versus Poststructuralism.'

40 See my longer discussion of these issues in my 'Telling our Stories.'

41 Hennessey, *Materialist Feminism*, 78.

42 Frisch, 'The Memory of History,' 16. The exploration of the construction of memory was explored earlier by Grele, *Envelopes of Sound.*

43 For more on this, see Salazar, 'A Third World Women's Text'; Sommer, 'Not Just a Personal Story'; and Cruikshank, 'Myth and Tradition as Narrative Framework.'

44 For a discussion of silences and jokes, see Passerini, 'Work, Ideology and Working-Class Attitudes to Fascism.'

45 On individual scripts, see Grele, *Envelopes of Sound*; on collective scripts, see Bodnar, 'Power and Memory in Oral History.' For further discussion on the way in which collective scripts reflected workplace paternalism, see Sangster, 'The Softball Solution.'

46 Oakley, 'Interviewing Women.'

47 Stacey, 'Can There Be a Feminist Ethnography?' See also Patai, 'U.S. Academics and Third World Women,' and Finch, 'It's Great to Have Someone to Talk to.'
48 Stacey, 'Can There Be a Feminist Ethnography?'
49 On the problems of pluralism masking power, see Gordon, 'Response to Joan Scott' and 'On Difference.'
50 Tilley, 'People's History and Social Science History,' 443.
51 Barrett, 'The Concept of Difference.'
52 Stanley, 'Recovering Women in History from Feminist Deconstruction.'

CHAPTER 1 Peterborough

1 *Examiner*, 7 July 1937.
2 Ibid.
3 Jones and Dyer, *Peterborough: The Electric City*, 8.
4 Ibid., 43.
5 The labour force participation rate is shaped by many factors; the size of a city, the rural/urban divide, family size and age of children, social security available, cultural attitudes, and many other items. Much of this information (for example, family size) is not consistently available here, so my conclusions are tentative. From oral evidence, it does appear that the school-leaving age was rather laxly enforced in the interwar period. On factors shaping the participation rate, see Woods and Ostry, *Labour Policy and Labour Economics in Canada*, 312–13.
6 On the census as a changing and socially constructed piece of historical evidence, see Hakim, 'Census Reports as Documentary Evidence.' For some of the problems in looking at census data relating to women in the labour force over time owing to changing categorization, see Denton and Ostry, *Historical Estimates of the Canadian Labour Force*, chap. 2.
7 Canada, Dominion Bureau of Statistics, *Census of Canada* (hereafter cited as *Census*); see 1961, vol. 3, table 34, for age. The 11% comes from *Census*, 1931, vol. 7, table 40, which gives Ontario figures. No consistent statistics are listed for Peterborough on a number of issues, including age and marital status for women in the workforce.
8 *Canadian Textile Journal*, 25 Oct. 1921.
9 *Census*, 1931, vol. 7, table 57.
10 This is an estimate based on two sources. First, I used the census to judge the number of women and men who appear to have been employed in the electrical and food industries; and second, by the late 1930s, one oral

source claimed that women represented 13% of CGE workers. See Keifer, 'Women in Peterborough During World War II.' Again, without access to wage lists or company sources, these statistics can never be accurate.

11 An estimate, again, taken by counting women listed in clerical work in each industrial category from the *Census*, 1921, vol. 4, table 3, and 1941, vol. 7, table 9 (256), listing clerical workers overall in the city. Since even the categories counted changed over time, I can only make an estimate. On the increasing number of female clerical workers in this period, see Lowe, *Women in the Administrative Revolution.*

12 *Census*, 1911, vol. 1; 1921, vol. 4; and 1931, 1941, and 1951. The most dramatic drops came between 1911 and 1921, and from 1941 to 1951. In between these periods, the numbers were fairly stable.

13 Collins, 'Women and Domestic Service in Peterborough.'

14 Fox and Fox, 'Occupational Gender Segregation of the Canadian Labour Force,' 14. By segregation, Fox and Fox mean the degree to which men and women are employed in different occupations.

15 Although GE employed about half of Peterborough's manufacturing workforce, it had fewer women than the textile mill. In the industry as a whole, women constituted about 20% of the workforce; at GE, it was probably about 10–15%. See Guard, 'The "Woman Question" in Canadian Unionism,' 127. For an analysis of the U.S. industry, see Schatz, *The Electrical Workers*, and Milkman, *Gender at Work.*

16 Forestall, 'All That Glitters Is Not Gold.'

17 As Dionne Brand points out, for instance, black women were more likely than white women to work for wages and were more likely to be concentrated in domestic service (Brand, *No Burden to Carry*).

18 *Census*, 1931, vol. 5, table 37.

19 Ibid. Again, such detailed information on wages was given only for 1931 for Peterborough, so it is difficult to measure changes over time.

20 Morton, 'Labour, Politics and Peterborough, 1914–23,' 35.

21 Interviews with EG, 21 March 1990, and Susan E, Feb. 1990.

22 Jones and Dyer, *Peterborough: The Electric City*, 8.

23 Canada, Department of Labour, *Labour Organization in Canada, 1920–40.*

24 Since wage lists exist only for 1934 for the Bonnerworth and Auburn mills, I compared these to listings in the city directories to come to this conclusion. No further analysis could be done, because the city assessment rolls for these years were destroyed.

25 Interview with Edna M, 27 June 1989.

26 There were a few houses rented out by Dominion Woollens, but no extensive housing tracts were built and rented by the company.

27 Interview with Claire M, Feb. 1990.

28 Peterborough Centennial Museum and Archives (hereafter cited as PCMA), Clipping File. A petition was presented to the council in 1924 to prevent a Chinese restaurant from setting up downtown.

29 Interview with Chris L, 25 July 1991.

30 For example, the 1941 census (table 31) indicates that Native women were 0.8% of the female population in the county and that almost all Native women lived in the rural areas, not in the city.

31 See Frakenberg, *White Women, Race Matters*, for a discussion of the way in which race privilege often remains unseen and taken for granted.

32 Outboard Marine Company interviews, Joan B, 1990.

33 Interview with Eldon H, 27 Nov. 1990.

34 PCMA, Clipping File, 'A Pioneer Race', n.d. [probably just after World War II]. Thanks to Andrew McDonald for pointing this out to me. In a similar vein, an article in the *Canadian Textile Journal*, 25 Oct. 1921, reassured businessmen that the city had 'reliable' labour of a 'good type' because it was primarily British in origin.

CHAPTER 2 Schooling Girls for Women's Work

1 Interview with Lilly A, 28 Aug. 1989.

2 Hunt, *Lessons for Life*.

3 Bradbury, 'Gender at Work at Home,' 119, 133.

4 Pat Carlen uses the term in *Women, Crime and Poverty* to note acceptance of the dominant and respectable norms of behaviour.

5 Sutherland, 'We Always Had Things to Do.'

6 As historians of childhood have shown, the very notion of childhood has altered over time, molded by different economic roles of children, household configurations, and social understandings of youth. See Parr's introduction to her *Childhood and Family in Canadian History*.

7 Coulter, 'Teen-agers in Edmonton.'

8 On the latter topic, the two classics are Kett, *Rites of Passage*, and Gillis, *Youth and History*. For an analysis of the missing gender and class perspective in studies of youth, see Coulter, 'Teen-agers in Edmonton'; on the family economy, see Bradbury, *Working Families*; and on child-centered reform, see Sutherland, *Children in English Canadian Society*, or, for a more critical view from the perspective of class, Bullen, 'J.J. Kelso and the "New Child-savers."' On school reform, see *Prentice, The School Promoters*; Houston and Prentice, *Schooling and Scholars in Nineteenth-Century Ontario*; and Curtis, *Building the Educational State*. On gender and twentieth-century education, see Heap and Prentice, *Gender and*

Education in Ontario. This is not a comprehensive list of works in these areas.

9 Sutherland, 'Listening to the Winds of Childhood.'
10 Outboard Marine Oral History Project, interview with Ellen R, May 1990.
11 This equation is all the more forcefully made if the person feels that her life has been 'successful' because of her perceived upward social mobility. On the notion of dominant 'scripts' informing interviews, see Grele, *Envelopes of Sound,* and Sangster, 'Telling Our Stories.'
12 Although statistics are not available for Peterborough, the Ontario ones offer useful comparisons, In 1931, for example, 15% of the Ontario family heads who were born in Canada were female. Two-thirds of these were widows, but the other one-third included separated, divorced, and deserted women. See *Census,* 1931, vol. 5, table 92. Also, in Peterborough, Children's Aid Society records are more likely to reveal single-parent households with children. Even if women experienced different family forms during their childhood (for example, living with relatives while fathers went elsewhere looking for work), they tended to emphasize their time in the more traditional nuclear family; this way of remembering may well indicate the ideological power and pre-eminence of this image of the family.
13 Roberts, *A Woman's Place,* 11.
14 Sutherland, 'We Always Had Things to Do,' 112.
15 For the feminist psychoanalytic view, which explores the creation of gender identity in the family, see Chodorow, *The Reproduction of Mothering.* A critique of the class and race bias of this theory is found in Spelman, *Inessential Woman,* chap 4. On socialization, see Mackie, *Constructing Women and Men.*
16 As many studies have indicated, it is difficult to 'label' women in relation to their class backgrounds. When I refer to a blue-collar family, the major adult breadwinner or breadwinners are in a blue-collar occupation; the same rule applies to the term white-collar family. In some cases, there were earners from both, especially where skilled working-class fathers had daughters who went into clerical work. I have tried to indicate these situations.
17 Bullen, 'Hidden Workers,' and Bird, 'Hamilton Working Women in the Period of the Great Depression.'
18 On family strategies, see Bradbury, *Working Families.* Recent debates on this issue have emphasized that these strategies may have been unconscious and ad hoc as much as conscious planning. Moreover, the word 'strategies' should not be equated only with consensual and equal

decision making; power relations and lack of choice also characterized familial economic relations. See Tilley, Folbre, and Smith's comments in 'Family Strategy,' and Comacchio's review of *Working Families.*

19 Interview with Jane M, Feb. 1990.

20 Interview with Laura H., 29 Aug. 1989. Such a collective voice may also reflect a pattern of women's oral histories – the tendency to put one's memories in a familial and collective context rather than in an individual one. See Bertaux-Wiame, 'The Life History Approach to Internal Migration,' 193.

21 Interview with Lorna C, 13 Feb. 1990.

22 Interview with Isabel G, 19 March 1990.

23 Sutherland, 'We Always Had Things to Do,' 112.

24 Interview with Lilly A, 28 Aug. 1989.

25 Porter, 'Time, Life Course and Work in Women's Lives,' 7.

26 See Nasaw, 'The Little Mothers,' and Bullen, 'Hidden Workers.'

27 Ontario, Sessional Papers, *Report of the Department of Education*, 1921, 100–1; 1926, 88–9; 1931, 98–9; and 1936, 86–7.

28 In her study of Edmonton, Rebecca Coulter found an increase in part-time work for youth in the interwar period. Similar statistics on age groups are not available for this city, but the same pattern may apply.

29 Interview with Barbara C, 28 Aug. 1989.

30 Interview with Harriet I, 17 July 1989.

31 See, for example, *Labour Gazette*, Jan. 1931, 96.

32 Caplan, *Don't Blame Mother.*

33 The Children's Aid Society of Peterborough (hereafter cited as CAS), Board Minutes, 17 Nov. 1926.

34 Interview with Carol H, 22 Aug. 1989.

35 Interview with Lilly A, 28 Aug. 1989.

36 Interview with June H, 31 July 1989.

37 Interview with Barbara C, 28 Aug. 1989.

38 Harrigan, 'The Schooling of Boys and Girls in Canada.'

39 Ontario, Sessional Paper, *Report of the Department of Education*, 1931, 94–5. Of the 470, there were 195 with 'family heads' in commerce and the professions, 72 in agriculture, 116 in skilled trades, 32 in labouring occupations, 47 in 'other' occupations, and 8 with no occupation listed. I have assumed that in the majority of cases the occupation listed was that of the father. Unfortunately, these figures are not given in every respect, so I cannot trace them consistently over time.

40 Interview with Amelia H, 28 Aug. 1989.

41 The nature and availability of employment had an important bearing on

school attendance; see Gaffield and Levine, 'Dependency and Adolescence on the Canadian Frontier.' Statistics on Depression school attendance are provincially based; see Harrigan, 'The Schooling of Boys and Girls in Canada,' 805.

42 Interview with Sam E, 25 Aug. 1989.

43 Interview with Ethel M, 22 Aug. 1989.

44 Interview with June H, 31 July. 1989.

45 Interview with Lilly A, 28 Aug. 1989.

46 Interview with Laura H, 29 Aug. 1989.

47 Interview with Mary E, 25 Aug. 1989.

48 *Examiner*, 22 Dec. 1936.

49 Peterborough County Board of Education, Minutes, 1 Dec. 1931.

50 The *Examiner*, 5 Jan. 1932, noted a Kiwanis-sponsored camp for undernourished children who needed extra health care; attendance was 246.

51 CAS Board Minutes, 1 June 1926.

52 PCMA, Oral History Transcripts, interview with FR.

53 For a discussion of this argument in relation to British women and education, see McLaren, *Ambitions and Realizations*, 39.

54 Interview with Thelma A, June 1989.

55 For example, the women did not want this experience linked to their names, since it might hurt other family members. In contradiction to Harrigan, Strong-Boag (*The New Day Recalled*) argues that the practice of sending sisters out to work so that brothers could be educated was common in this period. Even if Harrigan is correct about boys' and girls' equal participation in school, it is evident that women did not always perceive their opportunities or rights to be the same as those of their brothers.

56 Interview with Monica K, 4 Dec. 1989.

57 Jackson and Gaskell, 'White Collar Vocationalism.'

58 Heap, 'Schooling Women for Home or Work?'

59 Danylewycz, 'Domestic Science Education in Ontario.'

60 Interview with Phyllis P, June 1991.

61 Willis, *Learning to Labour*.

62 For example, S. Humphries, *Hooligans or Rebels*.

63 Interview with Joy D, 26 July 1990.

64 Barman, 'Knowledge Is Essential for Universal Progress but Fatal to Class Privilege.'

65 Roome, 'Amelia Turner and Calgary Labour Women.'

66 Peterborough County Board of Education, School Board Minutes, 29 Sept. 1939 and 12 Dec. 1940.

67 Interview with Gina V, 11 July 1989.

68 Interview with Rosa B, 2 Aug. 1989.

69 Russell, 'The Hidden Curriculum of School,' and Gaskell, 'Course Enrolment in High School.'

70 Interview with Claire M, Feb. 1990.

71 On cultural alienation, see Willis, *Learning to Labour*, and McRobbie, 'Working-Class Girls and the Culture of Femininity.'

72 Interview with Dot H, 23 Aug. 1989.

73 Gaskell, 'Course Enrolment in the High School.'

74 County of Peterborough, Lang Archives, Mothers Allowance Board Minutes, 30 June 1934, 29 June 1935.

75 CAS Board Minutes, 13 Feb. 1934.

76 CAS Board Minutes, Annual Meeting, 20 April 1937. On the tradition of using such children as cheap labour, see Parr, *Labouring Children*, and Bullen, 'J.J. Kelso and the "New Child-savers."'

77 Interview with Veronica L, 24 Aug. 1989. The use of the word 'invited' is telling here.

78 Strong-Boag, *The New Day Recalled*, and Vipond, 'The Image of Women in Mass Circulation Magazines of the 1920s.'

79 Tinkler, 'Learning through Leisure.'

80 For a more contemporary exploration of this theme, see Hudson, 'Femininity and Adolescence.'

81 *Examiner*, 25 May 1933. Even the Protestant churches associated with the progressive Social Gospel upheld a traditional view of woman's maternal urges and her primarily domestic role. See Hallett, 'Nellie McClung and the Fight for the Ordination of Women in the United Church of Canada.'

82 The actual responses of children and their families to such attempts at reform and regulation is open to debate. Some argue that these attempts were unwelcome and were resisted. See Bullen, 'J.J. Kelso and the "New Child-savers,"' and Strange, 'From Modern Babylon to a City upon the Hill.'

83 Pederson, 'Building Today for the Womanhood of Tomorrow.'

84 Archives of Ontario, Mercer Reformatory Records, RG 23, case file 8111 (1938).

85 Sangster, 'Pardon Tales from Magistrate's Court.'

86 Interview with Pamela M, 24 June 1991.

87 On this point, see also Chunn, *From Punishment to Doing Good*.

88 Despite the importance of youth wages to the family of the first cohort, it is a simplification and distortion to imply that working-class children were valued for their productive power and middle-class children for

their personalities, with the former increasingly being 'sentimentalized' by the mid-twentieth century, as portrayed in Zelizer, *Pricing the Priceless Child.*

89 Roberts, *A Woman's Place,* 10.

90 Cohen, *Women's Work, Markets and Economic Development in Nineteenth-Century Ontario.*

91 Synge, 'The Transition from School to Work.'

92 For discussion of these theories, see McLaren, *Ambitions and Realizations,* or MacDonald, 'Socio-Cultural Reproduction and Women's Education.' I have simplified these theories in this sentence; Marxist theories of social reproduction in education do not simply argue that 'education was imposed on the working class.'

93 McLaren, *Ambition and Realizations.*

94 Coulter, 'Teen-Agers in Edmonton.'

95 Interview with Lilly A, 28 Aug. 1989.

CHAPTER 3 Packing Muffets for a Living

1 Interview with Harriet I, 17 July 1989.

2 Interview with Doris B, 12 Dec. 1989.

3 Interview with Janet R, 23 July 1989.

4 Interview with June H, 31 July 1989.

5 Interview with Herman B, June 1989.

6 For a similar discussion, see Hareven, *Family Time and Industrial Time,* chap. 5.

7 Interview with Marilyn B, 8 Feb. 1990.

8 Interview with May D, 25 Aug. 1989.

9 Interview with Dot H, 23 Aug. 1989.

10 Interview with Dot H, 23 Aug. 1989, and with May D, 25 Aug. 1989.

11 Interview with Barbara C, 28 Aug. 1989.

12 Interview with HN, 1 Nov. 1990.

13 Interview with Joy D, 26 July 1990.

14 Interview with Rosa B, 2 Aug. 1989.

15 Glucksmann, *Women Assemble.*

16 Ibid., 154.

17 Interview with Mona G, 21 Aug. 1989.

18 Interview with EH, 27 Nov. 1990.

19 Interview with Herman B, June 1989.

20 Interview with Morris H, 18 July 1989.

21 Glucksmann, *Women Assemble,* 220.

22 Interview with Christine M, Feb. 1990.
23 Interview with Doris B, Feb. 1990.
24 Outboard Marine Oral History Project, interview with Joan B. Women who wore glasses were sometimes asked for a note from their eye doctor saying that they could handle the work.
25 Interview with Mona G, 21 Aug. 1989.
26 Interview with Hilary P, 23 Aug. 1989.
27 Interview with Edna M, 27 June 1989.
28 Interview with Eleanor T, Jan. 1990.
29 Interview with Thelma A, June 1989.
30 Interview with Joan J, 25 Aug. 1990.
31 Interview with Jane M, Feb. 1990.
32 Interview with Joan J, 25 Aug. 1990.
33 Ibid.
34 Interview with PH, 9 Aug. 1990.
35 Interview with Molly W, March 1990.
36 Lowe, 'Mechanization, Feminization and Managerial Control in the Early Twentieth-Century Canadian Office,' 178.
37 Ibid. I have changed the phrasing of Lowe's quote.
38 Lowe, *Women in the Administrative Revolution*. See also American studies such as Davies, *Woman's Place Is at the Typewriter*. While authors such as Lowe have analysed the feminization of clerical work, I am more interested in how these women experienced their daily work and how they compared it to production work in the factory.
39 Interview with Ethel M, 22 Aug. 1989.
40 Rosemary Pringle's contemporary research on secretaries argues that authority relations between men and women are situated in, and understood with, a familial and sexual discourse (Pringle, 'Bureaucracy, Rationality, and Sexuality').
41 Ibid.
42 Interview with Sandra D, 5 July 1989.
43 Interview with Ethel M, 22 Aug. 1989.
44 Interview with Henrietta G, 24 July 1989.
45 Interview with Lorna C, 13 Feb. 1990.
46 Phillips and Taylor, 'Sex and Skill,' 55, 65.
47 Barrett, *Women's Oppression Today*; 168–70.
48 Heron and Storey, *On the Job*; Braverman, *Labor and Monopoly*; S. Wood, *The Degradation of Work?*; Thompson, *The Nature of Work*; Edwards, *Contested Terrain*; and Burawoy, *Manufacturing Consent.*
49 Milkman, *Gender at Work.*

50 Interview with Peter F, June 1989.
51 Interview with Herman B, June 1989.
52 Interview with Peter F, June 1989.
53 Valverde, 'Giving the Females a Domestic Turn,' 621.
54 Rainnie, *The Woollen and Worsted Industry*, 46.
55 The American woollen industry, concentrated in the north of the United States, did have higher hourly rates than the Canadian one, but during the Depression it had lower weekly rates because of short time. See Canada, *Report of the Royal Commission on the Textile Industry*, 1937 (hereafter cited as *1937 Report*), 174.
56 For example, a comparison of wages in the manufacturing industry done for the Royal Commission on the Textile Industry showed that women's wages in the woollen industry ranked eighteenth among forty-one occupations for women, whereas men's wages were thirty-seventh among forty occupations for men (*1937 Report*, 280–1).
57 Parr, *The Gender of Breadwinners*, 75.
58 These statistics were given to Nancy Keifer by a retired GE employee, Donald Smith, for an undergraduate paper at Trent (see Keifer, 'The Recruitment of Women into the Work Force in Peterborough During World War II'). By the time I asked for figures, Mr Smith was not available, and no one at the company would give me any statistics, saying they were not available. By 1961, women were again about 10 per cent of the workforce. See United Electrical, Radio and Machine Workers of America, Local 524 Archives (hereafter, UE Local 524) Records, 'Summary of All CGE Shops 1961 Hourly Earnings.' Of 1,971 workers (1,746 on men's codes and 225 on women's codes), the men's codes average about $2.55 an hour, the women's about $2.25.
59 UE Local 524 Records, 'Genelco Brief to the Ontario Regional War Labour Board,' 19 July 1943.
60 Ibid.
61 National Archives of Canada, United Electrical, Radio and Machine Workers of America, National Records, MG 28-I-190, 'Submission of National UE to Hon. Charles Daley, Minister of Labour, re Female Employees Fair Remuneration Act, 1951,' 23 March 1955.
62 Pamela Sugiman found that the War Labour Board also lacked sympathy for equal pay in the auto industry (Sugiman, 'Labour's Dilemma,' chap. 3).
63 Pierson, 'Gender and the Unemployment Insurance Debates in Canada.' See also Strong-Boag, 'Girl of the New Day,' and Coulter, 'Young Women

and Unemployment in the 1930s.' This theme is dealt with at greater length in chapter 8.

64 A more extensive discussion of the unions' responses to the sexual division of labour is discussed in chapter 7.

65 For a strong defence of the 'managerial control' argument (and an attack on Walby), see Savage, 'Trade Unionism, Sexual Regulation and the State.'

66 Lown, *Women and Industrialization.*

67 For this limited definition, see Seccombe, 'Patriarchy Stabilized.'

68 Interview with EG, 21 March 1990.

69 Interview with Sam E, 25 Aug. 1989.

70 Phillips and Taylor, 'Sex and Skill,' 55.

71 The classic view here is J. Humphries, 'Class Struggle and the Persistence of the Working-Class Family.' An opposing view is given by Barrett and McIntosh, 'The Family Wage.' For a subsequent debate, see Brenner and Ramas, 'Rethinking Women's Oppression,' and Lewis, 'A Debate on Sex and Class.' See also H. Hartmann, 'Capitalism, Patriarchy and Job Segregation,' and Walby, *Patriarchy at Work.*

72 M. May, 'Bread before Roses.'

73 Rothbart, 'Homes Are What Any Strike Is About.'

74 Rose, 'Gender Antagonism and Class Conflict.'

75 On the active role of male workers or unions in creating the sexual division of labour, see Milkman, 'Organizing the Sexual Division of Labour.' For an opposing view, see Savage, 'Trade Unionism, Sex Segregation and the State.'

76 Interview with HN, 1 Nov. 1990.

77 Seccomb, 'Patriarchy Stabilized,' 55.

78 Interview with Terrance O, Aug. 1989.

79 Interview with Marilyn B, 8 Feb. 1990.

80 Sangster, 'The Dark Side of Family Life.'

81 Interview with PH, 9 Aug. 1990.

82 Willis, 'Shop Floor Culture,' 197.

83 Collinson and Collinson, 'Sexuality in the Workplace,' 107.

84 Gray, 'Sharing the Shop Floor,' 80.

85 Interviews with Monica K, 4 Dec. 1989; June H, 31 July 1989; and May D, 25 Aug. 1989. The ulcer comment is interesting because the assumption is that a wage-earning wife would put him under more stress and aggravate his ulcer. Later in the interview, she implied that his reaction was linked to pride.

86 As Wally Seccombe points out in 'Patriarchy Stabilized,' a materialist analysis of the rule of the father points to his traditional right to make primary decisions about property, children, and his wife. Many critiques of the concept of patriarchy claim that if one rejects an essentialist view (as one should), there is no clear rationale for its existence. I would suggest that this power and its concurrent privileges remain an important rationale.

87 Interview with May D, 25 Aug. 1989.

88 Outboard Marine Oral History Project, interview with Ellen R.

89 Interview with Harriet I, 17 July 1989.

90 Outboard Marine Oral History Project, interview with Ellen R.

91 For women who worked until the 1960s and 1970s, this *appeared* to be confirmed by what they called the dangers of 'women's lib' ideas that challenged the division of labour in the workplace. As one blue-collar woman from Outboard Marine said, 'When women's lib came in ... they [men] played dirty with you. [Before], men would come around and say they would help you lift something, as women were not supposed to lift more than a certain amount. When women's lib came in, men said lift it yourself; you're supposed to be able to do what a man can' (Outboard Marine Project, interview with Brenda M).

92 Interview with PH, 9 Aug. 1990.

93 Interview with Andrea E, 10 July 1989. The final comment about the 'old school' is a recognition that the interviewer probably thinks differently, as well as a recognition that the sexual division of labour has now been challenged in the workplace.

94 Interview with Hilary P, 3 Aug. 1989.

95 Interview with Annie B, 25 July 1989.

96 Interview with May D, 25 Aug. 1989.

97 Ibid.

98 Interview with Claire M, Feb. 1990.

99 Kessler-Harris, *A Woman's Wage*, 7–8.

100 Interview with Hilary P, 23 Aug. 1989.

101 Interview with Sandra D, 5 July 1989.

102 Collinson and Knights, 'Men Only.' Although these authors draw on poststructuralist theory to develop this idea, they do not emphasize the multiple and unstable identities as many poststructuralists do but, rather, ultimately opt for a more existential conclusion.

103 Interview with Thelma A, June 1989.

104 Interview with Lorna C, 13 Feb. 1990.

105 Milkman, 'Organizing the Sexual Division of Labour,' 107.

106 Interview with Deanna C, 24 July 1991.

107 Lown, *Women and Industrialization*, 219.

108 Beechey, *Unequal Work*, 146.

109 As many critics have pointed out, the Foucauldian notion of a network or grid of diffuse powers, and Foucault's emphasis on ascending not descending power, on the exercise not possession of power, does not adequately explain the origins of all social relations. As Nancy Harstock notes, this is 'power without any headquarters.' See Harstock, 'Foucault on Power,' and Hennessey, *Materialist Feminism and the Politics of Discourse*, 19–20.

110 Reiger, *The Disenchantment of the Home*, 23.

CHAPTER 4 Women's Work Culture, Women's Identities

1 *GE Works News*, 25 June 1948.

2 My definition is taken from Benson, *Counter Cultures*. On women's work culture, see also Cooper, *Once a Cigar Maker*, and Lamphere, *From Working Daughters to Working Mothers*. For contemporary studies that discuss this concept, see Westwood, *All Day Every Day*, and Pollert, *Girls, Wives, Factory Lives*.

3 Historians studying working-class housewives have also shown how social practices, cultural values, and a shared economic environment shaped a distinct culture for women working in the home. See Cameron, 'Bread and Roses Revisited'; Ross, 'Not the Sort to Sit on the Doorstep'; and Morton, 'Men and Women in a Halifax Working-Class Neighbourhood.'

4 Westwood, *All Day Every Day*.

5 This debate has some affinity to earlier debates over whether a distinct women's 'culture' existed. For an earlier symposium on this, see DuBois et al., 'Politics and Culture in Women's History.' A more recent discussion is found in Fox-Genovese, 'Socialist-Feminist American Women's History.'

6 See, for example, Benson, *Counter Cultures* and Lamphere, 'Bringing the Family to Work.' The suggestion that we take into account the psychological theories of Chodorow and others that women have different 'relational' capacities based on the gendering of character structure in the family is made in Sugiman, 'Labour's Dilemma,' but it is also implicit in some other writing on work culture.

7 Livingstone and Luxton, 'Gender Consciousness at Work.'

8 Kessler-Harris, 'Gender Ideology in Historical Reconstruction,' and Turbin, 'Beyond Dichotomies.'

9 Butler's *Gender Trouble* is one extreme example of such writing, though Riley's *Am I That Name* also stresses fluctuating identities.

10 Hewitt, 'Illusions of Freedom,' 83. Similar concerns are expressed by others, for example, Macdonnel, *Theories of Discourse*, especially pp. 120–1, and Felski, 'Feminism, Post-modernism and the Critique of Modernity.'

11 The best overview of these years is Strong-Boag, *The New Day Recalled*. For American overviews that cover the same period and offer insights on popular culture (which was shared by Canadians through movies, for instance) see Ware, *Holding Their Own*; S. Hartmann, *The Home Front and Beyond*; and Wandersee, *Women's Work and Family Values*.

12 Strong-Boag, *The New Day Recalled*, 85.

13 On increasing pressures towards heterosexuality, see Rapp and Ross, 'The Twenties Backlash,' and Duggan 'The Social Enforcement of Heterosexuality and Lesbian Resistance.'

14 Vipond, 'The Image of Women in Mass Circulation Magazines.'

15 Interview with Doris B, Feb. 1990.

16 On the late-nineteenth- and early-twentieth-century family, see Coontz, *The Social Origins of Private Life*. On sexuality and companionate marriage, see Simmons, 'Modern Sexuality and the Myth of Victorian Repression'; E.T. May, *Great Expectations*; and Strong-Boag, *The New Day Recalled*.

17 Dodd, 'Women in Advertising'; Arnup, 'Educating Mothers'; and Strong-Boag, 'Intruders in the Nursery.' For an analysis of the emergence of professional experts, see also Reiger, *The Disenchantment of the Home*.

18 Gee, 'The Life Course of Canadian Women' and 'Female Marriage Patterns in Canada.'

19 For example, while both middle- and working-class women experienced the dominant message that motherhood was central to women's identity, their understanding of the domestic ideal may have differed. For working-class women, their difficult management of a subsistence budget, longer workday, lack of privacy, close neighbourhood existence, and different ideas about family responsibilities ensured a domestic existence quite different from that of middle-class women. On working-class women and the ideal of domesticity in the 1920s, see Morton, 'Men and Women in a Halifax Working-Class Neighbourhood.'

20 Interview with Adele T, 23 July 1989.

21 Ryan, 'The Movie Moderns of the 1920's,' 122, 128. See also Haskell, *From Reverence to Rape,* and E.T. May, *Great Expectations,* chap. 4.

22 E.T. May, *Homeward Bound,* chap. 2. See also Ware, *Holding Their Own.*

23 On the importance of dress, language, and gesture as symbols used by women in varying ways to make statements about their lives and values, see Hall, 'Disorderly Women,' and Peiss, *Cheap Amusements.*

24 Outboard Marine Oral History Project, (hereafter cited as OMP), interview with Joan B, 1990.

25 Interview with Lucy P, 12 July 1989.

26 Interview with Claire M, Feb. 1990.

27 As Ruth Pierson has noted, the wartime adoption of pants created some jitters about women's femininity. See Pierson, *They're Still Women After All,* chap. 4.

28 Interview with Rosa B, 2 Aug. 1989.

29 Interview with Gina V, 11 July 1989.

30 Interview with May D, 25 Aug. 1989.

31 Interview with HN, 1 Nov. 1990.

32 Interview with Molly W, March 1990.

33 On the YWCA, see Pederson, 'Keeping Our Girls Good,' and Mitchinson, 'The YWCA and Reform in the 19th Century.'

34 Strange, 'The Perils and Pleasures of the City.'

35 Trent University Archives, Peterborough YWCA Papers, Assistant Secretary's Report, 1921–2.

36 Ibid., Annual Report of 1920, 1921.

37 Ibid., General Secretary's Report, Dec. 1922.

38 Ibid., General Secretary's Report, Oct. 1921.

39 Shaw-Cullen and Lee, *Changing Lives in Changing Times,* 35.

40 Pedersen, 'Building Today for the Womanhood of Tomorrow.'

41 *GE Works News,* 24 March 1950 and 9 Nov. 1951.

42 Interview with Ethel M, 22 Aug. 1989, and with Anne Marie B, Aug. 16 1989.

43 Peiss, *Cheap Amusements.* On attempts of the middle class to control working-class leisure, see Rosenzweig, *Eight Hours for What We Will.*

44 A local murder case involved a peeping tom who was a nightly visitor to one of the city's parking spots for young couples on Gordon Avenue in the west end. Police surmised that he was caught and was murdered with a blow to the head. The murderer was never found (Peterborough *Examiner,* 27 July 1934).

45 Interview with Joy D, 26 July 1990.

46 Interview with Lucy P, 12 July 1989.

47 Interview with Eleanor T, Jan. 1990.

48 Ibid. It is crucial to note the limitations of oral history here: most women would not stress their misbehaviour as much as their respectability.

49 Sangster, 'Pardon Tales from Magistrates Court.' See also Odem, 'Single Mothers, Delinquent Daughters and the Juvenile Court.'

50 Interview with May D, 25 Aug. 1989.

51 Interview with Barbara C, 28 Aug. 1989.

52 Ibid.

53 Synge, 'The Transition from School to Work.'

54 Interview with Jane M, Feb. 1990.

55 Interview with Harriet I, 17 July 1989.

56 Lynd and Lynd, *Middletown*.

57 Interview with Dorothy H, 23 Aug. 1989.

58 Interview with Sam E, Aug. 1989.

59 'Girls arrive in the factory and become women on the shopfloor' (Westwood, *All Day Every Day*, 11).

60 Interview with Sarah L, 3 Dec. 1990.

61 Interview with Marilyn B, 8 Feb. 1990.

62 Interview with May D, 25 Aug. 1989.

63 Interview with WH, July 1989.

64 OMP, interview with Joan B, 1990.

65 Interview with Doris B, Feb. 1990.

66 Interview with Lorna C, 13 Feb. 1990.

67 *Tic Talk*, Dec. 1956. On marriage humour in the interwar period, see Snell, 'Marriage Humour and Its Social Functions.'

68 Interview with Edna M, 27 June 1989.

69 Interview with Lucy P, 12 July 1989.

70 Sugiman, 'Labour's Dilemma,' chap. 4.

71 Interview with Lorna C, 13 Feb. 1990.

72 Interview with Julia N, Aug. 29, 1989.

73 Interview with Susan E, 25 Aug. 1989.

74 Interview with Judith T, 23 July 1989.

75 Peterborough Centennial Museum, Oral History Transcripts, interview with B. Cordery, 28 July 1978. Workers who started in the 1930s did not mention this practice.

76 Interview with Laura H, 29 Aug. 1989.

77 Interview with Susan E, 25 Aug. 1989. Perhaps they were also implying the need for his family or spouse to 'humanize' him as well.

78 Interview with Beatrice G, 25 June 1991.

79 Interview with Donna B, 25 June 1991.

80 Interview with Susan E, 25 Aug. 1989.
81 OMP, interview with Brenda M, 1990.
82 Interview with Eleanor T, Jan. 1990.
83 Cavendish, *On the Line*, 56.
84 Interview with Lilly A, 28 Aug. 1989.
85 Interview with Edna M, 27 June 1989.
86 Pamela Sugiman refers to these explicitly as 'gendered strategies' used not only as coping mechanisms but also in the creation of resistance (Sugiman, 'Labour's Dilemma,' 8).
87 OMP, interview with Joan B, 1990. Ironically, many of these workplaces also set up incentive systems in the 1940s which offered money prizes for workplace suggestions to improve production.
88 Interview with Andrea E, 10 July 1989.
89 On oral history as a method of analysing how working-class values can be used as a means of encouraging respect for authority, see Passerini, 'Italian Working-Class Culture between the Wars.'
90 Interview with Emma C, 27 June 1990.
91 OMP, interview with Barb S, 1990.
92 Buroway, *Manufacturing Consent*, especially chap. 5.
93 Interview with Lucy P, 12 July 1989.
94 Interview with Christine M, Feb. 1990.
95 Westwood, *All Day Every Day*, and Pollert, *Girls, Wives, Factory Lives*. For a critique of Pollert, see Beechey, *Unequal Work*, chap. 5.
96 For example, Tentler, *Wage-Earning Women*; Hareven, *Family Time and Industrial Time*; Scott and Tilley, *Women, Work and Family*; Wandersee, *Women's Work and Family Values*; Klacynska, 'Why Women Work'; Yan's-McLaughlin, 'Italian Women and Work'; Iacovetta, 'From Contadina to Worker'; and Brandt, 'Weaving it Together.'
97 Turbin, 'Reconceptualizing Family, Work, and Labor Organizing' and 'Beyond Dichotomies.'
98 Baron, 'Gender and Labor History,' 7. See also Kessler-Harris, 'Gender Ideology in Historical Reconstruction.'
99 Feldberg and Glenn, 'Male and Female.'
100 Ava Baron argues that we must overcome the tendency to dichotomize women: 'Research that emphasizes the sameness of women and men potentially subsumes women workers' experiences under men's but research that highlights women's differences runs the risk of essentialism' (Baron, 'Gender and Labor History,' 22).
101 Westwood, *All Day Every Day*, 6.
102 Kessler-Harris, 'Gender Ideology in Historical Reconstruction,' 36.

CHAPTER 5 Maintaining Respectability, Coping with Crises

1 Outboard Marine Oral History Project, interview with Brenda M, 1990.
2 Hembold, 'Beyond the Family Economy,' 633.
3 For discussion of concepts of respectability in the nineteenth century, see R. Gray, *The Labour Aristocracy in Victorian Edinburgh,* and B. Palmer, *Working-Class Experience,* 57–61. For studies that look more at women, see Reiger, 'Clean, Comfortable and Respectable,' and Ross, 'Not the Sort to Sit on the Doorstep.' Two Canadian works that discuss notions of women's respectability are Morton, 'Men and Women in a Working-Class Neighbourhood in Halifax,' and Parr, *The Gender of Breadwinners.*
4 B. Palmer, *Working-Class Experience,* 229–36.
5 Ross, 'Not the Sort to Sit on the Doorstep,' 38–9.
6 For a discussion of such a 'reformulation' of respectability in the nineteenth century, see Bailey, 'Will the Real Bill Banks Please Stand Up?' and on respectability as a 'two-edged sword,' see B. Palmer, *Working-Class Experience.*
7 For one example of the discussion of the analysis of silences in interviews, see Passerini, 'Work Ideology and Working-Class Attitudes to Fascism.'
8 To note only one example, during the Second World War the paper referred to the increasing problem of street harassment of night workers by obnoxious 'curb-cruisers' (*Examiner,* 26 May 1942).
9 Even if people were not regular church attenders, they saw occasional church attendance (for marriages, baptisms) and adherence to 'Christian ideas' as important markers of respectability. In her study of nineteenth-century Ontario, Lynn Marks notes that the working classes were not as likely to be church members as the middle classes, though membership was also crucially shaped by marital status and gender (Marks, 'Ladies, Loaders, Knights and Lasses').
10 Roberts, *A Woman's Place,* 4.
11 Interview with Morris H, 18 July 1989.
12 Interview with Joy D, 26 July 1990.
13 Interview with Marilyn B, 8 Feb. 1990.
14 Interview with Carol H, 22 Aug. 1989.
15 Frankenberg, *White Women, Race Matters,* 229.
16 Interview with Maggie H, 26 July 1989. This woman is drawing on a common discourse (especially during this time period) which Ruth Frankenberg terms 'colour and power evasiveness.' In opposition to

unacceptable biological ideas of racial difference, people tried to emphasize the sameness of all people, regardless of race or ethnicity, but this
also had the effect of denying the power differences that did exist. See
Frankenberg, *White Women, Race Matters,* 142–3.

17 B. Palmer, *Working-Class Experience,* 29–35.

18 Ross, 'Not the Sort to Sit on the Doorstep,' 39.

19 Interview with Doris B, Feb. 1990.

20 Interview with Beatrice G, 25 June 1991.

21 Interview with Patricia M, 20 June, 1991.

22 Interestingly, a woman who was outspoken on union and political issues
in one workplace was assumed to be nonconformist in her sexual life as
well. This became a reason for other women to view her apprehensively.

23 Interview with Robert A, 14 July 1989, and with Lynn D, 27 June 1989.

24 On the nineteenth century, see Fingard, *The Dark Side of Life in Victorian
Halifax.* A British study of the twentieth-century underclass is Jeremy
White's *The Worst Street in North London.*

25 As Mark Rosenfeld points out, male railway workers engaged in both
respectable and rough behaviour. This was socially approved, as long as
the activities took place in the appropriate social space. A drinking binge
while 'on the road' was quite acceptable for the man who then went to
church on Sunday. This leeway, of course, was easier for men than
women (Rosenfeld, 'She Was a Hard Life,' 134).

26 Morton, 'Men and Women in a Working-Class Halifax Neighbourhood.'

27 Interview with Laura H, 29 Aug. 1989.

28 Strong-Boag, 'Canada's Early Experience with Income Supplement,' and
Little, 'The Regulation of Ontario Single Mothers.'

29 Interview with Annie B, 25 July 1989.

30 Sangster, 'Pardon Tales from Magistrate's Court.'

31 Archives of Ontario (hereafter cited as AO), Dept of Labour Records,
RG 7, 8–1, Textile Probe file, Mrs S. to David Croll, 27 Feb. 1936.

32 Interview with Beatrice G, 25 June 1991.

33 *Examiner,* 22 Dec. 1936.

34 City of Peterborough, Council Minutes for 1929 and 1933. GE employees
numbered 1,725 in 1929, and 978 in 1933.

35 National Archives of Canada, Dept of Labour Records, RG 27, vol. 2119,
National Registration of Persons on Relief, Peterborough, Sept. 1938. This
lists the number of employable women as 73 and men as 222, with a total
of 1,296 on relief (partially employable and unemployable). By January
1939, there were 2,227 on relief in total, of whom 97 were employable
women and 473 employable men; the rest (about 1,500) were considered

dependents. The numbers finally went down by 1940 to a total of 1,341 on relief.

36 As discussed below, census and other survey figures are notoriously unreliable. For example, the 1931 census (vol. 6, app. 1, table 3) noted that of wage earners *20 and over*, 7% of women earners in the city were unemployed and 15% of men were unemployed *on 1 June 1931*. This obviously left out teenagers and first-time earners who had never found jobs.

37 Hobbs, 'Gendering Work and Welfare,' chap. 5.

38 The 1931 census (vol. 6, app. 1, table 7) shows the number of earners who had lost time over the year as much higher than the number officially listed as unemployed. In the period from June 1930 to June 1931, 25% of the women who lost time did so for 'all causes,' and 13% because they had no job. ('All causes' included temporary lay-off, accident, illness, strikes, etc.) Ontario statistics show higher rates of unemployment for women in manufacturing, service, and trade than those listed for this city (see tables, 5, 11, and 19 in the same census volume). Failing precise statistics drawn from Peterborough, these must be used to indicate some degree of the dislocation women suffered.

39 Cassidy, *Unemployment and Relief in Ontario*, 29.

40 Hobbs, 'Gendering Work and Welfare,' chap. 6. See also Cohen, 'Women at Work in Canada during the Depression.'

41 Peterborough County Board of Education, Board Minutes, 6 June 1933. A 5% salary cut was instituted in 1932. In 1933 the board recommended a further 15% cut for teachers and 10% for other employees. Since women teachers were already paid less than men, the Women Teachers of the Public Schools wrote and asked that women be given only a 12.5% cut. In 1930 a female first-class teacher was making $950–$1,700, an equivalent male $1,600–$2,300; the Depression salary cuts would have reduced some starting teachers' salaries to those of factory workers. An interview with a former teacher indicated that some members on the board were not even superficially sympathetic: 'One member just sat there with a smirk on his face like we were dirt under his feet' (quoted in Robinson, 'A History of Peterborough Teachers').

42 Interview with a former teacher, quoted in Robinson, 'A History of Peterborough Teachers'; interview with Morris H, 18 July 1989.

43 Interview with Andrea E, 10 July 1989.

44 Peterborough Centennial Museum and Archives, Oral History Transcripts, interview with FR.

45 Coulter, 'Young Women and Unemployment in the 1930s.'

46 The YWCA had operated a referral service for domestic work since 1898. As one local historian noted, 'The Association [in Peterborough] tended to view unemployment or low wages as a personal circumstance which could be overcome through individual training and attitude' (Lee, 'Maternal Reform').

47 This is supported by both oral and quantitative evidence. The decline in the number of women in domestic service since 1911 was, of course, a result of other factors, such as the changing nature of domestic work, organization of the household, etc. In 1911, 43% of employed women in the city were in manufacturing and only 17% in domestic service. By 1921, the number of women in domestic service had fallen by 4%. By 1931, only 10% of the female workforce was employed in domestic service, though the number of women in this work had climbed slightly from 1921: from 177 to 215. The percentage of women in domestic service in the city is actually smaller than overall Ontario figures.

48 In the mid-1930s, for instance, when hundreds of women were using the employment bureau, a mere 45 were collecting relief (City of Peterborough, Relief Committee Minutes, 6 Aug. 1937 and 9 Sept. 1938).

49 *Examiner*, 11 Sept. 1935.

50 Cassidy, *Unemployment and Relief in Ontario*, 252.

51 Pierson, 'Gender and the Unemployment Insurance Debates,' 103.

52 Hobbs, 'Gender in Crisis.'

53 *Examiner*, 22 Feb. 1934.

54 Willis, 'Shop Floor Culture, Masculinity and the Wage Form,' 197.

55 Pierson, 'Gender and the Unemployment Debates.'

56 Interview with Penny H, 26 July 1989.

57 Interview with May D, 25 Aug. 1989.

58 *Examiner*, 5 July 1932 and 3 Dec. 1938.

59 *Examiner*, 28 Jan. 1931, notes the formation of the relief association and the fact that 191 families had gone to the charity board in January alone. By 1932, there were, on average, at least 500 families on relief; by the late 1930s there were almost 800 (with 2,000–3,000 people all dependent on relief).

60 City of Peterborough, Relief Committee, Minutes, 7 April 1938.

61 AO, Dept. of Public Welfare, RG 29, acc. 10889, vols. 9 and 12. The Peterborough rate was smaller than that for Guelph or Sudbury, for example.

62 For example, Alderman G.N. Gordon complained privately to the provincial government about the CAS: first, that the salary of the first woman superintendent was 'too much money' for a small town; second,

that maintenance costs for CAS wards – sometimes with delinquent
fathers – were unfairly placed on the city. 'We are sick and tired of CAS
officers and the way they are running things in Toronto ... Unless the CAS
is more reasonable, I am going to get people on Council to starve it out'
(AO, Dept of Public Welfare, RG 29, ac. 769-23-5-3, box 61, file 2424,
Gordon to Eric Cross, Minister, 12 Jan. 1938 and 28 Dec. 1939).

63 City of Peterborough, Relief Committee, Minutes, 17 June 1936; 6 May
1936; 6 Aug. 1936.

64 Ibid., 6 Dec. 1932. This notes that the Ontario inspector for relief urged
the committee, in the process of reorganizing the relief association, to
appoint one unemployed man to the board.

65 *Examiner*, 1 May 1936.

66 At the beginning of the Depression, some council members were
especially concerned about providing work for the city's skilled tradesmen (*Examiner*, 9 Sept. 1931).

67 Children's Aid Society of Peterborough, Board Minutes (hereafter CAS
Board Minutes), 9 Dec. 1939.

68 Trent University Archives, Joseph Wearing Papers, the speech 'Depression Blues' [*c.* 1934].

69 Interview with Lynn D, 27 June 1989.

70 On the last example, see Peterborough County Board of Education,
School Board Minutes, 29 Sept. 1939.

71 *Examiner*, 22 Feb. 1934.

72 Ibid.

73 Creese, 'The Politics of Dependence,' and Sangster, *Dreams of Equality*.

74 *Examiner*, 31 July 1934.

75 *Examiner*, 6 Sept. 1934.

76 Milkman, 'Women's Work and Economic Crisis,' 81.

77 Interview with Mary E, 25 Aug. 1989.

78 Interview with Lorna C, 13 Feb. 1990.

79 AO, Mercer Reformatory Records, RG 23, reel 13.

80 Interview with Donna B, 25 June 1991.

81 Ibid.

82 Again, precise figures are not available for Peterborough, but Ontario
figures show that more female-headed households (61%) had children
earning than male-headed households did (55%). See *Census*, 1931, vol. 5,
table 38. This would accord with the findings of nineteenth-century
studies such as McLean, 'Single Again.'

83 Interview with Shirley B, 8 Aug. 1991.

84 Almost every decade revealed one or two sensational bigamy cases. See *Examiner*, 11 Oct. 1930; 10 May 1942; 13 July 1954; 5 April 1955.

85 County of Peterborough, Lang Archives, Mothers' Allowance Board Records, Board Minutes, 30 March 1935.

86 On nineteenth-century widows, see Bradbury, 'Surviving as a Widow in 19th Century Montreal,' and McLean, 'Single Again.' While some of the strategies for widows remained the same in the twentieth century (calling on relatives for help, relying on children's earnings, taking in boarders), other strategies, such as keeping animals, would have changed.

87 CAS Board Minutes, Nov. 1934, Annual Meeting.

88 CAS Board Minutes, 7 Dec. 1937.

89 Little, 'The Regulation of Ontario Single Mothers.'

90 The 1921 census (vol. 3, table 26) shows that 14% of all families in the city were 'female-headed,' with 565 women listed as widows. The 1931 census (vol. 2, table 30) shows that there were 977 widows in the city, and the 1941 census lists 1,804 widows in the city and county combined. All these numbers suggest the small proportion of women actually collecting the allowance. Sessional papers for the 1930s, for instance, indicate that from 60 to 100 women were collecting the allowance for the city and county (and the Depression would have forced more women to resort to the allowance).

91 County of Peterborough, Lang Archives, Mothers' Allowance Board Records, Board Minutes, 9 Oct. 1932.

92 Little, 'The Regulation of Ontario Single Mothers.'

93 Interview with Pamela M, 24 June 1991.

94 See Forbes, 'Rum in the Maritime Economy,' for a discussion of women's engagement in similar activities.

95 *Examiner*, 26 Jan. 1929.

96 *Examiner*, 26 Jan. 1929 and 13 Oct. 1933.

97 *Examiner*, 27 Oct. 1930.

98 For example, one woman was incarcerated for 'peculiar' behaviour, including the use of loud bad language in public, reckless bicycle riding, and dressing like a child or in male clothes, and thus making a 'nuisance' of herself (AO, Mercer Records, case files, reel 6, no. 5690).

99 By the 1950s, housewives had replaced domestic workers as the dominant occupational group.

100 *Examiner*, July 26 1930 and 13 May 1932.

101 For example, between 1920 and 1960, the proportion of all charges (n - 616) by occupation was as follows: domestics, 39%; housewives, 35%;

factory workers, 8%; waitresses, 2.6%; white collar, 4.1%, plus other. Factory workers accounted for 7% of vagrancy charges, 8% of street-walking charges, 17% of disorderly house/bawdy house charges, 11% of theft charges, and 5% of liquor intoxication charges.

102 On the current relationship between women, poverty and crime, see Carlen, *Women, Crime and Poverty*. On the nineteenth-century, see Fingard, *The Dark Side of Life in Victorian Halifax*; Strange, 'The Velvet Glove'; and Price, 'Raised in Rockhead, Died in the Poorhouse.'

103 AO, Mercer Records, case files 9291.

104 *Examiner*, 25 May 1927 and 26 Jan. 1929.

105 For example, the arrest and arraignment statistics for the 1920s and 1930s indicate that the magistrate sometimes sentenced only a few nonsupport cases every year.

106 *Examiner*, 11 Feb. 1929.

107 *Examiner*, 10 April 1926.

108 *Examiner*, 11 Aug. 1925.

109 *Examiner*, 12 Jan. 1931.

110 *Examiner*, 2 Nov. 1939.

111 *Examiner*, 5 Jan. 1943.

112 Statistics taken from the jail registers (which are inadequate because they show only the men arrested) nonetheless indicate that charges doubled from the thirties to the forties, and more than tripled in the fifties (from 14 to 29 to 112).

113 Children's Aid Society of Peterborough, Clipping Scrapbooks. For example, an article of 7 June 1956 notes an increase in the number of unwed mothers, but also that the percentage of these women within the population was still very low. A slight increase in single mothers from 1951 to 1961 was also noted in an *Examiner* article of Oct. 1961.

114 Statistics on wife assault are very unreliable because so many cases were mediated informally. The 'Magistrate's Court' column in the newspaper does not always accord with the jail registers. For example, on 12 Aug. 1942 the *Examiner* noted three wife-assault cases and one nonsupport case before magistrate, and these are not recorded in the register.

115 See the cases of abused wives killing husbands in desperation, *Examiner*, 22 Nov. 1943 and 5 Nov. 1948.

116 *Examiner*, 15 Nov. 1928.

117 *Examiner*, 23 Jan. 1939.

118 Sangster, 'The Dark Side of Family Life.'

119 *Examiner*, 19 Feb. 1926.

120 *Examiner*, 6 May 1942.

121 Interview with Betty L, 27 June 1989.
122 *Examiner*, 22 Jan. 1940.

CHAPTER 6 Accommodation at Work

1 Interview with Penny H, 26 July 1989.
2 Interview with Joy D, 26 July 1990.
3 Collinson, *Managing the Shopfloor*, 221.
4 Baron, 'Gender and Labor History,' 16.
5 Joyce, *Work, Society and Politics*, 94.
6 Interview with May D, 25 Aug. 1989.
7 Interview with Dot H, 15 March 1990.
8 Interview with Gayle W, March 1990.
9 Interview with Ethel M, 22 Aug. 1989.
10 Outboard Marine Oral History Project (hereafter cited as OMP), interview with Joan B, 1990.
11 Interview with Jack D, 10 April 1991.
12 Interview with Peter F, June 1989.
13 Parr, *The Gender of Breadwinners*, 35.
14 Interview with Joy D, 26 July 1990.
15 Interview with Henrietta G, 24 July 1989.
16 Interview with Rosa B, 2 Aug. 1989.
17 Eagleton, *Ideology*, 34.
18 OMP, interview with Jill R, 1990.
19 Interview with Lynn D, 27 June 1989.
20 Interview with Doreen C, 24 July 1991.
21 Interview with Henrietta G, 24 July 1989.
22 Archives of Ontario (hereafter cited as AO), Dept of Labour, RG 7-57, 3, Industrial Relations file, pre-1936.
23 Interview with Herman B, June 1989.
24 The women's attitudes towards benefits were also shaped by their age and the length of their employment. Still, many industries at the time relied on generalizations about all women workers. For example, General Electric in the United States assumed that women were interested in 'sociability not security' (Schatz, *The Electrical Workers*, 22).
25 AO, Dept of Labour, RG 7-57, Miss Finlay's report, 1927. Westclox's paid vacations were the most expensive and attractive of its benefits. In the 1927 study, only about one-third of the companies surveyed had paid vacations.
26 *Industrial Canada*, June, Sept., and Oct. 1935 and Aug. 1936.

27 It also needs to be compared with industries of other size and wealth. Companies like Imperial Oil were much larger and able to sustain expensive benefits. As Nelson points out for the United States, only a minority of the larger companies ever became really involved in welfare plans; many smaller companies continued to deal with unions in a different way – with active intimidation (Nelson, *Workers and Managers*, 116).

28 Interview with Doris B, 12 Dec. 1990.

29 AO, Dept of Labour, RG 7-57, 3, Industrial Relations file, pre-1936.

30 Ibid.

31 On paternalism in Britain, see Joyce, *Work, Society and Politics*, and Lown, *Women and Industrialization*. See also Reid, 'Industrial Paternalism,' and Dellheim, 'The Creation of a Company Culture.' American studies range from those starting with the mid-nineteenth-century textile mills to those extending their focus into the twentieth century. See Scranton, 'Varieties of Paternalism'; Hall, *Like a Family*; Hareven, *Family Time and Industrial Time*; Meyer, *The Five Dollar Day*; and Budner, *Pullman*. The best recent book is Zahavi, *Workers, Managers and Welfare Capitalism*.

32 Lown, 'Not So Much a Factory, More a Form of Patriarchy.' Lown argues that 'paternalism is only one of many and varying forms of legitimation that holders of patriarchal power adopt' (35–6).

33 Lown, *Women and Industrialization*, 3.

34 Brandes, *American Welfare Capitalism*; Nelson, *Managers and Workers*, and Brody, *Workers in Industrial America*. Nelson, for example, sees paternalism and welfare capitalism as distinct and claims that in some situations, traditional paternalism 'deterred' the adoption of welfare work (*Managers and Workers*, 115).

35 Interview with Mona G, 21 Aug. 1989.

36 Ibid.

37 Interview with Laura H, 29 Aug. 1989.

38 Interview with Christine M, Feb. 1990.

39 Interview with Edna M, 27 June 1989.

40 Interview with Peter F, June 1989.

41 Interview with Edna M, 27 June 1989.

42 This is not an ahistorical claim that women are by nature conciliatory, but rather a suggestion that in this time period women often did learn mediating roles in the family. While labour historians have documented women's different work cultures and approaches to resistance, there is

less study of women's distinct methods of accommodation in the workplace. More recent feminist literature on women's methods of organizing has suggested that our gendered experience can produce different methods of organizing (see Wine and Ristock, *Women and Social Change*). It is also worth noting that a contemporary study of activist women suggests different conclusions from mine about the relationship between family and work (see Sachs, *Caring by the Hour*).

43 Purcell, 'Female Manual Workers,' 49.
44 Interview with Doris B, Feb. 1990.
45 Phillips, 'Women in the Outboard Marine Family,' 27.
46 Brandes, *American Welfare Capitalism*, 140.
47 On distinct programs for women, see Nelson, *Managers and Workers*. On nineteenth-century paternalism and the protection of women's respectability, see Parr, *The Gender of Breadwinners*, chap. 2. In *Workers, Managers and Welfare Capitalism*, Zahavi argues that Endicott Johnson defended the morality and respectability of wage-earning mothers primarily because these women's labour was needed in his factory – indicating the malleability of paternalism according to the needs of capital. In the context of the Peterborough labour market, married women were not a crucial necessity to the company (at least, not until the war years), so the company could endorse the family wage and ignore the issue of wage-earning mothers.
48 For more details, see Sangster, 'The Softball Solution.'
49 Interview with Herman B, June 1989.
50 Interview with Andrea E, 10 July 1989.
51 OMP, interview with Ellen R, 1990.
52 OMP, interview with Kathy S, 1990.
53 Interview with Doris B, 12 Dec. 1990.
54 Interview with Harriet I, 17 July 1989.
55 Interview with Christine M, Feb. 1990.
56 Gelber, 'Working at Playing.' American sports historians point to the commercialization of sports in this period, but this was not so visible in a smaller community. See Dyreson, 'The Emergence of Consumer Culture and the Transformation of Physical Culture,' and Betke, 'The Social Significance of Sport in the City.'
57 Mott, 'One Solution to the Urban Crisis.'
58 For this erroneous view, see Melchers, 'Sports in the Workplace.' On the increasing use of recreation programs by companies in the Second World War, see 'Industrial Recreation, Canadian Style,' *Recreation*, Dec. 1944.

Fones-Wolf argues that U.S. companies *renewed* their interest in welfare capitalism during the war (see her 'Industrial Recreation, the Second World War and the Revival of Welfare Capitalism').

59 Lenskyj, *Out of Bounds.* See also her 'Femininity First.'
60 For a similar suggestion, see Adilman, 'Baseball, Business and the Workplace.'
61 Interview with Harriet I, 17 July 1989.
62 Peterborough *Examiner*, Clipping, n.d. [1990]. This was an interview with a wartime member of an industrial softball team.
63 Tomlinson, 'Good Times, Bad Times and the Politics of Leisure.'
64 Brandes, *American Welfare Capitalism.*
65 'How GE Spreads Its News,' *Financial Post*, 2 April 1955.
66 *Tic Talk*, June 1954.
67 *Tic Talk*, June 1944.
68 Ads for GE products made this point, though obviously in a general way. The Peterborough plant made few 'domestic' products. For a discussion of companies like GE that promoted consumerism among their workers, see Cumbler, *Working-Class Community in Industrial America.*
69 *Tic Talk*, June 1954.
70 *Tic Talk*, Dec. 1966.
71 *Tic Talk*, Sept. 1959.
72 *Tic Talk*, Sept. 1959.
73 Lamphere, 'Bringing the Family to Work.'
74 Interview with Marilyn B, 8 Feb. 1990.
75 Interview with Robert A, 14 June 1989.
76 Interview with Wendy L, 6 Aug. 1990.
77 Interview with Amelia H, 28 Aug. 1989.
78 Burawoy, *Manufacturing Consent*, 106.
79 Interview with Susan E, 25 Aug. 1989. This quote also indicates how women's own informal codes of conduct, discussed in chapter 4, were not always oppositional to the company's interests. The interviewee said that she did try to help her get the machine going again later.
80 Interview with Henrietta G, 24 July 1989.
81 Ibid.
82 Davies, *Women's Place Is at the Typewriter*, 155.
83 Pringle, 'Bureaucracy, Rationality, Sexuality,' 169. See also her *Secretaries Talk.* Although Pringle's research was done in the 1980s, her description here bears a remarkable resemblance to the relations just described in this chapter.
84 Heron, *Working in Steel*, 110.
85 Heron and DeZwaan, 'Industrial Unionism in Eastern Ontario.' It is

important to note that many of the businesses (except for GE) in this city were, like Westclox, small enough to facilitate the cultivation of paternalism.

86 There are a number of poststructuralist critiques of the concept of ideology. Foucault's views have influenced many others. His objection was (1) that ideology implies the existence of another more 'real' or 'truthful' reality (and he was not a fan of any truth claims); (2) that it is linked to a Marxist view of a material economic determinant; and (3) that it rests on the notion of a humanist view of the 'subject' (Foucault, 'Truth and Power,' 118). A second major critique is Laclau and Mouffe's *Hegemony and Socialist Strategy*, which draws extensively on Gramsci but ultimately rejects any notion that classes *a priori* exist (outside their construction in political discourses) or are progressive agents of change. In *The Politics of Truth*, Barrett also critiques the 'descriptive' and 'critical' Marxist definitions of ideology, again because of ideology's link to ideas of class primacy and material determination, and because of its inadequate theorizing of power. Barrett seems to want to hold onto aspects of the Marxist 'critical' definition of ideology, seeing ideology 'tied to the exercise of power and domination,' but she downplays the questions of where that power is centralized, why, and in whose interest. Although Barrett's view influenced this chapter, I am ultimately more indebted to writers such as Holub, who argues (in my simplified words) that 'Foucault shows how power exists; Gramsci why it exists' (*Antonio Gramsci*, 200).

87 Holub, *Antonio Gramsci*, 200. Holub points out that both Foucault and Gramsci were concerned with power and the production of consent from below, though in the last instance their analysis differed in terms of causality. On Gramsci and feminism, see also O'Brien, 'Hegemony and Superstructure.'

88 Armstrong and Armstrong, *Theorizing Women's Work*, 45.

89 On hegemony, see Gramsci, *Selections from Prison Notebooks*; Bocock, *Hegemony*; and Boggs, *The Two Revolutions*.

90 Eagleton, *Ideology*, 114 (I have paraphrased his actual words).

91 Ibid., 117.

92 National Archives of Canada, IUE Collection, 28-I-264, vol. 83, P. Drysdale to G. Hutchens, President, IUE, 15 Sept. 1969.

CHAPTER 7 Resistance and Unionization

1 *Examiner*, 2 Sept. 1925.

2 Klein and Roberts, 'Beseiged innocence.'

3 Quoted in Phillips, 'Women in the Outboard Marine Family,' 25.

4 Peterborough Centennial Museum and Archives, Quaker Oats Collection, Staff Lists file, 15 April 1920.

5 National Archives of Canada (hereafter cited as NA), Dept. of Labour, RG 27, Strikes and Lockouts, vol. 382, file 54.

6 Ibid., vol. 420, file 240.

7 Interview with KM, 7 Aug. 1990.

8 Interview with Joan J, 25 Aug. 1990.

9 Interview with RP, 19 March 1989.

10 *Examiner*, 2 Sept. 1919.

11 Morton, 'Labour, Politics and Peterborough.'

12 Canada, Dept of Labour, 'Labour Organization in Canada, 1920–40.'

13 See NA, Dept of Labour, RG 27, Strikes and Lockouts, vol. 320, file 143.

14 Because the working class was scattered over a number of wards, citywide voting allowed trade unionists to 'plump' for their own, which aided the election of labour men.

15 Morton, 'Labour, Politics and Peterborough,' 3.

16 *Examiner*, 20 Jan. 1920: 'Labour council endorses a resolution of the Hamilton Labour Council that women only work 8 hours a day.' Overall, women are hardly ever mentioned in labour council meetings.

17 Naylor, *The New Democracy*, chap. 5. For example, there is little evidence of an active female presence in the local ILP that elected Thomas Tooms (see University of Toronto, Rare Books Room, Woodsworth Memorial Collection, Tooms files).

18 Canada. *Report of the Royal Commission on the Textile Industry*, 1937, chap. 9, esp. pp. 170–5.

19 NA, Royal Commission on Price Spreads, RG 33-18/111, vol. 39, has wage lists for 1934 for the Bonnerworth and Auburn mills.

20 A comparison of the 1931 census figures for wages for male weaving with estimates of wages given by J.L. Cohen at the 1937 Industry and Labour Board hearings indicates a small drop in wages. Similarly, for female spinners, wages remained largely stagnant over these years.

21 Archives of Ontario (hereafter cited as AO), Dept of Labour, RG 7, box 15, 1-1, W. Stevens to David Croll, 3 Feb. 1936; C. Stone to Croll, 27 Feb. 1936.

22 NA, Royal Commission on Textiles, RG 33-20, Barrett to Dawson, 22 Nov. 1932, quoted in *Report of Royal Commission on Textiles*, 171.

23 NA, Royal Commission on Textiles, RG 33-20, vol. 74, 'Manual of the Textile Industry.' Through the Depression, employment remained at a fairly stable 800 in Dominion Woollens in Peterborough.

24 Ibid., vol. 33, report of G. Evans for Bank of Montreal on Dominion Woollens.

25 Interview with Robert A, 14 June 1989. G.N. Gordon also gave this opinion to various politicians.

26 Interview with HN, 1 Nov. 1990.

27 Interview with May D, 25 Aug. 1989.

28 Interview with June H, 31 July 1989.

29 Interview with Rosa B, 2 Aug. 1989.

30 Interview with Joy D, 26 July 1990.

31 Interview with Edith F, 26 June 1989.

32 Ibid.

33 Parr, *The Gender of Breadwinners*, chap. 5.

34 *Examiner*, 10 August 1937, and NA, Dept of Labour Papers, RG 27, Strikes and Lockouts, vol 388, file 176, clippings.

35 Interview with Doris B, 12 Dec. 1990.

36 *Examiner*, 6 July 1937.

37 *Examiner*, 5 July 1937.

38 *Examiner*, 10 July 1937. See also *Globe and Mail*, 17 July 1937.

39 *Examiner*, 29 July 1937.

40 *Examiner*, 29 July 1937.

41 Interview with Dorothy H, 23 Aug. 1989.

42 *Examiner*, 10 Aug. 1937.

43 *Examiner*, 21 Aug. 1937.

44 Interview with Joy D, 26 July 1990.

45 NA, J.L. Cohen Papers, MG 30-A94, vol. 11, Elmer Hickey to Cohen, 14 Sept. 1937.

46 Interview with June H, 31 July 1989.

47 Interview with Dorothy H, 23 Aug. 1989, and with Joy D, 26 July 1990.

48 Interview with BH, Aug. 1990.

49 *Examiner*, 29 July 1937.

50 Ibid.

51 *Examiner*, 3 July 1937.

52 Phillips, 'Women in the Outboard Marine Family,' 39.

53 Interview with BH, Aug. 1990.

54 *Examiner*, 10 Aug. 1937.

55 AO, Dept of Labour Records, RG 7, 8-I, box 4, Minimum Wage Statistics, 'Draft Copy: Memorandum re Establishment of Minimum Wage Schedule in Textile Industry,' 1 Sept. 1937.

56 Ibid.

57 AO, Dept of Labour Records, RG 7, 8-I, box 4, 'Proceedings in Textile Industry,' Peterborough, 1 Oct. 1937.

58 Ibid.

59 Ibid., 37–8.

60 All the quotations in this passage are from the interview with Rosa B, 2 Aug. 1989.

61 Extremely revealing is Rosa's claim that her close friend also continued to work. Yet other glaring evidence (her friend's arrest notice in the paper, confirmed by a family member) says otherwise.

62 Interview with June H, 31 July 1989.

63 Interview with Amelia H, 28 Aug. 1989.

64 Interview with Dorothy H, 23 Aug. 1989.

65 Bertaux-Wiame, 'The Life History Approach to Internal Migration.'

66 Interview with Edith F, 26 June 1989.

67 For example, see the discussion of the 1974 Fleck strike in Maroney, 'Feminism at Work.'

68 Pringle, *Secretaries Talk*, 200.

69 NA, United Electrical, Radio and Machine Workers of America, National Records (hereafter UE National), MG-I-190, Reel 2336, National Executive Minutes, 5 Feb. 1938.

70 The profit-sharing plan was introduced in the late 1930s – as unionization increased in the United States – along with other benefits, such as pensions.

71 NA, Dept of Labour, RG 27, vol. 345, 'Employment in Plants Engaged in War Industry,' 1943.

72 Interview in *Monitor* (employee newspaper), May 1977, quoted in Phillips, 'Women in the Outboard Marine Family,' 12.

73 *Examiner*, 4 Sept. 1941.

74 Palmer, 'Sexuality and War Plants.'

75 Pierson, *They're Still Women After All*. As Pierson points out, fears about sexual promiscuity in the armed forces were directed particularly at working-class women.

76 *Examiner*, 22 Feb. 1943. I am indebted to Julie Guard for this reference.

77 The presence of two girl welders made big news in the plant paper, the *Works News*, Feb. 1943 and May 1943.

78 Pierson, *They're Still Women After All*.

79 *Examiner*, 12 and 15 May 1942.

80 *UE News*, 5 Sept. 1944.

81 NA, Dept of Labour, RG 27, vol. 105, file V-24-1, W.I. Hetherington to Rex Eaton, 13 Oct. 1943.

82 Ibid.
83 United Electrical, Radio and Machine Workers of America, Local 524, Archives (hereafter cited as UE Local 524), Genelco files, radio script.
84 *UE News*, 9 Dec. 1944.
85 Hunter, *Which Side Are You On Boys?* 140.
86 Loth, *Swope of GE.*
87 Interview with David S, Nov. 1992.
88 Schatz, *The Electrical Workers.*
89 NA, UE National, MG 28-I-190, reel 2339, B. Ward to R. Russell, 6 Sept. 1945.
90 Ibid.
91 Ibid., Bob Ward to George Harris, 8 Feb. 1945.
92 Abella, *Nationalism, Communism and Canadian Labour*, 139.
93 Ibid., 158.
94 Turk, 'Surviving the Cold War.'
95 Kannenberg, 'From World War to Cold War.'
96 Guard, 'The "Woman Question" in Canadian Unionism.'
97 For a good discussion of seniority in the electrical industry, see Schatz, *The Electrical Workers*, chap 5.
98 UE Local 524, Genelco Early History file. In the first agreement, lay-off was affected by length of service, ability, skill, and family status and number of dependents; there was a point system that gave employees status by marital situation, number of dependents, etc. By 1945, the company had agreed to remove the family status clause. On the second issue, see General Membership Meeting, 29 Oct. 1946.
99 UE Local 524, Local bulletin, 19, 21 Oct. 1948. Protests immediately after the war are not apparent from the minutes, except for the Induction Motors issue, discussed below.
100 NA, UE National correspondence, MG 28-I-190, reel 2339, C.O. O'Donnell to I. Wilson, 14 June 1949. See also UE Local 524, Executive Minutes, Morton report on girls meeting, 13 June 1949.
101 Quoted in Guard, 'The "Women Question" in Canadian Unionism,' 154.
102 NA, UE National correspondence, MG 28-I-190, Jackson to O'Donnell, 16 June 1949. See also the heated replies, 30 June 1949, and letter from Jackson to Morton, 7 July 1949.
103 The Canadian UE liked to stress its autonomy from the U.S. leadership but maintained fairly centralized control over its own locals (Coldwell, 'The United Electrical, Radio and Machine Workers of America').
104 *UE News*, 18 March, 6 May, and 20 May 1949.
105 UE Local 524, pamphlet file.

106 Ibid.

107 *UE News*, 25 March 1949.

108 Interview with RP, 19 March 1989.

109 It is significant that Morton was not perceived as the women's advocate in this issue. 'Did you see John Morton fighting for the girls in induction motors?' the UE charged rhetorically in a pamphlet.

110 It is interesting to note that in Schatz's study, in one workplace, many women and people of colour voted against the UE; this, he suggests, may have been in part because the UE, organized earlier, now looked like the 'establishment.' Here, however, the UE was recently organized and had a stronger reputation for militancy and for defending the rights of the most marginalized workers.

111 *UE News*, 21 Oct. 1949.

112 See also *Works News*, 28 Oct. 1949.

113 *GE Works News*, 28 Oct. 1949.

114 Legal reforms in the 1960s allowed the possibility of taking a company to court to force an arbitration settlement.

115 UE Local 524, Genelco Early History file.

116 *UE News*, 21 Aug. 1953.

117 NA, Dept of Labour, RG 27, vol. 851, file 8-3-18-3, Independent Report by J.L. Cohen to the Board.

118 See chapter 3 for this example. UE Local 524, Genelco Brief to the Ontario Regional War Labour Board, 19 July 1943.

119 Ibid.

120 NA, UE National, MG 28-I-190, reel 2336, District 5 Minutes, 30 April 1944.

121 NA, UE National, MG 28-I-190, C.S. Jackson to area reps, 'Brief on Problems of Working Women,' 14 July 1955.

122 Interview with PH, 9 Aug. 1990.

123 *UE News*, 20 May 1949.

124 NA, UE National, MG 28-I-190, reel 2362, 'How to Tackle Job and Rate Discrimination against Women,' 1955.

125 Some equal pay gains were notably made in the war years at electrical plants. See articles on Rodgers Tubes and Leland Electric in *UE News*, 30 March 1945 and 19 Dec. 1944.

126 NA, UE National, MG 28-I-190, reel 2336, Minutes of Annual Convention, 8–11 Oct. 1953.

127 UE Local 524, Submission of UE to Board of Conciliation, 1953–4.

128 UE Local 524, Executive Minutes, 11 July 1949.

129 Interview with RP, 19 March 1989.

130 UE Local 524, Sullivan to Jackson, 28 Feb. 1949, and Sullivan to Wren, 1 Feb. 1949.

131 UE Local 524, Grievance files, 1949.

132 UE Local 524, Grievance files, 30 May 1960 and 24 Nov. 1954.

133 The union argued that 'the moral climate in Peterborough was beyond her control' (quoted in Guard, 'The "Woman Question,"' 229).

134 *Voice of the Worker*, June/July 1961 and Oct. 1961. The board had denied her UIC even though she could have taken light work during a pregnancy.

135 UE Local 524, Pamphlet file.

136 Interview with Thelma A, June 1989.

137 Interview with Ramona H, 29 Nov. 1989.

138 A second UE local in Peterborough, Local 527, was a composite local for Raybestos, Peterborough Lock, and the Peterborough Marble Works. The UE also tried to organize (unsuccessfully) Westclox. It lost Outboard Marine to a Steelworkers campaign in the 1950s. The extent of UE organizing, as one interviewee commented, made the UE appear formidable and dangerous to Peterborough employers.

139 *Examiner*, speech by Sam Baron, 5 Sept. 1950.

140 *Examiner*, 27 Sept. 1950.

141 *Examiner*, 7 Aug. 1951.

142 *Examiner*, 27 March 1953. The speaker was James Fraser of the Chamber of Commerce.

143 Interview with AG, 21 March 1990.

144 Interview with RP, 19 March 1989.

145 *Works News*, 28 Oct. 1949.

146 Machinery and Allied Products Institute, *The GE Approach to Industrial Relations*, and Northrup, 'The Case for Boulwarism.'

147 Interview with RP, 19 March 1990.

148 'Organizing for Enterprise,' *Canadian Business*, Oct. 1954.

149 Kannenberg, 'From World War to Cold War,' argues that this is precisely what happened to the United States.

150 More than one male interviewee remembers physical confrontations.

151 Guard, 'The "Woman Question,"' 240.

152 For example, in Peterborough, the auxiliary tried to hold socials for the plant women, and in one case a union activist, Kathy How, later became an auxiliary activist.

153 Interview with AG, 21 March 1990.

154 GE, of course, had also long fostered the notion that its policies and wage levels supported a male-breadwinner model. See chapter 3.

155 Interview with RP, 19 March 1989.

156 *UE News*, 2 Jan. 1953.

157 UE Local 524, Pamphlet file, 'Calling All UE Girls.'

158 *UE News*, 14 Oct. 1955.

159 Interview with KM, 7 Aug. 1990.

160 Ibid.

161 As Dorothy Sue Cobble argues, we must develop a more inclusive, less middle-class definition of feminism that recognizes the various sites and means of women's resistance to their inequality. Sue Cobble, 'Re-thinking the Doldrum Years.'

162 Interview with Kathy L, Aug. 1990.

163 Guard, 'The "Woman Question,"' 319.

164 *UE News*, 23 Oct. 1953.

165 Interview with RP, 19 March 1989.

166 Interview with Joan J, 25 Aug. 1990.

167 Ibid.

168 Janiewski, *Sisterhood Denied.*

169 Interview with Edith F, 26 June 1989.

CHAPTER 8 Doing Two Jobs

1 Interview with Patricia M, 20 June 1991.

2 Interview with Doreen C, 24 July 1991.

3 Interview with Beatrice G, 25 June 1991.

4 Iacovetta, *Such Hard-Working People*, 92–3. As Veronica Strong-Boag points out, the image of more middle-class women going out to work masked the reality that most married wives were working because their families needed their wages. Women in higher income brackets were actually less likely to be in the workforce.

5 Jill Matthews points to five areas of paid work already done by women: the private sale of skills such as laundering and child minding; the sale of home produce, such as food and crafts; the provision of lodging; the operation of small businesses, such as sewing or music lessons; and outwork done for industry (Matthews, 'Deconstructing the Masculine Universe').

6 National Archives of Canada (hereafter, NA), Dept of Labour, RG 27, Women's Bureau Papers (hereafter, WB), vol. 4171, submission of the OFL to Royal Commission on the Status of Women.

7 Krashinsky, *Day Care and Public Policy in Ontario*, 7–8, table 1.

8 NA, RG 27, WB, vol. 1904, 9 Nov. 1960, memo. This memo on married women workers noted that 19% of married women worked and that 'this should not exceed 25%.' Similarly, the Gordon commission completely

miscalculated the increase in female labour (see *Canadian Business*, Feb. 1958).

9 Between 1941 and 1961, high school enrolment doubled in Canada (Harrigan, 'The Schooling of Boys and Girls in Canada'). Similar expansion of high school enrolment was visible in Peterborough.

10 Armstrong and Armstrong, *The Double Ghetto*.

11 Department of Labour, *Women at Work*, 23–5. Surveys offered contradictory evidence on the extent to which part-time work was a choice for women. On women's part-time work, see Julie White, *Women and Part-Time Work*. Ann Duffy and Norene Pupo also discuss the question of voluntary/involuntary part-time work, and they note that part-time work 'boomed' in this era, especially for female workers (Duffy and Pupo, *Part-Time Paradox*, 44).

12 As noted earlier, there is no continuous historical data on the labour force activity of married women for Peterborough in the censuses. In 1951, women who were married, divorced, or widowed were 38% of women workers. By 1961, they were 51% (*Census*, 1951, vol. 5, table 18; *Census*, 1961, vol. 3:1, table 13). By 1976, the figure was 62%, and the most rapidly increasing group in the labour force was that of women aged 25 to 44 (Hobbs, *Working Trends*, 18–19).

13 Interview with Ramona H, 29 Nov. 1989.

14 Interview with Suzanne I, July 1991.

15 Interview with Francis M, 21 June 1991.

16 Interview with Donna B, 25 June 1991.

17 Interview with Eleanor T, Jan. 1990.

18 NA, Canadian Food and Allied Workers, MG 28-I-186, vol. 23, Canada Packers Local 293, Collective Agreement.

19 UE Local 524, Summary of Payroll Reports, 1961.

20 Calculated from *Census*, 1961, vol. 3:3, table 27.

21 NA, IUE Collection, 28-1-264, vol. 83, P. Drysdale to G. Hutchens, 15 Sept. 1969. The issue was taken up by other women outside the factory, who wrote to the Ontario Women's Bureau complaining that such a rollback would be discriminatory. Since it was the codes rather than individual women that were targeted, it was not deemed discriminatory (AO, Dept of Labour, RG 7, Women's Bureau Correspondence, series 8, box 1).

22 This is also the conclusion of Pamela Sugiman in her analysis of UAW women in the postwar period, though the auto plants she studied also saw more ethnic diversity in the workforce, which was not so apparent here (Sugiman, 'Labour's Dilemma,' chap. 5).

23 Guard, 'The "Woman Question" in Canadian Unionism,' 131.

24 Interview with Eleanor T, Jan. 1990.

25 Outboard Marine Oral History Projects, interview with Brenda M. She may have been referring to a union function having a bar, not a meeting having one, but the two were associated in her mind.

26 Interview with Beatrice G, 25 June 1991.

27 Interview with Donna B, 25 June 1991.

28 Interview with Isabel G, 19 March 1990.

29 Pierson, *They're Still Women After All.*

30 See, for example, studies done by the Ontario Women's Bureau relating to employment counselling in the 1960s (AO, Dept of Labour, RG 7, Women's Bureau, 7-1-0, file 1371, 'What Women Think about Working'). In another survey, teachers and student teachers were surveyed; while a high number (75–81%) planned to marry and have children, 64% of the current teachers and 93% of the student teachers planned to return to work (Ibid., vol. 8, Employment Counselling file).

31 Department of Labour, Women's Bureau, *Occupational Histories of Married Women Working for Pay.*

32 Interview with Doreen C, 24 July 1991.

33 Ursel, *Private Lives, Public Policy*, 230.

34 Interview with Henrietta G, 24 July 1989.

35 Interview with Corinne L, July 1991.

36 Interview with Doris B, 12 Dec. 1990.

37 Canada, Department of Labour, *Survey of Married Women Working for Pay.* The majority of women earned between $1,000 and $2,000 and 60% of their husbands earned less than $2,000. By the 1970s the National Council of Welfare estimated that 51% of two-spouse families would fall below the poverty line if the wives did not work (National Council of Welfare, *Women and Poverty*, 20).

38 Interview with Deborah A, 24 June 1991.

39 Outboard Marine Oral History Project, interview with Ellen R, 1990.

40 Interview with Monica K, 4 Dec. 1989.

41 Interview with Corinne L, July 1991.

42 Interview with Beatrice G, 25 June 1991.

43 Interview with Pamela M, 24 June 1991.

44 Interview with Patricia M, 20 June 1991.

45 Interview with Jean R, 9 July 1991.

46 Interview with Shirley M, 8 Aug. 1991.

47 Interview with Francis M, 21 June 1991.

48 Interview with Donna B, 25 June 1991.

49 Other women who had working mothers made similar observations, but

only if they saw some measure of choice or enjoyment, or a measure of economic independence, coming from their mothers' wage work. This would accord with Kathleen Gerson's more contemporary research on working mothers and daughters, *Hard Choices.*

50 Interview with Eleanor T, Jan. 1990.

51 The federal Women's Bureau research showed that the notion that women constantly moved in and out of the workforce was false. About 80% of women did withdraw at the time of marriage or pregnancy, but there was still strong continuity in their working lives: 40% of those surveyed were at their original job, 79% at their second job. See Canada, Department of Labour, Women's Bureau, *Occupational Histories of Married Women Working for Pay,* 25–9.

52 NA, RG 27, WB, vol 4171, Briefs to the Royal Commission on the Status of Women, Study done by Hickling-Johnston on Status of Women in Canada.

53 Canada, Department of Labour, *Survey of Married Women Working for Pay,* 59.

54 Ibid.

55 E.T. May, *Homeward Bound.*

56 'Why Some Women Never Marry,' *Chatelaine,* Nov. 1954; 'A Minister's Frank Words for Brides and Grooms,' Ibid., May 1954. Articles such as these support the contention that it was not only domesticity but this combined with compulsory heterosexuality and pronatalism that made this era oppressive for many women.

57 Rutherford, *When Television Was Young,* 332, 200.

58 I recognize that historians of popular culture have argued persuasively that these visual images can be 'read' on different and possibly even subversive levels. On portrayals of women in Hollywood movies, see Haskel, *From Reverence to Rape,* and French, *On the Verge of Revolt.*

59 Interview with Jean R, 9 July 1991.

60 Jane Ursel suggests that the turn to women's productive labour occurred with relatively little 'notice and controversy' (*Private Lives, Public Policy,* 234). The debate, however, was ongoing and fairly extensive.

61 Strong-Boag, 'Women with a Choice.' This fixation with middle-class women was apparent in discussions of gender discrimination as well. One female writer critical of the Royal Commission on the Status of Women maintained that Canadian 'women had little to complain about.' All the examples she used were of more privileged, middle-class and professional women ('Do Women's Rights Have Wrongs?' *Globe and Mail,* 26 Jan. 1967).

62 'I Quit My Job to Save My Marriage,' *Chatelaine,* June 1955.

63 As Franca Iacovetta has pointed out, some female immigrants had a very high labour force participation rate, thus contradicting this stereotype (Iacovetta, 'From Contadina to Worker').

64 *Canadian Business*, June 1961, cited a poll by the Canadian Institute of Public Opinion: 72% of women and 58% of men thought that a married woman should be able to work *if there are no small children*; 37% of the men said no married woman should work (my emphasis).

65 'The Many Lives of Modern Woman,' *Chatelaine*, Aug. 1952.

66 'A Minister's Frank Words,' *Chatelaine*, May 1954.

67 Interview with Francis M, 21 June 1991.

68 *Examiner*, 6 and 15 March 1950.

69 On mother blaming, see Breines, 'The 1950s: Gender and Some Social Science,' and Caplan, *Don't Blame Mother*.

70 Interview with Suzanne I, July 1991.

71 Sangster 'Doing Two Jobs.'

72 'Will Married Women Go to War Again?' *Saturday Night*, 30 Jan. 1951.

73 Interview with Lita Rose Betcherman, Sept. 1993.

74 Interview with Phyllis P, July 1991.

75 The founding president stated in the 1960s that claims of sex discrimination in the university were wrong, 'behind the times' (*Examiner*, 14 Jan. 1966). Yet the university historian admits that there was an 'unwritten policy against the appointment of spouses' (the sentence *should* read 'female spouses'). See Cole, *Trent*.

76 Interview with Doreen C, 24 July 1991.

77 Interview with Ethel M, 22 Aug. 1989.

78 Interview with Corinne L, July 1991.

79 NAC, RG 27, WB, vol. 1904, 38-11-3-4, Maternity Protection for Women Workers, 1967. The doctors consulted offered varying opinions. Some admitted that women could return to work six weeks after the birth, especially since breast feeding was less prevalent; others urged women to remain home.

80 Interview with Eleanor T, Jan. 1990.

81 Ibid.

82 Report of a Board of Arbitration, 'In the matter of a dispute between local 293, United Packinghouse, Food and Allied workers and the Quaker Oats Company of Canada,' 22 June 1960. Mary Eady was the head of the CLC's Women's Bureau. My thanks to Bill Hickey for giving me a copy of this arbitration from his files.

83 Interview with Beatrice G, 25 June 1991.

84 Canada, Department of Labour, *Survey of Married Women Working for Pay*.

85 Interview with Shirley M, 8 Aug. 1991, and with Dianna M, 26 June 1991. These comments indicate the extent to which women themselves internalized and wrestled with elements of 'maternal' ideology.

86 Interview with Doris B, 12 Dec. 1990.

87 Interview with Vera B, 11 July 1991, and with Dianna M, 26 June 1991.

88 Canada, Department of Labour, *Survey of Married Women Working for Pay*, 60.

89 Interview with Shirley M, 8 Aug. 1991.

90 Interview with Beatrice G, 25 June 1991.

91 Pierson, *They're Still Women After All*, and S. Prentice, 'Workers, Mothers, Reds.'

92 AO, Dept. of Public Welfare, RG 29, box 21, file 878 (717-12-6-2), draft of memo from Minister of Public Welfare to Minister of Education, 27 June 1949.

93 There were some nursery school programs, but these were part-time and not geared towards mothers with full-time jobs.

94 *Examiner*, 20 July 1966.

95 Interview with CAS official, in Muller, 'Daycare in Peterborough.'

96 Interview with Dianna M, 26 June 1991.

97 Interview with Joan J, 25 Aug. 1990.

98 Interview with Vera B, 11 July 1991.

99 Interview with Heather M, 19 July 1991.

100 Interview with Francis M, 21 June 1991.

101 Interview with Shirley M, 8 Aug. 1991 and with Francis M, 21 June 1991.

102 Interview with Beatrice G, 25 June 1991.

103 Heitlinger, *Women's Equality, Demography and Public Policies*, 222.

104 Interview with Doreen C, 24 July 1991.

105 Interview with Beatrice G, 25 June 1991.

106 Kessler-Harris, *Out to Work*.

107 Interview with Eleanor T, Jan. 1990.

108 Coontz, *The Social Origins of Private Life*, 304.

CONCLUSION: From Working Daughter to Working Mother

1 Interview with Berna D, 25 June 1991.

2 O'Brien, 'Hegemony and Superstructure,' 97.

3 This emphasis is drawn from Eagleton, *Ideology*, 7.

4 Gerson and Peiss, 'Boundaries, Negotiation, Consciousness,' 318.

5 Parr, *The Gender of Breadwinners*.

Bibliography

ARCHIVAL SOURCES

ARCHIVES OF ONTARIO
Department of Labour Records, RG 7
Department of Public Welfare, RG 29
Mercer Reformatory Records, RG 23

CAMBRIDGE CITY ARCHIVES
Dominion Woollens Records

CHILDREN'S AID SOCIETY OF PETERBOROUGH
Board minutes
Clipping Scrapbooks

CITY OF PETERBOROUGH
Council Minutes
Relief Committee Minutes

COUNTY OF PETERBOROUGH, LANG ARCHIVES
Mothers' Allowance Board Records

NATIONAL ARCHIVES OF CANADA
Canadian Food and Allied Workers, MG 28-I
Canadian Labour Congress Papers, MG 28-I-103
Department of Labour Papers, RG 27
IUE Collection, 28-I-264
J.L. Cohen Papers, MG-30 A-94
Royal Commission on Price Spreads Records, RG 33-18/111

Royal Commission on Textiles Records, RG 33-20
United Electrical, Radio and Machine Workers of America, National Records,
  MG 28-I- 190

PETERBOROUGH CENTENNIAL MUSEUM AND ARCHIVES
Clipping File
Oral History Transcripts
Quaker Oats Collection

PETERBOROUGH COUNTY BOARD OF EDUCATION
School Board Minutes

TRENT UNIVERSITY ARCHIVES
Joseph Wearing Papers
Peterborough YWCA Papers

UNITED ELECTRICAL, RADIO AND MACHINE WORKERS OF AMERICA, LOCAL 524
Records

UNIVERSITY OF TORONTO, RARE BOOKS ROOM
Woodsworth Memorial Collection
Tooms Files

NEWSPAPERS AND MAGAZINES

Canadian Business
Canadian Textile Journal
Chatelaine
Financial Post
GE Works News
Industrial Canada
Labour Gazette
Peterborough *Examiner*
Tic Talk
UE News
Voice of the Worker

GOVERNMENT DOCUMENTS

Canada. Department of Labour. *Labour Organization in Canada.* Ottawa
  1920–40

- Department of Labour. *Survey of Married Women Working for Pay in Eight Canadian Cities*. Ottawa 1958
- Department of Labour. *Women at Work*. Ottawa 1964
- Department of Labour, Women's Bureau. *Occupational Histories of Married Women Working for Pay in Eight Canadian Cities*. Ottawa 1958
- Dominion Bureau of Statistics. *Census of Canada*. Ottawa 1911–61
- *Report of the Royal Commission on the Textile Industry*. Ottawa 1937
Ontario. Sessional Papers. *Report of the Department of Education*. Toronto 1921–51

OTHER SOURCES

Abella, Irving. *Nationalism, Communism and Canadian Labour*. Toronto 1973
Adilman, Melvin. 'Baseball, Business and the Workplace: Gelber's Thesis Re-examined.' *Journal of Social History* 23, no. 2 (Winter 1989)
Alcoff, Linda. 'Cultural Feminism versus Post-structuralism.' *Signs* 13 (3) (1988)
Alexander, Sally. 'Women, Class and Sexual Difference in the 1830s and 1840s: Some Reflections on the Writing of Feminist History.' *History Workshop Journal* 17 (Spring 1984)
Alexander, Sally, and Barbara Taylor. 'In Defence of Patriarchy.' In Raphael Samuel, ed., *People's History and Socialist Theory*. London 1981
Armstrong, Pat, and Hugh Armstrong. 'Beyond Sexless Class and Classless Sex: Towards Feminist Marxism.' *Studies in Political Economy* (Winter 1983)
- *The Double Ghetto: Canadian Women and Their Segregated Work*. Toronto 1986
- *Theorizing Women's Work*. Toronto 1990
Arnup, Katharine. 'Educating Mothers: Government Advice to Women in the Inter-war Years.' In Arnup, A. Lévesque, and R. Pierson, eds., *Delivering Motherhood: Maternal Ideologies and Practices in the 19th and 20th Centuries*. London 1990
Bailey, Peter. 'Will the Real Bill Banks Please Stand Up? Towards a Role Analysis of Mid-Victorian Working-Class Respectability.' *Journal of Social History*, Spring 1979
Barman, Jean. 'Knowledge Is Essential for Universal Progress but Fatal to Class Privilege: Working People and the Schools in Vancouver in the 1920s.' *Labour/Le Travail* 22 (1988)
Baron, Ava. 'Gender and Labor History: Learning from the Past, Looking to the Future.' In Baron, ed., *Work Engendered: Toward a New History of American Labor*. Ithaca 1991

- ed. *Work Engendered: Toward a New History of American Labor.* Ithaca 1991
Barrett, Michele, et al. *Ideology and Cultural Production.* London 1979
- *Women's Oppression Today: Problems in Marxist Feminist Analysis.* London 1980
- 'The Concept of Difference.' *Feminist Review* 20 (1987)
- *The Politics of Truth: From Marx to Foucault.* Stanford 1991
- 'Words and Things: Materialism and Method in Contemporary Feminist Method.' In Barrett and Anne Phillips, eds., *Destabilizing Theory: Contemporary Feminist Debates.* Stanford 1992
Barrett, Michele, and Mary McIntosh. 'The Family Wage: Some Problems for Socialists and Feminists.' *Capital and Class* 9, no. 12 (summer 1980)
Beechey, Veronica. *Unequal Work.* London 1987
Bennett, Judith. 'Feminism and History.' *Gender and History* 1, no. 3 (Autumn 1989)
Benson, Susan Porter. *Counter Cultures: Saleswomen, Managers and Customers in American Department Stores, 1890–1940.* Urbana 1988
Benston, Margaret. 'The Political Economy of Women's Liberation.' *Monthly Review,* September 1969
Bertaux-Wiame, Isabel. 'The Life History Approach to Internal Migration: How Men and Women Came to Paris between the Wars.' In Paul Thompson, ed., *Our Common History: The Transformation of Europe.* Atlantic Highlands, NJ, 1982
Betke, Carl. 'The Social Significance of Sport in the City.' In A.R. McCormack and I. Macpherson, eds., *Cities in the West.* Ottawa 1975
Bird, Pat. 'Hamilton Working Women in the Period of the Great Depression.' *Atlantis* 8, no. 2 (Spring 1983)
Blewett, Mary. *Men, Women and Work: Class, Gender and Protest in the New England Shoe Industry, 1790–1910.* Urbana 1988
Bliss, Michael. 'Privatizing the Mind: The Sundering of Canadian History, the Sundering of Canada.' *Journal of Canadian Studies* 26, no. 4 (Winter 1991–92)
Bocock, Robert. *Hegemony.* London 1986
Bodnar, John. 'Power and Memory in Oral History: Workers and Managers at Studebaker.' *Journal of American History* 75, no. 4 (1989)
Boggs, Carl. *The Two Revolutions: Gramsci and the Dilemmas of Western Marxism.* Boston 1984
Bradbury, Bettina. 'Women's History and Working-Class History.' *Labour/Le Travail* 19 (Spring 1987)
- 'Surviving as a Widow in 19th Century Montreal.' *Urban History Review,* Feb. 1989

- 'Gender at Work at Home: Family Decisions, the Labour Market and Girls' Contributions to the Family Economy.' In G. Kealey and G. Patmore, eds., *Canadian and Australian Labour History: Towards a Comparative Perspective*. St John's 1990
- *Working Families: Age, Gender and Daily Survival in Industrializing Montreal.* Toronto 1993

Bradley, Harriet. *Women's Work, Men's Work: A Sociological History of the Sexual Division of Labour in Employment.* Minneapolis 1989

Brand, Dionne. *No Burden to Carry: Oral Narratives of Black Working Women in Ontario, 1920s to 1950s.* Toronto 1991

Brandes, Stuart. *American Welfare Capitalism, 1880–1940.* Chicago 1976

Brandt, Gail C. '"Weaving It Together": Life Cycle and the Industrial Experience of Female Cotton Workers in Quebec, 1910–50.' *Labour/Le Travail* 7 (1981)

Braverman, Harry. *Labor and Monopoly Capital: The Degradation of Work in the Twentieth Century.* New York 1974

Breines, Wini. 'The 1950s: Gender and Some Social Science.' *Sociological Inquiry* 56, no. 1 (1986)

Brenner, J., and M. Ramas. 'Rethinking Women's Oppression.' *New Left Review,* 144 (March/April 1984)

Brody, David. *Workers in Industrial America: Essays on the Twentieth-Century Struggle.* New York 1980

Bruner, J. 'Life as Narrative.' *Social Research* 54 (1987)

Budner, Stanley. *Pullman: An Experiment in Industrial Order and Community Planning.* New York 1979

Buhle, Mari Jo. 'Gender and Labor History.' In Alice Kessler-Harris and J.C. Moody, eds., *Perspectives in Labor History.* De Kalb: Northern Illinois University Press, 1989

Bullen, John. 'Hidden Workers: Child Labour and the Family Economy in Late Nineteenth Century Urban Ontario,' *Labour/Le Travail* 18 (Fall 1986)
- 'J.J. Kelso and the 'New Child-savers': The Genesis of the Children's Aid Movement in Ontario.' In R. Smandych et al., eds., *Dimensions of Childhood: Essays on the History of Children and Youth in Canada.* Winnipeg 1991

Burawoy, Michael. *Manufacturing Consent: Changes in the Labor Process under Monopoly Capitalism.* Chicago 1979

Butler, Judith. *Gender Trouble: Feminism and the Subversion of Identity.* New York 1990

Cameron, Ardis. 'Bread and Roses Revisited: Women's Culture and Working-Class Activism in the Lawrence Strike of 1912.' In Ruth Milkman, ed., *Women, Work and Protest.* Boston 1985

Canning, Kathleen. 'Feminist History and the Linguistic Turn: Historicizing Discourse and Experience.' *Signs* 19, no. 2 (Summer 1994)

Caplan, Paula. *Don't Blame Mother: Mending the Mother-Daughter Relationship.* New York 1989

Carlen, Pat. *Women, Crime and Poverty.* Philadelphia: 1980

Cassidy, Harry. *Unemployment and Relief in Ontario, 1929–32.* Toronto 1932

Cavendish, Ruth. *On the Line.* London 1982

Chodorow, Nancy. *The Reproduction of Mothering: Psychoanalysis and the Sociology of Gender.* Berkeley 1978

Chunn, Dorothy. *From Punishment to Doing Good: Family Courts and Socialized Justice in Ontario, 1880–1940.* Toronto 1992

Cobble, Dorothy Sue. 'Re-thinking the Doldrum Years: Working Class Feminism in the 1940s.' Paper presented at the 8th Berkshire Conference, Rutgers, 1990

Cockburn, Cynthia. *Brothers: Male Dominance and Technological Change.* London 1983

Cohen, Marjorie. *Women's Work, Markets and Economic Development in Nineteenth-Century Ontario.* Toronto 1988

– 'Women at Work in Canada during the Depression.' Paper presented at the Blue Collar Conference, Windsor, May 1979

Coldwell, Douglas. 'The United Electrical, Radio and Machine Workers of America, District 5, Canada, 1937–56.' MA thesis, University of Western Ontario, 1976

Cole, A.O.C. *Trent: the Making of a University.* Peterborough 1992

Collins, Mark. 'Women and Domestic Service in Peterborough, 1880–1930.' Honours paper, Trent University, 1985

Collinson, David. *Mananging the Shopfloor: Subjective Masculinity and Workplace Culture.* New York 1992

Collinson, David, and Margaret Collinson. 'Sexuality in the Workplace: The Domination of Men's Sexuality.' In Jeff Hearn et al., eds. *The Sexuality of Organization.* London 1989

Collinson, David, and David Knights. '"Men Only": Theories and Practices of Job Segregation in Insurance.' In D. Knights and H. Willmott, eds., *Gender and the Labour Process.* Aldershot, England 1986

Comacchio, Cynthia. Review of *Working Families* in *Labour/Le Travail* 33 (Spring 1994)

Coontz, Stephanie. *The Social Origins of Private Life.* New York 1988

Cooper, Patricia. *Once a Cigar Maker: Men, Women and Work Culture in American Cigar Factories, 1900–1919.* Urbana 1992

Coulter, Rebecca. 'Young Women and Unemployment in the 1930s: The Home Service Solution.' *Canadian Women's Studies* 7, no. 4 (Winter 1986)
– 'Teen-Agers in Edmonton, 1921–31: Experiences of Gender and Class.' PhD thesis, University of Alberta, 1987
Coward, Rosalind. *Female Desire.* New York 1985
Crapanzano, Vincent. 'Life Histories.' *American Anthropologist* 86, no. 4 (1984)
Creese, Gillian. 'The Politics of Dependence: Women, Work and Unemployment in the Vancouver Labour Movement before World War II.' In G. Creese and V. Strong-Boag, eds., *British Columbia Reconsidered: Essays on Women.* Vancouver 1992
Cruikshank, Julie. 'Myth and Tradition as Narrative Framework.' *International Journal of Oral History* 9, no. 3 (1988)
Cumbler, John. *Working-Class Community in Industrial America: Work, Leisure and Struggle in Two Industrial Cities, 1880–1930.* Westport 1979
Curtis, Bruce. *Building the Educational State, Canada West, 1836–71.* London 1988
Danylewycz, Marta. 'Domestic Science Education in Ontario, 1900–1940.' In Ruby Heap and Alison Prentice, eds., *Gender and Education in Ontario.* Toronto 1991
Davies, Margery. *Woman's Place Is at the Typewriter: Office Work and Office Workers, 1870–1930.* Philadelphia 1982
de la Coeur, Lykke, Cecilia Morgan, and Mariana Valverde. 'Gender Regulation and State Formation in Nineteenth-Century Canada.' In A. Greer and I. Radforth, eds., *Colonial Leviathan: State Formation in Mid-Nineteenth-Century Canada.* Toronto 1992
Dellheim, Charles. 'The Creation of a Company Culture: Cadburys, 1861–1931.' *American Historical Review* 92, no. 1 (1987)
Delphy, C. *Close to Home: A Materialist Analysis of Women's Oppression.* London 1984
Denton, Frank, and Sylvia Ostry. *Historical Estimates of the Canadian Labour Force.* Ottawa 1967
Diamond, Irene, and Lee Quinby. *Feminism and Foucault: Reflections on Resistance.* Boston 1988
Dodd, Dianne. 'Women in Advertising: The Role of Canadian Women in the Promotion of Domestic Electrical Technology in the Interwar Period.' In M. Gosztonyi Ainley, ed., *Despite the Odds: Essays on Canadian Women and Science.* Montreal 1990
DuBois, Ellen, et al. 'Politics and Culture in Women's History: A Symposium.' *Feminist Studies,* 6, no. 1 (Spring 1980)

Duffy, Ann, and Norene Pupo. *Part-Time Paradox: Connecting Gender, Work and Family.* Toronto 1992

Duggan, Lisa. 'The Social Enforcement of Heterosexuality and Lesbian Resistance in the 1920s.' In Amy Swerdlo and Hanna Lessinger, eds., *Class, Race and Sex: The Dynamics of Control.* Boston 1983

Dyreson, Mark. 'The Emergence of Consumer Culture and the Transformation of Physical Culture: American Sport in the 1920s.' *Journal of Sport History* 16, no. 3 (Winter 1989)

Eagleton, Terry. *Ideology: An Introduction.* London 1991

Edwards, R. *Contested Terrain: The Transformation of the Workplace in the Twentieth Century.* New York 1979

Eisenstein, Z., ed. *Capitalist Patriarchy and the Case for Socialist Feminism.* New York 1979

Feldberg, Roslyn, and Evelyn Glenn. 'Male and Female: Job versus Gender Models in the Sociology of Work.' *Social Problems* 26, no. 5 (June 1979)

Felski, Rita. 'Feminism, Post-modernism and the Critique of Modernity.' *Cultural Critique* 13 (Fall 1989)

Finch, Janet. 'It's Great to Have Someone to Talk to: The Ethics and Politics of Interviewing Women.' In C. Bell and H. Roberts, eds., *Social Researching: Politics, Problems, Practice.* London 1984

Fingard, Judith. *The Dark Side of Life in Victorian Halifax.* Potters Lake 1989

Flax, Jane. 'Postmodernism and Gender Relations in Feminist Theory.' *Signs* 12, no. 4 (Summer 1987)

Fones-Wolf, Elizabeth. 'Industrial Recreation, the Second World War and the Revival of Welfare Capitalism, 1934–60.' *Business History Review* 69, no. 2 (Summer 1986)

Forbes, Ernie. 'Rum in the Maritime Economy.' In his *Challenging the Regional Stereotypes.* Fredericton 1989

Forestall, Nancy. 'All That Glitters Is Not Gold: The Gendered Dimensions of Work, Family and Community Life in the Northern Ontario Goldmining Town of Timmins, 1909–1950.' PhD thesis, University of Toronto, 1993

Foucault, M. 'Truth and Power.' In Colin Gordon, ed., *Power/Knowledge: Selected Interviews and Other Writings, 1972–1977.* New York 1980

Fox, Bonnie, ed. *Hidden in the Household: Women's Domestic Labour under Capitalism.* Toronto 1980

– 'Conceptualizing Patriarchy.' *Canadian Review of Sociology and Anthropology* 25, no. 2 (1988)

Fox, Bonnie, and John Fox. 'Occupational Gender Segregation of the Canadian Labour Force, 1931–1981.' *Canadian Review of Sociology and Anthropology* 24, no. 2, (1987)

Fox-Genovese, Elizabeth. 'Socialist-Feminist American Women's History.' *Journal of Women's History* 1, no. 3 (1990)

Frager, Ruth. *Sweatshop Strife: Class, Ethnicity and Gender in the Jewish Labour Movement of Toronto, 1900–39.* Toronto 1992

Frakenberg, Ruth. *White Women, Race Matters: The Social Construction of Whiteness.* Minneapolis 1993

Fraser, Nancy, and Linda Gordon. 'A Genealogy of Dependency: Tracing a Keyword of the U.S. Welfare State.' *Signs* 19, no. 2 (1994)

French, Brandon. *On the Verge of Revolt: Women in American Films of the 1950s.* New York 1978

Frisch, Michael. 'The Memory of History.' *Radical History Review* 25

Gabin, Nancy. *Feminism and the Labor Movement: Women and the United Auto Workers, 1935–75.* Ithaca 1990

Gaffield C., and D. Levine. 'Dependency and Adolescence on the Canadian Frontier.' *History of Education Quarterly*, Spring 1978

Gaskell, Jane. 'Course Enrolment in High School: The Perspective of Working-Class Females.' *Sociology of Education* 58 (January 1985)

Gee, Ellen. 'Female Marriage Patterns in Canada: Changes and Differentials.' *Journal of Comparative Family Studies* 11, no. 4 (1980)

– 'The Life Course of Canadian Women: A Historical and Demographic Analysis.' *Social Indicators Research*, August 1986

Geiger, Susan. 'What's So Feminist about Women's Oral History?' *Journal of Women's History* 2, no. 1 (1990)

Gelber, Stephen. 'Working at Playing: The Culture of the Workplace and the Rise of Baseball.' *Journal of Social History*, Summer 1983

Gerson, Judith, and Kathy Peiss. 'Boundaries, Negotiation, Consciousness: Reconceptualizing Gender Relations.' *Social Problems*, 32 (1984)

Gerson, Kathleen. *Hard Choices: How Women Decide about Work, Career, and Motherhood.* Berkeley 1985

Gillis, John. *Youth and History: Tradition and Change in European Age Relations, 1770–Present.* New York 1974

Gluck, Sherna Berger, and Daphne Patai, eds. *Women's Words: The Feminist Practice of Oral History.* New York 1991

Glucksmann, Miriam. *Women Assemble: Women Workers and the New Industries in Inter-war Britain.* London 1990

Gordon, Linda. 'Response to Joan Scott.' *Signs* 15, no. 4 (1990)

– 'On Difference.' *Genders* 10 (Spring 1991)

Gramsci, Antonio. *Selections from Prison Notebooks.* New York 1970

Gray, R. *The Labour Aristocracy in Victorian Edinburgh.* Oxford 1976

Gray, Stan. 'Sharing the Shop Floor.' *Canadian Dimension*, June 1984

Grele, Ronald. *Envelopes of Sound.* Chicago 1975

Guard, Julie. 'The "Woman Question" in Canadian Unionism: Women in the UE, 1930s to 1960s.' PhD thesis University of Toronto, 1994

Hakim, Catherine. 'Census Reports as Documentary Evidence: The Census Commentaries, 1801–1951.' *Sociological Review* 28, no. 3 (1980)

Hall, Jacqueline Dowd. *Like a Family: The Making of a Southern Cotton Mill World.* Chapel Hill 1987

– 'Disorderly Women.' In Ellen Du Bois, ed., *Unequal Sisters: A Multicultural Reader in U.S. Women's History.* New York 1990

Hallett, Mary. 'Nellie McClung and the Fight for the Ordination of Women in the United Church of Canada.' *Atlantis* 4, no. 2 (Spring 1979)

Hareven, Tamara. *Family Time and Industrial Time: The Relationship between Family and Work in a New England Industrial Community.* New York 1982

Harrigan, Patrick. 'The Schooling of Boys and Girls in Canada.' *Journal of Social History* 23, no. 4 (Summer 1990)

Harstock, N. 'Foucault on Power: A Theory for Women?' In Linda Nicholson, ed., *Feminism and Postmodernism.* New York 1990

Hartmann, Heidi. 'Capitalism, Patriarchy and Job Segregation.' In Z. Einsenstein, ed., *Capitalist Patriarchy and the Case for Socialist Feminism.* New York 1979

– 'The Unhappy Marriage of Marxism and Feminism.' In *Women and Revolution.* Boston 1981

Hartmann, Susan. *The Home Front and Beyond: Women in the 1940s.* Boston 1982

Haskell, Molly. *From Reverence to Rape: The Treatment of Women in the Movies.* New York 1974

Heap, Ruby. 'Schooling Women for Home or Work? Vocational Education for Women in Ontario in the Early Twentieth Century: The Case of the Toronto Technical High School, 1892–1920.' In Heap and Alison Prentice, eds., *Gender and Education in Ontario.* Toronto 1991

Heap, Ruby, and Alison Prentice, eds. *Gender and Education in Ontario.* Toronto 1991

Heitlinger, Alena. *Women's Equality, Demography and Public Policies: A Comparative Perspective.* London 1993

Hembold, Lois. 'Beyond the Family Economy: Black and White Working Class Women during the Great Depression.' *Feminist Studies* 13, no. 3 (Fall 1987)

Hennessey, Rosemary. *Materialist Feminism and the Politics of Discourse.* New York 1993

Heron, Craig. *Working in Steel: The Early Years in Canada, 1883–1935.*
Toronto 1988

Heron, Craig, and George DeZwaan. 'Industrial Unionism in Eastern Ontario:
Gananoque, 1918–21,' *Ontario History,* September 1985

Heron, Craig, and Robert Storey, eds. *On the Job: Confronting the Labour
Process in Canada.* Montreal 1986

Hewitt, Marsha. 'Illusions of Freedom: The Regressive Implications of Postmodernism.' In Ralph Miliband and L. Panitch, eds., *Socialist Register.* 1993

Hobbs, Margaret. *Working Trends: Women in Peterborough.* Peterborough
1982

– 'Gender in Crisis: The Anti-Feminist Assault on the Wage-Earning Woman
in Canada in the 1930s.' Paper presented at the Berkshire Conference on
Women, 1990

– 'Gendering Work and Welfare: Women's Relationship to Employment,
Unemployment and Social Policy during the Great Depression.' PhD thesis,
University of Toronto, 1994

Holub, Renate. *Antonio Gramsci: Beyond Marxism and Postmodernism.*
London 1992

Houston, Susan, and Alison Prentice. *Schooling and Scholars in Nineteenth-
Century Ontario.* Toronto 1988

Hudson, Barbara. 'Femininity and Adolescence.' In Angela McRobbie and
Mica Nava, eds., *Gender and Generation.* London 1984

Humphries, Jane. 'Class Struggle and the Persistence of the Working-Class
Family.' *Cambridge Journal of Economics* 1, no. 3 (1977)

Humphries, Stephen. *Hooligans or Rebels: An Oral History of Working-Class
Childhood and Youth, 1889–1939.* Oxford 1981

Hunt, Felicity, ed. *Lessons for Life: The Schooling of Girls and Women, 1850–
1950.* Oxford 1987

Hunter, Peter. *Which Side Are You On Boys? Canadian Life on the Left.*
Toronto 1988

Iacovetta, Franca. 'From Contadina to Worker: Southern Italian Immigrant
Working Women in Toronto, 1947–62.' In Jean Burnet, ed., *Looking into My
Sisters Eyes: An Exploration in Women's History.* Toronto 1986

– *Such Hard-working People: Italian Immigrants in Postwar Toronto.*
Montreal 1992

Iacovetta, Franca, and Mariana Valverde, eds. *Gender Conflicts: New Essays in
Women's History.* Toronto 1992

Jackson, Nancy, and Jane Gaskell. 'White Collar Vocationalism: The Rise of
Commercial Education in Ontario and British Columbia, 1870–1920.' In

Ruby Heap and Alison Prentice, eds., *Gender and Education in Ontario.* Toronto 1991

Jaggar, Alison. *Feminist Politics and Human Nature.* Totowa, NJ, 1983

Janiewski, Dolores. *Sisterhood Denied: Race, Gender and Class in a New South Community.* Philadelphia 1985

Jehlen, Myra. 'Patrolling the Borders.' *Radical History Review* 43 (Winter 1989)

Jones, Elwood, and Bruce Dyer. *Peterborough: The Electric City.* Burlington 1987

Jones, Jaqueline. *Labour of Love, Labour of Sorrow: Black Women, Work and the Family From Slavery to the Present.* New York 1985

Joyce, Patrick. *Work, Society and Politics.* London 1980

Kannenberg, Lisa Ann. 'From World War to Cold War: Women Electrical Workers and Their Union, 1940–55.' MA thesis, University of North Carolina, 1990

Kealey, Greg. 'Labour and Working-Class History in Canada: Prospects for the 1980s.' *Labour/Le Travail* 7 (1981)

Kealey, L., et al. 'Teaching Canadian History in the 1990s: Whose National History Are We Lamenting?' *Journal of Canadian Studies* 27, no. 2 (Summer 1992)

Keifer, Nancy. 'The Recruitment of Women into the Workforce in Peterborough during World War II.' Honours paper, Trent University, 1982

Kessler-Harris, Alice. *Out to Work: A History of Wage-Earning Women in the United States.* New York 1982

– 'Gender Ideology in Historical Reconstruction: A Case Study from the 1930s.' *Gender and History* 1, no. 1 (Spring 1989)

– 'A New Agenda for American Labor History: A Gendered Analysis of the Question of Class.' In A. Kessler-Harris and J.C. Moody, eds., *Perspectives in Labor History: The Problems of Synthesis.* De Kalb 1989

– *A Woman's Wage: Historical Meanings and Social Consequences.* Lexington 1990

Kessler-Harris, Alice, and J.C. Moody, eds. *Perspectives in Labor History: The Problems of Synthesis.* De Kalb 1989

Kett, Joseph. *Rites of Passage: Adolescence in America, 1880 to the Present.* New York 1977

Klacynska, Barbara. 'Why Women Work: A Comparison of Various Groups in Philadelphia, 1910–40.' *Labor History* (Winter 1976)

Klein, Alice, and Wayne Roberts. 'Beseiged Innocence: The "Problem" and Problems of Working Women – Toronto, 1896–1914.' In Janice Acton et al., eds., *Women at Work: Ontario, 1880–1930.* Toronto 1974

Krashinsky, Michael. *Day Care and Public Policy in Ontario.* Toronto 1977

Laclau, Ernesto, and Chantal Mouffe. *Hegemony and Socialist Strategy: Towards a Radical Democratic Politics.* London 1985

Lamphere, Louise. 'Bringing the Family to Work: Women's Culture on the Shop Floor.' *Feminist Studies* 11, no. 3 (1985)

– *From Working Daughters to Working Mothers: Immigrant Women in a New England Industrial Community.* Ithaca 1987

Lee, Alissa. 'Maternal Reform: The Peterborough YWCA and Its Industrial Work.' Honours paper, Trent University, 1990

Lenskyj, Helen. *Out of Bounds: Women Sport and Sexuality.* Toronto 1986

– 'Femininity First: Sport and Physical Education for Ontario Girls, 1890–1930.' In Morris Mott, ed., *Sports in Canada.* Toronto 1989

Lewis, Jane. 'A Debate on Sex and Class.' *New Left Review* 149 (January/February 1985).

Little, Margaret Hillyard. 'The Regulation of Ontario Single Mothers during the "Dirty" Thirties.' Paper presented at the Canadian Historical Association, Charlottetown, 1992

Livingstone, D.W., and Meg Luxton. 'Gender Consciousness at Work: Modification of the Male Breadwinner Norm among Steelworkers and Their Spouses.' *Canadian Review of Sociology and Anthropology* 26, no. 2 (1989)

Loth, David. *Swope of GE.* New York 1958

Lowe, Graham. 'Mechanization, Feminization and Managerial Control in the Early Twentieth-Century Canadian Office.' In Craig Heron and Robert Storey, eds., *On the Job: Confronting the Labour Process in Canada.* Montreal 1986

– *Women in the Administrative Revolution.* Toronto 1987

Lown, Judy. 'Not So Much a Factory, More a Form of Patriarchy: Gender and Class during Industrialization.' In E. Gamarnikow, ed., *Gender, Class and Work.* London 1985

– *Women and Industrialization: Gender at Work in Nineteenth-Century England.* London 1990

Lynd, R.S., and H.M. Lynd. *Middletown: A Study in American Culture.* New York 1959

MacDonald, Madeleine. 'Socio-Cultural Reproduction and Women's Education.' In Rosemary Deem, ed., *Schooling for Women's Work.* London 1980

Macdonnel, Diane. *Theories of Discourse: An Introduction.* Oxford 1986

Machinery and Allied Products Institute. *The GE Approach to Industrial Relations.* New York 1962

Mackie, Marlene. *Constructing Women and Men: Gender Socialization.* Toronto 1987

McLaren, Arlene Tigar. *Ambitions and Realizations: Women in Adult Education.* London 1985

McLean, Lorna. 'Single Again: Widows' Work in the Urban Family Economy, Ottawa, 1871.' *Ontario History* 83, no. 2 (June 1991)

McRobbie, Angela. 'Working-Class Girls and the Culture of Femininity.' In Women's Studies Group, *Women Take Issue.* Birmingham 1978

Marks, Lynn. '"Ladies, Loaders, Knights and Lasses": The Social Dimensions of Religion and Leisure in 19th Century Small Town Ontario.' PhD thesis, York University, 1992

Maroney, Heather Jon. 'Feminism at Work.' *New Left Review* 141 (September/October 1983)

Matthews, Jill. 'Deconstructing the Masculine Universe: The Case of Women's Work.' In Women and Labour Publications, *All Her Labours: Working It Out.* Sydney 1984

May, Elaine Tyler. *Great Expectations: Marriage and Divorce in Post-Victorian America.* Chicago 1980

– *Homeward Bound: American Families in the Cold War Era.* New York 1988

May, Martha. 'Bread before Roses: American Workingmen, Labor Unions and the Family Wage.' In Ruth Milkman, ed., *Women, Work and Protest.* New York 1985

Melchers, Ronald. 'Sports in the Workplace.' In Jean Harvey and Hart Cantelon, eds., *Not Just a Game: Essays in Canadian Sport Sociology.* Ottawa 1988

Meyer, Stephen. *The Five Dollar Day: Labor Management and Social Control in the Ford Motor Company, 1908–21.* Albany 1981

Milkman, Ruth. 'Women's Work and Economic Crisis: Some Lessons of the Great Depression.' *Review of Radical Political Economics* 8 (Spring 1976)

– 'Organizing the Sexual Division of Labour: Historical Perspectives on "Women's Work" and the American Labor Movement.' *Socialist Review* 49 (January/February 1980)

– *Gender at Work: The Dynamics of Job Segregation by Sex during World War II.* Urbana 1987

Mitchell, Juliet. *Women's Estate.* London 1971

Mitchinson, Wendy. 'The YWCA and Reform in the 19th Century.' *Histoire Sociale* 12, no. 24 (November 1979)

Morton, Suzanne. 'Labour, Politics and Peterborough, 1914–23.' Honours paper, Trent University, 1985

– 'Men and Women in a Halifax Working-Class Neighbourhood in the 1920s.' PhD thesis, Dalhousie University, 1990

- 'Separate Spheres in a Separate World: African Nova Scotian Women in Late-19th Century Halifax County.' *Acadiensis* 22, no. 2 (Spring 1993)
Mott, Morris. 'One Solution to the Urban Crisis: Manly Sports and Winnipeggers, 1900–14.' *Urban History Review* 12, no. 2 (1983)
Muller, Theresa. 'Daycare in Peterborough.' Honours paper, Trent University, 1991
Nasaw, David. 'The Little Mothers.' In Nasaw, *Children of the City: At Work and at Play*. New York 1985
National Council of Welfare. *Women and Poverty*. Ottawa 1979
Naylor, James. *The New Democracy: Challenging the Social Order in Industrial Ontario, 1914–25*. Toronto 1991
Nelson, Daniel. *Managers and Workers: Origins of the New Factory System in the United States, 1880–1920*. Madison 1975
Northrup, H. 'The Case for Boulwarism.' *Harvard Business Review* 41 (September/October 1963)
Oakley, Anne. 'Interviewing Women: A Contradiction in Terms.' In Helen Roberts, ed., *Doing Feminist Research*. London 1981
O'Brien, Mary. 'Hegemony and Superstructure: A Feminist Critique of Neo-Marxism.' In Jill McCalla Vickers, ed., *Taking Sex into Account*. Ottawa 1984
Odem, Mary. 'Single Mothers, Delinquent Daughters and the Juvenile Court in Early 20th Century Los Angeles.' *Journal of Social History* 25, no. 1 (1991)
Palmer, Bryan. *The Making of E.P. Thompson: Marxism, Humanism and History*. Toronto 1980
- *Descent into Discourse: The Reification of Language and the Writing of Social History*. Philadelphia 1990
- *Working-Class Experience*. Toronto 1992
Palmer, Nancy. 'Sexuality and War Plants in the 1940s: Working Women "Invade" Male Factories.' Paper presented at the 9th Berkshire Conference on Women, Vassar, 1993
Parr, Joy. *Labouring Children: British Immigrant Apprentices to Canada, 1869–1924*. London 1980
- *The Gender of Breadwinners*. Toronto 1991
- ed., *Childhood and Family in Canadian History*. Toronto 1982
Passerini, Luisa. 'Italian Working-Class Culture between the Wars: Consensus to Fascism and Work Ideology.' *International Journal of Oral History* 1, no. 1 (February 1980)
- 'Work, Ideology and Working-Class Attitudes to Fascism.' In Paul Thompson, ed., *Our Common History: The Transformation of Europe*. New Jersey 1982

Patai, Daphne. 'U.S. Academics and Third World Women: Is Ethical Research Possible?' In Sherna Gluck and Patai, eds., *Women's Words*. New York 1991

Pederson, Diana. 'Keeping Our Girls Good: The YWCA of Canada, 1870–1920.' MA thesis, Carleton University, 1981

– 'Building Today for the Womanhood of Tomorrow: Businessmen, Boosters and the YWCA, 1890–1930.' *Urban History Review* 15, no. 3 (1987)

Peiss, Kathy. *Cheap Amusements: Working Women and Leisure in Turn-of-the-Century New York*. Philadelphia 1986

Phillips, Anne, and Barbara Taylor. 'Sex and Skill: Notes towards a Feminist Economics.' In *Waged Work: A Reader*. London 1986

Phillips, Margaret. 'Women in the Outboard Marine Family.' Honours paper, Trent University, 1990

Pierson, Ruth Roach. *'They're Still Women after All': The Second World War and Canadian Womanhood*. Toronto 1986

– 'Gender and the Unemployment Insurance Debates in Canada.' *Labour/Le Travail* 25 (Spring 1990)

– 'Colonization and Canadian Women's History.' *Journal of Women's History* 4, no. 2 (Fall 1992)

Pollert, Anna. *Girls, Wives, Factory Lives*. London 1981

Porter, Marilyn. 'Time, Life Course and Work in Women's Lives.' *Women's Studies International Forum* 14, nos. 1–2 (1991)

Prentice, Alison. *The School Promoters: Education and Social Class in Mid-Nineteenth-Century Upper Canada*. Toronto 1977

Prentice, Susan. Toronto's Postwar Daycare Fight. *Studies in Political Economy* 30 (Autumn 1989)

Price, Jane. 'Raised in Rockhead, Died in the Poorhouse: Female Petty Criminals in Halifax.' In Phil Girard and Jim Phillips, eds., *Essays in the History of Canadian Law*, vol. 3, *Nova Scotia*. Toronto 1990

Pringle, Rosemary. *Secretaries Talk: Sexuality, Power and Work*. London 1989

– 'Bureaucracy, Rationality, and Sexuality: The Case of Secretaries.' In Jeff Hearn et al., eds., *The Sexuality of Organization*. London 1989

Purcell, Kate. 'Female Manual Workers: Fatalism and the Reinforcement of Inequalities.' In David Robbins, ed., *Inequalities*. London 1982

Rainnie, G.F., ed. *The Woollen and Worsted Industry*. Oxford 1965

Raphael, Samuel, ed. *People's History and Socialist Theory*. London 1981

Rapp, Rayna, and Ellen Ross. 'The Twenties Backlash: Compulsory Heterosexuality: The Consumer Family and the Waning of Feminism.' In Amy Swerdlo and Hanna Lessinger, eds., *Class, Race and Sex: The Dynamics of Control*. Boston 1983

Reid, Donald. 'Industrial Paternalism: Discourse and Practice in Nineteenth-Century French Mining and Metallurgy.' *Comparative Studies in Society and History* vol. 27 (1985)

Reiger, Kareen. *The Disenchantment of the Home: Modernizing the Australian Family, 1880–1940*. Melbourne 1985

– 'Clean, Comfortable and Respectable: Working-Class Aspirations and the Australian 1920 Royal Commission on the Basic Wage.' *History Workshop*, Spring 1989

Report of a Board of Arbitration. 'In the Matter of a Dispute between Local 293, United Packinghouse, Food and Allied Workers and the Quaker Oats Company of Canada.' 22 June 1960

Riley, Denise. *Am I That Name: Feminism and the Category of 'Woman' in History*. Minneapolis 1988

Roberts, Elizabeth. *A Woman's Place: An Oral History of Working-Class Women, 1890–1940*. Oxford 1984

Robinson, Julie. 'A History of Peterborough Teachers.' Honours paper, Trent University, 1989

Roome, Patricia. 'Amelia Turner and Calgary Labour Women.' In L. Kealey and J. Sangster, eds., *Beyond the Vote: Canadian Women and Politics.* Toronto 1989

Rose, Sonya. 'Gender Antagonism and Class Conflict: Exclusionary Strategies of Male Trade Unionists in Nineteenth Century Britain.' *Social History* 13, no. 2 (May 1988)

Rosenau, Pauline. *Postmodernism and the Social Sciences, Insights, Inroads, Intrusions.* Princeton 1992

Rosenfeld, Mark. '"It Was a Hard Life": Class and Gender in the Work and Family Rhythms of a Railway Town, 1920–50.' *Canadian Historical Association Report.* 1988

– '"She Was a Hard Life": Work, Family and Community Politics and Ideology in a Railway Ward of a Central Ontario Town, 1900–60.' PhD thesis, York University, 1990

Rosenzweig, Roy. *Eight Hours for What We Will: Workers Leisure in an Industrial City, 1870–1920.* New York 1983

Ross, Ellen. 'Fierce Questions and Taunts: Married Life in Working-Class London, 1870–1914.' *Feminist Studies* 8, no. 3 (Fall 1982)

– 'Not the Sort to Sit on the Doorstep: Respectability in Pre–World War I London.' *International Labor and Working-Class History* 27 (Spring 1985)

Rothbart, Ron. 'Homes Are What Any Strike Is About: Immigrant Labor and the Family Wage.' *Journal of Social History* 23, no. 2 (Winter 1989)

Rowbotham, Sheila. *Women, Resistance and Revolution.* London 1972
– 'The Trouble with Patriarchy.' In R. Samuel, ed., *People's History and Socialist Theory.* Boston 1981
– *Dreams and Dilemmas.* London 1983
Russell, Susan. 'The Hidden Curriculum of School: Reproducing Gender and Class Hierarchies.' In M. Barrett and R. Hamilton, eds., *The Politics of Diversty.* London 1986
Rutherford, Paul. *When Television Was Young: Primetime Canada, 1952–67.* Toronto 1990
Ryan, Mary. 'The Movie Moderns of the 1920s.' In Lois Scharf and Joan Jenson, eds., *Decades of Discontent: The Women's Movement, 1920–40.* Westport, Conn., 1983
Sachs, Karen. *Caring by the Hour: Women, Work and Organizing at Duke Medical Centre.* Urbana 1988
Sangster, Joan. *Dreams of Equality: Women on the Canadian Left.* Toronto 1989
– 'The Softball Solution: Women Workers and Male Managers in a Peterborough Clock Factory.' *Labour/Le Travail* 32 (1993)
– 'Pardon Tales from Magistrate's Court: Women, Crime and the Courts in Peterborough County, 1920–60.' *Canadian Historical Review* (1993)
– 'The Dark Side of Family Life: Women, Wife Battering and the Courts in Small-town Ontario.' Paper presented at the Carleton History of the Family Conference, May 1994
– 'Telling Our Stories: Feminist Debates and the Use of Oral History.' *Women's History Review* 3, no. 1 (1994)
– 'Doing Two Jobs: The Wage-Earning Mother in Post-war Ontario, 1945–70.' In Joy Parr, ed., *A Diversity of Women* (forthcoming)
Sargent, Lydia, ed. *Women and Revolution: A Discussion of the Unhappy Marriage of Marxism and Feminism.* Boston 1981
Savage, Mike. 'Trade Unionism, Sexual Regulation and the State: Women's Employment in the "New Industries" in Interwar Britain.' *Social History* 13, no. 2 (May 1988)
Schatz, Ronald. *The Electrical Workers: A History of Labor at General Electric and Westinghouse, 1923–60.* Urbana 1983
Scott, Joan. 'Experience.' In Judith Butler and Scott, eds., *Feminists Theorize the Political.* New York 1992
Scott, Joan, and Louise Tilley. *Women, Work and Family.* New York 1978
Scranton, Phillip. 'Varieties of Paternalism: Industrial Structures and the Social Relations of Production in American Textiles.' *American Quarterly* 36 (Summer 1984)

Seccombe, Wally. 'The Housewife and Her Labour under Capitalism.' *New Left Review*, 83 (1974)

– 'Patriarchy Stabilized: The Construction of the Male Breadwinner Wage Norm in Nineteenth Century Britain.' *Social History* 11, no. 1 (January 1986)

Shaw-Cullen, Lisbeth, and Alissa Lee. *Changing Lives in Changing Times: Peterborough Women and the YWCA, 1891–1991*. Peterborough 1991

Simmons, Christina. 'Modern Sexuality and the Myth of Victorian Repression.' In K. Peiss, ed., *Passion and Power: Sexuality in History*. Philadelphia 1989

Snell, James. 'Marriage Humour and Its Social Functions, 1900–39.' *Atlantis* 11, no. 2 (Spring 1986)

Sommer, Doris. 'Not Just a Personal Story.' In Bella Brodski and Celeste Schenck, eds., *Life/Lines: Theorizing Women's Autobiography*. Ithaca 1988

Spelman, Elizabeth. *Inessential Woman: Problems of Exclusion in Feminist Thought*. Boston 1988

Stacey, Judith. 'Can There Be a Feminist Ethnography?' In Sherna Gluck and Daphne Patai, eds., *Women's Words*. New York 1991

Stanley, Liz. 'Recovering Women in History from Feminist Deconstruction.' *Women's Studies International Forum* 13, nos. 1–2 (1990)

Stansell, Christine. *City of Women: Sex and Class in New York, 1789–1890*. New York 1986

– 'Response to Joan Scott.' *International Labor and Working-Class History* 31 (Spring 1987)

Strange, Carolyn. 'The Velvet Glove: Maternalistic Reform at the Andrew Mercer Reformatory for Females.' MA thesis, University of Ottawa, 1983

– 'From Modern Babylon to a City upon the Hill: The Toronto Social Survey Commission of 1915 and the Search for Sexual Social Order in the City.' In Roger Hall, ed., *Patterns of the Past: Interpreting Ontario's History*. Toronto 1988

– 'The Perils and Pleasures of the City: Single, Wage-earning Women in Toronto, 1880–1930.' PhD thesis, Rutgers University, 1991

Strong-Boag, Veronica. 'Canada's Early Experience with Income Supplement: The Introduction of Mothers Allowances.' *Journal of Canadian Studies* 24 (1979)

– 'Girl of the New Day: Canadian Working Women in the 1920s.' *Labour/Le Travail* 4 (1979)

– 'Intruders in the Nursery: Child Care Professionals Reshape the Years One to Five.' In Joy Parr, ed., *Childhood and Family in Canadian History*. Toronto 1982

- *The New Day Recalled: Lives of Girls and Women in English Canada, 1919–39.* Toronto 1988
- '"Women with a Choice": Canada's Wage-earning Wives and the Construction of a Middle Class, 1945–60.' Paper presented at the Canadian Historical Association, Charlottetown, 1992

Sugiman, Pamela. 'Labour's Dilemma: The Meaning and Politics of Worker Resistance in a Gendered Setting. A Case Study of Southern Ontario Auto Industry and the UAW Canadian Region (1939–79).' PhD dissertation, University of Toronto, 1991

Sutherland, Neil. *Children in English-Canadian Society: Framing the Twentieth-Century Consensus.* Toronto 1976
- '"Listening to the Winds of Childhood": The Role of Memory in the History of Childhood.' *Canadian History of Education Bulletin* 5 (1988)
- 'We Always Had Things to Do: The Paid and Unpaid Work of Anglophone Children between the 1920s and the 1960s.' *Labour/Le Travail* 25 (Spring 1990)

Synge, Jane. 'The Transition from School to Work: Growing Up Working-Class in Early 20th Century Hamilton.' In K. Ishwaran, ed., *Childhood and Adolescence in Canada.* Toronto 1979

Tentler, Louise. *Wage-Earning Women: Industrial Work and Family Life in the United States, 1900–1930.* New York 1979

Thompson, Paul. *The Nature of Work: An Introduction to Debates on the Labour Process.* London 1983

Tilley, Louise. 'People's History and Social Science History.' *Social Science History* 7, no. 4 (1983)

Tilley, Louise, Nancy Folbre, and Daniel Scott Smith. 'Family Strategy: A Dialogue.' *Historical Methods* 20, no. 3 (Summer 1987)

Tinkler, Penny. '"Learning through Leisure": Feminine Ideology in Girls' Magazines, 1920–50.' In Felicity Hunt, ed., *Lessons for Life: The Schooling of Girls and Women, 1850–1950.* Oxford 1987

Toews, John. 'International History after the Linguistic Turn.' *American Historical Review* 92, no. 4 (1987)

Tomlinson, Alan. 'Good Times, Bad Times and the Politics of Leisure.' In Hart Cantelon et al., eds., *Leisure, Sport and Working Class Culture.* Toronto 1988

Tress, D. 'Comment on Flax's Postmodernism and Gender Relations in Feminist Theory.' *Signs* 14, no. 1 (1988)

Turbin, Carole. 'Reconceptualizing Family, Work, and Labor Organizing: Women in Troy, 1860–90.' *Review of Radical Political Economics* 16 (Spring 1984)
- 'Beyond Dichotomies: Interdependence in Mid-Nineteenth Century

Working Class Families in the United States.' *Gender and History* 1, no. 3 (Autumn 1989)

Turk, Jim. 'Surviving the Cold War: A Study of the United Electrical Workers in Canada.' *Canadian Oral History Association Journal* 4, no. 2 (1980)

Ursel, Jane. *Private Lives, Public Policy: 100 Years of State Intervention in the Family*. Toronto 1992

Valverde, Mariana. 'Giving the Females a Domestic Turn: The Social, Legal and Moral Regulation of Women's Work in the British Cotton Mills, 1820–50.' *Journal of Social History* 21, no. 4 (Summer 1988)

Vipond, Mary. 'The Image of Women in Mass Circulation Magazines of the 1920s. 'In S. Mann Trofimenkoff and Alison Prentice, eds., *The Neglected Majority: Essays on Canadian Women*. Toronto 1977

Walby, Sylvia. *Patriarchy at Work*. Minneapolis 1987

Walzer, Michael. 'The Politics of Foucault.' In David Hoy, ed., *Foucault: A Critical Reader*. Oxford 1986

Wanderesee, Winnifred. *Women's Work and Family Values, 1920–40*. Boston 1981

Ware, Susan. *Holding Their Own: American Women in the 1930s*. Boston 1982

Weedon, Chris. *Feminist Practice and Poststructuralist Theory*. Oxford 1987

Westwood, Sallie. *All Day Every Day: Factory and Family in the Making of Women's Lives*. London 1984

White, Jeremy. *The Worst Street in North London: Campbell Bunk, Islington between the Wars*. London 1986

White, Julie. *Women and Part-time Work*. Ottawa 1983

Willis, Paul. *Learning to Labour: How Working-Class Kids Get Working-Class Jobs*. Farnborough 1977

– 'Shop Floor Culture, Masculinity and the Wage Form.' In J. Clarke et al., eds., *Working-Class Culture: Studies in History and Theory*. New York 1979

Wine, Jeri, and Janice Ristock, eds., *Women and Social Change*. Toronto 1991

Wood, Ellen. 'The Politics of Theory and the Concept of Class: E.P. Thompson and His Critics.' *Studies in Political Economy* 9 (Fall 1982)

Wood, Stephen, ed. *The Degradation of Work? Skill, Deskilling and the Labor Process*. London 1982

Woods, H.D., and S. Ostry. *Labour Policy and Labour Economics in Canada*. Toronto 1972

Yans-McLaughlin, Virginia. 'Italian Women and Work.' In Milton Cantor and B. Laurie, eds., *Class, Sex and the Woman Worker*. Westport 1977

Zahavi, Gerald. *Workers, Managers and Welfare Capitalism*. Urbana 1988

Zelizer, Viviana. *Pricing the Priceless Child: The Changing Social Value of Children*. New York 1985

Picture Credits

Index